The Synoptic Gospels

The Biblical Seminar
31

The SYNOPTIC GOSPELS

A Sheffield Reader

edited by
Craig A. Evans &
Stanley E. Porter

Sheffield
Academic Press

Published by Sheffield Academic Press Ltd
Mansion House
19 Kingfield Road
Sheffield, S11 9AS
England

Printed on acid-free paper in Great Britain
by The Cromwell Press
Melksham, Wiltshire

British Library Cataloguing in Publication Data

A catalogue record for this book is available
from the British Library

ISBN 1-85075-732-1

CONTENTS

Preface to the Series

This Series, of which *The Synoptic Gospels* is one, collects what the Series editors believe to be the best articles on the topic published in the first 50 issues (1978–1993) of *Journal for the Study of the New Testament*. Founded in 1978, with one issue in its inaugural year, *JSNT* was produced from 1979 to 1990 in three issues a year, and then, from 1991 to the present, in four issues a year. The continuing success of the journal can be seen in several ways: by its increasing circulation, by its increased publication schedule, by its fostering of a significant supplement series, which has now reached its one-hundredth volume (JSNT Supplement Series), by its public exposure and influence within the scholarly community, and, most of all, by the quality of the essays it publishes. This volume contains a representative group of such articles on a specific area of New Testament studies.

Once it was decided that such a Series of volumes should be issued, the question became that of how the numerous important articles were going to be selected and presented. The problem was not filling the volumes but making the many difficult choices that would inevitably exclude worthy articles. In the end, the editors have used various criteria for determining which articles should be reprinted here. They have gathered together articles that, they believe, make significant contributions in several different ways. Some of the articles are truly ground-breaking, pushing their respective enquiry into new paths and introducing new critical questions into the debate. Others are assessments of the critical terrain of a particular topic, providing useful and insightful analyses that others can and have built upon. Others still are included because they are major contributions to an on-going discussion.

Even though back issues of *JSNT* are still in print and these essays are available in individual issues of the journal, it is thought that this kind of compilation could serve several purposes. One is to assist scholars who wish to keep up on developments outside their areas of specialist research or who have been away from a topic for a period of time and wish to re-enter the discussion. These volumes are designed to be representatively selective, so that scholars can gain if not a thorough grasp of all of the developments in an area at least significant insights into major topics of debate in a field of interest. Another use of these volumes is as textbooks for undergraduates, seminarians and even graduate students. For undergraduates, these volumes could serve as useful readers, possibly as supplementary texts to a critical introduction, to provide a first exposure to and a sample of critical debate. For seminary students, the same purpose as for undergraduates could apply, especially when the seminarian is beginning critical study of the New Testament. There is the added use, however, that such material could provide guidance through the argumentation and footnotes for significant research into a New Testament author or topic. For graduate students, these volumes could not only provide necessary background to a topic, allowing a student to achieve a basic level of knowledge before exploration of a particular area of interest, but also serve as good guides to the detailed critical work being done in an area. There is the further advantage that many of the articles in these volumes are models of how to make and defend a critical argument, thereby providing useful examples for those entering the lists of critical scholarly debate.

Many more articles could and probably should be reprinted in further volumes, but this one and those published along with it must for now serve as an introduction to these topics, at least as they were discussed in *JSNT*.

Craig A. Evans   Stanley E. Porter
Trinity Western University   Roehampton Institute London
Langley, B.C. Canada   England

ABBREVIATIONS

AB	Anchor Bible
ANRW	*Aufstieg und Niedergang der römischen Welt*
ASNU	Acta seminarii neotestamentici upsaliensis
AusBR	*Australian Biblical Review*
BAGD	W. Bauer, W.F. Arndt, F.W. Gingrich and F.W. Danker, *Greek–English Lexicon of the New Testament*
BDF	F. Blass, A. Debrunner and R.W. Funk, *A Greek Grammar of the New Testament*
BETL	Bibliotheca ephemeridum theologicarum lovaniensium
Bib	*Biblica*
BJRL	*Bulletin of the John Rylands University Library of Manchester*
BSac	*Bibliotheca Sacra*
BTB	*Biblical Theology Bulletin*
BZNW	Beihefte zur *ZNW*
CBQ	*Catholic Biblical Quarterly*
CBQMS	*Catholic Biblical Quarterly*, Monograph Series
CGTC	Cambridge Greek Testament Commentary
EKKNT	Evangelisch-Katholischer Kommentar zum Neuen Testament
EvQ	*Evangelical Quarterly*
ExpTim	*Expository Times*
FRLANT	Forschungen zur Religion und Literatur des Alten und Neuen Testaments
HNT	Handbuch zum Neuen Testament
HTKNT	Herders theologischer Kommentar zum Neuen Testament
HTR	*Harvard Theological Review*
ICC	International Critical Commentary
Int	*Interpretation*
JAAR	*Journal of the American Academy of Religion*
JBL	*Journal of Biblical Literature*
JETS	*Journal of the Evangelical Theological Society*
JJS	*Journal of Jewish Studies*
JR	*Journal of Religion*
JSNT	*Journal for the Study of the New Testament*
JSNTSup	*Journal for the Study of the New Testament*, Supplement Series
JSOT	*Journal for the Study of the Old Testament*
JSOTSup	*Journal for the Study of the Old Testament*, Supplement Series
JSPSup	*Journal for the Study of the Pseudepigrapha*, Supplement Series
JTS	*Journal of Theological Studies*

LCL	Loeb Classical Library
LSJ	Liddell–Scott–Jones, *Greek–English Lexicon*
NCB	New Century Bible
NEB	*New English Bible*
NICNT	New International Commentary on the New Testament
NICOT	New International Commentary on the Old Testament
NIGTC	The New International Greek Testament Commentary
NovT	*Novum Testamentum*
NovTSup	*Novum Testamentum* Supplements
NTAbh	Neutestamentliche Abhandlungen
NTD	Das Neue Testament Deutsch
NTS	*New Testament Studies*
OBO	Orbis biblicus et orientalis
RB	*Revue biblique*
RevQ	*Revue de Qumran*
RNT	Regensburger Neues Testament
RSR	*Recherches de science religieuse*
RSV	Revised Standard Version
SBL	Society of Biblical Literature
SBLDS	SBL Dissertation Series
SBLMS	SBL Monograph Series
SBLSP	SBL Seminar Papers
SBM	Stuttgarter biblische Monographien
SBT	Studies in Biblical Theology
SC	Sources chrétiennes
SE	*Studia Evangelica* I, II, III (= TU 73 [1959], 87 [1964], 88 [1964], etc.)
SNTSMS	Society for New Testament Studies Monograph Series
SNTU	Studien zum Neuen Testament und seiner Umwelt
SR	*Studies in Religion/Sciences religieuses*
ST	*Studia theologica*
TDNT	G. Kittel and G. Friedrich (eds.), *Theological Dictionary of the New Testament*
THKNT	Theologischer Handkommentar zum Neuen Testament
TS	*Theological Studies*
TU	Texte und Untersuchungen
TynBul	*Tyndale Bulletin*
VT	*Vetus Testamentum*
WMANT	Wissenschaftliche Monographien zum Alten und Neuen Testament
WUNT	Wissenschaftliche Untersuchungen zum Neuen Testament
ZNW	*Zeitschrift für die neutestamentliche Wissenschaft*
ZTK	*Zeitschrift für Theologie und Kirche*

MATTHEW

JSNT 6 (1980), pp. 2-16

SON AND SERVANT: AN ESSAY ON MATTHEAN CHRISTOLOGY

David Hill

The closest approach to a comprehensive statement from a redactional-critical perspective on Matthean christology is to be found in the central section of J.D. Kingsbury's book *Matthew: Structure, Christology, Kingdom*[1] which sets forth, in revised form, views first published in articles in various scholarly journals. The author makes a strong and, in the opinion of most of his reviewers, convincing case for the claim that the title 'Son of God' is the central and dominant term in Matthew's christology. It extends to every phase of Jesus' life: conception, birth, infancy; baptism and temptation; public ministry; death, resurrection and exaltation—it is the natural complement of the thoroughly Matthean 'my Father', and represents the most exalted confession of Matthew's community. The words 'God with us' in 1.23 constitute Matthew's 'thumbnail definition' of the predication 'Son of God' (p. 53), and indeed the rest of the Gospel may be seen as an elaboration of the implications of the phrase (as the closing paragraph, 28.16-20, suggests). As to the title 'Kyrios', Kingsbury accepts Bornkamm's thesis that for Matthew this is a divine name of majesty, but he insists that it is nonetheless an auxiliary christological title the function of which is 'to attribute to Jesus divine authority in his capacity as Messiah, Son of David, Son of God or Son of Man' (p. 105). Probably the most provocative of Kingsbury's

1. (Philadelphia: Fortress Press, 1975; London: SPCK, 1976), pp. 49-127. (Page references for quotations are given in the text.) The substance of these two chapters on Matthean christology is reproduced, in abbreviated form, in Kingsbury's later book, *Matthew: A Commentary for Preachers and Others* (Philadelphia: Fortress Press, 1977; London: SPCK, 1978), pp. 30-57. (It should be noted that this book is not in any sense a conventional commentary on the Gospel: it is composed of three essays on Matthean theology, preceded by a chapter which discusses the nature and purpose of the Gospel.)

suggestions is his view that 'Son of Man' largely coincides with 'Son of God' in terms of content, but is to be distinguished from the latter primarily on a formal basis: 'Son of Man' is a public title or term, whereas 'Son of God' is confessional. 'Except for such transcendent personalities as God (3.17; 17.5), Satan (4.3, 6) and demons (8.29), only those who confess Jesus, never enemies or unbelievers (unless it be in blasphemy), assert the truth that Jesus is the Son of God' (p. 55): but 'Son of Man' is the title with which Jesus confronts the world (Jews first, and then Gentiles) and particularly his opponents and unbelievers. Here the evidence is being subjected to Procrustean treatment. It may be true that on many occasions Matthew employs 'Son of Man' when Jesus confronts enemies and unbelievers, but is it credible that the scribe (8.19) is being cast in the role of opponent because he evokes the logion, 'The foxes have holes and the birds of the air have nests: but the Son of man has nowhere to lay his head'? After all, his stance in relation to Jesus is no worse, probably better, than the would-be follower who is described in 8.21 as 'another of the disciples'. Again, is it credible that Matthew can use 'Son of Man' at 20.28 (the ransom logion) only because it is the mother of James and John (i.e. an unbeliever or opponent?) whose request provokes the utterance? (Mark also uses 'Son of Man' when James and John themselves make the request that provokes the saying, a saying which many regard as authentic.) Kingsbury observes that 'Matthew's primary interest in the Son of Man title has to do with its association with the Parousia' (p. 114), in the description of which the confessional 'Son of God' and the public 'Son of Man' terms coalesce—thus explaining or explaining away the exceptions to his distinction between the titles. This claim has a certain validity on the basis of statistics, but it would be more accurate to say simply that Matthew shows a special interest in the Parousia. Since statements about Jesus' role in the Parousia are almost exclusively attributed to Jesus himself rather than to someone else, it ought not to surprise us that the term 'Son of Man' occurs frequently in these statements as the term by which Jesus traditionally referred to himself. That is to say: Kingsbury is right in seeking to establish a formal distinction between 'Son of Man' and 'Son of God' as a confessional term (for which Kyrios must substitute when believers address the Son of God vocatively): but the formal function of 'Son of Man' is not only public, nor does it always have opponents in view; it is simply the peculiar way of referring to himself attributed to Jesus by the tradition (whether genuine or not) and accepted without question by Matthew.

Three observations on Kingsbury's discussion of the prominence of the 'Son of God' title are in order at this point. (1) There is a degree of circularity to the argument: themes are related to the 'Son of God' christology and then their recurrence is used to argue for the significant role of that christology when the designation is not evident. For instance, it is because 'Son of God' is not a public title that the almost total absence of the designation from 4.17–10.42 can be accounted for, since in these chapters Jesus is heavily engaged with the crowds and their leaders! (2) I am not convinced that 'God with us' functions in its Matthean context as a succinct definition of the significance of 'Son of God',[2] and therefore I am unconvinced by the argument which Kingsbury builds upon that assertion (for I find no other foundation for it), namely that it is as 'Son of God' that Jesus is designated as the one in whom God draws near to people with his eschatological Rule (p. 68). (3) On a more general note: no rationale is provided for the view that *one* christological title needs to be understood as 'most exalted', 'foremost', 'principal' or 'preeminent' (pp. 67, 99, 162), yet this seems to serve as a methodological presupposition of the investigation. It is not my intention to dispute the prominence of the 'Son of God' title in Matthean christology, but to question the accuracy and adequacy of Kingsbury's claim that 'Son of God' has such primacy in Matthew that all other christological themes and titles require to be regarded as secondary to it or as subsumed under it. Already weaknesses have been hinted at in his treatment of the 'Son of Man' designation, but the christological theme to which I want to direct fuller consideration is that of 'Servant'. But first we must see what Kingsbury has to say on that term.

'The Servant' in Kingsbury's Discussion

Because Matthew makes use, at 8.16-17 and 12.15-21, of formula quotations taken respectively from Isaiah 53 and 42 in order to picture Jesus

---

2. The phrase 'God with us' is, in the Old Testament, a semi-technical expression of God's assisting presence with individuals (see W.C. van Unnik, 'Dominus Vobiscum', in A.J.B. Higgins [ed.], *New Testament Essays: Studies in Memory of T.W. Manson* [Manchester: University of Manchester Press, 1959], pp. 270-73). In Matthew's use of it (cf. also 18.20 and 28.20) the sense of the divine presence—saving, instructing and encouraging—is dominant, but is not linked, implicitly or explicitly, to any specific christological title.

as fulfilling the role of Servant through his healing ministry to Israel, and because the affinity between 12.18 on the one hand and 3.16-17 (the baptismal words) and 17.5 (the Transfiguration word) on the other is so striking, Kingsbury is forced to face the question as to the relationship in Matthew's Gospel between 'Servant' christology and 'Son of God' christology. He offers four reasons in defence of his view that Matthew intends the Servant christology to be subsumed under his Son of God christology and not the reverse.

1.   The term παῖς occurs in Matthew's Gospel only at 12.18. This argument has conclusive significance only if the importance of a christological theme is measured by a word-count of the explicit references to it.

2.   In the mixed quotations at 3.17 and 17.5 which combine words taken from Psalm 2 and the Servant song of Isaiah 42, Matthew employs the Servant song both times only in order to enhance his 'Son of God' christology. This view provokes two comments: (a) What if the Isaiah reference is the predominant or only one in 3.17 and 17.5, as some scholars are prepared to affirm? (b) To say, as Kingsbury does, that the verb εὐδόκησα was *certainly* interpreted by Matthew in terms of the conviction that Jesus is the one in whom God brings his rule to human kind is to proceed too far too fast. The verb εὐδόκησα enunciates Jesus' right relationship to God for the reception of the Spirit, and of the seven texts listed in support of Kingsbury's certainty about the Matthean meaning of εὐδόκησα (1.23; 4.17, 23; 9.35; 12.18; 24.14 and 28.18b-20) all but two—1.23 ('God with us') and 12.18 (taken from an Isaiah quotation)—have to do with Jesus' preaching of the Kingdom and his healing and teaching ministry and seem quite irrelevant to any argument about the 'Son of God' title. It is on the basis of his presuppositions about the content of the texts rather than on what the texts explicitly affirm that Kingsbury can say that 3.17 and 17.5 employ the servant theme only to enhance the 'Son of God' christology.

3.   Matthew ascribes to Jesus 'Son of God' a ministry of healing. One of the two pieces of direct evidence adduced to support this claim is already found in Mark (Mt. 8.29 = Mk 5.7) and can therefore tell us nothing about Matthew's special interests, and the other (14.22-23) certainly contains the redactional

ἀληθῶς θεοῦ υἱὸς εἶ, but that may be ambiguous and, in any case, the pericope in which it occurs is not a healing narrative but the account of a nature miracle. The indirect supporting evidence (pp. 61-62) is nothing more than special pleading. It is therefore very doubtful that Matthew attributes a healing ministry to Jesus as 'Son of God'.

4. Matthew associates both the forgiveness of sins and death on the cross with Jesus 'Son of God', not with Jesus as 'Servant'. The interpolation into Mt. 27.38-54 of vv. 40 and 43 shows that Matthew is intent on stressing the fact that Jesus hangs on the cross and dies in his status as the 'Son of God' because it is only the death of God's perfectly obedient (v. 40) and trusting (v. 43) Son that accomplishes the forgiveness of sins. But are perfect obedience to and absolute trust in God in the midst of a death that accomplishes atonement exclusively pointers to divine Sonship? Is there no indebtedness to ideas from the Servant song, Isaiah 53? Furthermore, when Kingsbury lists as the primary passages relating to Matthew's doctrine of forgiveness 1.21, 20.28 and 26.18 he fails to recognize the fact that none of these verses links forgiveness to the 'Son of God' title. 1.21 speaks of *Jesus* being so named because he will save his people from their sins: 20.28, the ransom saying, is a '*Son of Man*' logion, and in 26.18, the saying over the eucharistic cup, Jesus speaks and uses no title, and what he says may recall Isaiah 53. In short, Kingsbury's attempt to assume that Jesus accomplishes atonement as 'Son of God' is not convincing on the basis of the evidence he presents. Once again, it is possible to detect a tendency to read into the title 'Son of God' what the author wants to read out of it.

Very little then is left of the four-pronged argument which affirms that 'Servant' christology is intended by Matthew to be subsumed under his 'Son of God' christology. I would not argue for the reverse: my contention would be that 'Servant' christology (with input from other titles too) gives *content* to a 'Son of God' christology and, on the whole, Kingsbury's treatment of the 'Son of God' title is singularly weak in giving content to it, save in terms of authority, if healing and atonement themes are withdrawn in accordance with the preceding argument. Statistics of usage, rather than content, seem ultimately to be the basis for Kingsbury's claim for the centrality and pre-eminence of the 'Son of God' term in Matthean christology.

It is true that Kingsbury devotes two pages (pp. 93-95) to a consideration of the 'Servant' title and at an early point says that 'Matthew's adaptation in 12.18-21 of the text of Isaiah is tantamount to a summary of the ministry of Jesus Messiah, here called "Servant" (12.18a)' (p. 94), but he immediately proceeds to negate the importance of that remark by asserting that 'if this observation seems to suggest that Matthew attaches great importance in his Gospel to the title "Servant", it must be balanced by the recognition that he develops no "Servant christology" as such. On the contrary, everything that is said of the Servant in the words of Isaiah in 12.18-21 Matthew otherwise says in much more detail of Jesus as the Son of God.' Even the points made about Jesus and his ministry in vv. 14-17 of ch. 12 (withdrawal, healings, reticence about his identity) are all made or accord well with references made elsewhere to Jesus as 'Son of God'. For instance, Kingsbury says that 'the Matthean emphasis in 12.15b that Jesus... heals them "all"...calls to mind other scenes in the first Gospel in which mass healings are ascribed to Jesus as Messiah Son of God', yet none of the five passages listed in support contains any reference to Jesus' healing by virtue of his being or being recognized and called 'Son of God', but 8.16-17 is included, though that is drawn from Isaiah 53 with reference to the 'Servant'. Again, in alluding to the unobtrusiveness of Jesus depicted in 12.16b (which is the thematic link which binds the Isaiah quotation to its context, cf.12.19) Kingsbury claims that while this is 'a trait that is typical of the Matthean Jesus almost across the board, it is especially reminiscent, however, of 16.20, where Jesus, confessed by Peter to be the Messiah Son of God (16.16), "warns" (ἐπετίμησεν) his disciples not to tell anyone that he is this Messiah' (p. 94). Is 12.16 especially reminiscent of that? Only if one is predisposed to link the theme of Jesus' reticence about himself to appearances of the 'Son of God' title.

In examining the Old Testament quotation itself Kingsbury asserts that in 12.18a-b the accent falls not on the word 'Servant' *per se*, but on 'God' (cf. the threefold use of μου), but surely that is a matter of opinion: of v. 18b he says that it reflects editorial assimilation to 3.17 and 17.5; yes, indeed: but most exegetical opinion will oppose Kingsbury's view that these are passages in which Matthew quotes Isaiah 42 not to enhance a 'Servant' christology but to present Jesus in definitive fashion as 'Son of God'. According to our author, 12.18c, 'I will put my Spirit upon him', alludes to the empowerment of Jesus 'Son of God' at his baptism, whereas most unbiased interpreters would claim that Spirit-endowment relates primarily to Servanthood. And 12.18d, 'and he shall proclaim justice to the Gentiles', is said to find its concrete articulation in 28.20 where Matthew focuses on the resurrected Son of God as he enjoins 'all nations' to 'observe all that I have commanded you'. Another view of the function of 12.18d will be offered later in this paper, but suffice it to say at this juncture that even if the promise is articulated concretely in 28.20 we cannot be certain that it is as 'Son of God' rather than as risen Lord that Jesus speaks in that passage. Finally, and I quote,

> The description of the Servant's ministry to Israel in 12.20 and to the nations in 12.21 calls to mind, on the one hand, the appeal of the Son of God to the weary and heavy-ladened (cf. 11.28) and his compassion for the harassed and driven (9.36) and, on the other hand, the commission that he, the exalted Son of God, gives to his followers, namely, to go and make disciples of all the Gentiles (note the change in the translation of ἔθνη; cf. 28.19; also 24.14; 26.13).

Of the five supporting references in that statement only one, 11.28, has any clear or certain connection with Jesus' status as 'Son of God'! In the light of these parallels to what is said in the quotation from Isaiah—which amount to very little indeed, in my opinion—Kingsbury concludes

> that Matthew's purpose with the Servant-passage 12.18-21 is manifestly not to establish an independent christological strain in his Gospel, but to stress the fact that, again, in Jesus Messiah, the Son of God, OT prophecy concerning the Servant has reached its fulfilment (cf. 12.17). In the last analysis, the role this Servant-passage plays in the Gospel is to enrich Matthew's more comprehensive picture of Jesus as the Son of God (p. 95).

Is that an adequate assessment of the significance of the longest formula quotation in the Gospel? What if there is already present before 12.18-21, *and* after it, a 'Servant' strain in Matthew's christology? What if a number of passages in addition to 12.18-21 affirm that in Jesus Old Testament prophecy concerning the 'Servant' is fulfilled? In short, is the 'Servant' theme merely an enrichment of the picture of Jesus as 'Son of God'?

Evidence of the Servant-Motif

What passages in Matthew's Gospel may we consider as evidence pointing to a 'Servant' theme in his christology? Among the many solutions proposed to the intriguing problem presented by the words Ναζωραῖος κληθήσεται in 2.23 the suggestion originally proposed by G.H. Box[3] deserves 'serious consideration', in the view of Barnabas Lindars.[4] The proposal is that Ναζωραῖος represents נְצִירֵי (*qere* נְצֹרֵי) of Isa. 49.6, a word traditionally vocalized as a passive participle ('the preserved [from נצר = guard] of Israel'), but which could be interpreted as an adjective from *nēṣer* ('branch') of Isa. 11.1, or even as a patronymic 'Nazorean' (*nasorai*) applied by Jewish-Christian exegetes (employing legitimate Jewish exegetical methods) to Jesus. In the latter case the verse would read, 'It is too light a thing that you should be my servant to raise up the tribes of Jacob and a Nazorean to restore Israel'. Although some support for this suggestion is provided by the word κληθήσεται which, though not found in the Hebrew text of Isa. 49.6, is found in the LXX in the form κληθῆναι, the proposal must at best be regarded as only a possibility: but if a trace of Isa. 49.6 is present, then in this text from ch. 2 of Matthew's Gospel Jesus is represented as the Servant of God, formed in the womb and commissioned by God to fulfil his purpose of restoring Israel and making her 'the light of the nations'—and Nazareth in Galilee is in the category of a Gentile place, cf. 4.15—so that Yahweh's salvation might reach the ends of the earth.

With Mt. 3.15 we are on somewhat firmer ground. The words of the heavenly voice at Jesus' baptism are reminiscent of Isa. 42.1 and may, at least in the opinion of some, echo, as well as Gen. 22.2, the words of Ps. 2.7. But the 'Servant' reference is not subsumed under the 'Son of God' theme as Kingsbury's view concerning the significance of ἀγαπητός and ἐν ᾧ εὐδόκησα seeks to prove. Indeed, the real accent in the baptismal words is on Jesus' manifestation as the one endowed with the Spirit, and that, in my opinion, makes it more likely that the allusion to the Servant is dominant. If it be said that the voice in the Baptism-scene is not specially Matthean, being derived from Mark, the special significance of the Isaiah/Psalms quotation for Matthew is clear from the fact that he repeats it in full again (unlike Mark) in the Transfiguration narrative, presumably to make the *bat qol* speak the same words on both occasions and therefore to underline the Servant allusion: 'in whom I am well pleased' applies to the Servant who is also

3.   G.H. Box, *St Matthew* (Century Bible; London: Oxford University Press, 1922), p. 89.

4.   B. Lindars, *New Testament Apologetic* (London: SCM Press; Philadelphia: Westminster Press, 1961), p. 195.

the Son: the 'Servant' theme is not simply used, as Kingsbury thinks, to enhance the 'Son of God' christology. The disciples are bidden to hear the Son: but the Son, even in his glory, is the Servant of God.

In the case of 8.17, which refers to Jesus' healing ministry, we are on firm terrain. This formula citation of Isa. 53.4 is quite different from the LXX (which has spiritualized the meaning) but close to the Hebrew and may, as Stendahl suggests,[5] be Matthew's own rendering of it. The sense of the Hebrew נשא, namely, 'took upon himself' or 'bore'—which allows the verse to be interpreted in terms of Jesus' (substitutionary) suffering in Acts 8.32-33 (cf. 1 Pet. 2.22-25)—is altered by Matthew to 'took away' or 'carried off' (cf. ἐβάστασεν) so that the passage may find its fulfilment in Jesus' healings: his deeds of power are a manifestation of his mercy, obedience and lowliness—the lowliness of the Servant who does not lose his might, but uses it not for himself, but in the service of the rejected (the leper, 8.1-4), the despised (the Gentile centurion's servant, 8.5-13) and the sick (Peter's mother-in-law and others, 8.14-16). We may be certain that for Matthew—and the formula-quotation is redactional—Jesus heals as 'Servant' (as well as, perhaps, 'Son of David' and as Shepherd of Israel). It is very difficult to accept Kingsbury's remark that 8.16-17 'serves to illustrate the healing ministry of Jesus, Son of God' (p. 63).

We turn now to Mt. 12.18-21, a passage which, as we have seen, Kingsbury deals with quickly and ineffectively. Two facts may be stated concerning this quotation from Isa. 42.1-4. It is the longest citation from the Old Testament in the entire Gospel of Matthew, a fact which immediately suggests that the ideas expressed in it were important to the evangelist. And secondly, it is the most divergent from all traditional texts, agreeing with neither the Massoretic text nor the LXX, with neither any known Targum nor version. This state of affairs Lindars[6] attributes to its having a long history of apologetic use in the Church, and Stendahl[7] to the interpretative work of the 'school' behind Matthew, and Gerhard Barth[8] to the editorial work of the evangelist himself. For reasons which will emerge as we discuss the passage I am inclined to

---

5. K. Stendahl, *The School of St Matthew* (ASNU, 20; Uppsala and Lund: Gleerup, 1954; repr. 1968), p. 107.

6. Lindars, *New Testament Apologetic*, pp. 147-50.

7. Stendahl, *The School of St Matthew*, pp. 107-10.

8. In G. Bornkamm, G. Barth and H.J. Held, *Tradition and Interpretation in Matthew* (London: SCM Press; Philadelphia: Westminster Press, 1963), pp. 125-28.

think that the last-mentioned view is the most likely. The opening words of v. 18 'Behold my servant' (ἰδοὺ ὁ παῖς μου) correspond to the עבדי הן of the Hebrew text, but what immediately follows reveals a strong echo of the words of the heavenly voice at the baptism of Jesus (3.17) which are repeated at 17.5. The alterations from the original text look like the work of one who was intentionally reshaping the quotation to make it correspond with these two heavenly utterances which express, if they do not in fact stress, the Servanthood of Jesus. The text then makes two promises about the Servant who has been chosen: he will possess or be endowed with the Spirit of God, and he will proclaim justice or judgment (κρίσις) to the Gentiles or the nations. Are these promises of any importance to Matthew in the context in which he places the citation, or are they simply included because they stand between the opening words of the Isaiah passage and the verse 'he will not wrangle or cry aloud, nor will any one hear his voice in the streets' (the wording of which is entirely intelligible as an interpretation of the Hebrew text by Matthew himself, since, by its emphasis on the Servant's lowliness, it clarifies his immediate purpose in introducing the quotation, namely, the withdrawal of Jesus, his refusal to put himself forward in the face of Pharisaic opposition and plotting, and his avoidance of self-advertisement as Messiah)?

In answering this question we would draw attention to the interesting and cumulatively convincing argument by Lamar Cope[9] that the necessary fulfilment in Jesus of the two promises made concerning the Servant accounts for the Matthean construction of the rest of ch. 12. The miraculous healing briefly narrated in v. 22 leads to the Pharisees' charge that Jesus is acting in collusion with Beelzebul, a charge which Jesus deals with by asking the source of the Pharisees' healing power and by posing the alternative that his healings are signs of the Kingdom: 'But if it is by the Spirit of God that I cast out demons, then the kingdom of God has come upon you' (12.28). After offering the analogy about how to rob a strong man, Jesus goes on to speak of the blasphemy against the Holy Spirit. For the Pharisees' speech against Jesus himself, Son of Man, there could be forgiveness, but to impugn the power by which he works, namely the Holy Spirit, is unforgivable because it is tantamount to blasphemy. The guilt of the Pharisees is thus established, and in the attack on them which is couched in the metaphor

9.   O.L. Cope, *Matthew: A Scribe Trained for the Kingdom of Heaven* (CBQMS, 5; Washington: Catholic Biblical Association, 1976), pp. 36-52.

'good tree—good fruit: bad tree—bad fruit' *their* fruit is their spoken blasphemy against the Spirit: 'by your words you will be justified, and by your words you will be condemned' (12.37). 'From the miracle story which introduced the debate to the closing sentence...the Beelzebul controversy in Matthew has shown a consistent, highly-organized argument which has been constructed as support for the claim that the line in the Isaiah citation "I will pour out my spirit upon him" applies to Jesus'.[10]

But what of the second promise, 'he will proclaim justice or judgment (κρίσις) to the Gentiles'? This Cope links with the 'sign' pericope (vv. 38-42). The men of Nineveh, a fine example of Gentiles, had been preached to by Jonah and 'lo, a greater than Jonah is here': and the function of Jonah was the announcing of κρίσις, justice or forensic judgment to the Ninevites—'Yet forty days and Nineveh will be overthrown' (Jn 3.4). Jesus is greater than Jonah and will announce (ἀπαγγελεῖ: future) justice to the Gentiles or nations when, as Son of Man, he has taken his place as messianic king and announces the final judgment of the nations in 25.31-46. Cope regards v. 42 as irrelevant, included simply because it was part of the tradition employed by Matthew: but it need not be so, for the 'queen of the South' (Sheba) is as good an example of Gentiles as the Ninevites, and she too passed judgment, albeit positive, on Solomon than whom Jesus is greater too, and both vv. 41 and 42 contain the words ἐν τῇ κρίσει—a future judgment scene in which the Gentiles will fare better than the scribes and Pharisees. Verse 45b 'So shall it be also with this evil generation' is the clue to the reason for vv. 43-45 being added in this context: for it is 'an evil and adulterous generation that seeks for a sign' (v. 39) and Gentiles will arise at the judgment 'with this generation' and pass condemnation on it (vv. 41, 42). The present state of this generation is bad by reason of its ignorance and opposition to Jesus, but its fate at the judgment will be even worse: 'and the last state of that man becomes worse than the first: so shall it be also with this evil generation'.

The redactional thread by which Matthew has organized thus far his ch. 12 has been shown to lead from the citation of Isa. 42.1-4 forward to the Beelzebul narrative and its fulfilment of the first promise to be the chosen Servant Messiah and to 'the sign of Jonah' passage (v. 40 being regarded as inauthentic to the original text of the Gospel)[11] and the fulfilment of the second promise. The chapter concludes with the

---

10. Cope, *Matthew*, pp. 39-40.
11. Stendahl, *The School of St Matthew*, pp. 132-33.

pericope concerning the desire of Jesus' family to see him. Does this fit
into the structure of the rest in relation to the Isaiah quotation? Yes, says
Cope, because the crux of the incident, for Matthew, is the answer to the
family's request, 'And stretching out his hand towards his disciples, he
said, "Here are my mother and my brothers! For whoever does the will
of my Father in heaven is my brother, and sister, and mother"'(vv. 49-
50). The disciples are brothers and sisters, but Jesus is the son of the
Father, and the word used in the citation in 12.18 παῖς can mean either
servant or 'son' as the Isaianic words from the baptism-narrative would
remind the reader: in short, Jesus is the 'son/servant' of the citation and
all of 12.22-50 is an example of the common Jewish *Stichwort* method
of exegesis which shows that the promises of the Isaianic prophecy are
fulfilled in him.

But there is still more to be discovered from the citation. As said
above, v. 19 ('he will not wrangle...') interprets Jesus' withdrawal from
controversy and recognition as an acting out of that gentleness and lowliness which are attributed to him at 11.29 (πραῢς καὶ ταπεινὸς
τῇ καρδίᾳ), but what of v. 20: 'he will not break a bruised reed or
quench a smouldering wick'? This might be regarded as referring to the
sick in 12.15, but because of the close connection between the words
and 'until he bring justice to victory' (a conscious and theological interpretation of Isa. 42.3c and 4b, with influence from Hab. 1.4 on εἰς
νῖκος) the thought cannot be only of the sick. Rather, it is on the comprehensive sense of the saving work of Jesus directed towards the weak,
the lost and the broken, those who are characterized elsewhere by
Matthew alone as 'harassed and helpless' (9.36) and 'those who labour
and are heavy laden' (11.28). The vocation of the Servant, the goal of
his activity, is the victorious establishment and carrying forward of
God's justice, a justice which graciously and savingly seeks out and
intervenes on behalf of the weak, the despised, the rejected and helpless,
on behalf of their dignity and their rights. For this reason, the Gentiles,
or the nations, will have cause to hope in his name, to hope for just
judgment (cf. 21.31-46) and for a share in his saving mission (cf. 21.43;
24.14 and 26.18-20).

It would be difficult, in my view, to overestimate the significance of
the citation of Isa. 42.1-4 in Mt. 12.18-21. Not only does it express
Matthew's conception of the role of Jesus as Servant and the nature of
his ministry in obedient lowliness and mercy: it contributes, if Cope is
correct, to the structuring of all ch. 12 by the evangelist, and, as we have

hinted, what it says about Jesus' vocation as Servant underlies much else that comes to expression in various parts of the Gospel.

A Scandinavian Contribution

In the final section of this paper I want to direct attention to the work of a prominent Scandinavian scholar whose contribution to the understanding of Matthew's christology is neglected by Kingsbury, that of Birger Gerhardsson.[12] Gerhardsson is concerned to discover the way in which Matthew presents Jesus to his readers and he claims that the ethical dimension is of primary significance for the first evangelist's christology. After discussing the baptism and temptation of Jesus as revelatory narratives which disclose that Jesus is the promised Son who takes upon himself the task of being the 'Servant of God', as the quotation from Isaiah in chs. 8 and 12 show, Gerhardsson suggests that Matthew presents the work of Jesus in Israel, which begins with evidences of success and ends with destruction, in terms of contrasting categories drawn from Old Testament, late Jewish and early Christian tradition, categories such as 'blessing' and 'curse', 'God with' and 'God not with', 'mighty and powerful' contrasted with 'weak and powerless', 'to receive good at the hand of God' and 'to receive evil' (Job 2.10), and the rabbinic contrast between 'the portion of the good' and 'the portion of the evil, the punished, the chastised'. (Incidentally, these contrasts figured frequently in Jewish discussions concerning the examples in sacred tradition of the ideal 'just' or 'righteous' man [e.g. Abraham, David, Hezekiah, Job] and the traits of the ideal Servant of God.) Accordingly, the life's work of Jesus falls into two periods—the period of his strength and success when, with sovereign ἐξουσία, he teaches with wisdom (5.1–7.27) and carries out the mighty acts of power (δυνάμεις, 8.1–9.34; cf. 13.54), and the period of his defeat and ultimate humiliation. God deals to his Son both 'the portion of the good' and 'the portion of the chastised' (in weakness, humiliation and destruction) and both portions are accepted by the Son in perfect obedience.

12. B. Gerhardsson, 'Gottes Sohn als Diener Gottes: Messias, Agapē und Himmelsherrschaft nach dem Matthäusevangelium', *ST* 27 (1973), pp. 73-106. Also important are his 'Jesus livré et abandonné d'après la passion selon Saint Matthew', *RB* 76 (1969), pp. 206-27, and 'Sacrificial Service and Atonement in the Gospel of Matthew', in R. Banks (ed.), *Reconciliation and Hope* (Festschrift L. Morris ; Exeter: Paternoster Press, 1974), pp. 25-35.

The period when 'God is with him', the period of his ἐξουσία, is characterized by meekness (Mt. 11.29), which recalls the meekness (πραΰς: LXX of Num. 12.3) of Moses, 'servant of the Lord' (Deut. 34.5); Jesus' service of God (λατρεύειν, 4.10) is based on the principle of not seeking his own, but seeking the things of God (i.e. his kingdom and righteousness, 6.33), a principle which comes to its most poignant expression in the logion 'The Son of man came not to be served, but to serve, and to give his life as a ransom for many' (20.28). In addition to observing that the Servant passage of Isaiah 53 has contributed to the formation of this saying, we may point out that, since the verb διακονεῖν occurs here in both the active and the passive and can mean only 'serve' or 'attend to', it does not primarily refer to service of God, but to service given to men. The death 'as a ransom for many' is the voluntary and climactic act of obedience in a life which is marked throughout by service, service which is to be emulated by disciples (note the ὥσπερ): the λατρεία, the worship of God in practice becomes the service of men: that Jesus should seek not his own but the well-being of others is a fundamental law of the Kingdom. In a word: love, the love that identifies with sinners and tax-collectors, the weary and heavy laden, that heals the sick and helpless, the love that fulfils the vocation of the Servant of the Lord characterizes the period of Jesus' ἐξουσία when God is with him.

When we consider the period in which the 'portion of chastisement' falls to Jesus we discover the same attitude of filial obedience. At certain times of threat Jesus withdraws (ἀναχωρεῖν)—a Matthean redactional motif (12.4-5; 14.12-13; 15.21; cf. 2.14, 22)—presumably to avoid an untimely end, and in the moment of acute testing, the trial scenes, he is silent (26.63; 27.14), thus embodying the attitude of Abraham in his supreme test (Gen. 22.2-3) so often cited by the rabbis as the noblest response to tribulation, and also fulfilling Isa. 53.7 'like a sheep that before its shearers is dumb, so he opened not his mouth'. The silence is broken by Jesus only to confirm his identity before the rulers of Israel and the representative of the Roman hegemony and to engage in prayer on the cross where he dies as the perfect example of the righteous or just man abandoned by God (Wis. 2.18-20: Mt. 27.43). Even when God deals to him the lot of 'the curse', when God is 'not with' him, when he is forsaken, Jesus shows that perfection which can be summarized in the commandment, 'Thou shalt love the Lord thy God with all thy heart (27.33-34), with all thy soul (27.38-50) and with all thy might or substance', for even his clothes were divided (27.25-27): even in death, the giving of his life as a spiritual sacrifice, Jesus serves God not out of fear, but out of love which is the only right way for *the* Servant to serve. But it does not end there: as the Servant of the Lord is 'to be exalted and lifted up and be very high' (Isa. 52.13), so, in his resurrection, Jesus is again given ἐξουσία, πᾶσα ἐξουσία (Mt. 28.18) wherewith he enables his disciples to take upon themselves the yoke of his teaching and themselves to enter into the vocation of the Servant of the Lord which is διακονία grounded in love.

By putting 'servant-hood' in this broader perspective Gerhardsson has impressively demonstrated the rightness of the title which he gives his article *Gottes Sohn als Diener Gottes* ('God's Son as Servant of God') and, at the same time, has shown how in Matthew's presentation of his entire career Jesus exemplifies the Servant par excellence. In my view this approach gets to grips with Matthew's understanding of Jesus at a depth and with a sensitivity which Kingsbury's rather statistical and superficial discussion of the title does not.

When we put together the possibly implicit and explicit references to the Servant passages, the suggestion of Lamar Cope that ch. 12 is intentionally structured by Matthew around Isa. 42.1-4 and Gerhardsson's argument that Matthew sets out to present Jesus as the Son of God who takes it upon himself to be the perfect Servant of God in all things, we shall, I think, want to say more than that the Servant theme is used to enhance Matthew's dominant 'Son of God' christology (so Kingsbury): we shall, I hope, wish to say that the Servant theme gives the necessary content to Matthew's 'Son of God' christology, a content without which 'Son of God' is a strangely empty title, as it is on Kingsbury's evidence when that evidence is properly scrutinized and evacuated of what does *not* (except for Kingsbury) belong to it. Matthew's dominant christological title may indeed be 'Son of God': I think it is, but the sonship is expounded, given content, possibly even validated, by Matthew (more clearly than by Mark) in terms of Jesus' servant-hood in general and by his exemplification of *the* Servant, *Ebed Yahweh* (עבד יהוה).

JSNT 48 (1992), pp. 23-42

MATTHEW AND THE COMMUNITY OF THE DEAD SEA SCROLLS

Akio Ito

A few years ago G.N. Stanton could write: 'There is an urgent need for full-scale commentaries [on Matthew], for Matthew has not been as well served as have the other three Gospels'.[1] However, a steady stream of commentaries on Matthew has appeared since then.[2] Although all these commentaries differ from each other in purpose, scope, format and readership, they agree, at least, on one point: the question of Matthew (and his church) and the community of the Dead Sea Scrolls has never been raised.[3] It may seem strange to draw attention to this fact, since more than two decades ago W.D. Davies concluded from his painstaking analysis that the DSS do not offer us an important background to Matthew's Gospel, especially the Sermon on the Mount.[4] His work on

---

1. G.N. Stanton, *The Interpretation of Matthew* (London: SPCK; Philadelphia: Fortress Press, 1983), p. 16.

2. To mention some: W.D. Davies and D.C. Allison, Jr, *A Critical and Exegetical Commentary on the Gospel according to Saint Matthew* (Edinburgh: T. & T. Clark, 1988–); J. Gnilka, *Das Matthäusevangelium* (Freiburg: Herder, 1986–88); U. Luz, *Das Evangelium nach Matthäus* (Zürich: Benziger Verlag; Neukirchen–Vluyn: Neukirchener Verlag, 1985–). On a smaller scale there are: D.A. Carson, 'Matthew', in F.E. Gaebelein (ed.), *The Expositor's Bible Commentary* (Grand Rapids: Zondervan, 1984), VIII, pp. 3-599; R.T. France, *Matthew* (Leicester: Inter-Varsity Press; Grand Rapids: Eerdmans, 1985).

3. Exceptionally Gnilka mentions it only in passing (*Das Matthäusevangelium*, II, p. 532).

4. W.D. Davies, *The Setting of the Sermon on the Mount* (Cambridge: Cambridge University Press, 1964), pp. 208-56. Note that this monograph has been recently reprinted by the Scholars Press.

possible backgrounds to Matthew's Gospel is well-known for its main thesis, that is, the Jamnian setting of the Sermon on the Mount (and the whole Gospel), but it is a thorough investigation. He goes through all the possible backgrounds in detail, including the DSS, and rejects all but one as an important setting for Matthew's Gospel. As far as I am aware, no-one has challenged this negative part of Davies's work although there are those who argue against his main thesis.[5] This may not be surprising if we bear in mind the separation in time between Matthew and the community of the DSS; while the scholarly consensus dates Matthew's composition of the Gospel between 80–100 CE,[6] the community of the DSS was destroyed by the Romans almost certainly before 70 CE. Consequently Matthew and his church could hardly be engaged in a dialogue with the community of the DSS. Therefore, Davies could conclude that 'much material in the tradition upon which Matthew drew in the *SM* [Sermon on the Mount] was probably concerned with a dialogue between Jesus, the disciples and Qumran'.[7] In other words, he denies the possibility of a direct dialogue between Matthew and the community of the DSS, but accepts the possibility of an indirect relationship between them via Jesus and the disciples. This short essay is not intended to challenge Davies's conclusion that the DSS did not form an important background to Matthew's Gospel. I shall rather question the possibility of an indirect relationship between Matthew (and his church) and the community of the DSS, despite the possible parallels between Matthew and the DSS, because we cannot find anything in Matthew distinctively characteristic of the DSS. It is more likely that Matthew (and his church) and the community of the DSS belong to a broadly apocalyptic stream of the Judaism of the time. First of all I shall briefly survey the Matthaean parallels to the DSS, and then turn to the assessment of these parallels.

---

5.   E.g. Luz, *Matthäus*, I, p. 71.

6.   As a matter of fact, I am inclined to date Matthew's Gospel before 70 CE. Cf. Carson, 'Matthew', pp. 19-21; France, *Matthew*, pp. 28-30; R.H. Gundry, *Matthew* (Grand Rapids: Eerdmans, 1982), pp. 599-609.

7.   Davies, *The Setting*, p. 255.

The Possible Matthaean Parallels[8]

1. Matthew 5.3

οἱ πτωχοὶ τῷ πνεύματι (the poor in spirit); עוי רוח (1QH 14.3; 1QM 14.7)[9]

The usual conclusion from a source-critical study of Mt. 5.3 and Lk. 6.20 is that 'in spirit' in the Matthaean version is redactional.[10] If this is correct, the question we must answer is whether Matthew's addition of 'in spirit' was somehow influenced by its Hebrew equivalent in the DSS or not. As Davies[11] argues (*contra* K. Schubert), it is probably wrong to conclude that this parallel between Matthew and the DSS 'indicates a conscious awareness of Essene thought and an intention of Jesus to make clear his stand against their sect'.[12] It is questionable whether Matthew's addition has greatly changed the meaning of the traditional 'the poor'. Although there is no exact wording in the Hebrew Bible, both οἱ πτωχοὶ τῷ πνεύματι and its Hebrew equivalent can be fully understood within the semantic sphere of 'the poor' in the Hebrew Bible.[13]

8.　All of the following are covered in Davies's treatment of the subject in his *The Setting* (pp. 208-56). The list is not intended to be exhaustive. I attempt to focus on those parallels which are not found in the other Gospels.

9.　Although it is common to refer to this phrase in these passages as a parallel to the Matthaean phrase (e.g. H. Braun, *Qumran und das Neue Testament* [Tübingen: Mohr, 1966], p. 13; Davies and Allison, *A Critical and Exegetical Commentary*, I, p. 444; J. Dupont, 'Les πτωχοὶ τῷ πνεύματι de Matthieu 5,3 et les 'nwy rwh de Qumrân', in J. Dupont, *Etudes sur les Evangiles Synoptiques* [Leuven: Leuven University Press, 1985], II, pp. 779-92; Luz, *Matthäus*, p. 206), D. Flusser refers to [nk]'y rwh (1QH 18.15) as a parallel expression ('Blessed are the Poor in Spirit...', in D. Flusser, *Judaism and the Origins of Christianity* [Jerusalem: Magnes, 1988], pp. 102-14). Unless otherwise noted, I use E. Lohse, *Die Texte aus Qumran* (Darmstadt: Wissenschaftliche Buchgesellschaft, 1964) for the Hebrew text of the DSS.

10.　E.g. Davies and Allison, *A Critical and Exegetical Commentary*, I, p. 442; Luz, *Matthäus*, I, p. 200; G. Strecker, *Die Bergpredigt* (Göttingen: Vandenhoeck & Ruprecht, 1984), p. 33; C.M. Tuckett, 'The Beatitudes: A Source-Critical Study', *NovT* 25 (1983), p. 197.

11.　Davies, *The Setting*, p. 251.

12.　K. Schubert, 'The Sermon on the Mount and the Qumran Texts', in K. Stendahl (ed.), *The Scrolls and the New Testament* (New York: Harper & Brothers, 1957), pp. 121-22.

13.　See, e.g., Pss. 12.6; 14.6; 22.25; 37.14; 69.30; 70.6; 86.1 (MT); Isa. 61.1. Note also a fixed expression, עני ואביון (πτωχὸς καὶ πένης LXX) in Pss. 34.10; 36.14; 39.18; 69.6; 85.1; 108.22.

Nevertheless, at this stage we cannot completely deny the possibility that Matthew added 'in spirit' to the traditional 'the poor' because of his knowledge or the indirect influence of its Hebrew equivalent in the DSS.

2. *Matthew 5.33-35*

Again you have heard that it was said to the men of old, 'You shall not swear falsely, but shall perform to the Lord what you have sworn [lit. render your oaths to the Lord]'. But I say to you, Do not swear at all, either by heaven, for it is the throne of God, or by the earth, for it is his footstool, or by Jerusalem, for it is the city of the great King.

[   ] וא[שר יזכיר דבר בשם הנכבד על כול ה]

[The one w]ho makes an oath in the honoured name...(1QS 6.27b).[14]

Swear, nor by Aleph and Lamedh [i.e. *el, elohim*], nor by Aleph and Daleth [i.e. *adhonai*], but with an oath of agreement by the curses of the covenant. Even the Law of Moses let him not mention, for [...] and if he were to swear and then transgressed his oath, 'he would profane the name'. But if he swears by the curses of the covenant before the judges, if he transgresses his oath, he becomes guilty and confesses and makes restitution, but does not bear sin and shall not die (CD 15.1-5).[15]

Although both the Matthaean passage and the DSS seem to agree on prohibition of certain forms of swearing and their concern for the divine names, it is not at all easy to interpret the three passages cited above in view of the texts which apparently legitimate swearing (e.g. Mt. 26.63-64; 1QS 5.8; Mt. 23.16-22).[16]

Although the parallel is close, the prohibition in Matthew's Gospel is more absolute than those in the DSS because the DSS explicitly permit a certain form of oath (i.e. 'the curses of the covenant'). Furthermore,

14. P. Wernberg-Møller, *The Manual of Discipline* (Leiden: Brill, 1957), p. 31. W.H. Brownlee translates it as : 'and he] who mentions anything in the Honored Name against any [...' (*The Dead Sea Manual of Discipline* [New Haven: American Schools of Oriental Research, 1951], p. 28); L.H. Schiffman's translation runs as: 'Who]ever shall swear anything by the Honored Name for any [...]' (*Sectarian Law in the Dead Sea Scrolls* [Chico, CA: Scholars Press, 1983], p. 133); G. Vermes's rendering is: 'If any man has uttered the [Most] Venerable Name...' (*The Dead Sea Scrolls in English* [London: Penguin Books, 3rd edn, 1987], p. 70).

15. C. Rabin, *The Zadokite Documents* (Oxford: Oxford University Press, 1954), pp. 70-72.

16. Cf. Schiffman, *Sectarian Law*, pp. 133-54; C. Milikowsky, 'Law at Qumran: A Critical Reaction to L.H. Schiffman', *RevQ* 46 (1986), pp. 237-49, esp. p. 247.

there is the probability that Matthew preserves the authentic tradition of Jesus' prohibition of swearing in Mt. 5.33-37.[17]

3. *Matthew 5.43*

> You have heard that it was said, 'You shall love your neighbour and hate your enemy'.

> ...as He commanded through Moses and through all his servants the prophets. He [i.e. a member of the community] shall love everything which He has chosen, and hate everything which He has rejected... He shall love each one of the sons of light according to his lot in the council of God, and hate each one of the sons of darkness according to his guilt at the time of God's vengeance (1QS 1.3-4, 9-10).[18]

Mt. 5.43 is usually regarded as redactional.[19] *Prima facie* this parallel is significant since we cannot find any other text which explicitly commands hatred for one's enemy. Hence, it can be argued that Matthew contrasts Jesus' love command with the command of hatred in the DSS.[20]

Here we must be cautious, since none of the antitheses seems to be directed against the community of the DSS or any other particular group in Judaism.[21] Furthermore, although we cannot find any explicit command of hatred for the enemy in the Hebrew Bible, there are similar sentiments found there.[22] Besides, the command to hate one's enemy may not have to be understood as a positive command to hate, but in a permissive sense: 'You need not love your enemy'.[23] If so, it follows

---

17. So that Jesus' prohibition is distinct from those parallel prohibitions in the DSS. Cf. Luz, *Matthäus*, I, p. 282; Strecker, *Die Bergpredigt*, pp. 81-82; A. Ito, 'The Question of the Authenticity of the Ban on Swearing (Mt. 5.33-37)', *JSNT* 43 (1991), pp. 5-13.

18. Wernberg-Møller, *The Manual of Discipline*, p. 22.

19. Davies and Allison, *A Critical and Exegetical Commentary*, I, p. 549; Gnilka, *Das Matthäusevangelium*, I, pp. 180, 190; Luz, *Matthäus*, I, p. 306; Strecker, *Die Bergpredigt*, p. 90.

20. So Gnilka, *Das Matthäusevangelium*, I, pp. 190-91; Schubert, 'The Sermon on the Mount', pp. 120-21.

21. Davies and Allison, *A Critical and Exegetical Commentary*, I, p. 550.

22. Cf. J. Piper, *'Love Your Enemies'* (SNTSMS, 38; Cambridge: Cambridge University Press, 1979), pp. 32-35. Gundry considers that Matthew formulated Mt. 5.43b on the basis of Ps. 139.21-22 (*Matthew*, pp. 96-97).

23. J. Jeremias, *New Testament Theology* (London: SCM Press, 1971), p. 213-14 n. 3. Davies and Allison follow him (*A Critical and Exegetical Commentary*, I, p. 550). *Contra* Luz, *Matthäus*, I, p. 311 n. 47; Strecker, *Die Bergpredigt*, p. 91.

that 'hate your enemy' functions simply to stress a limitation of the love of one's neighbour.[24] This coincides with the fact that the love command of Lev. 19.18 cited in Mt. 5.43a is by no means a command of limitless love which even includes the non-Israelite enemies.[25] Nevertheless, the possibility that Matthew was influenced by the DSS here cannot be excluded completely at this stage.

4. *Matthew 5.48*

> You, therefore, must be perfect, as your heavenly Father is perfect. (Cf. 19.21: Jesus said to him, 'If you would be perfect, go, sell what you possess and give to the poor, and...')[26]

> ...according to His perfect ways, and... And the priests bless all the men of God's lot who walk perfectly in all His ways, and... May he establish his steps for walking in perfection in all God's ways...so that upright ones may achieve insight in the knowledge of the Most High and the wisdom of the sons of Heaven and the perfect in way become wise...and a perfect way of life as a pleasing freewill offering...as a Holiest of Holy and a house of community consisting of Israel who walk in integrity [lit. perfection]...The property of the holy men who walk in integrity [lit. perfection]—their property must not be mixed with the property of the men of deceit who have not purified their way by separating themselves from deceit and by walking in a perfect way... (1QS 1.13; 2.2; 3.9; 4.22; 9.5, 6, 8, 9).[27]

It is usually held that these three occurrences of the adjective τέλειος ('perfect') in Matthew's Gospel are redactional.[28] Since 1QS puts far more emphasis upon perfection than Matthew, Matthew's use of the adjective (only three times!) does not seem significant in indicating some connection between Matthew's Gospel and the DSS although it is significant that only Matthew among the Evangelists makes use of this adjective.

24. Davies and Allison, *A Critical and Exegetical Commentary*, I, p. 550.

25. Piper, *'Love Your Enemies'*, pp. 27-32.

26. There are the only three occurrences of the word in the four Gospels. Cf. Lk. 6.36 and Mk 10.21 // Lk. 18.22.

27. Wernberg-Møller, *The Manual of Discipline*, pp. 22-35.

28. For Mt. 5.48, see, e.g., Davies and Allison, *A Critical and Exegetical Commentary*, I, p. 563; Gnilka, *Das Matthäusevangelium*, I, p. 189; R.A. Guelich, *The Sermon on the Mount* (Waco, TX: Word Books, 1982), p. 233; Luz, *Matthäus*, I, p. 306; Strecker, *Die Bergpredigt*, p. 96.

5. *Matthew 13.35*

> This was to fulfil what was spoken by the prophet: 'I will open my mouth
> in parables, I will utter what has been hidden since the foundation of the
> world (ἐρεύξομαι κεκρυμμένα ἀπὸ καταβολῆς [κόσμου])'.
> ἀνοίξω ἐν παραβολαῖς τὸ στόμα μου,
> φθέγξομαι προβλήματα ἀπ᾽ ἀρχῆς (Ps. 77.2 LXX).

> אפתחה במשל פי
> אביעה חידות מני־קדם
> I will open my mouth in a parable;
> I will utter dark sayings from of old... (Ps. 78.2 MT).

If we compare the Matthaean citation with the LXX text of Ps. 77.2 and
the MT of Ps. 78.2, we can conclude that the ἐρεύξομαι of the
Matthaean text is derived from the אביעה of the MT, but it is not easy to
determine the origin of the κεκρυμμένα of Mt. 13.35.[29] Yet we can
say that the Matthaean κεκρυμμένα is closer to חידות of the MT than
the προβλήματα of the LXX. Here we might be justified in seeing a
parallel between the Matthaean figure of Jesus as the revealer of
something hidden[30] and the Teacher of Righteousness depicted in the
following passage:

> And when it says, *so that he can run who reads it* [Hab. 2.2], the interpre-
> tation of it concerns the Teacher of Righteousness, to whom God made
> known all the mysteries of the words of his servants the prophets (כול רזי
> דברי עבדיו הנבאים). *For there is yet a vision...* (1QpHab 7.3-5).[31]

It is somewhat significant that Matthew's Gospel and the DSS attribute
a similar revelatory function to Jesus and the Teacher of Righteousness
respectively. As far as we are concerned, the question is to what extent
this was a distinctive idea among the Jews of the day. If it was common
at the time, we cannot use this as a clue to linking Matthew with the
DSS. This parallel notion seems to indicate their affinity to the
apocalyptic strand of Judaism. We shall have to come back to this later.

---

29. Cf. Davies and Allison, *A Critical and Exegetical Commentary*, I, p. 52, II,
pp. 425-26; Gnilka, *Das Matthäusevangelium*, I, pp. 496-97; R.H. Gundry, *The Use
of the Old Testament in St Matthew's Gospel* (NovTSup, 18; Leiden: Brill, 1967),
pp. 118-19; Luz, *Matthäus*, II, pp. 336-37.

30. Certainly we can find this notion in other Gospels as well: e.g. Lk. 10.21-22
(// Mt. 11.25-27).

31. M.P. Horgan, *Pesharim: Qumran Interpretation of Biblical Books* (CBQMS,
8; Washington: The Catholic Biblical Association of America, 1979), p. 16.

6. Matthew 13.36-43

> Then he [Jesus] left the crowds and went into the house. And his disciples
> came to him, saying, 'Explain to us the parable of the weeds of the field'.
> He answered, 'He who sows the good seed is the Son of man; the field is
> the world, and the good seed means the sons of the kingdom; the weeds
> are the sons of the evil one, and the enemy who sowed them is the devil;
> the harvest is the close of the age, and the reapers are angels. Just as the
> weeds are gathered and burned with fire, so will it be at the close of the
> age. The Son of man will send his angels, and they will gather out of his
> kingdom all causes of sin and all evildoers, and throw them into the
> furnace of fire; there men will weep and gnash their teeth. Then the
> righteous will shine like the sun in the kingdom of their Father. He who
> has ears, let him hear.'[32]

> In His power are the qualities of all things, He being the one who sustains
> them in all their doings. He created man to rule over the earth, designing
> two spirits for him in which to walk until the time fixed for His visitation,
> namely the spirits of truth and of deceit. From a spring of light [emanate]
> the generations of truth and from a well of darkness [emerge] the genera-
> tions of deceit. And in the hand of the prince of lights is the rule over all
> the sons of righteousness, and in the ways of light they walk. In the hand of
> the angel of darkness is all the rule over the sons of deceit, and in the ways
> of darkness they walk. By the angel of darkness [comes] the aberration of
> all the sons of righteousness, and all their sins, their offences, their guilt,
> and their iniquitous deeds [are caused] by his reign, according to God's
> mysteries, during the period fixed by Him. All their afflictions and their
> times of suffering [are caused] by the ascendency of his hostility. All the
> spirits which are allotted to him, [strive] to trip up the sons of light, but
> Israel's God and His true angel help all the sons of light (1QS 3.17-24).[33]

We can detect a somewhat similar dualistic idea in these passages. This
parallel idea on its own is probably not significant enough in understanding a possible connection between Matthew and the DSS. Yet this
parallel implies an apocalyptic background to both Matthew and the
DSS although the extent to which each is dependent on it varies.

---

32. Cf. Mt. 13.47-50, 52.

33. Wernberg-Møller, *The Manual of Discipline*, p. 25. This dualistic passage
continues up to 4.26. For a comparison between this passage and John's dualism, see
J.H. Charlesworth, 'A Critical Comparison of the Dualism in 1QS 3.13–4.26 and the
"Dualism" Contained in the Gospel of John', *NTS* 15 (1968–69), pp. 389-418, repr.
in J.H. Charlesworth (ed.), *John and the Dead Sea Scrolls* (repr. New York:
Crossroad, 1990), pp. 76-106.

7. *Matthew 16.17-19*

> And Jesus answered him, 'Blessed are you, Simon Bar-Jona! For flesh and blood has not revealed this to you, but my Father who is in heaven. And I tell you, you are Peter, and on this rock I will build my church, and the powers of death [lit. the gates of Hades] shall not prevail against it. I will give you the keys of the kingdom of heaven, and whatever you bind on earth shall be bound in heaven, and whatever you loose on earth shall be loosed in heaven.'

> When these become in Israel—the council of the community being established in truth—an eternal plant, a holy house consisting of Israel, and a most holy congregation consisting of Aaron, true witness about uprightness, chosen by [divine] pleasure to atone for the earth and to punish the impious—then that is the tested wall, the costly cornerstone. Its foundations shall neither be shaken nor be dislodged from their place, a most holy dwelling consisting of Aaron... (1QS 8.5-8).[34]

> A support is at my right hand, on a firm rock is the way of my footstep. It shall not be shaken on account of anything, for the truth of God is... (1QS 11.4).[35]

> For Thou wilt set the foundation on rock and the framework by the measuring-code of justice (1QH 6.26).[36]

> Thou hast made me like a strong tower, a high wall, and hast established my edifice upon rock... (1QH 7.8).[37]

Similar symbolism is used for the church in Matthew 16 and for the community in the DSS. This parallel is not especially significant, partly because the parallel is not exact and partly because the terminology was probably derived from the Hebrew Bible, for example Ps. 118.22, Isa. 28.16-17.

---

34. Wernberg-Møller, *The Manual of Discipline*, p. 33. See also יסוד היחד (1QS 7.17, 18; 8.10) which means literally 'the foundation of the community', but is variously translated.

35. Wernberg-Møller, *The Manual of Discipline*, p. 38.

36. Vermes, *The Dead Sea Scrolls in English*, p. 183.

37. Vermes, *The Dead Sea Scrolls in English*, p. 184. Cf. O. Betz, 'Felsenmann und Felsengemeinde: Eine Parallele zu Mt. 16.17-19 in den Qumranpsalmen', repr. in O. Betz, *Jesus—Der Messias Israels* (WUNT, 42; Tübingen: Mohr, 1987), pp. 99-126.

8. Matthew 18.10

> See that you do not despise one of these little ones; for I tell you that in heaven their angels always behold the face of my Father who is in heaven.

> Those whom God has chosen He has established as an eternal possession. He has bestowed upon them a share in the lot of the holy ones. With the sons of heaven He has united their assembly for a council of community. Their assembly is a house of holiness for an eternal plant during every... (1QS 11.7-8).[38]

The reference to angels is probably not significant by itself since angelic beings are mentioned in various apocalyptic texts, including the book of Daniel. Nevertheless, this may be significant in connection with parallels 5 and 6 above.

9. Matthew 18.15-17

> If your brother sins against you, go and tell him his fault, between you and him alone. If he listens, you have gained your brother. But if he does not listen, take one or two others along with you, that every word may be confirmed by the evidence of two or three witnesses. If he refuses to listen to them, tell it to the church; and if he refuses to listen even to the church, let him be to you as a Gentile and a taxcollector.

> They shall admonish one another in t[ruth], humility, and affectionate love. He must not speak to him with anger or with a snarl, or with a [stiff] neck...[in] a spirit of ungodliness, and he must not hate him...of his heart, for he shall admonish him at once, so that he does not bear sin because of him; nor must anyone bring up any case against his neighbour before the Many without proof before witnesses (1QS 5.25–6.1).[39]

> And as to that which He said: 'Thou shalt not take vengeance nor bear rancour against the children of thy people'—every man of the members of the covenant who brings against his neighbour an accusation [lit. word] without reproving before witnesses and brings it up when he grows angry or tells his elders to make him contemptible, he is one who takes vengeance and bears rancour—although it is expressly written [lit. not is written but]: '*He* taketh vengeance on *His* adversaries, and *He* reserveth wrath to *His* enemies'—namely, if he held his peace at him from one day

---

38. Wernberg-Møller, *The Manual of Discipline*, pp. 38-39. Wernberg-Møller notes the fact that 'both *qdwšym* and *bny šmym* refer to angels is realized by most scholars' (*The Manual of Discipline*, p. 152 n. 17). Also Brownlee, *The Dead Sea Manual of Discipline*, p. 45 nn. 14-16.

39. Wernberg-Møller, *The Manual of Discipline*, p. 29.

to the next, and spoke about him when he got angry with him, and it was in
a capital matter that he testified against him; because he did not carry out
the commandment of God, who said to him: 'Thou shalt surely reprove
thy neighbour and not bear sin because of him' (CD 9.2-8).[40]

The somewhat similar disciplinary measures are found in both Matthew's
Gospel and the DSS. The measures to be taken are not exact enough to
connect them with each other. It is natural to create some sort of
disciplinary measures once a religious community is established with a
view to sustaining it. The bigger question is whether it was a common
practice to form a religious community; were the church (of Matthew)[41]
and the community of the DSS distinctive phenomena at the time?

Assessment of the Possible Matthaean Parallels

As we go through the list above, it becomes apparent that some parallels
appear more significant than others. It depends on our interpretation of
respective passages of both Matthew and the DSS whether in a certain
pair of passages we find a striking parallel or not.

Here I shall first briefly summarize the survey and then give an
assessment of it. According to my survey parallels 1, 3 and 5 may be
significant in detecting a possible connection between Matthew (and his
church) and the community of the DSS. In addition to these, parallels 6
and 8 may be significant in connection with parallel 5. Parallels 1 and 3
concern verbal parallels while parallel 5 concerns the thought world.

First, we turn to the former category, that is 1 and 3. These parallels
create a problem for us because they point to opposite attitudes of
Matthew[42] toward the community of the DSS; parallel 1 implies a
favourable attitude while parallel 3 points to an antagonistic one.[43]
Although it is certainly possible both to accept one aspect and to reject

40. Rabin, *The Zadokite Documents*, p. 44.
41. There are no other occurrences of ἐκκλησία in the four Gospels apart from
those in Mt. 16.18; 18.17.
42. Here I assume that both 'in spirit' and 'hate your enemies' are redactional, as
is usually understood.
43. Since Schubert seems to take both of them as reliable evidence for a possible
connection between Jesus (of Matthew) and the community of the DSS, he asserts
that Jesus (of Matthew) was both opposed to and aligned with the community of the
DSS ('The Sermon on the Mount', pp. 118-28). Behind this conclusion appears to
lie his assumption that Matthew's parallels to the DSS are traditional.

the other of the same religious group, it seems unlikely that Matthew accepted the self-designation of the community of the DSS (i.e. 'the poor in spirit') and rejected its command of hatred for the enemy at the same time. Then should we abandon both of them as unreliable parallels, or take one of them as reliable? In view of the alternative interpretation of 'hate your enemy' and the redactional origin of the phrase[44] we are inclined not to understand the phrase 'hate your enemy' as a reliable parallel to establish a connection between Matthew and the community of the DSS. With respect to parallel 1 it is questionable whether Matthew's addition of 'in spirit' has greatly changed the meaning of the traditional 'the poor' in view of the background of the Hebrew Bible. It is also hard to imagine how Matthew could become acquainted with the Hebrew phrase in the DSS in view of the separation in time between Matthew's composition and the destruction of the community of the DSS. Therefore, we can conclude that parallels 1 and 3 do not provide us with any positive information about a possible relation between Matthew and the community of the DSS.

Now we must turn to parallel 5 (possibly together with parallels 6 and 8).[45] Broadly speaking, from this parallel we might be justified in categorizing both Matthew and the DSS as apocalyptic. In this connection the similarity between *pesher* exegesis of the DSS and Matthew's use of the Hebrew Bible is significant.[46] Certainly we must be aware of the debate over the matter of definition[47] and the relation between the DSS and the apocalyptic movement.[48]

---

44. Having granted the redactional origin of the phrase, Gnilka still considers that Matthew made use of the *Auslegungstradition* in the DSS (*Das Matthäusevangelium*, I, pp. 190-91). One cannot but wonder in what way Matthew had an access to the command of hatred for the enemy in the DSS. Is Matthew a former member of the community of the DSS, or a friend of a former member? It is possible, but is it likely?

45. Note that the Matthaean parallels 6 and 8 may be traditional.

46. K. Stendahl, *The School of St Matthew, and its Use of the Old Testament* (Philadelphia: Fortress Press, 2nd edn, 1968). Although his hypothesis of 'the school of Matthew' is not convincing, it is his contribution that drew our attention to the similarity between *pesher* exegesis of the DSS and Matthew's use of the Hebrew Bible.

47. Cf. R.E. Sturm, 'Defining the Word "Apocalyptic"', in J. Marcus and M.L. Soards (eds.), *Apocalyptic and the New Testament* (JSNTSup, 24; Sheffield: JSOT Press, 1989), pp. 17-48.

48. Cf. J.J. Collins, 'Was the Dead Sea Sect an Apocalyptic Movement?', in L.H. Schiffman (ed.), *Archaeology and History in the Dead Sea Scrolls* (JSPSup, 8; Sheffield: JSOT Press, 1990), pp. 25-51.

I shall now turn to the fact overlooked by Davies; none of the possible Matthaean parallels to the DSS concerns prominent characteristics of the DSS. Irrespective of the question whether we consider these possible Matthaean parallels striking or not, we should not disregard this fact. However close or striking parallels may appear, we cannot conclude definitively that Matthew (and his church) had any contact with the community of the DSS unless these parallels are related to the distinctive characteristics of the DSS (or their community), owing to our lack of information about Judaism of that era.

What then are the distinctive characteristics of the DSS and their community? P.R. Davies enumerates three issues in which the people of Qumran differed from their fellow-Jews at the time. First of all they observed a different calendar: while the rest of the nation followed the lunar calendar, the solar calendrical system was observed at Qumran.[49] The difference in calendar must have been highly significant for the Jews of the day. The second major respect in which the community of the DSS is different from its fellow-Jews was their refusal to participate in the temple cult.[50] This is certainly connected with the first because different calendars fix festivals on different dates. Besides, the community of the DSS did not consider the high priests of Jerusalem to be qualified. It follows that they rejected sacrifice as such, since the Mosaic Law prohibited sacrifice outside the chosen sanctuary, that is Jerusalem; the community could not offer a sacrificial worship at Qumran.[51] Finally, the people at Qumran differed from their fellow-Jews in their interpretation of the Law. It is difficult to ascertain the precise extent of the differences since we know too little about interpretation of the Law outside Qumran at the time. Generally speaking, the community of the DSS was more strict than their fellow-Jews in this respect, for example in regulations concerning marriage (CD 4.19–5.7) and the Sabbath (CD 10.14–11.18).[52]

If I am right in considering that these aspects are prominent characteristics of the community of the DSS, what can be said about the possible

---

49. P.R. Davies, *Qumran* (Grand Rapids: Eerdmans, 1982), pp. 83-86; S. Talmon, 'The Calendar of the Covenanters of the Judean Desert' and 'Yom Hakippurim in the Habakkuk Scroll', in his *The World of Qumran from within* (Jerusalem: Magnes; Leiden: Brill, 1989), pp. 147-99. Note that there is a possibility that the solar calendrical system is older than the lunar system among Jews.

50. Davies, *Qumran*, pp. 86-87.

51. Cf. 1QS 8.3-4; 9.4-5; 4QFlor 1.6-7.

52. Davies, *Qumran*, pp. 87-88.

Matthaean parallels to the DSS? We can conclude without hesitation that Matthew (and his church) does not share the first two characteristics of the DSS; Matthew reveals nowhere in his Gospel his awareness that Jesus and the disciples have any dispute over the calendar[53] or the temple cult.[54]

However, in reference to the third aspect we detect some similarity; both Matthew and the DSS interpret the Mosaic Law, or at least parts of it, more strictly than contemporary Jews. For instance, we can understand the Antitheses (Mt. 5.21-48) as 'not only...but also' sayings which demand more than the Law requires.[55] In addition to the Antitheses E.P. Sanders draws our attention to a layer of the Matthaean material which presents to us a Jesus who 'calls his followers to be more righteous than the Pharisees *by the same standard*'.[56] If he is right in interpreting the relevant passages in Matthew as super-Pharisaic,[57] does it follow that Matthew and the DSS share a common view of the Law to a certain extent?

Here we must face the problem of lack of material. First, we lack relevant material outside the New Testament and the DSS which is as old as Matthew and the DSS. As I have noted above, the extent of the differences cannot be determined precisely owing to the lack of material, although we might be able to say that the community of the DSS differed from its contemporaries in interpretation of the Law. The same thing can be said about Matthew as well. Secondly, it is seldom that both Matthew and the DSS refer to the same subject in the Mosaic Law. While Matthew presents 'a strict interpretation' of the Law in the

53. We should not overlook the danger of argument from silence. However, in this case we can be almost certain that the Jesus of Matthew and the disciples (and Matthew's church) had no dispute over the question of calendar with the Jewish authorities. Among the writings of the New Testament it is only John's Gospel which implies affinity with the DSS with regard to the calendar (cf. A. Jaubert, 'The Calendar of Qumran and the Passion Narrative in John', in Charlesworth [ed.], *John and the Dead Sea Scrolls*, pp. 62-75).

54. Cf. Mt. 5.23-24; 8.4; 12.6-7. I interpret these passages as referring to priority of other things over the temple cult without denying the validity of the temple cult as such. The question whether Matthew's church in practice participated in the temple cult or not depends on the date of Matthew's composition.

55. E.P. Sanders, *Jesus and Judaism* (London: SCM Press, 1985), p. 260.

56. Sanders, *Jesus and Judaism*, p. 261 (emphasis original). He refers to Mt. 5.17-20, 43-48; 6.1-8, 16-18; 18.15-18; 23.5-7, 23-26.

57. Due to the complex nature of the problem and the limitation of space we cannot discuss Matthew and the Mosaic Law in detail here.

Antitheses, the DSS do not refer to the subjects dealt with in the Antitheses, except for divorce; it is questionable whether the DSS imply a similar interpretation of the same subjects.

As far as I am aware, divorce, the purity/food laws and the Sabbath are the only subjects to which both Matthew and the DSS refer. Yet with regard to divorce the Matthaean passages (5.31-32; 19.3-9) are parallel to Lk. 16.18 and Mk 10.1-12 respectively, apart from the notorious exceptive clauses. The passage in the Temple Scroll (11QT 57.17-19) simply prohibits divorce without exception.[58] Hence we cannot claim a point of contact between Matthew and the DSS in reference to divorce. As to the purity/food laws it can hardly be argued that Matthew is strict in interpreting them (Mt. 15.11, 17-19), although Matthew is probably more conservative here than Mark (cf. Mk 7.19b).[59]

Similarly the Sabbath is not a promising subject since we have far too little material to determine the precise extent of similarity in their view on the Sabbath. It is often argued that Matthew presents a more conservative attitude to the Sabbath than the other Evangelists, but it is not at all certain that Matthew (and his church) is strict in observing the Sabbath commandment. There is an interesting reference to the Sabbath in the Matthaean eschatological discourse: 'Pray that your flight may not be in winter or on a sabbath'[60] (24.20). This reference to the Sabbath is apparently open to two opposite interpretations. One interpretation is that this reference to the Sabbath reflects Matthew's (and his church's) strict observance of the Sabbath; they cannot escape on a Sabbath because they observe the Sabbath strictly.[61]

---

58. CD 4.19-21 may simply refer to the practice of polygamy. *Contra* H. Hübner, *Das Gesetz in der synoptischen Tradition* (Göttingen: Vandenhoeck & Ruprecht, 2nd edn, 1986), pp. 66-67; Sanders, *Jesus and Judaism*, pp. 257-59.

59. With regard to the interpretation of Mt. 15.11, 17-19, see B. Lindars, 'All Foods Clean: Thoughts on Jesus and the Law', in B. Lindars (ed.), *Law and Religion* (Cambridge: James Clarke, 1988), pp. 65-66; E.P. Sanders, *Jewish Law from Jesus to the Mishnah* (London: SCM Press; Philadelphia: Trinity Press International, 1990), p. 28. Both scholars, in fact, refer to their interpretation of Mk. 7.15 without reference to 7.19b, which almost certainly coincides with their interpretation of Mt. 15.11, 17-19.

60. 'Nor on a sabbath' (μηδὲ σαββάτῳ) does not appear in the Markan passage (Mk 13.18).

61. E.g. R. Hummel, *Die Auseinandersetzung zwischen Kirche und Judentum im Matthäusevangelium* (Munich: Chr. Kaiser Verlag, 1966), p. 41; E. Schweizer, *Das Evangelium nach Matthäus* (NTD, 2; Göttingen: Vandenhoeck & Ruprecht, 1981), p. 295.

The other interpretation of 'nor on a sabbath' is that it refers to the physical hindrances to flight posed by the Sabbath arising 'from the sabbatarian scruples of the Jews, e.g. shutting of gates of the cities, difficulty in procuring provisions, etc.'[62] If so, the reference to the Sabbath in Mt. 24.20 does not reflect strict observance of the Sabbath on the part of Matthew and his church. I am inclined to take the latter interpretation.

Even if the former sabbatarian interpretation of Mt. 24.20 was a correct one, Matthew and the DSS present somewhat different approaches to the Sabbath. While the relevant material in CD defines what should be avoided on the Sabbath,[63] Matthew shows little or no interest in such a halakhic matter.[64] From this we can probably say that Matthew and the DSS have basically different approaches to the Mosaic Law in general. If this generalization is justified, we can conclude that Matthew and the DSS are not similar enough in interpretation of the Law to point to their close relationship although both of them are strict in their interpretation of certain parts of the Mosaic Law.

Closely connected with the concerns for interpretation of the Mosaic Law, there are two related matters to which we must pay attention because they imply apocalyptic background both to Matthew and to the DSS. One is their positive attitude to 'scribes', which seems to indicate the presence of the scribal function both in Matthew's church and in the community of the DSS. In Matthew the word 'scribe' appears in a

---

62. R. Banks, *Jesus and the Law in the Synoptic Tradition* (SNTSMS, 28; Cambridge: Cambridge University Press, 1975), p. 102. Followed by D.A. Carson, 'Jesus and the Sabbath in the Four Gospels', in D.A. Carson (ed.), *From Sabbath to Lord's Day* (Grand Rapids: Zondervan, 1982), p. 74; France, *Matthew*, p. 341. In a somewhat similar line: G.N. Stanton, '"Pray that your Flight may not be in Winter or on a Sabbath" (Matthew 24.20)', *JSNT* 37 (1989), p. 26.

63. CD 10.14-19 reads:

> Let no man do work on the Friday from the time when the orb of the sun is distant from the gate by its own fulness... And on the Sabbath day, let no man speak a lewd or villainous word. Let him not lend anything to his neighbour. Let him not shed blood for property and gain. Let him not speak of matters of labour and work to be done on the morrow... (Rabin, *The Zadokite Documents*, p. 52).

64. We find two controversy stories about the Sabbath in Matthew (12.1-8, 9-14) which have parallels in both Mark (2.23-28; 3.1-6) and Luke (6.1-5, 6-11). However one may interpret the Matthaean passages, Matthew's Jesus is far from being strict with regard to observance of the Sabbath.

positive light in two of its 19 occurrences. These 'good scribes' are the 'scribe who has been trained [lit. discipled] for the kingdom of heaven' (13.52) and those who have been sent by Jesus ('I') along with prophets and wise men (23.34).[65] In view of the other occurrences which refer to Jesus' opponents, it seems significant that Matthew refers to 'scribe' positively. These 'good scribes' seem to indicate the presence of the scribal function in his church. Or the Evangelist may have regarded himself as the 'Christian scribe'. If so, we may be allowed to attribute the composition of the quotation formula, for example, and even of the whole Gospel, to the scribal function. With regard to the community of the DSS it is evident that it is a 'scribal' community with its own 'scriptorium'.[66]

The other point of contact is 'the continuance of inspired literary activity in the biblical mode'[67] found in the DSS. The community of the DSS did not share the sages' perception that the Hebrew canon was a closed corpus; the people of the DSS considered themselves as continuing to live in the time of inspired literary activity of the biblical prophets.[68] As we have seen in the previous section (in connection with parallel 5), Matthew had a similar perspective.[69] This similar prophetic perspective can be connected with the presence of the scribal function in Matthew's church and the community of the DSS. It may be precisely the scribal function of the respective communities to undertake inspired literary activity in the biblical mode.

If we pay more attention to this aspect of Matthew, its several features can be explained. The Matthaean fulfilment theme may have originated from the scribes of Matthew's church who were conscious of living in the age of fulfilment when the close of the age was near (13.39, 40, 49;

---

65. In the Lukan parallel (11.49) it is 'the Wisdom of God' who will send and it is 'prophets and apostles' who will be sent.

66. For scribes and the DSS, see D.E. Orton, *The Understanding Scribe* (JSNTSup, 25; Sheffield: JSOT Press, 1989), pp. 121-33. The whole of Orton's work deals with the question of Matthew's scribal ideal in the apocalyptic context, which is relevant to the point I am making here.

67. Talmon, *The World of Qumran*, p. 31.

68. This is particularly evident in 1QpHab 7.1-17 (cited as parallel 5 above). S. Talmon argues that the people of the DSS 'perceived themselves as standing within the orbit of the biblical era and their community as the rejuvenated embodiment of biblical Israel' ('Between the Bible and the Mishna', in Talmon, *The World of Qumran*, pp. 21-52. The citation is from p. 25).

69. See also Mt. 11.25-27 // Lk. 10.21-22.

24.3; 28.20). This fulfilment theme is also related to the Emmanuel theme (1.23; 18.19, 20; 28.20), which was first introduced by the quotation of Isa. 7.14 in 1.22-23. Further, the fulfilment theme is connected with interpretation of the Mosaic Law in Matthew through Jesus' 'fulfilment' of the Law and the prophets in 5.17.[70]

Does this apocalyptic aspect of Matthew shed any light on Matthew's church and its circumstances? One thing can be provisionally inferred from this: Matthew's church was facing a critical moment in its history. By analogy with the community of the DSS, we might be able to say that Matthew's church was facing a persecution of some sort by mainstream Judaism.[71] Even if this is too rash a conclusion from the evidence, we can certainly say that Matthew's church was struggling for survival in the midst of a predominantly antagonistic world. If Matthew was composed after 70, it could be the predominantly pagan Roman world in which Matthew's church had to struggle for survival.

In spite of this similar apocalyptic perspective shared by Matthew and the DSS in distinction from the sages, this can scarcely be evidence for a close relationship between Matthew (and his church) and the community of the DSS. It is not difficult to infer from a vast amount of the apocalyptic literature that such a perspective was widespread among the Jews of the day. Rather, the sages' notion that the Hebrew canon was a closed corpus may have originated in their encounter with the emerging Christian church. As a result of this measure against the Christian church they may well have excluded elements of Jewish apocalyptic/messianic movements from the scope of their 'orthodox Judaism'.

To sum up, my conclusion is somewhat ambivalent. On the one hand, Matthew (and his church) and the community of the DSS did not seem to have a close (either direct or indirect) relationship, partly because the parallels do not concern the three distinctive characteristics of the DSS, and partly because the Matthaean parallels seem redactional. On the other hand, various possible parallels between Matthew's Gospel and the DSS (e.g. the revelatory function of Jesus and the Teacher of Righteousness, interpretation of the Hebrew prophets, strict interpretation of the Law,

70. We can further mention the 'expanded' eschatological discourse in Mt. 24–25 for Matthew's strong concern for the imminent End.

71. It is not difficult to infer from Matthew that Matthew's church was under some sort of persecution (e.g. Mt. 5.11-12 // Lk. 6.22-23; Mt. 10.17-25 [Lk. 12.11-12; 6.40] Mt. 24.9-14 // Mk 13.9-13 // Lk. 21.12-19), but it is almost impossible from the text to decide who the chief persecutor(s) was/were and other details of the circumstances.

the presence of the scribal role and the open canon, etc.) seem to point to a common apocalyptic background. It follows, then, that both Matthew (and his church) and the community of the DSS probably belonged to a broadly apocalyptic stream of the Judaism of the time, although they did not have a close relationship with each other.

If I am correct so far, Davies's presupposition that Jesus, the disciples and the community of the DSS engaged in dialogue may be questionable, at least on the basis of Matthew's Gospel;[72] it can hardly be inferred from this study that Matthew drew upon a tradition concerned with dialogue between Jesus, the disciples and the community of the DSS because we cannot find a definite point of contact between Matthew's Gospel and the DSS.

In spite of this negative finding, my conclusion that both Matthew (and his church) and the community of the DSS belonged to a broadly apocalyptic stream of the Judaism of the time explains a number of the parallels between Matthew's Gospel and the DSS. Although we know so little about pre-70 Judaism and the changes brought about by the destruction of the temple in 70 CE, these parallels seem to indicate that Matthew and the DSS share a similar milieu influenced by apocalypticism. If so, it could be concluded that Matthew's church, like the community of the DSS, was struggling for survival in the midst of a predominantly antagonistic world.

72. There is no denying that the existence of this dialogue is arguable on the basis of other material.

JSNT 21 (1989), pp. 3-36

THE FIGURE OF JESUS IN MATTHEW'S STORY: A LITERARY-CRITICAL PROBE

Jack Dean Kingsbury

The question of the christology of Matthew's Gospel continues to spark debate. There is as yet no agreement in scholarly circles as to where the center of this christology lies.[1] Among recent developments in biblical studies, interpreters have increasingly been analyzing the Gospels from the standpoint of literary, or narrative, criticism.[2] One result of the application of this method is that biblical scholars have been made aware of the rhetorical device of 'ideological (evaluative) point of view'.[3] The principle burden of this essay is to argue that sensitivity to the way in

---

1. To illustrate this, one need only compare with one another, for example, my own understanding of Matthew's christology (*Matthew: Structure, Christology, Kingdom* [London: SPCK; Philadelphia: Fortress Press, 1975]) and that of H. Waetjen (*The Origin and Destiny of Humanness* [Corte Madera, CA: Omega Books, 1976]), of R. Pregeant (*Christology beyond Dogma: Matthew's Christ in Process Hermeneutics* [Missoula, MT: Scholars Press; Philadelphia: Fortress Press, 1978]), of J. Meier (*The Vision of Matthew* [New York: Paulist, 1979]), of B.M. Nolan (*The Royal Son of God* [OBO, 23; Göttingen: Vandenhoeck & Ruprecht, 1979]), of D. Hill ('Son and Servant: An Essay on Matthean Christology', *JSNT* 6 [1980], pp. 2-16), and of R.H. Fuller and P. Perkins (*Who is This Christ?* [Philadelphia: Fortress Press, 1983], ch. 7).

2. For a brief but comprehensive explanation of literary-critical technique and how it has been applied in the last years to the Gospel according to Mark, cf. D. Rhoads, 'Narrative Criticism and the Gospel of Mark', *JAAR* 50 (1982), pp. 411-34; cf. further D. Rhoads and D. Michie, *Mark as Story* (Philadelphia: Fortress Press, 1982).

3. Perhaps the first biblical scholar to demonstrate with what gain the notion of 'point of view' can be applied to gospel-narratives is N. Petersen, in his already classic article '"Point of View" in Mark's Narrative' (*Semeia* 12 [1978], pp. 97-121).

which 'Matthew'[4] employs this device in narrating his gospel-story will corroborate the claim I have advanced on other grounds that Matthew's christology is preeminently a Son-of-God christology.[5] Through the vehicle of the title Son of God, Matthew calls attention to the unique filial relationship that Jesus has with God and to the soteriological implications associated with this.

Two further goals are also in view. The one is to trace the flow of Matthew's story and, in so doing, to show that this flow is such as to commend the threefold division of Matthew I have set forth elsewhere.[6] These three divisions present Jesus to the reader (1.1–4.16), describe his ministry to Israel and Israel's response to him (4.17–16.20), and tell of his journey to Jerusalem and of his suffering, death, and resurrection (16.21–28.20). They culminate in the respective pericopes on the baptism of Jesus (3.13-17), on Peter's confession (16.13-20), and on the great commission (28.16-20). The latter pericope is likewise the culmination of Matthew's entire story. As I see it, the great strength of this outline is that it takes proper account of the fact that Matthew is not merely a collection of speeches embedded in a framework but does instead constitute a narrative composition.

The third goal of this essay is to discuss the way in which Matthew makes use of 'the Son of man'. The evidence suggests that Matthew does not employ this designation to set forth the identity of Jesus as such, that is, to specify for the reader 'who Jesus is'. Still, he does make of it a technical term, or title, in the sense that it applies to Jesus in a manner in which it can be applied to no other human being. As Jesus designates himself as the Son of man, he points to himself as 'the man', or 'the human being' (earthly, suffering, vindicated), and asserts his divine authority in the face of opposition. For purposes of translation, perhaps one can capture its force by rendering it as 'this man', or 'this human being'. Overall, the function of 'the Son of man' in Matthew's story is to direct attention to the twin elements of conflict and vindication which characterize Jesus' interaction with the 'public', or 'world'.

A final preliminary word is in order. In principle, I concur with the oft-repeated assertion that the question of christology is larger than the

---

4.   On my decision to use 'Matthew' as the designation by which to refer to both the 'reliable narrator' and the 'implied author', cf. below in the body of this essay.

5.   Cf. Kingsbury, *Matthew*, chs. 2–3.

6.   Cf. Kingsbury, *Matthew*, ch. 1.

analysis of titles of majesty.[7] By the same token, I am also of the conviction that this question cannot be solved apart from such analysis. In the First Gospel, for example, titles are used with plan and purpose and occur at strategic points in the course of the narrative. The task, therefore, is to examine the major titles Matthew ascribes to Jesus while at the same time keeping an eye on the flow of the story Matthew tells. This task I shall undertake in sections I-V of this essay.

I

One becomes aware, in reading the First Gospel, that the story is being told by a 'speaker', or 'voice'. This voice is the 'narrator'.[8] In addition, behind this story there emerges the author as he arranges for himself, through the medium of the story, to be seen. This 'literary version' of the author, or 'second self', is the 'implied author'.[9] Because the narrator in the story of the First Gospel proves himself not to be at odds with the implied author but, on the contrary, to espouse the same system of values, he may be said to be 'reliable'.[10] And because the narrator does in fact espouse the values of the implied author, I shall refer to both in this essay, so as to retain a familiar nomenclature, simply as 'Matthew'.[11]

I just alluded to the circumstance that Matthew, in narrating his story, creates a world, not only of events, but also of values. Specifically, Matthew imbues his story with an 'ideological (evaluative) point of view' (i.e., with a particular way of construing reality; a system of attitudes, beliefs, values, and norms), which the reader, in order to involve

7. On this point, cf., e.g., the comments by Rhoads ('Narrative Criticism', pp. 417-18) and L.E. Keck ('Jesus in New Testament Christology', *AusBR* 28 [1980], pp. 1-20).

8. Cf. S. Chatman, *Story and Discourse* (Ithaca: Cornell University Press, 1978), pp. 146-51.

9. Cf. W.C. Booth, *The Rhetoric of Fiction* (Chicago: University of Chicago Press, 1961), pp. 70-76.

10. The comments of R. Fowler (*Loaves and Fishes* [SBLDS, 54; Chico, CA: Scholars Press, 1981], p. 229 n. 23) on the element of 'reliability' in the Gospel according to Mark apply as well to the Gospel according to Matthew.

11. In this connection, the remark of Rhoads ('Narrative Criticism', p. 422) to the effect that, in the Gospel according to Mark, there is little or no distance between the reliable narrator and the implied author because both advocate the same values is likewise true in the case of the Gospel according to Matthew and is the reason I am taking the liberty of referring to both narrator and implied author as 'Matthew'.

himself in Matthew's story, contracts to adopt.[12] By the same token, Matthew develops his story in such a fashion that the evaluative point of view of Jesus, the protagonist of his story, will be in alignment with his own.[13] Hence, as Matthew describes it there is only one correct way in which to view things: the way of Jesus, which is likewise Matthew's own way.[14]

But true as this is, it is crucial to observe that Matthew makes yet another move in the manner in which he operates with 'evaluative (ideological) point of view'. If Matthew aligns the evaluative point of view of Jesus with that of himself, he goes further and makes certain that there is also an alignment in his story between the evaluative points of view of Jesus and of himself on the one hand and the evaluative point of view of God on the other. By authorial design, Matthew establishes God's conception of reality, his system of values or 'will', as being normative for the story he tells.

How does Matthew go about bringing God's evaluative point of view to bear upon the story? One thing Matthew does not do: he does not deal with God in the same fashion in which he deals with the other characters of his story. With respect to the latter, Matthew assumes the posture of the 'omniscient narrator'.[15] As an invisible observer, he is present in each scene of his story, and the characters, including Jesus, have no thoughts, feelings, or motives to which he is not privy. With respect to God, however, Matthew does not permit the reader to imagine that he has 'unmediated access' either to heaven, God's abode,[16] or to his 'mind'.[17] There are no scenes in Matthew's story whose settings are in

12. Cf. B. Uspensky, *A Poetics of Composition* (Berkeley: University of California Press, 1973), pp. 8-16; Booth, *Rhetoric of Fiction*, pp. 73-74; Chatman, *Story and Discourse*, pp. 151-58.

13. Petersen demonstrates this relative to Mark ('Point of View', pp. 97-121), and it is equally the case relative to Matthew.

14. Regarding the notion that Gospel texts admit of only two ideological points of view, the 'true' and the 'untrue', cf. J.M. Lotman, 'Point of View in a Text', *New Literary History* 6 (1975), pp. 341-43.

15. On this score, Petersen's discussion of Mark ('Point of View', pp. 105-18) pertains also to Matthew.

16. Cf. Mt. 5.16, 34, 45; 6.1, 9; 7.11, 21; 10.32-33; 12.50; 16.17; 18.10, 14, 19; 23.22.

17. Even at 3.17 and 17.5, to which we shall return, God does not speak 'freely' but in words drawn from the Old Testament.

heaven, and 'inside views' about what is transpiring in the 'heart' of God are rare—if they can be said to be present at all.

Nonetheless, Matthew shows in at least three ways that it is God's evaluative point of view which governs his story. The first way is oblique: Matthew indicates, by means of the genealogy he situates at the head of his story (1.1-7) and by means of such parables as those which Jesus speaks against Israel (12.28–22.14), that God is the guiding agent of the whole of the history of salvation, of which the life of Jesus is a part, and that God is therefore the one who establishes the prevailing norms of this history and of the story of Jesus. The second way is obtrusive: Matthew arranges for God to communicate in direct fashion his 'will' or his 'thinking' to other characters. For example, at the baptism (3.17) and at the transfiguration (17.5) God himself enters the world of Matthew's story as 'actor' in order to address other characters. Similarly, God also communicates directly with other characters when the 'angel from the Lord' appears to Joseph to instruct him (1.20, 24; 2.13, 19) or to the women at the tomb (28.2, 5-7) to convey to them a message.

Still, the primary way in which Matthew shows that it is God's evaluative point of view which is normative for his story is by having Jesus, the protagonist of his story, and subsidiarily also John the Baptist (3.3; 11.10), 'reliably' espouse this point of view. Matthew accomplishes this both with and without the aid of the Old Testament. Concerning Matthew's use of the latter, he informs the reader from the outset of his story that he holds Old Testament Scripture to be the word of God: it is, for instance, 'that which has been spoken *by the Lord [God]* through the prophet' (1.22; 2.15). Because Scripture attests to the purposes of God, it is hardly coincidental that Old Testament quotations and allusions occur as a matter of course in the mouth of Jesus but only infrequently or with 'perverse intent'[18] in the mouths of other characters. Correlatively, it is likewise no coincidence that Matthew himself prominently identifies, by means of the 'formula quotations' that are peculiar to his story, some ten occurrences associated in some way with the life of Jesus as being the fulfillment of divine prophecy.[19] Of course to these formula quotations one must also add the other Old Testament

18. Cf., e.g., Mt. 4.5-6; 19.3, 7; 22.23-24.
19. Cf. Mt. 1.22-23; 2.15, 17-18, 23; 4.14-16; 8.17; 12.17-21; [13.14-15]; 13.35-36; 21.4-5; 17.9-10.

references that mark Jesus' life as the fulfillment of prophecy. On balance, Matthew's procedure is clear: by cloaking the life of Jesus and many of his words in the aura of Old Testament Scripture, Matthew establishes Jesus as the thoroughly reliable exponent of God's evaluative point of view.

But Matthew also reveals through sayings of Jesus which do not rely on the Old Testament that God's evaluative point of view is determinative of the fabric of his story. For one thing, Jesus lets it be known that what he himself is about is singularly to serve the purposes of God (cf. 3.14-15; 4.1-11). Indicative of this, for example, are his references to God as 'my Father' and to himself as 'the Son',[20] his awareness that it is 'divine necessity' (δεῖ) that dictates his passion,[21] and his utterance of such programmatic statements as 'All things have been delivered to me by my Father... ' (11.27; cf. 28.18) or 'My Father... not as I will, but as you will' (26.39, 42). For another thing, Jesus teaches his disciples that for them, too, God's will is normative. He does this, for instance, by speaking of God as 'your Father'[22] and of them as being the 'sons of God',[23] and by instructing them to pray, 'Our Father... let your will be done'.[24] And finally, Jesus furthermore makes it plain that also in the case of Israel and the nations, the standards by which they will be judged are those which God sets.[25]

The literary-critical recognition that Matthew tells a story in which he posits God's evaluative point of view as normative is of paramount significance for the study of the christology of the First Gospel. As I stated, a vigorous debate continues in scholarly circles over where the center of Matthean christology lies. But if it be granted that God's evaluative point of view is normative in the First Gospel, it follows that the center of Matthew's christology must lie with God's understanding of Jesus, that is, with the way in which God 'thinks' about Jesus (cf. 16.23e). By authorial choice, Matthew has fashioned a narrative in which he establishes neither his own (i.e., the reliable narrator's) evaluative point of view regarding Jesus as normative nor even Jesus' evalua-

20. Cf. Mt. 7.21; 10.32-33; 11.27; 12.50; 15.13; 16.17; 18.10, 14, 19, 35; 20.23; 25.34, 41; 26.29, 39, 42; 11.27; 21.38; 24.36; 28.19.
21. Cf. Mt. 16.21; 26.54.
22. Cf., e.g., Mt. 5.45, 48; 6.1, 4, 6, 8, [9], 14, 15, 18, 26, 32; 7.11.
23. Mt. 5.45; cf. 5.9; 13.38.
24. Mt. 6.10; cf. 7.21; 12.50.
25. Cf. Mt. 15.1-14; 21.43; 25.32, 34, 41.

tive point of view regarding himself, but, again, God's evaluative point of view regarding Jesus. Once this is seen, the avenue of approach to Matthew's christology becomes clear. The task is to ascertain both how God 'thinks' about Jesus in Matthew's story and what place Matthew gives to this understanding of Jesus as he moves the reader through the plot of his story.

II

The chief aim of Matthew in the first main part of his gospel-story (1.1–4.16) is to present Jesus to the reader. The shape of the narrative is such that it reaches its culmination in God's declaration at the baptism of his evaluative point of view concerning Jesus' identity, that is, of how he 'thinks' about Jesus (3.17; 16.23e). This is the normative understanding of Jesus against which all other understandings are to be measured.

Matthew begins with the genealogy of Jesus (1.1-17) and informs the reader by the way he introduces it of the evaluative point of view concerning Jesus' identity which he, as narrator, would have it convey: Jesus is 'Christ', 'Son of David', and 'Son of Abraham' (1.1). Because the reader trusts Matthew to be a reliable narrator and Matthew does not betray that trust, the reader accepts these designations as correctly applying to Jesus and as constituting Matthew's initial description of him. With respect to the genealogy as such, the key to its overall meaning is the concluding verse (1.17): the whole of Israel's history has been so guided (by God) that the promises which were made to Abraham and to King David and which ostensibly had come to nought in the Babylonian captivity have attained to their fulfillment in the coming of the Messiah.

The manner in which Matthew employs the term χριστός ('Anointed One', 'Christ', 'messiah'; 1.1, 16, 17) is also instructive. One can already observe in the genealogy the twin features that will characterize it throughout Matthew's story, namely, its diversity of use and need for definition. As for its diversity of use, χριστός serves in 1.1 as a personal name ('Jesus *Christ*') that is also a title ('Jesus [who is] *messiah*'), but in 1.16 and 1.17 it serves only as a title ('messiah'). And as for its need for definition, if in 1.1 χριστός is interpreted in terms of 'Son of David' and 'Son of Abraham', elsewhere it also refers to Jesus as the 'Coming One' (11.2-3) or as the 'King of Jews' (2.2, 4) or as the 'Son of God' (16.16, 20; 26.63, 68). χριστός thus proves to be a general title for Jesus

in Matthew's story, and one must look to the immediate or wider context to know how to construe it.

As has been noted, Matthew also designates Jesus in the genealogy as
the 'Son of Abraham' (1.1, 2, 17). In light of both the genealogy and a
passage such as 8.11, what this title connotes is that in Jesus, who is the
messiah, the entire history of Israel, which began with 'father Abraham',
reaches its culmination, and the Gentiles, too, find blessing.

With the final link, Matthew 'breaks' his genealogy (1.16). He does
not write that Joseph fathered Jesus but that Joseph is 'the husband of
Mary, from whom Jesus was born... ' This 'break' raises the question:
How can Jesus legitimately be called 'Son of David' (1.1) if Joseph son
of David (1.20) is not his father? Matthew's answer is that Joseph, as
instructed by the angel of the Lord, gives Jesus his name and hence
adopts him into the line of David (1.20-21, 24-25).

Matthew insists later in his story that Jesus, in the line of David, fulfills
in his ministry the eschatological expectations associated with David.
This Jesus does mainly by healing,[26] but also by 'taking possession' of
Jerusalem and the temple (21.1-11, 12-17). The fact is striking that
whereas the Jewish leaders refuse even to entertain the idea that Jesus is
the Son of David (12.23-24; 21.15) and the Jewish crowds, while they
toy with the thought, nevertheless dismiss it,[27] for certain persons it constitutes their evaluative point of view concerning Jesus. We refer to the
blind men whom Jesus heals (9.29; 20.30-31), the Gentile woman who
appeals to him (15.22), and the children in the temple who acclaim him
(21.15). These persons, however, are all 'no-accounts', and by contrasting them with the crowds and their leaders, Matthew invites the
reader to identify with them and to distance himself from the latter:
these no-accounts 'see' and 'confess' the truth to which Israel is 'blind',
namely, that Jesus is indeed its Davidic messiah.[28]

Following the birth of Jesus, the Magi arrive in Jerusalem and
inquire after him: 'Where', they ask, 'is he who is born King of the
Jews?' (2.1-2). 'King of the Jews' is consequently the evaluative point of

26. Mt. 9.27-31; 15.21-28; 20.29-34; 21.14; cf. also 12.22-24.

27. At 12.23, the question the crowds pose anticipates a negative answer (cf.
μήτι), and in 21.9-11 the crowds who hail Jesus as the Son of David declare that this
means to them that he is the prophet from Nazareth of Galilee.

28. Cf. further J.D. Kingsbury, 'The Title "Son of David" in Matthew's
Gospel', *JBL* 95 (1976), pp. 591-602.

view concerning Jesus' identity of the Magi, and since they have come to offer him their sincere 'worship' (2.2, 11), Matthew urges the reader to accept this title, too, as correctly applying to Jesus.

Unlike the Magi, Herod and all Jerusalem react with fear to the news that the messiah, the King of the Jews, has been born (2.2-4). Indeed, Herod hatches a plot calculated to find the child and have him killed (2.7-8, 13, 16). In Herod's eyes, the one who is the King of the Jews is in effect a pretender to the throne of Israel, an insurrectionist. Accordingly, Herod's evaluative point of view coincides with the one Pilate will later take when he hands Jesus over to be crucified for being the King of the Jews even though he himself does not believe Jesus to be an insurrectionist (27.11-44). Matthew indicates the truth of the 'King of the Jews' title especially well in the scenes of Roman and Jewish mockery to which Jesus submits during his passion: Jesus is in fact the King of the Jews, yet not as a national-political figure laying claim to the throne of Israel but, ironically, as the one who 'saves others' by 'not saving himself' and hence by enduring, in obedience to God, suffering that leads to death (27.27-31, 41-42).

God himself foils the plot of King Herod, by directing the Magi through a dream not to return to Herod (2.12) and by dispatching an angel to Joseph to instruct him in a dream to flee to Egypt and to remain there until Herod dies (2.13-14). After Herod's death, the angel from the Lord again comes to Joseph in a dream and commands him to return to Israel (2.19-21), and, warned by God through still another dream, Joseph settles in Nazareth (2.22-23).

In the next segment of his story, Matthew focuses on John the Baptist (3.1-12). John is Elijah *redivivus* (11.14; 17.10-13), and he fulfills the prophecy associated with Elijah by summoning Israel to baptism and to repentance in view of the imminent inbreaking of the Kingdom of Heaven. Knowing himself to be the forerunner of another, John prophesies that the 'Coming One' who is mightier than he and who will execute judgment to salvation and to condemnation is about to appear (3.11-12). The 'Coming One', then, constitutes John's evaluative point of view concerning Jesus' identity.

The pericope on the baptism of Jesus follows (3.13-17). In accord with John's prophecy, Jesus suddenly arrives at the Jordan river, and although John would have it otherwise, Jesus enjoins him to baptize him (3.13-15). After he has been baptized, Jesus goes up from the water, and, thus removed from John (3.16a), he becomes the recipient of two

revelatory events. In the first event, the heavens open and Jesus sees the
Spirit of God descend upon him, empowering him (3.16). In the second
event, a voice from heaven announces in words heard by Jesus and
apparently by such transcendent beings as Satan as well (cf. 4.3, 6):
'This is my beloved Son, in whom I take delight!' (3.17).

God's empowerment of Jesus with his Spirit and especially his
announcement from heaven bring the entire first part of Matthew's story
to its culmination. With these events, God enters the world of Matthew's
story as 'actor' and personally marks Jesus out to be his supreme agent.[29]
In his announcement, God sets forth, in words drawn from Gen. 22.2,
Ps. 2.7, and Isa. 42.1, his evaluative point of view concerning Jesus'
identity: Jesus is his only, or unique, Son ('my beloved Son') whom he
has chosen for eschatological ministry. To get at the meaning of the key
designation 'my Son', a look at Psalm 2 is revealing. Here it is the king-
designate from the house of David who on the day of his coronation is
termed God's 'anointed' (LXX: χριστός) and God's 'son' (Ps. 2.2, 6-7).
What, then, does 'my Son' in the words of 3.17 connote? It connotes
that Jesus, the messiah-king from the line of David (and of Abraham
[1.2-6]), is the royal Son of God. So understood, God's designation for
Jesus can be seen to overlap in meaning with the other designations we
have encountered: 'messiah' ('Coming One'[30]), 'Son of Abraham', 'Son
of David', and 'King of the Jews'. At the same time, 'my Son', or 'Son
of God', also transcends the others in significance, for Matthew imbues
it with a quality the others do not possess in like measure. This quality is
that it attests to the unique filial relationship that Jesus has with God:
Jesus is conceived by God's Spirit (1.18, 20) and empowered by God's
Spirit (3.16) so that he is Emmanuel, or 'God with us' (1.23), the one
who reveals God (11.27) and is God's agent of salvation.[31] In Matthew's
story, God himself dictates that Jesus is preeminently the Son of God.

The occurrence of God's baptismal announcement does not come as a
complete surprise to the reader. Not only has Matthew alluded to the
truth that Jesus is God's Son,[32] but twice he has stated it: in the formula

---

29. To use an expression coined by Booth (*Rhetoric of Fiction*, p. 18), God
confers his 'badge of reliability' upon Jesus.

30. Cf. Mt. 3.11-12 to 11.2-3.

31. Cf. Mt. 11.27a; 1.20-23; 4.23; 26.28; 27.54; 28.18b.

32. Cf., e.g., Mt. 1.16, 18, 20, 25; and the expression 'the child and [with] his
mother' throughout ch. 2.

quotations of 1.22-23 ('they shall call his name Emmanuel... God with us') and of 2.15 ('Out of Egypt have I called my son'). The thing to observe, however, is that these formula quotations are of the nature of a comment that Matthew directs to the reader alone. The reason God's baptismal announcement of Jesus' divine sonship is climactic is because it is central to the action of Matthew's story and is not merely a part of its frame.[33]

Empowered by the Spirit at the baptism, Jesus Son of God is led by the Spirit into the desert to be tested by Satan (4.1-11). Three times Satan entices Jesus to break faith with God and hence disavow his divine sonship. But Jesus resists Satan's temptations and demonstrates that he, the Son of God, both knows and does the Father's will.

To conclude the first main part of his story (1.1–4.16), Matthew tells of Jesus' return to Galilee and the completion of his 'preliminary' travels (cf. 4.12-13 with 2.22b-23). If Joseph had settled in Nazareth after the return from Egypt (2.22-23), Jesus now leaves Nazareth and moves to Capernaum (4.12-16), which becomes 'his own city' (9.1). He is thus poised to begin his public ministry.

III

In the second main part of his story (4.17–16.20), Matthew highlights Jesus' ministry to Israel (4.23; 9.35; 11.1) and Israel's reaction to him (11.6; 13.57). If in the first main part Matthew presents Jesus to the reader and arranges for the narrative to culminate in God's baptismal announcement that Jesus is his Son, he so shapes the second main part that it reaches its culmination in the confession of Peter on behalf of the disciples that, again, Jesus is God's Son (16.13-20). In the first main part, God enters the world of Matthew's story as 'actor' and himself declares in the hearing of Jesus and apparently of such transcendent beings as Satan as well what his evaluative point of view concerning Jesus' identity is, that is, how he 'thinks' about Jesus. In the second main part, Peter shows by means of the confession he makes at Caesarea Philippi that the disciples' evaluative point of view concerning Jesus' identity, that is, how they 'think' about him, has been brought 'into alignment'

33. On the matter of the 'frame' of a story, cf. Uspensky, *Poetics of Composition*, pp. 137, 165; J. Anderson, 'Point of View in Matthew: Evidence' (unpublished paper; SBL Group on Literary Aspects of the Gospels and Acts, 1981), pp. 6, 15-16.

ɩt of God. To sketch the movement of Matthew's narrative in pect is now our task.

The major summary-passages 4.23, 9.35, and 11.1 indicate how Matthew conceives of Jesus' public ministry to Israel: it is one of teaching, preaching, and healing. Jesus commences his ministry by proclaiming, 'Repent, for the Kingdom of Heaven is at hand!' (4.17). He next calls his first disciples (4.18–22), thus surrounding himself with eye- and ear-witnesses. Followed by the disciples and attracting huge crowds (4.23-25), he ascends a mountain and there programmatically teaches the will of God (5.1–7.29). Then, wandering in the area of Capernaum and traveling across the sea of Galilee and back, he performs ten mighty acts of deliverance, at the same time setting forth the nature and the cost of discipleship (8.1–9.34). At the height of his activity, he commissions the twelve to a ministry in Israel modeled on his own, one of preaching and healing though not of teaching (9.35–10.42).

The last of Matthew's three major summaries of Jesus' public activity occurs at 11.1. In the section 11.2–16.20, which comprises of the latter half of the second main part of Matthew's story (4.17–16.20), the tenor of the plot changes. No longer does the motif of Jesus' teaching, preaching, and healing dominate the flow of events (4.23; 9.35; 11.1). Instead, it is the motif of repudiation, which is coupled in turn with the motif of wonderment and speculation about the identity of Jesus. The two pericopes that call attention to these twin motifs are John the Baptist's question and Jesus' answer (11.2-6) and Jesus' rejection at Nazareth (13.53-58). These two pericopes stand out for two reasons: they are strategically located as far as the latter half of the second main part of Matthew's story is concerned (11.2–16.20); and each one contains both a question having to do with Jesus' identity (11.3; 13.55) and a prominent reference to 'taking offense' at him (11.6; 13.57).

To trace the flow of Matthew's story in the section 11.2–16.20, it is important to note that as a result of Jesus' widespread activity of teaching, preaching, and healing (4.17–11.1), his fame spreads, throughout Palestine and even Syria (4.24-25; 9.31; 11.2, 4; 14.1). Still, the spread of Jesus' fame and the thronging to him of the crowds are no indication that Israel has 'accepted' him. Quite the contrary, Israel repudiates him (11.2–12.50), a circumstance of which Matthew has forewarned the reader.[34] Jesus' response to his repudiation is to declare

---

34. Mt. 2.3; 3.7-12; cf. 9.34 with 9.27-30; also 10.5-42.

Israel to be obdurate and to give public demonstration of this by addressing the crowds 'in parables', that is, in speech they cannot understand (13.1-35). By contrast, he pronounces the disciples 'blessed' (13.16-17) and explains to them the mysteries of the Kingdom of Heaven (13.11, 36-52). Nor does Jesus fare any better in his home town of Nazareth; when the people hear him teach in the synagogue, they take offense at him (13.53-58). Even more ominously, news reaches Jesus that John the Baptist has been beheaded (14.1-12), and this prompts him to embark on a series of journeys[35] that take him to deserted places, back and forth across the sea, and into Gentile lands.[36]

It was stated above that people in Israel also react to Jesus' public ministry in 11.2–16.20 by wondering or speculating about his identity. Thus, John the Baptist, expecting Jesus to execute final judgment (cf. 3.7-12), asks by way of the disciples he sends to him, 'Are you the Coming One [messiah], or do we await another?' (11.2-3). The crowds, having witnessed a healing of Jesus, query one another, though in a manner that anticipates a negative reply, 'This man cannot be the Son of David, can he?' (12.23). The home-town people of Nazareth, hearing Jesus teach in their synagogues, wonder in astonishment even as they take offense at him, 'Is not this the carpenter's son?' (13.55). Herod Antipas, taking notice of the reports about Jesus, speculates, 'This is John the Baptist; he has been raised from the dead, and therefore these miraculous powers are at work in him!' (14.2). And the disciples, having watched Jesus walk on the water, calm the wind, and rescue Peter from drowning, worship Jesus and affirm, 'Truly you are the Son of God!' (14.33). In so doing, they in effect give answer to the earlier question they themselves had raised in an equally perilous situation at sea, 'What sort of man is this, that even winds and sea obey him?' (8.27).[37]

All of these conflicting thoughts about Jesus Matthew combines into two contrasting positions which he juxtaposes in the climactic pericope of the second main part of his story, namely, that of the confession of Peter at Caesarea Philippi (16.13-20). To begin with, Jesus asks the

---

35. It is to 'forewarn' the reader that Jesus will take evasive action in the face of danger prior to the coming of his 'hour' (cf. 14.13–16.20) that Matthew reports in 12.14-15, as he also does here in 14.13, that Jesus 'departed from there'.

36. Cf. Mt. 14.13, 22, 34; 15.21, 29 (33), 39; 16.4c-5, 13.

37. By juxtaposing the pericope on the Gadarene demoniacs (8.28-34) with this pericope on the stilling of the storm (8.23-27), Matthew communicates to the reader 'in advance' what the answer to the disciples' question is (cf. 8.29 with 8.27).

disciples who the public imagines him to be, and they reply, 'Some say John the Baptist, others say Elijah, and others Jeremiah or one of the prophets' (16.13-14). In other words, the evaluative point of view concerning Jesus' identity which the public holds is that he is a prophet of some stature or another (cf. 21.11, 26, 46). This understanding of Jesus, however, is false, on three counts: (a) Jesus cannot be John the Baptist, Elijah, Jeremiah, or one of the prophets because John, who is himself 'Elijah', is the forerunner of Jesus (11.10, 14), and it is the task of Jeremiah and the prophets to 'foretell' of Jesus (2.17; 11.13; 13.17); (b) the answer that Jesus is a prophet evokes no 'blessing' from Jesus (16.17); and (c) what is most important, to think of Jesus as a prophet does not square with God's 'thinking' about Jesus (3.17; 16.23e).

In antithesis to his first question, Jesus next asks the disciples who they understand him to be, and Peter replies on behalf of all, 'You are the messiah, the Son of the living God!' (16.16). This answer of course is correct, for two of the same reasons the other answer is wrong: (a) it evokes from Jesus a 'blessing' (16.17); and (b) it squares with the way God 'thinks' about Jesus (3.17; 16.17, 23e). Accordingly, Matthew brings the second main part of his story, in which he tells of Jesus' ministry to Israel and of Israel's reaction to him (4.17–16.20), to its culmination by showing that, whereas the public in Israel does not 'receive' Jesus and falsely conceives of him as being a prophet, the disciples confess him aright to be the Son of God and so reveal that their evaluative point of view concerning Jesus' identity is 'in alignment' with that of God.

IV

Matthew devotes the third main part of his story (16.21–28.20) to Jesus' journey to Jerusalem and to his suffering, death, and resurrection. To alert the reader to this, Matthew makes prominent use of three passion-predictions (16.21; 17.22-23; 20.17-19), which are the counterpart to the three summary-passages he employs in the second main part of his story (4.23; 9.35; 11.1). Of interest is the way in which Matthew lends cohesion to this third main part of his story. He begins it by narrating the first of the three passion-predictions (16.21), in which he states that Jesus 'goes' to Jerusalem. This reference to 'going' is no idle comment, for with it Matthew signals the reader that Jesus will continue his travels, at first within Galilee (16.21–18.35) and then away from there into the regions of Judea beyond the Jordan (19.1–20.16) and finally on to Jerusalem (20.17–28.15 [16-20]). Consequently, Jesus' journey to Jerusalem and his presence there and in its environs serve as the 'framework' by means of which Matthew binds together the materials that make up the third main part of his story, and punctuating this framework are the three passion-predictions that sound the theme of this part.

If in its first and second main parts Matthew's story culminates, respectively, in God's announcement of his evaluative point of view concerning Jesus' identity (3.17) and in Peter's statement of the disciples' evaluative point of view concerning Jesus' identity (16.16), it culminates in its third main part, first, in the declaration by the Roman soldiers of their evaluative point of view concerning Jesus' identity (27.54) and, secondly, in Jesus' meeting with the eleven disciples in Galilee and the commission he gives them (28.16-20). A brief review of Matthew's story will make this clear.

Following Peter's confession of Jesus at Caesarea Philippi, Matthew has Jesus charge the disciples to tell no one that he is the messiah Son of God (16.16, 20). Why this prohibition? Because although the disciples know who Jesus is, they are as yet in no position to 'make disciples of all nations', for they are ignorant of the central purpose of his mission.

The central purpose of Jesus' mission is his suffering, and this is the first thing he tells the disciples in the section 16.21–28.20. Peter's response to Jesus' word is to reject out of hand the notion that he must suffer (16.22), and Jesus, in turn, reprimands Peter for this (16.23). Still, six days later Jesus leads Peter, James, and John atop a high mountain. There he is suddenly transfigured before them, and from a cloud that overshadows them a voice exclaims, 'This is my beloved Son in whom I take delight; hear him!' (17.1-5). As at the baptism, this voice is that of God, and within the context of Matthew's story it 'confirms' the validity of Peter's recent confession by showing that it was in fact 'in alignment' with God's 'thinking' about Jesus (cf. 17.5 with 16.16). But correct as this is, more significant is the circumstance that God does not simply repeat his baptismal proclamation but expands it, through the injunction to 'hear him' (17.5). The stress, then, lies on this injunction, and necessarily so, for what the disciples must grasp in 16.21–28.20 is the truth of the very word of Jesus Peter has repudiated, namely, that about his passion (16.21-23). At what point the disciples will finally grasp this truth the reader learns in the command to silence Jesus gives the disciples: not until after he has been raised from the dead are the three to tell anyone about their experience atop the mountain (17.9).

As Jesus is outside Jericho on his way to Jerusalem, Matthew portrays him, in the presence of a great crowd, as healing two blind men who appeal to him as the 'Son of David' to open their eyes (20.29-34). Like the previous two blind men (9.27-31) and the Gentile woman (15.22), these 'no-accounts' 'see' what the Jewish crowds and their leaders cannot: that Jesus is Israel's Davidic messiah. The evaluative point of view concerning Jesus' identity of these no-accounts underlines the guilt that Israel incurs because of its 'blindness'.

The 'blindness' of the Jewish crowds and their leaders also manifests itself in the pericopes on Jesus' entrance into Jerusalem (21.1-11) and on his cleansing the temple (21.12-17). As Jesus approaches Jerusalem, the crowds surround him and hail him as the 'Son of David' (21.9). But despite this, when the people of Jerusalem ask the crowds who this man entering the city is, they reply, 'This is the prophet Jesus, from Nazareth of Galilee' (21.10-11). Just as the disciples had said when questioned by Jesus at Caesarea Philippi, the evaluative point of view of the crowds concerning Jesus' identity is that he is merely a prophet (16.13-14). In a related vein, when Jesus cleanses the temple and the children there acclaim him as being the 'Son of David', the leaders of the Jews become incensed at this (21.15). Like the crowds, they, too, are blind to Jesus' Davidic messiahship. Unlike the crowds, they will not even countenance the thought that he could be so much as a prophet, for they hold him to be in league with Satan (9.34; 12.22-29).

But however valid it may be to look upon Jesus as being the Son of David, of itself this evaluative point of view proves to be insufficient. This is the thrust of Matthew's pericope on the question about David's son (22.41-46). In debate with the Pharisees, Jesus confounds them with a problem of antinomy. The question he puts to them is: How is it possible for the messiah to be both the 'son' of David and the 'lord' of David when these two views are ostensibly contradictory? Although Jesus leaves the answer to be inferred, the reader of Matthew's story can well supply it: the messiah is the 'son' of David because he stands in the line of David (1.1, 6, 25); at the same time, the messiah is also the 'lord' of David because he is, as God's evaluative point of view concerning him dictates (3.17; 17.5), the Son of God and therefore of higher station and authority than David.

Matthew places Jesus, during his stay in Jerusalem prior to his passion, in the temple teaching, debating, and speaking in parables (21.12–23.39). The parables Jesus tells bespeak judgment against Israel because of its repudiation of John the Baptist (21.28-32) and of himself (21.33-46) and warn the 'implied reader' of Matthew's story against comporting himself in a manner that is contrary to the 'norms' that befit life in the sphere of God's rule (22.1-14). Of particular interest is the second of these parables, that of the wicked husbandmen (21.33-46).

Jesus addresses this parable to the 'chief priests and the elders of the people', that is, Jewish officialdom associated with the Sanhedrin (21.23, 28, 33). In it Jesus sketches God's dealings with Israel in the history of salvation. He portrays God as the 'owner of the vineyard' and himself as 'the son' whom the owner calls 'my son' and whom the wicked tenant-farmers kill (21.37-39). Quoting from scripture, Jesus likewise predicts that this 'stone-son' whom the 'builders' reject God will place 'at the head of the corner', that is, vindicate through the miraculous act of the resurrection (21.42).

Noteworthy is the fact that by having the 'owner of the vineyard' designate 'the son' as 'my son', Jesus adopts for himself in this parable the evaluative point of view concerning his identity which God had enunciated at both the baptism and the transfiguration (3.17; 17.5). Accordingly, Jesus is making himself out to be the Son of God, even while he is making the Jewish leaders out to be the murderous tenant-farmers. Because these identifications are by no means lost on the Jewish leaders and they reject them (21.45), they want to arrest Jesus (21.46). Ironically, however, in wanting to arrest Jesus, which is tantamount to denying the truth-claim of his parable, the Jewish leaders are unwittingly disavowing God's evaluative point of view concerning Jesus' identity. Without doubt they have grasped Jesus' parable intellectually, but they remain blind as to who he is for they will not, and cannot, accept his claim of being the Son of God.

The parable of the wicked husbandmen points ahead to the pericope on Jesus' trial before the Sanhedrin (26.57-68). At his trial, Jesus again faces the chief priests and the elders of the Jews (26.57, 59). As the presiding officer of the Sanhedrin, the high priest is privy to the claim to be the Son of God which Jesus had advanced in allegorical form in his parable. When, therefore, the high priest asks Jesus, '...are you the messiah, the Son of God?' (26.63), he is at once reformulating Jesus' claim in non-allegorical terms and aiming to turn it against him in order to destroy him. Moreover, from his own standpoint the high priest succeeds, for Jesus' reply is affirmative ('[So] you have said'; 26.64; cf. 27.43). In consequence of Jesus' reply, the Sanhedrin, at the instigation of the high priest, condemns Jesus to death for blasphemy (26.65-66). And therein lies the irony of Jesus' fate. In the case of Jesus, the irony is that although he is made to die for committing blasphemy against God, his 'crime' has been to dare to 'think' about himself as God has revealed, at his baptism and transfiguration, that he does in truth 'think' about him (3.17; 17.5; 21.37; 26.63-64). In the case of the high priest and the Sanhedrin, the irony is that in condemning Jesus to death for blaspheming God, they are alleging that they know the 'thinking' of God; yet even while alleging that they have such knowledge, they are effectively disavowing it.

Bent on having Jesus put to death, the Jewish leaders deliver him to Pilate (27.1-2). At issue in the hearing before Pilate is whether Jesus is the 'King of the Jews [Israel]' (27.11, 29, 37, 42). Matthew has Jesus affirm that he is (27.11). In the ears of Pilate, this means that Jesus is an insurrectionist (27.37), a charge which the Jewish leaders support (27.12) but which Pilate discounts completely even though he accedes to it (27.18, 23-24, 26). Wherein the truth of Jesus' affirmation lies Matthew shows in the two scenes of Roman and Jewish mockery: Jesus is indeed the King of the Jews (Israel), yet not as an insurrectionist but, ironically, as the one who 'saves others' by himself submitting to suffering and death in obedience to God (27.27-31, 42).

Upon the death of Jesus, Matthew tells of the occurrence of super-natural portents (27.51-53) in response to which the Roman soldiers guarding Jesus exclaim, 'Truly this man was the Son of God!' (27.54). As characters who appear on the scene only briefly, it is not for the soldiers but for the reader to grasp the full import of their words. In this regard, three things stand out.

The first thing that stands out is that this acclamation of the Roman soldiers constitutes a vindication of Jesus' claim to be the Son of God (21.37; 26.63-64). In condemning Jesus to death at his trial and in blas-pheming and mocking him as he hangs upon the cross, the Sanhedrin in the one instance and the passers-by and the Jewish leaders in the other instance repudiate Jesus' claim to be the Son of God (26.63-66; 27.39-43). Against the backdrop of this repudiation, the soldiers' acclamation becomes a counter-assertion, evoked by God himself through the super-natural portents he causes to occur, that, on the contrary, Jesus 'truly' was the 'Son of God' (27.51-54).

The second thing that stands out is that the verb in this acclamation is in the past tense ('was'; 27.54). In that the Roman soldiers say that Jesus was the Son of God, their acclamation calls attention to the fact that the cross marks the end of Jesus' earthly ministry. The end, however, is at the same time the culmination, for the cross is the place where Jesus 'pours out' his blood for the forgiveness of sins (26.28) and thus 'saves' his people from their sins (1.21). In the cross, Jesus atones for sins (20.28) and supersedes the temple and the Jewish cult (27.51) as the 'place' of salvation.

And the last thing that stands out is that with this acclamation of the Roman soldiers, Matthew brings the entire third main part of his story (16.21–28.20) to its initial climax. In attesting Jesus to be the Son of God, the Roman soldiers 'think' about Jesus as God 'thinks' about him (3.17; 17.5; 16.23e), so that their evaluative point of view concerning Jesus' identity can be seen to be 'in alignment' with that of God. Moreover, in contrast, for example, to Peter's confession on behalf of the disciples, no comment of any kind, narrative or otherwise, which can function as a command to silence follows the soldiers' acclamation.[38] The reason is apparent: whereas Peter and the disciples at Caesarea Philippi correctly understood who Jesus is but were as yet ignorant of his passion, the Roman soldiers acclaim Jesus to be the Son of God at that juncture where he has completed his passion and, in fact, the whole of his earthly ministry. In consequence of this, the way is, in principle, now open for the task of 'going and making disciples of all nations'. And since the soldiers are themselves Gentiles, they attest in this way, too, that the time for embarking upon this universal mission is at hand.

Matthew's concluding pericope (28.16-20) is the major climax, not only of the third main part of his story (16.21–28.20), but also of his entire story. The Jesus who meets the eleven disciples atop the mountain in Galilee stands forth as the crucified but resurrected Son of God. Thus, he is the resurrected Son of God whose eschatological glory God revealed 'proleptically' to Peter, James, and John on the mountain of the transfiguration (17.2, 5). Still, even as the resurrected Son of God, he remains the crucified Son of God ('the one who has been, and remains, the crucified'; 28.6; 27.54). Indeed, he is the rejected 'stone-son' whom God has placed 'at the head of the corner', that is, raised from the dead and exalted to universal lordship (21.37, 42; 28.28). He is, in fact,

---

38. Cf. Mt. 27.54 with 16.16, 20; also 17.5, 9.

Emmanuel, or 'God with us', the Son conceived of the Spirit in whom God will abide with the disciples until the consummation of the age (1.20, 23; 28.20).

The disciples, in seeing Jesus Son of God as the resurrected one who remains the crucified one (28.6-7, 10, 17), see him in new perspective. In the boat at sea and in the regions of Caesarea Philippi, the disciples confessed Jesus to be the Son of God and therefore confessed aright 'who he is' (14.33; 16.16), but they did not as yet know of the central purpose of his mission, which was his passion. Atop the mountain of the transfiguration, God 'confirmed' to Peter, James, and John that the disciples' confession of Jesus was indeed valid ('in alignment' with his own 'thinking'), but he also enjoined them to 'hear' Jesus (17.5), that is, he called upon them to pay heed to the very word of Jesus concerning his passion to which Peter had taken umbrage (16.21-22; cf. 17.10-13). Here on the mountain in Galilee, it is the crucified, albeit also resurrected, Son of God who appears to the eleven (28.6, 16). Seeing Jesus as such, the disciples now comprehend, not only what they had earlier perceived as well, namely, that he is the Son of God, but also the central purpose of his mission, namely, his death on the cross and the salvation from sins he thereby accomplished. Still, this insight does not of itself guarantee that a 'post-Easter disciple' is as a matter of course immune to the affliction of doubt, or little faith (28.17; cf. 14.28-33). Nonetheless, equipped with this insight, the disciples are not again commanded by Jesus, as previously, to silence concerning him (16.20; 17.9), but are instead commissioned to go and make of all nations his disciples (20.19). In pursuit of this commission, the disciples move from Easter into the world Jesus described for them in his eschatological discourse of chs. 24–25.

V

Why does Matthew tell his story about Jesus along these lines? The answer lies in the effect this story is calculated to have upon the 'implied reader'.

In the first main part of Matthew's story (1.1–4.16), the reader looks on as Matthew guides events to that point where God enters the world of the story as 'actor' in order to announce his evaluative point of view concerning Jesus: Jesus is his royal Son, whom he has chosen (and empowered) for messianic ministry (3.17). In the second main part of his story (4.17–16.20), Matthew describes for the reader the ministry of Jesus to Israel and Israel's reaction to him. Whereas the Jewish leaders think of Jesus as being in league with Satan and do not so much as raise the question of his identity, the Jewish public concludes that he is a prophet (16.14). By contrast, the disciples confess him to be the Son of God (16.16). The confession of the disciples thus constitutes the climax of this part of Matthew's story, for they give expression to an evaluative point of view concerning Jesus' identity which is 'in alignment' with that of God.

In the third main part of Matthew's story (16.21–28.20), the reader follows along as Matthew tells of Jesus' journey to Jerusalem and his suffering, death, and resurrection. At the moment Jesus dies, God causes a series of supernatural portents to occur in response to which the Roman soldiers guarding Jesus acclaim him as truly having been the Son of God (27.54). This acclamation marks the initial culmination of this third part of Matthew's story, for against the background of Israel's abject repudiation of Jesus, Gentiles give expression to an evaluative point of view concerning Jesus' identity which is also 'in alignment' with that of God. Still, the ultimate culmination both of this part and of the whole of Matthew's story comes in the final scene. Here the disciples see Jesus Son of God as the resurrected one who nonetheless remains the crucified one. Although the disciples had earlier correctly confessed Jesus to be the Son of God, insight into the central purpose of his ministry, death on the cross accomplishing salvation from sins, had eluded them. In seeing Jesus Son of God as the crucified and resurrected one, the disciples now comprehend, not only who he is, but also what he was (and is) about. In consequence of this, Jesus does not, as previously, command them to silence concerning his identity (16.20; 17.9), but commissions them to go and make of all nations his disciples (28.19).

The reader finds himself or herself at the end of Matthew's story 'standing in the shoes' of the disciples. He or she views Jesus and his ministry as they do, that is, 'in alignment' with the 'thinking' of God (16.23e). The commission Jesus gives the disciples assumes the form of direct address. Hence, as the disciples receive this commission, the 'implied reader', too, receives it. Accordingly, one reason Matthew tells his story along the lines he does is to bring the reader's 'thinking' about Jesus 'into alignment' with God's 'thinking' about him and to invite the reader to look upon himself or herself as being a disciple of Jesus and to regard the commission Jesus addresses to the disciples as also being addressed to him or her: 'Go therefore and make disciples of all nations...'

VI

Thus far, I have treated the story Matthew narrates apart from the obvious fact that he not infrequently depicts Jesus, beginning with 8.20, as referring to himself as 'the Son of man'. In the final sections of this essay, I should like to turn to the question of the significance of this designation.

I have argued above that Matthew has, by authorial choice, made God's evaluative point of view normative as far as his story is concerned. This recognition is of no little consequence for properly assessing the importance that Matthew attaches to 'the Son of man'. Because 'the Son of man' occurs exclusively on the lips of Jesus, it is tempting to interpret this as indication that this designation dominates the understanding of Jesus Matthew would project through the medium of his story. But if it is correct that Matthew, as implied author, has fashioned a story in which he aligns both the evaluative point of view of the narrator and that of Jesus with the evaluative point of view of God, it follows that what will be weightiest in Matthew's presentation of Jesus is the understanding of him which God conveys. As we have observed, God twice enters the world of Matthew's story as 'actor' in order to announce that Jesus is his beloved Son (3.17; 17.5). Clearly, therefore, Matthean christology must be adjudged to be preeminently a Son-of-God christology, and the interpreter dare not lose sight of this in ascertaining the meaning and function of 'the Son of man'.

The first thing to observe about 'the Son of man' in Matthew's story is that it is different in nature from such major titles[39] as χριστός ('messiah'), 'King of the Jews (Israel)', 'Son of David', and 'Son of God'. It stands in a class apart from these, for it does not function 'confessionally' to inform the reader of Jesus' identity, that is, of 'who Jesus is'.

The two personal names Jesus bears in Matthew's story are 'Jesus' and χριστός ('Christ').[40] At 1.1, Matthew conjoins the two to form the

---

39. As I have shown elsewhere (*Matthew*, pp. 103-13), κύριος ('Lord') is not, strictly speaking, a major title in Matthew but an 'auxiliary christological title'.

40. Cf. Mt. 1.1, 16, 21, 25.

name 'Jesus Christ'.[41] At the basis of this fuller name is the assertion that 'Jesus is the Christ (messiah)'.[42]

Of significance is the circumstance that Matthew places christological titles in apposition to the names 'Jesus' and 'Jesus Christ' and to the name and title χριστός in order to apprise the reader of the identity of Jesus. Therefore through the vehicle of this grammatical device, as well as the parallel wording found in 2.2 and 2.4,[43] the reader learns that Jesus is the King of the Jews (27.37), or that (Jesus) messiah is the Son of David,[44] the Son of Abraham (1.1), the King of the Jews (2.2, 4), and the Son of God (16.16; 26.63-64). By contrast, never does the reader ever find 'the Son of man' standing in apposition to 'Jesus', 'Jesus Christ', or χριστός. What this suggests is that if the titles 'Son of David', ('Son of Abraham'), 'King of the Jews', and 'Son of God' prove themselves to be related to one another by being related to 'Jesus', 'Jesus Christ', and χριστός, it is apparent that 'the Son of man' does not belong to this family. If the purpose of these former titles is to inform the reader of 'who Jesus is', the purpose of 'the Son of man' must lie elsewhere.

Another indication that 'the Son of man' does not function to inform the reader of 'who Jesus is' is the fact that although Jesus frequently uses it in public in order to refer to himself, the thought occurs neither to the Jews nor to the disciples to identify him as such. Consider the Jews. In the full hearing of the crowd(s)[45] and of the Jewish leaders,[46] Jesus designates himself as 'the Son of man'. Still, when the question of the identity of Jesus arises, the leaders and the public regard him as being, not 'the Son of man', but either as one who is in collusion with 'Beelzebul'[47] or as a 'prophet',[48] namely, 'John the Baptist',[49] 'Elijah',

41. The correct reading at 1.18 and 16.21 is not 'Jesus Christ' but 'Christ' ('messiah') in the first instance and 'Jesus' in the second.

42. Cf. Mt. 1.16; 27.17, 22.

43. Cf. 2.2, 'Where is he who is born King of the Jews?' with 2.4, 'Where is the messiah born?'

44. Mt. 1.1; cf. 22.42, 45.

45. Cf. Mt. 8.20 with 8.18; 9.6 with 9.8 (also 9.2); 11.19 with 11.7 and 11.16.

46. Cf. Mt. 8.20 with 8.19; 9.6 with 9.3; 12.8 with 12.2; 12.32 with 12.24; 12.40 with 12.38.

47. Cf. Mt. 12.22-24; also 9.34.

'Jeremiah', or 'one of the prophets' (16.14). Or take the disciples. In their hearing, too, Jesus repeatedly calls himself 'the Son of man' throughout 4.17–16.20.[50] But despite this, when the disciples confess Jesus in the boat on the sea or when Jesus puts to them the question of his identity in the regions of Caesarea Philippi, they do not affirm him to be 'the Son of man' but the 'Son of God' (14.33; 16.15-16).

To stay with this passage of Peter's confession in the regions of Caesarea Philippi, the first of the two questions Jesus asks the disciples reveals in especially telling fashion that 'the Son of man' does not serve in Matthew's story to specify Jesus' identity. In that Matthew has Jesus ask the disciples who 'men' say that 'the Son of man' is (16.13), he shows that 'the Son of man' is not meant to clarify for the reader who Jesus is but must itself be clarified.

Further indications that 'the Son of man' functions other than to set forth the identity of Jesus can be found in the pericope on the trial of Jesus before the Sanhedrin (26.57-68). This pericope turns on the question of Jesus' identity. Noteworthy is the fact that although Jesus has openly referred to himself as the Son of man on several occasions heretofore in Matthew's story,[51] the high priest does not ask him whether he is the Son of man but whether he is 'the Messiah, the Son of God' (26.63).

The reply Jesus gives to the question of the high priest is also noteworthy. Jesus first responds with an assertion: '(So) you have said' (26.64). This assertion is affirmative in nature, so that in making it Jesus publicly avows that his own conception of himself is that he is indeed the messiah, the Son of God. Evidence of the affirmative nature of this assertion is ready to hand. To begin with, so long as the testimony brought against Jesus at his trial is false, he remains silent (26.59-63a). But the moment the high priest asks him whether he is the messiah, the Son of God, Jesus breaks his silence and speaks out (26.63b-64). This striking contrast between 'remaining silent' and 'speaking out' leads the reader to postulate a parallel contrast between the giving of false testimony and the posing of a question wherein the truth is expressed.

48. Mt. 21.11, 46.

49. Mt. 16.14; cf. 14.2.

50. Cf. Mt. 8.20 with 8.18; 10.23 with 10.5; 12.8 with 12.1; 13.41 with 13.36; 16.13.

51. Cf. nn. 45 and 46.

Asked to assert the truth of his identity, Jesus replies in the affirmative.

In the second place, Jesus' assertion '(So) you have said' can also be seen to be affirmative in nature because the source from which the high priest has got his question is none other than Jesus himself. As I noted above, what the high priest does at the trial is to take the claim to be the Son of God which Jesus advanced in his parable of the wicked husbandmen (21.37) and to direct it back at Jesus in the form of a question that places Jesus' answer under oath (26.63). In replying '(So) you have said' to the high priest, Jesus is therefore reaffirming his own claim to be the Son of God (21.37). For him to reply otherwise than in the affirmative would be for him to make of himself an 'unreliable character' and to place himself at odds with God's evaluative point of view concerning his identity.[52]

Accordingly, Jesus' immediate response to the question of the high priest is such as to assert the fact that he is indeed the messiah, the Son of God. Following this assertion, Jesus makes a solemn prediction in which he tacitly refers to himself as 'the Son of man' (26.64). As far as Jesus' identity is concerned, this Son-of-man reference appears to convey virtually nothing to those who hear it. What suggests this is the scene of mockery that accompanies Jesus' condemnation to death (26.67-68). In this scene, the members of the Sanhedrin identify Jesus, not as 'the Son of man', but as the 'messiah' (26.68). As in the case of 16.20 as well, 'messiah' here is an abbreviation for 'the messiah, the Son of God' (cf. 26.63; 16.16). Ignoring, therefore, Jesus' tacit reference to himself as 'the Son of man', the members of the Sanhedrin revert to the high priest's identification of Jesus as the messiah, the Son of God, and mock Jesus as such. In this crucial pericope, therefore, Matthew once again shows that he does not employ 'the Son of man' to explain 'who Jesus is'.

Still another observation that weighs heavily against the notion that 'the Son of man' informs the reader of the identity of Jesus is the circumstance that although Matthew makes liberal use of what may be termed the 'predication formula', in no case does he do so in conjunction with 'the Son of man'. As I define it, a 'predication formula' is a statement (even if conditional) or a question which attributes to Jesus some name, designation, or title of majesty in the interest of divulging

52. Cf. Mt. 26.63 with 21.37; 17.5; and 3.17.

'who he is'.[53] The following is a representative list of the predication formulas found in Matthew: (1) God affirms, 'This is my beloved Son' (3.17; 17.5); (2) the devil and, at the cross, the passers-by tempt Jesus with the words, 'If you are the Son of God...' (4.3, 6; 27.40); (3) through his disciples, John the Baptist asks Jesus, 'Are you the Coming One?' (11.3); (4) the crowds ask in amazement, anticipating a negative reply, 'This isn't the Son of David, is it?' (12.23; cf. 22.42, 45); (5) the people at Nazareth query one another, 'Is this not the son of the carpenter?' (13.55); (6) Herod declares to his servants, 'This is John the Baptist' (14.2); (7) Jesus discloses his identity to the anxious disciples by calling out, 'Take heart, it is I [Jesus];[54] have no fear' (14.27); (8) Peter confesses on behalf of the disciples, 'You are the messiah, the Son of the living God' (16.16; cf. 14.33); (9) the crowds shout aloud their perception of Jesus, 'This is the prophet Jesus, from Nazareth of Galilee' (21.11); (10) Jesus predicts in his eschatological discourse, 'For many will come in my name, saying, "I am the Messiah"' (24.5); (11) the high priest asks and Jesus responds affirmatively, '"... tell us whether you are the messiah, the Son of God"... "(So) you have said"' (26.63-64); (12) Pilate asks and Jesus responds affirmatively, '"Are you the King of the Jews?"... "(So) you say"' (27.11); (13) Pilate asserts by means of the charge the soldiers place above the head of the crucified Jesus, 'This is Jesus, the King of the Jews' (27.37; cf. 27.42); (14) the Jewish leaders mock Jesus as he hangs upon the cross, '... for he said, "I am the Son of God"' (27.43); and (15) the Roman soldiers affirm, 'Truly this was the Son of God' (27.54).

If one scans this list, one notices at once that the spectrum of characters who utter these predication formulas ranges from transcendent beings (God, Satan) to human beings (Jesus, John the Baptist, disciples, crowds, opponents, Roman soldiers) and that the designations, which have as their purpose to identify Jesus, are, in terms of evaluative points of view Matthew sanctions, both true ('Jesus', 'Coming One', 'messiah', 'Son of David', 'King of the Jews [Israel]', 'Son of God') and false (Jesus is 'John the Baptist' or a 'prophet' or simply the 'son of the carpenter'). In view of this broad and varied use of the predication

---

53. For a discussion of this rhetorical phenomenon, cf. E. Norden, *Agnostos Theos* (Leipzig: Teubner, 1913), pp. 177-201.

54. Cf. V. Howard, *Das Ego Jesu in den synoptischen Evangelien* (Marburger Theologische Studien, 14; Marburg: Elwert, 1975), p. 84.

formula in Matthew, it is highly significant that not a single example of its use contains 'the Son of man', and this despite the fact that Jesus frequently and openly speaks of himself as such. No one, neither transcendent being nor human being, says or asks of Jesus, 'This is (You are; Are you? Is this?) the Son of man'. The obvious inference to be drawn from this would seem to be that 'the Son of man' does not specify for the characters in Matthew's story 'who Jesus is'.

A final reason for believing that the function of 'the Son of man' in Matthew is not to tell the reader of the identity of Jesus has to do with its conspicuous absence from the first main part of Matthew's story (1.1–4.16). Rhetorically, this first main part functions principally as 'frame' material[55] to present Jesus to the reader so that the reader will know 'who Jesus is' throughout the rest of the story. This explains why the major designations by means of which Matthew makes Jesus known to the reader all stand out prominently in this part: 'Jesus', 'Jesus Christ', 'messiah', 'Son of David', 'King of the Jews', and 'Son of God' (also 'Son of Abraham', 'Emmanuel', 'one who shepherds'). This likewise explains why this entire first part reaches its culmination in the highly dramatic pericope on the baptism, in which God himself declares Jesus to be his beloved Son and in so doing gives expression to the evaluative point of view concerning Jesus' identity which the reader is to regard as being normative for Matthew's story (3.17). In contrast to the designations just cited and particularly to that of the Son of God, Matthew does not introduce 'the Son of man' into his story until as late as 8.20. Then, too, when he does introduce it, he does so unobtrusively, for the reader does not anticipate its sudden use and the focus of the text is neither on the term itself nor on the topic of Jesus' identity but on the theme of discipleship. Literarily, it is difficult to see from the way in which Matthew first acquaints the reader with 'the Son of man' that it is calculated to inform the reader of 'who Jesus is'.

VII

If on the one hand 'the Son of man' differs in nature from such major terms as χριστός, 'King of the Jews', 'Son of David', and 'Son of God' in so far as it does not function confessionally to set forth the identity of Jesus, it cannot be doubted, on the other hand, that Matthew

55. Cf. Uspensky, *Poetics of Composition*, p. 137.

would have the reader construe it as a technical term, or title. At least three factors combine to make this clear. For one thing, the use to which Matthew puts 'the Son of man' is such that, overall, it reflects the peculiar contours of the ministry of Jesus: Jesus designates himself as 'the Son of man' in association with his earthly activity,[56] with his suffering, death and resurrection,[57] and with his anticipated parousia.[58] The upshot is that 'the Son of man' is a term that applies to Jesus in a way in which it cannot be applied to any other human being. For another thing, 'the Son of man' is also unique because it constitutes the 'phraseological point of view'[59] of Jesus exclusively: it occurs solely in his mouth; it is always definite in form ('the' Son of man);[60] and when Jesus employs it, he does so to refer to himself alone. And thirdly, Jesus fulfills Old Testament prophecy in his capacity as 'the Son of man',[61] which is further indication that 'the Son of man' possesses a status that is comparable to that of the other major titles.[62]

VIII

It has been concluded thus far that 'the Son of man' is a title in Matthew but that it does not apprise the reader of 'who Jesus is'. What, then, does it mean? How does it function? And what impact does Matthew's use of it have upon his story? To get at these questions, 'the Son of man' may be defined as the title by means of which Jesus refers to himself 'in public' or in view of the 'public' (or 'world') in order to point to himself as 'the man', or 'the human being' (earthly, suffering, vindicated), and to assert his divine authority in the face of opposition.

'The Son of man' describes Jesus in Matthew as 'the man', or 'the human being' (earthly, suffering, vindicated); for purposes of translation, one can perhaps capture its force by rendering it as 'this man', or 'this

56. Cf. Mt. 8.20; 9.6; 11.19; 12.8; 13.37; 16.13.

57. Cf. Mt. 12.40; 17.9, 12, 22; 20.18, 28; 26.2, 24, 45.

58. Cf. Mt. 10.23; 13.41; 16.27-28; 19.28; 24.27, 30, 37, 39, 44; 25.31; 26.64.

59. Cf. Uspensky, *Poetics of Composition*, ch. 2.

60. Cf. C.F.D. Moule, 'Neglected Features in the Problem of "the Son of Man"', in *Neues Testament und Kirche* (Festschrift Rudolf Schnackenburg; ed. J. Gnilka; Freiburg: Herder, 1974), pp. 419-22.

61. Cf. Mt. 12.40; 13.41-43; 16.27; 24.29-31, 37-39; 25.31; 26.24, 64.

62. Cf., e.g., Mt. 1.22-23; 2.1-6, 15; 3.17; 11.2-6; 12.17-21; 17.5; 21.4-5, 9; 21.33-46; 22.44; 23.38-39; 26.31.

human being'.[63] But, be that as it may, Matthew indicates in three passages in particular what 'the Son of man' means. At 11.19, for example, Jesus denounces this generation for dismissing the Son of man as the 'man' who is a glutton and a drunkard, a friend of tax collectors and sinners. At 9.6, Jesus declares that the Son of man has authority on earth to forgive sins and gives demonstration of this by healing a paralytic, whereupon the crowds respond by glorifying God for giving such authority to 'men' (9.8). And in the interpretation of the parable of the tares, Jesus first identifies the Son of man with the 'man' who in the parable has sown good seed (cf. 13.37 with 13.24) and then identifies this earthly Son of man with the future Son of man who will come at the consummation of the age to inaugurate the Great Assize (cf. 13.17 with 13.40-43).

Recognition of the fact that 'the Son of man' denotes 'the man' (this man) in Matthew dovetails neatly with what one can observe about the way in which this title functions. 'The Son of man' does not function, as has been pointed out, as a confessional title to set forth the identity of

---

63. For a discussion of linguistic considerations to take into account in dealing with the term 'the Son of man', cf. J. Fitzmyer, 'The New Testament Title "Son of Man" Philologically Considered', in *A Wandering Aramean* (SBLMS, 25; Missoula, MT: Scholars Press, 1979), pp. 143-60. The term ὁ υἱὸς τοῦ ἀνθρώπου, which has the two articles and hence, as C.F.D. Moule has reminded us (cf. 'Neglected Features', pp. 419-22; also *The Origin of Christology* [Cambridge: Cambridge University Press, 1977], p. 11 n. 1), is definite in form, means literally 'the son of the man (human being)' or, more simply, 'the man (human being)' (cf. already J. Wellhausen, *Einleitung in die drei ersten Evangelien* [Berlin: Georg Reimer, 1905], p. 40). The question, however, is how to render this term in translation so that the reader understands the sense the interpreter believes it is meant to convey. Since in Matthew 'the Son of man' is, as I have argued above, to be construed as a title, the option is precluded according to which the term has no consistent meaning but may denote 'I' (or 'me') in one instance or 'a man' in another or be a christological title in yet another. For the present, the translational equivalent that seems to me to convey best the consistent meaning 'the Son of man' bears in Matthew is 'this man', or 'this human being' (although they envisage primarily the historical Jesus, the discussions of the meaning of 'the Son of man' by J.P. Brown ['The Son of Man: "This Fellow"', *Bib* 58 (1977), pp. 361-87] and Moule [*Christology*, p. 15] are perhaps pertinent; cf. also the note by B. Lindars ['The New Look on the Son of Man', *BJRL* 63 (1980), p. 456 n. 1]). Unfortunately, the recent volume by B. Lindars (*Jesus Son of Man* [London: SPCK, 1983]) was not available to me in the writing of this article.

Jesus, but as a 'public title'.[64] In my use of the term 'public title', I have
two things in mind. The first thing is that it is principally with an eye to
the 'world', Jews and Gentiles and especially opponents, that Jesus designates himself as the Son of man. To verify this, consider the following.
In the earthly Son-of-man sayings, it is in view of the Jewish public
(16.13) or of the world (13.36-37) or in the audience of the crowds,[65] of
some of the scribes,[66] and of the Pharisees[67] that Jesus refers to himself
as the Son of man. In the suffering Son-of-man sayings, it is to some of
the scribes and Pharisees (12.38, 40) or to the disciples but in view of
Judas,[68] of 'men'[69] and 'sinners' (26.45), of the Jewish leaders (20.18),
of Gentiles (20.19), and of the rulers of the Gentiles (20.25, 28) that
Jesus speaks of himself as the Son of man. And in the future Son-of-man
sayings, it is in view of all the nations (Israel, the Gentiles, the Jewish
leaders, but also the disciples)[70] that Jesus calls himself the Son of man.
This orientation towards the 'world' in Jesus' use of the Son of man is
the one thing that, again, marks this title as 'public' in nature.

The second thing I have in mind in designating the Son of man as a
'public title' is the curious phenomenon touched on earlier. This phenomenon is that Jesus can, on the one hand, openly speak of himself as
the Son of man in the full hearing of the Jewish leaders, the crowds, and
the disciples and yet, on the other hand, never be identified or even
addressed by these groups as such. Proof that these groups do not construe Jesus' identity in terms of the Son of man can be found in especially striking fashion in the pericope on Peter's confession, which is
climactic as far as the subject of Jesus' identity throughout the whole of
4.17–16.20 is concerned. In this pericope, Matthew shows that whereas
the Jewish public wrongly thinks of Jesus as being John the Baptist,
Elijah, Jeremiah, or one of the prophets, the disciples, represented by
Peter, rightly know him to be the messiah, the Son of the living God
(16.13-16). The reason, of course, that Matthew does not so shape this
pericope as to present some segment of the Jewish public or the disciples

64. Cf. also Kingsbury, *Matthew*, pp. 113-22.
65. Cf. Mt. 8.18, 20; 9.6, 8; 11.7, 19.
66. Cf. Mt. 9.3, 6; also 8.19-20.
67. Cf. Mt. 12.2, 8, 24, 32.
68. Cf. Mt. 26.2, 24-25, 45-46.
69. Cf. Mt. 17.22; also 17.12.
70. Cf. Mt. 10.23; 13.41-43; 16.27-28; 19.28; 24.27, 30-31, 37-39, 44; 25.31-32;
26.64.

as identifying Jesus as the Son of man has to do with the meaning of this title. Describing Jesus as it does as 'the (this) man', 'the Son of man' can occur in Jesus' mouth frequently and in public and still not occasion the disclosure of his identity. To term the Son of man a 'public title', therefore, is also to envisage this phenomenon.

This leads me to consider a related matter of importance. Because the Son of man is a 'public title' that does not divulge the identity of Jesus, the question arises as to how, specifically, the reader is to construe the identity of Jesus Son of man. On this score, Matthew is unambiguous, directing the reader to the words of Peter. Who, then, is Jesus, the Son of man (16.13)? He is the Son of God (16.16). And lest one object that this answer is but the words of Peter, one will recall that the evaluative point of view Peter expresses in his confession is in accord with the evaluative point of view God has expressed at the baptism (3.17) and the transfiguration (17.5). Then, too, for the reader to recognize that the Son of man in Matthew is to be identified as the Son of God is also of benefit for gaining insight into yet another problem area. In the passages 16.27 and 25.34, the expressions 'his Father' and 'my Father' occur with reference to Jesus as the Son of man. Seen properly, these expressions likewise attest to the identity of Jesus, the Son of man: Jesus Son of man, in referring to God as 'my Father', tacitly bears witness thereby that he is the Son of God.

Associated with Jesus' use of the Son of man in Matthew is the assertion on his part of divine authority.[71] If we leave aside the passages 16.13 and perhaps 12.32, Jesus assumes to himself in the earthly Son-of-man sayings the power to forgive sins (9.6), to regulate the sabbath (12.8), to have table fellowship with tax collectors and sinners (11.19), and to raise up in the world sons of the Kingdom (13.37-38). Paradoxically, he also asserts his authority by embracing the life-style of 'itinerant radicalism' (8.19-20).[72] In the suffering Son-of-man sayings, Jesus evinces his authority by freely going the way of the cross in obedience to the will of God.[73] Indeed, as one who employs his authority not to be served but to serve, Jesus holds himself up as the example his

---

71. Cf. H.E. Tödt, *Der Menschensohn in der synoptischen Überlieferung* (Gütersloh: Gerd Mohn, 1959), p. 200.

72. Cf. G. Theissen, 'Itinerant Radicalism: The Tradition of Jesus Sayings from the Perspective of the Sociology of Literature', *Radical Religion* 2 (1975), pp. 84-93.

73. Cf. Mt. 17.22-23; 20.18-19; 26.24, 45, 56; also 16.21.

disciples are to emulate in their life together (20.28). And in the future
Son-of-man sayings, Jesus exercises his authority as the end-time judge
who ushers in the consummated Kingdom and inaugurates the Great
Assize.[74]

Also associated with the Son-of-man sayings in Matthew is a strong
emphasis on the element of opposition.[75] In regard to the earthly Son-of-
man sayings, such opposition comes to expression in numerous ways:
Satan stands forth as the cosmic antagonist of Jesus (13.37-39); 'men'
prove themselves to be ignorant of Jesus' true identity and imagine him
to be a prophet (16.13-14); 'this generation' repudiates Jesus (11.19); a
scribe wrongly attempts to arrogate to himself the right to become
Jesus' disciple (8.19-20); and the Jewish leaders charge Jesus with blasphemy (9.3, 6), accuse him of being in collusion with Satan (12.24, 32),
and take him to task because his disciples have allegedly acted unlaw-
fully on the sabbath (12.2, 8). In the suffering Son-of-man sayings, Jesus
speaks directly of the opposition he faces by predicting his death (12.39-
40), by telling his disciples of what his enemies will do to him,[76] and by
contrasting as opposites his will to serve with the will of the rulers of the
world to lord it over others (20.25-28). And in the future Son-of-man
sayings, Jesus sounds the note of opposition (but also of hope) by portraying himself as the judge who will hold the entire world accountable,
consigning some to condemnation and inviting others to share in the
bliss of God's presence.[77]

The objective of the preceding discussion has been to explain the
meaning and the function of 'the Son of man' in Matthew's Gospel. As
has been indicated, 'the Son of man' does not function 'confessionally'
to inform the reader of 'who Jesus is' but instead characterizes Jesus as
'the man', or 'the human being' (this man, or this human being). But
although 'the Son of man' does not denominate the identity of Jesus, it
is nonetheless a christological title, for it bears the unique stamp of Jesus'
life and ministry: earthly, suffering, and vindicated. In nature, the Son of
man is a 'public title', which is to say that Jesus employs it 'in public' or

74. Cf. Mt. 13.40-43; 16.27-28; 24.29-31; 26.31-46; 26.64.
75. Cf. F. Hahn, *Christologische Hoheitstitel* (FRLANT, 83; Göttingen:
Vandenhoeck & Ruprecht, 1963), p. 48.
76. Cf. Mt. 17.12, 22-23; 20.18-20; 26.2, 24, 45-46.
77. Cf. Mt. 10.23; 13.40-43; 16.27-28; 19.28; 24.29-31, 37-39, 43-44; 25.31-46;
26.64.

in view of the 'public', or 'world', and especially of his opponents. Typical of Jesus' use of this title is the assertion on his part of divine authority in the face of opposition.

This brings me to the final question of this study: What impact does Matthew's use of the title of the Son of man have upon his story? To answer this question, it is instructive to compare the overall role of this title with that of the family of titles at the head of which stands the 'Son of God'. Simply put, the title of the Son of God serves to identify Jesus for the reader. Thus, the first main part of Matthew's story culminates in God's announcement that Jesus is his Son (3.17), and the second main part culminates in the confession by Peter, which is in alignment with God's understanding of Jesus, that Jesus is God's Son (16.16-17). In the third main part of Matthew's story, Jesus appropriates God's understanding of him as his Son in the parable of the wicked husbandmen he addresses to the Jewish leaders (21.37-39), and from this parable, in turn, the high priest derives the question concerning Jesus' divine sonship on which Jesus' trial turns and for which he is condemned to death for blasphemy (26.63-64a). But despite this, upon Jesus' death the Roman soldiers, also uttering words that are in alignment with God's understanding of Jesus, likewise declare Jesus to be God's Son (27.54). The significance of their declaration is that with it Matthew has, in terms of narrating his story, guided it to a point where knowledge of the identity of Jesus also embraces, as far as the reader is concerned, a mature knowledge of the purpose of Jesus' earthly ministry. Finally, on a mountain in Galilee the disciples, to whom Jesus' identity had earlier been revealed (16.16; 14.33), see the resurrected Jesus as the crucified one (28.5-7) and hence comprehend at last not only who he is but also what he was about; accordingly, they receive from the resurrected Jesus, not a command to silence (16.20), but the commission to go and to make of all nations his disciples (28.16-20). Roughly parallel with this line of development (from 8.20 on), Jesus refers to himself in Matthew's story as the Son of man. In so doing, he does not divulge his identity but instead characterizes himself as 'the man', or 'the human being' (this man, or this human being). The purpose for which Jesus employs this title is multiple: to assert his divine authority in the face of public opposition, to tell his disciples what the 'public', or 'world' (Jews and Gentiles), is about to do to him, and to predict that he whom the world puts to death God will raise and that, exalted to universal rule, he will return in splendor as judge and consequently be seen by all as having been vindicated by God. Through Jesus' use of the public title of the Son of man, therefore, Matthew calls the reader's attention to the twin elements of 'conflict' and 'vindication'. In Matthew's purview, these mark the interaction of Jesus with the public, or world, that does not receive him as the one he is, namely, the Son of God.

JSNT 21 (1984), pp. 37-52

THE FIGURE OF JESUS IN MATTHEW'S STORY:
A RESPONSE TO PROFESSOR KINGSBURY'S
LITERARY-CRITICAL PROBE

David Hill

I

To be invited to respond to an essay on a Matthean topic written by
such an expert as Professor Kingsbury is an honour and I welcome the
opportunity to make some comments on this new attempt by him to
confirm his view that in Matthew's christology is preeminently a Son of
God christology. In other important publications[1] Kingsbury has sought
to establish this claim by using the methods and techniques of Gospel-
criticism which are familiar to all New Testament scholars. In the essay
before us he adopts an approach which is becoming increasingly fashionable (especially in the United States) and offers us a narrative reading
or literary-critical reading of Matthew which, it is claimed, corroborates
the dominance of the Son of God christology in the book.

This kind of reading of Matthew as 'story' or 'narrative' (rather than
'Gospel', since that term would probably introduce complicating considerations) requires or enables Kingsbury to lay aside altogether questions
about Matthew's sources and his redactional intention(s). There is no
comparison with Mark's narrative or Luke's: only Matthew's story as it
stands now is examined. That this is a quite valid approach to Matthew
is assured less by the fact that increasing numbers of scholars are
attracted to this way of reading biblical materials than by the fact that
there must have been some Christians for whom Matthew's form of the
Jesus-story was the only one they ever knew, heard or read: there was

---

1.   Most notably in *Matthew: Structure, Christology, Kingdom* (London: SPCK,
1976), and *Matthew* (Proclamation Commentaries; London: SPCK, 1978).

once an audience who had to read Matthew's story as Kingsbury reads it. To that extent it is immaterial whether Matthew wrote his story first or independently of other forms of the Jesus-story or in greater or lesser dependence on other forms of that story.

We, however, know that there is a relationship of some kind between Matthew's story and that of Mark as well as Luke's—and that knowledge depends upon literary investigation too—and therefore a reading of Matthew which does not take into account the writer's sources and, in particular, his redactional work cannot be regarded as an adequate reading of the story on which to build a claim about a special emphasis in Matthew's presentation of Jesus. That his literary-critical probe does not prove anything about Matthew's christology is implicitly accepted by Kingsbury; what it does, he argues, is to confirm what he sought to prove by the necessary investigative methods. In my view, the outcome of this reading of Matthew was never in doubt, not because Kingsbury presupposed his conclusions or cajoled evidence, but because a literary-critical reading of a narrative has an undeniably subjective element to it, and J.D. Kingsbury knows his mind very well on the matter of Matthean christology. Where my response depends on another narrative reading of Matthew's story the observations are likely to be as subjective as those of Kingsbury.

Given then that what Kingsbury sets out to do is a respectable and potentially interesting project for a scholar to take up (but with *limited* value because of the acknowledged interconnections between three forms of the Jesus-story), how satisfying and illuminating is this narrative reading of Matthew?

At the beginning of his essay Kingsbury draws upon the work of some of those scholars who have been analyzing gospel-material from the standpoint of literary, or narrative criticism in order to bring into play the rhetorical device of 'ideological (evaluative) point of view' (i.e. a way of looking at things). Matthew's point of view is adopted by the reader in order to involve himself in Matthew's story, which itself expresses Jesus' point of view. 'Hence as Matthew describes it there is only one correct way in which to view things: the way of Jesus, which is likewise Matthew's own way' (p. 50; all page numbers refer to the reprinted article by Kingsbury above). It would have been simpler to say (for the point is fairly obvious) that Matthew lets Jesus' point of view or way of looking at things come over, without obstruction, in his narrative. Since N. Petersen says exactly the same about Mark[2] one wonders if this transparency to Jesus' point of view is not a feature common to at least all three canonical versions of the Jesus-story. Be that as it may, it is surprising, in my view, that, after saying that for Matthew the only correct way of viewing things is Jesus' way, Kingsbury makes another move and claims (i) that Jesus' (and Matthew's) point of view is aligned with the evaluative point of view of God; and (ii) that 'By authorial design, Matthew establishes God's conception of reality, his system of values or "will" as being normative for the story he tells' (p. 50). This claim that God's point of view is the determinative one for Matthew's story is a highly significant one for the whole essay, and we must consider carefully the evidence Kingsbury uses to justify it. But before doing so, I have to admit that it was this very claim which made me think that the outcome of this probe, in relation to Matthew's view of Jesus, was already settled and delivered and would accord with what Kingsbury has strongly argued for elsewhere and by other means. Could anyone read Matthew (or Mark, or Luke) letting *Jesus'* point of view be normative and suggest that 'Son of God' was the dominant christology? It is of more than a little interest that when Petersen is discussing 'point of view' in Mark's narrative he does not make this move from Jesus' way of looking at things to God's; and yet Mark contains evidence (on which Petersen comments in such a way as to suggest that here lies the inspiration of Kingsbury's entire project[3]) which is parallel to some of that which is used by Kingsbury to validate his claim about the dominance of God's point of view in Matthew, evidence which would have allowed Petersen

2.   N. Petersen, '"Point of View" in Mark's Narrative', *Semeia* 12 (1978), pp. 97-121, especially p. 107.

3.   Petersen's statement deserves to be quoted in full: 'Although Mark never explicitly claims any title as his own, except for the name "Jesus" ("son of God" in 1.1 is textually suspect), his ideological, temporal and spatial, and psychological identification of his point of view with Jesus's, aligns him with the one appellation used only by Jesus, "son of Man". How this alignment is related to the other title of which he seems to approve, "son of God"... remains to be seen. At present, only my intuition tells me that the relationship is to be found in the distinction between the things of God and the things of men' ('Point of View', pp. 111-12). By this Petersen means to refer to Mk 8.33, which he used earlier (p. 107) to point out the ideological difference between Peter's point of view and Jesus', the latter being the evaluative one shared by Mark and Jesus.

(an acknowledged literary reader of Gospel material) to make the same claim with reference to Mark, if he had thought it right to do so. For example, if the baptism and transfiguration are, as Kingsbury claims, occasions when God himself directly enters the world of Matthew's story as 'actor' in order to address other characters (in this case, Jesus)—and are there any other equally direct entrances by God?—is this not the case also in Mark's story and in Luke's as well? Has Petersen just failed to see the significance of this for 'point of view', or is he correct in not allowing these and other factors to alter his conviction that Jesus' way of viewing things is the only right way in Mark's narrative?

Kingsbury, however, offers arguments to support his claim about the determinative point of view in Matthew. The first point is oblique: Matthew indicates by means of the genealogy with which he begins his story and by means of parables such as those which are spoken against Israel (21.28–22.14) that God is the guiding agent of the whole of the history of salvation, of which the life of Jesus is a part, and that therefore God is the one who establishes the prevailing norms of this history and of the story of Jesus. Even if this evidence were to permit the claim that God is the guiding agent of the history of salvation (something I think all the Gospel writers presupposed, even if they would not have expressed the belief in precisely these words), does that necessarily mean that he is the one who 'establishes the prevailing norms of this history and of Jesus' story'—whatever that means. It looks as if Kingsbury's language is chosen and calculated to advance his known position. But what are we to say of this oblique evidence that God's point of view governs the story? The genealogy solves the problem for Matthew of Jesus' relationship to the Old Testament and does so in terms of affirming continuity and fulfilment: the focus is on Jesus messiah emerging from Israel's history as its crown. The parables against Israel are *Jesus'* way of announcing what is really happening as a result of Israel's attitude to *himself*: the emphasis (in my view) remains on Jesus as prophet of God's judgment. In the passages cited by Kingsbury Matthew does not seem to me to be making a point (consciously or unconsciously) about God's guidance of or responsibility for salvation-history: it is Jesus who is the focus of interest. He fulfils the Old Testament and his messianic status is confirmed therefrom, and it is Jesus who proclaims and makes effective divine judgment. (Incidentally, I wonder if Matthew would have understood what we call 'salvation-history', and is it a category proper to a literary-critical reading of a text?)

Next Kingsbury appeals to the 'obtrusive' ways in which Matthew arranges for God to communicate his will or view to others. At the baptism (3.17) and transfiguration (17.5) God himself enters Matthew's story as 'actor'. In addition to observing that both Mark's story and Luke's contain the same intrusions (and that may lessen their significance in Matthew's narrative), I would say that it is not God's voice that is the dominant concern of the two incidents, but Jesus' identity: the narrator's point of view and God's point of view are aligned to affirm *who Jesus is*, not to establish God's conception of reality as normative for Matthew's story. That angelic messages to Joseph and to the women at the tomb are ways in which Matthew (and of course he is not the only writer of the Jesus-story to introduce these features) affirms divine intervention in what happens is true, but surely it is the happening (Jesus' birth and Jesus' resurrection)—in which God is involved—that is Matthew's real concern, rather than the desire to establish 'by authorial design' (which would surely require demonstration by references to other writers) that God's system of values or 'will' is normative for his story.

Kingsbury then proceeds to claim that the primary way in which Matthew shows that God's point of view is normative for his story is by having Jesus (and, subsidiarily, John the Baptist) reliably espouse that point of view; and that Matthew achieves this (a) with the aid of the Old Testament, and (b) without the aid of the Old Testament. Concerning (a), the formula-quotations and formula-citations, Kingsbury asserts that 'by cloaking the like of Jesus and many of his words in the aura of Old Testament Scripture Matthew establishes Jesus as the thoroughly reliable exponent of God's evaluative point of view' (p. 52). It is undeniably true that at 1.22 and 2.15 events take place to fulfil that which has been spoken *by the Lord* through the prophet: the ὑπὸ Κυρίου which is found in only these two formula citations is not repeated because, in my opinion, the Old Testament quotations refer to sonship, and Matthew wishes—in the birth narratives at any rate—to affirm Jesus' sonship to God/the Lord. The other formula-citations (in which the 'event' takes place in fulfilment of what was spoken *through* the prophet) and the other Old Testament quotations and allusions on Jesus' lips seem to have as their chief purpose for Matthew the desire to affirm that in his ministry Jesus fulfils the Old Testament. The focus is not on an old

formula but on a recent life.[4] I find it difficult to accept the idea that by
his formula citations, etc., Matthew is establishing Jesus as the truly
reliable exponent of God's point of view which, in turn, is normative for
his story. The citations, in Matthew's hand, are the means whereby he
links Jesus' life and ministry, in terms of fulfilment, to the Old Testament.
The central focus is on *Jesus* and *his* relationship to Israel's Scripture,
and that is not quite the same thing as 'God' or 'God's point of view'.

That God's point of view is determinative of the fabric of Matthew's
story is affirmed (b) by appeal to sayings of Jesus which do not relate to
the Old Testament: where he says he has to serve the purpose of God,
speaks of God as 'my father' and of himself as 'the son', acknowledges
the divine necessity of the passion, utters programmatic statements like
11.27 and 26.39-42; where he teaches disciples to treat God's will as
normative and to pray 'Our Father... let your will be done'; and when
he asserts that the standards by which Israel and the nations will be
judged are those which God sets. Once again it is a matter of where one
thinks the emphasis lies: certainly God's 'will' or point of view is carried
out, commanded, proclaimed, affirmed by Jesus, but three comments are
in order: (i) could any Jesus-story say or imply the contrary? (ii) the other
Jesus narratives we have say the same kind of thing (both about Jesus
and disciples); and (iii) the emphasis remains on Jesus throughout. Jesus'
way of looking at things aligns with God's, but in Matthew's story it is
not the latter which is being presented as normative or determinative,
but rather Jesus' point of view, with which, of course, Matthew agrees.

I cannot therefore agree that a literary-critical reading of Matthew's
story informs the reader that God's evaluative point of view governs the
narrative. It seems to me that in Matthew's narrative, taken as a whole,
the way of Jesus is the one correct point of view: on him, as it were, the
camera holds throughout. The God-orientation of the story is background, not foreground; it is of the greatest importance in a theological
reading of the narrative, but is not very obvious or determinative in a
literary reading of Matthew's story. Consequently I am not convinced
by Kingsbury's claim that, as far as christology in Matthew is concerned, it is God's evaluative point of view regarding Jesus (not Jesus'
point of view regarding himself) which is established by an authorial
choice which is discernible on a literary reading of the story.

4.   E. Schweizer, *The Good News according to Matthew* (London: SPCK;
Atlanta: John Knox, 1976), p. 27.

II

In the second part of his essay Kingsbury attempts to demonstrate that God's point of view about Jesus is normative for Matthew. In seeking to do this he has recourse to the divisions of the narrative which he has argued for elsewhere, and at the same time he implies that the findings of the literary-critical reading support his view of Matthew's structure. '[T]he flow of Matthew's story... is such as to commend the threefold division of Matthew I have set forth elsewhere' (p. 48)—and which has been quite severely criticized elsewhere.[5]

With so much of what Kingsbury writes here about the content of his first section (1.1–4.16) and the christological titles introduced in it I am in agreement, but I am not sure that the Spirit-empowerment and the identifying voice from heaven at Jesus' baptism 'bring the entire first part of Matthew's story to its culmination' (p. 56). That may be so if the first part does extend from 1.1 to 4.16. But this is to assume that the baptism of Jesus and his temptation belong structurally to the infancy narrative, rather than to the public ministry. In arguing thus in *Matthew: Structure, Christology, Kingdom* (p. 13) Kingsbury suggests that the weak and ambiguous particle δέ in 3.1 acts as a connective; but it may just as readily have a disjunctive force, and the deciding factor must be the context. And the context here at 3.1 is a jump of about thirty years (from the settlement at Nazareth to the beginning of the public ministry), the introduction of a completely new character (John the Baptist) and of a new (eschatological?) event solemnly introduced by the significant phrase 'in those days'. A literary-critical reading of the narrative will, I think, suggest to the open-minded that a fresh section starts, after the birth narratives, at 3.1. Furthermore, it is not by chance that in 3.2 Matthew places John the Baptist in parallel position to Jesus: he proclaims word-for-word the message which Jesus will proclaim in 4.17 (supposedly across the great structural divide), 'Repent, for the kingdom of God is at hand'. I would argue that with 3.1 the prologue has ended and the main body of the Gospel-story has commenced, and I think that a literary reading of the narrative would assent. But Kingsbury, interested of course in the Son of God declaration by God in 3.16, thinks that must be the climax to the first part of the story. He fails to observe

5. Most recently in R.H. Fuller and P. Perkins, *Who is This Christ?* (Philadelphia: Fortress Press, 1983), ch. 7.

that that christology has already been affirmed in 2.15 where the Old Testament words 'Out of Egypt have I called my son' are said to be spoken *by the Lord* through the prophet. That is the climax of the prologue; it is being reaffirmed, even more directly, early in the second major section of the narrative, at 3.16. But however important the divine declaration here may be, it designates more than Jesus' sonship. Kingsbury readily admits that the words of the divine voice recall Isa. 42.1 and possibly Gen. 22.2, as well as Ps. 2.7, but again (as in his earlier books) he lays no emphasis on the Isaiah references, and yet the 'This is...' may be a means of shifting the spotlight from Psalm 2 to Isa. 42.1 where God presents his servant in the third person: 'here is my servant...in whom I am pleased, upon whom I have put my spirit'. And I have argued elsewhere,[6] Matthew's interest in the Servant-of-the-Lord aspect of Jesus' sonship is clear from the two passages from the Servant songs of Isaiah which he uses as formula quotations, 8.17 and 12.18-21, the latter being the longest Old Testament citation in the entire Matthean story. A literary-critical reading of narrative must be alert to allusions and hints if it is to be sensitive, and there is a highly significant allusion to the Servant of the Lord in 3.16.

There are then three arguments to be set beside those of Kingsbury on his first section: (i) 1.1–4.16 is not a natural first section; chs. 1 and 2 (as prologue) in a sense stand outside the flow of the story (as part of the 'frame') which really commences at 3.1; (ii) Jesus' sonship finds divine expression in 2.15 (the climax of the prologue) and again at the baptism, which is the effective beginning of the story of the ministry; and (iii) the important baptismal announcement bears witness to Jesus as Servant of the Lord as well as Son of God. Incidentally, it is odd to find the formula quotations which lead up to the divine declaration in 3.16, namely 1.22-23 and 2.15, described as being 'of the nature of a comment that Matthew directs to the reader alone' (p. 57), whereas earlier the formula-quotations are taken as evidence that Matthew establishes Jesus as the thoroughly reliable exponent of God's point of view—an argument about which I have already expressed uneasiness.

---

6.   D. Hill, 'Son and Servant: An Essay on Matthean Christology', *JSNT* 6 (1980), pp. 2-16.

III

In the next section of his essay Kingsbury reviews what for him is the second major division of Matthew's story, 4.17–16.20; concerning this he concludes,

> Matthew brings the second main part of his story, in which he tells of Jesus' ministry to Israel and of Israel's reaction to him (4.17–16.20), to its culmination by showing that, whereas the public in Israel does not 'receive' Jesus and falsely conceives of him as being a prophet, the disciples confess him aright to be the Son of God and so reveal that their evaluative point of view concerning Jesus' identity is 'in alignment' with that of God. (p. 60)

The important verses for this conclusion are 14.33, where the disciples exclaim (after seeing Jesus walk on the water and rescue Peter), 'Truly you are the Son of God', and 16.16, which records Peter's confession, 'You are the messiah, the son of the living God'. It cannot be denied that on any kind of reading of Matthew's narrative the Caesarea Philippi incident is a climactic moment (as it is in Mark's story too), but are the words of Peter so unambiguously correct and, to use Kingsbury's terms, 'in alignment with God's point of view? Let us recall again the divine point of view expressed at the baptism and repeated, in exactly the same words, at the transfiguration: Jesus is the Servant-Son. Peter in fact is not 'in alignment' with that point of view and, because he refuses to countenance the way of suffering for the messiah-Son, is told by Jesus that he does not 'think the things of God', but rather 'thinks the things of men', that is, has a human or worldly point of view. It is striking that Kingsbury makes so little of the rebuke to Peter; the reason probably is his structural division of the story. His second main part ends at 16.20 (before the third occurrence of ἀπὸ τότε ἤρξατο[7]) which is in the middle of the Caesarea Philippi episode and dialogue, just before Jesus corrects Peter's expressed understanding of him. Admittedly Jesus does not say that Peter's confession is wrong; he implies that it is inadequate or inadequately understood: the element of necessary suffering is absent. Sonship is to be interpreted along Servant lines, as the divine voice had made clear. Consequently, in my view, Kingsbury is too positive in his

---

7. This Greek phrase acts as the marker for Kingsbury's three-fold division of the Matthean narrative; cf. *Matthew: Structure, Christology, Kingdom*, ch. 1.

evaluation of Peter's declaration; his structural division of Matthew's narrative permits or encourages this, as does the almost mechanical assumption that every time the Son of God title is uttered (as at 14.33), it is, in and of itself, *the* adequate or correct witness to Jesus' identity. But God's Son is God's Servant who 'took our infirmities and bore our diseases' (8.17), the one who suffers to save. The exclamations of the disciples and of Peter only partially reflect that understanding of who Jesus is, an understanding which is shared by Matthew and, as we will hope to demonstrate, by the Matthean Jesus.

On the matter of the structural division of Matthew's story I have drawn attention to the artificiality of a major division at 16.20; it is time now to observe that in this literary-critical probe of Matthew's narrative Kingsbury never comments on one of its most obvious literary features, viz. the repeated use of 'and when Jesus had finished these sayings... ' which occurs, as is well known, five times (7.28; 11.1; 13.53; 19.1; 26.1). It is not necessary to make this literary feature bear all the weight of an argument about the (new) pentateuchal-structure of Matthew; it is sufficient to recognize the repetitions (and they may be, as R.H. Gundry suggests,[8] no more than evidence of the author's desire to conform to Jewish convention about 'five-ness' in religious writings) and any unbiased literary reading would adjudge them to be intended markers or divisions in the story. Kingsbury ignores them and tries to validate his own threefold division by unconvincing claims about the climactic character of episodes where the Son of God title appears.

In his fourth section Kingsbury examines what for him is Matthew's third section, 16.21–28.20, and he claims that this part culminates in two events: (i) the declaration by the Roman soldiers concerning Jesus, 'Truly this man was the Son of God' (27.54); and (ii) the meeting of Jesus with the eleven disciples in Galilee and the commission he gives them (28.16-20). At the beginning of this section of his essay Kingsbury deals with the demand for secrecy which Jesus laid on his disciples after their recognition of his messiahship; the reason for this, it is claimed, is that the disciples, though they know who Jesus is (the Son of God), are not yet in a position to go and make disciples of all nations (by proclaiming their knowledge) because they are ignorant of the central purpose of Jesus' mission, which is his suffering. It seems to me odd that the

8.   R.H. Gundry, *Matthew: A Commentary on his Literary and Theological Art* (Grand Rapids: Eerdmans, 1982), pp. 10-11.

disciples can be said to have penetrated the truth about Jesus' identity while remaining totally ignorant of his mission's purpose. The fact is, as I have suggested, that they do *not* really know who Jesus is: their declarations do not contain the necessary element of suffering and therefore we find Jesus instructing them in it, almost against their will and belief. Kingsbury is driven to an indefensible solution to the secrecy demand because his major division of Matthew's narrative comes at the wrong place and because he assumes that 'son of the living God' on Peter's lips is a completely accurate witness to Jesus' identity. That that confession is inadequate or improperly understood is clear from Jesus' further teaching and by the repetition (in 17.5) of the divine voice which reaffirms the Servanthood of the son and adds, as if to correct misunderstandings, 'Listen to him'.

Before commenting on Kingsbury's use of the declaration made by the Roman soldiers, I wish to make an observation on the reply of Jesus to the high priest's accusing and unbelieving question, '... Are you the messiah, the Son of God?'. The response, 'so you have said' (σὺ εἶπας) or 'The words are yours' (NEB) is a very indirect form of affirmation: it is as if Matthew wishes to show Jesus distancing himself from the language and titles used by immediately appealing (with a strong adversative) to the Son of man designation and imagery. Kingsbury deduces from Jesus' reply in 26.64 that he is 'thinking' about himself as God has revealed that he 'thinks' about him (3.17; 17.5), that is, as Son of God. But what about 27.11 where the words σὺ λέγεις appear again as Jesus' reply to Pilate's question, 'Are you the king of the Jews?' The matter of the coherence of Jesus' view of himself and the divine disclosure about him in 3.17 and 17.5 is not at all as simple as Kingsbury's reliance on the appearances of the Son of God title would suggest.

As far as the declaration by the Roman soldiers is concerned, I hesitate about its climactic importance as expressed by Kingsbury. I cannot put out of my mind how powerfully climactic this Gentile confession is in Mark's story where, on seeing Jesus breathe his last, the centurion exclaims, 'Truly this man was the Son of God'. In Matthew what the soldiers see and what provokes their exclamation is no longer the unspectacular death of Jesus but a violent earthquake and its consequences. Thus the confession, though still important, loses a good deal of its dramatic force and impact on the reader. And I suspect that, read without any knowledge of Mark, this declaration in Matthew is not quite the climax Kingsbury makes of it. Given the astounding miracles which evoke the confession one is surprised not to be told that all Jerusalem spoke in the same vein—an idea which occurred to the author of the *Gospel of Peter* (8.2). It should be added, I think, that a literary reading of Matthew cannot grasp all that is probably involved in the writer's introduction of these seemingly fantastic happenings as Jesus dies.[9]

It is unlikely that anyone will wish to deny that 28.16-20 forms the climax of Matthew's whole story, irrespective of how it is thought the book is structured. But much of what Kingsbury says about this pericope I find very strange. He is concerned only with the identity of the one who comes and commissions. That the words 'I am with you always...' recall the Emmanuel prophecy employed at 1.23 is certainly true, but whether Matthew wishes the identification to be made with the precision that Kingsbury's words suggest is, I think, open to question. Even more questionable is the repeated affirmation that in this scene 'the disciples see Jesus Son of God as the resurrected one who remains the crucified one'. How does Kingsbury know that? That the resurrected one remains the crucified one (the one who has been, and remains the crucified) does not seem to me to be proved from the verses to which he appeals, 28.6, 10, 17; 27.54. The passage speaks only of 'Jesus'. Of course, the words 'the Son' appear in the baptismal formula, 'in the name of the Father, the Son and the Holy Spirit', but that does not by itself define the dominant christology of the section. A sensitive literary reading of the pericope could hardly miss the allusion to Dan. 7.13 in the declaration by Jesus in v. 18b, 'All authority in heaven and upon earth has been given to me'. Does not this suggest the enthronement or exaltation of Jesus as Son of Man at God's right hand in fulfilment of 26.64 ('... you will see...')? That this could be the main christological thrust of the climactic passage is a suggestion which Kingsbury cannot entertain because of his interpretation of the 'Son of Man' title, but even if his views on that designation were different he would not welcome the suggestion because of his commitment to the dominance of Son of God christology in Matthew's story and consequently to its dominance in the final and climactic episode. It is not at all as obvious to me as it is to Kingsbury (and he has quite remarkable knowledge as to what the disciples comprehended in this scene) that in 28.16-20 Jesus comes, commands and commissions solely or preeminently as Son of God.

9. Cf. J.P. Meier, *The Vision of Matthew: Christ, Church and Morality in the First Gospel* (New York: Paulist Press, 1979), pp. 33-35 and 204.

The fifth part of Kingsbury's essay concerns itself with the question of why Matthew tells his story in the way he does and offers as an answer the following: 'Matthew tells his story along the lines he does...to bring the reader's "thinking" about Jesus "into alignment" with God's "thinking" about him and to invite the reader to look upon himself or herself as being a disciple of Jesus' (p. 67) and as addressed by Jesus' commission. There is nothing remarkable about the suggestion that a Gospel-story writer desires to involve his readers in the action narrated and to draw them into discipleship to Jesus, but that this entails bringing the reader's thinking about Jesus 'into alignment' with God's thinking about him is, I think, less than certain. May we not say that Jesus' 'point of view' (both about himself and about God) is as creative of discipleship as the 'thinking' of God? As I have already said, I find it difficult to accepts Kingsbury's claim that in Matthew's story God's 'point of view' is, by authorial design, dominant, even normative. I discover now that he makes the same claim for Mark's story[10] but the supporting arguments are surprisingly weak.

IV

We come now to look at what Kingsbury has to say on the 'Son of man' designation. Although this designation must, on Kingsbury's presuppositions and arguments, be of less importance than 'Son of God', nevertheless he gives considerable attention to it.

(i) Unlike other titles such as 'Son of David' and 'king of the Jews', 'Son of man' in Matthew does not function confessionally, that is, to inform the reader of 'who Jesus is': even when it is used by Jesus in the presence of the Jews and the disciples they do not use it in return concerning him. The very strangeness of this state of affairs should arouse an alert reader to suspect that the writer is deliberately keeping the 'Son of man' for use by Jesus and no one else.

(ii) 'Son of man' is not used as a 'predication formula', and from this it is inferred that the term does not specify, for the characters of Matthew's story, 'who Jesus is'. Moreover we are told that 'literally, it is difficult to see from the way in which Matthew first acquaints the reader with "the Son of man" that it is calculated to inform the reader

10. J.D. Kingsbury, *The Christology of Mark's Gospel* (Philadelphia: Fortress Press, 1983), pp. 47-50.

of "who Jesus is"' (p. 73). But it does inform him of *who Jesus says he is*, for it is a self-designation, as Kingsbury readily admits when a little further on he states that it constitutes the 'phraseological point of view' of Jesus exclusively, and therefore must be construed as a technical term or title. One begins to suspect that a literary reading of Matthew is going to be unable by itself to solve the puzzle of this designation. It looks as if Matthew knew something more about the use and meaning of 'Son of man' than a purely narrative reading of his story is now able to supply. And in the end, Kingsbury (I think) implies that this is so; but it is with reference to 'Son of man' that he shows himself to be an insufficiently sensitive literary critic.

It is far from clear to me how a literary or narrative reading of Matthew leads to the interpretation of the 'Son of man' title which we are offered. The translational equivalent which, according to Kingsbury, best conveys the consistent meaning the 'Son of man' bears in Matthew, namely 'this man' or 'this human being', is simply not an available option. The Greek ὁ υἱὸς τοῦ ἀνθρώπου might, under strain, permit the definite rendering '*the* man', but it will not permit 'this man', for which there is perfectly acceptable Greek, οὗτος ὁ ἄνθρωπος. Even an appeal to the presumed underlying Aramaic form and its usage (and Kingsbury knows all about this evidence, though he stops short of admitting it here) will not yield the meaning 'this man' or 'this human being'; the best it will offer (if we must find a consistent meaning throughout the narrative) is 'a man' or 'a human being'. It is Kingsbury's requirement that the enigmatic words 'Son of man' be interpreted as a title that forces him beyond the acceptable and the permissible in his rendering ὁ υἱὸς τοῦ ἀνθρώπου; 'a man' or 'the man' (unless capitalized, and that imports other ideas) will not act as a title.

Whether or not 'Son of man' bears a consistent meaning in Matthew will be answered differently by scholars (and their answers will involve consideration of what is traditional and what is redactional in his use of the term), but it surely cannot be doubted that in the course of his narrative Matthew leaves one or two clues to understanding the puzzling phrase. The hesitant acceptance by Jesus of the title 'Son of God' in the high priest's unbelieving question is immediately followed by '... But from now on you will see the Son of man seated at the right hand of power and coming on the clouds of heaven' (26.64); this is undoubtedly an allusion to Dan. 7.13. Whether it complicates or simplifies the question about the meaning of 'Son of man', one cannot ignore this pointer to Daniel 7. An alert and sensitive literary reading of Matthew will take it into account. I find it astonishing that there is not a single reference to Daniel 7 in Kingsbury's entire discussion of 'Son of man'. In view of 26.64, is his literary reading of Matthew failing to admit literary evidence that may be awkward to combine with his neat solution? That Kingsbury can speak of 'Son of man' as bearing the unique stamp of Jesus' life and ministry—earthly, suffering and vindicated (p. 78)—and yet not refer to Daniel 7 is extraordinary.

Another clue as to the meaning of 'Son of man' is given by Matthew at 9.8 where, at the end of the story about the healing of the paralysed man (in the course of which we find 'But that you may know that the Son of man has power [ἐξουσία] on earth to forgive sins...') the crowds are made to 'glorify God who had given this power (ἐξουσία) to men'. The significance of this does not depend on comparison with Mark, though it is increased if Matthew used Mark. Whether what it suggests about Matthew's understanding of 'Son of man' (viz. that it signifies 'a man') can be linked with the pointer to Daniel 7 is not the question which a literary reading has to solve first; they are two pieces of literary evidence which a narrative reading must recognize in discussing the meaning of 'Son of man' in Matthew.

(iii) It is startling to be told that among the purposes for which Jesus (in Matthew's story) employs the 'Son of man' title is to assert his 'divine authority in the face of opposition' (p. 79). How can a title which (it is claimed) means 'this man' or 'this human being' be used by Jesus, or by Matthew of Jesus, to assert divine authority? I can only assume that Kingsbury is influenced by his knowledge of developments in Son-of-man *Forschung*, but is not admitting it. It does take more than a literary reading of Matthew (or Mark, or Luke) to solve the 'Son of man' problem.

(iv) Finally, it seems to me very strange that what Matthew is said to be conveying by Jesus' use of 'Son of man' (and that is *who Jesus says he is*) is so at odds with who he really is for Matthew, namely Son of God. If some 'servant of the Lord' content had been given by Kingsbury to 'Son of God', and if the Danielic overtones of 'Son of man' had been recognized and admitted, we would have had a much better-balanced statement about Matthew's christology, and something more like what Matthew himself, on any kind of reading, provides. Matthew's Jesus speaks of himself in terms of 'Son of man'; when the range of possible meanings for this designation are explored it becomes clear that it is not inconsistent with the divine declaration which affirms that his Sonship is interpreted in terms of Servanthood.

My concluding observation is a general one. Although I am not well-read in the literary approach to biblical materials (and that will partly excuse the failings of this response to Kingsbury's essay) I am sufficiently well-acquainted with its application to Old Testament materials, where it is providing very illuminating insights, to wonder why it is not proving so interesting and exciting when applied to the New Testament, and especially to the Gospels. Are New Testament scholars just again lagging behind their colleagues in Old Testament studies? Or are the methods of Gospel study too engrained for a fresh approach to make headway? Or is the Gospel genre peculiarly resistant to clarification by a literary or narrative reading? It would be absurd to give the impression that there are no valuable and sophisticated contributions in this area; there are, and perhaps the most recent is R.A. Culpepper's penetrating work on the Fourth Gospel.[11] But, in my view, this literary-critical probe of Matthew by Kingsbury is likely to be regarded as tentative.

11. R.A. Culpepper, *Anatomy of the Fourth Gospel: A Study in Literary Design* (Philadelphia: Fortress Press, 1983).

JSNT 25 (1985), pp. 61-81

THE FIGURE OF JESUS IN MATTHEW'S STORY:
A REJOINDER TO DAVID HILL

Jack Dean Kingsbury

David Hill's response to my 'The Figure of Jesus in Matthew's Story: A Literary-Critical Probe'[1] is uniformly negative. In what follows, my purpose is to discuss some of the issues Hill has raised apropos that article.

I

Hill's first objection takes aim at the literary-critical method itself. His contention is that it is burdened with an 'undeniably subjective element', so that 'a reading of Matthew which does not take into account the writer's sources and, in particular, his redactional work cannot be regarded as an adequate reading of the story on which to build a claim about a special emphasis in Matthew's presentation of Jesus'.[2] In other words, if a literary-critical approach to Matthew is not to be arbitrary, it needs to be placed under the control of source, and especially redaction, criticism.

In my article, I understand literary criticism to be an analysis of the narrative of Matthew. On this view, a 'narrative' is composed of a story and its discourse.[3] A 'story' is made up of settings, characters, and events that comprise the plot. In the case of Matthew, the story is of the life of Jesus from conception and birth to death and resurrection. The 'discourse' is the means whereby a story is put across. In the case of

---

1.   *JSNT* 21 (1984), pp. 3-36; responded to in D. Hill, 'The Figure of Jesus in Matthew's Story: A Response to Professor Kingsbury's Literary-Critical Probe,' *JSNT* 21 (1984), pp. 37-52. Both articles are reprinted above. The page numbers of the reprinted article are referred to in this response.

2.   Hill, 'Response', p. 82.

3.   Cf. S. Chatman, *Story and Discourse* (Ithaca: Cornell University Press, 1978).

Matthew, it encompasses the kind and style of language that is used, including the many rhetorical devices. It also encompasses such matters as, for example, the 'implied author' who stands behind the whole of the story, the 'narrator' (i.e. the 'voice') who tells the story, the 'implied reader' who understands and appropriately responds to the story, and the various aspects of 'point of view' (evaluative, phraseological, psychological, and spatial and temporal) which the narrator or any given character may adopt in the course of the story. So construed, a narrative like that of Matthew constitutes a 'world' that is peopled by characters and governed by a coherent system of values and beliefs. The person who hears or reads Matthew is invited to assume to the extent possible the role of the implied reader and to enter this world, to dwell within it, and at the end to take leave of it, perhaps changed.

From what has just been said, it is plain that in a literary-critical approach to Matthew the emphasis falls on the unity, or 'wholeness', of the text. By contrast, in a source- or redaction-critical approach the text is looked upon as a composite of tradition and redaction. The emphasis here is on distinguishing tradition from redaction so that one can ascertain how the evangelist has interpreted the sources or materials handed down to him. Not the wholeness of the text as such but the ability to disassemble it so as to lay bare whatever layers of tradition it contains is what counts most. The text in its totality constitutes the sum of layers of tradition.

The emphasis on the wholeness of the text in literary criticism means that one does not undertake to capture the peculiar shape of Matthean thought by endeavouring to isolate 'Matthean redaction'. Instead, one attends to the interplay of the constituent elements of Matthew's narrative, that is, the elements that comprise its story and its discourse. These elements are both recognizable and definable,[4] so that it is grossly inaccurate to portray literary criticism as being a method that cannot stand on its own and is devoid of adequate or verifiable controls. Accordingly, literary criticism, understood as the analysis of narrative, is not so 'undeniably subjective' that for it to make a contribution to Matthean studies its results must first pass the bar of source, and particularly redaction, criticism. Indeed, redaction criticism, burdened as it is not only with the uncertainties that currently surround competing source-hypotheses and the isolation of redaction but also with the

---

4.   Cf. Chatman, *Story and Discourse.*

misguided notion that traditional materials tell one little or nothing of the intention of the evangelist, is on the whole a considerably less stable method than is literary criticism. In any event, the allegation that, owing to the inherent subjectivity of the literary-critical method, I was free to employ it in my article so as simply to corroborate predetermined conclusions will not pass scrutiny. If I have properly applied the method, and those who practice it will surely test me on this, a more accurate assessment of my work is likely to be that through the independent application of different methods, the redaction-critical in 1975[5] and the literary-critical in the recent article, I have arrived at conclusions that in important respects are either the same or compatible.

II

Along with this question of method, the most crucial issue on which Hill and I part company has to do with 'evaluative point of view'. 'Evaluative point of view' denotes a particular way of looking at things. To the extent divulged by a story, the narrator and the various characters or groups of characters all have their respective evaluative points of view. Typically, these evaluative points of view give rise to conflict. For the implied reader to discern amid conflicting evaluative points of view the degree to which any single such point of view is to be construed as being 'true' or 'false', a story must, if it is to 'make sense', be governed by one, overarching, consistent evaluative point of view.

As Hill correctly observes, the pivotal assertion of my article is that it is the evaluative point of view of God which the implied author of Matthew has established as being normative in his story. The evaluative point of view of the narrator and of each character or group of characters is to be judged at any given juncture as being 'true' or 'false' to the degree that it is in alignment with, or diverges from, the evaluative point of view of God. Because Jesus, the protagonist, and the narrator espouse evaluative points of view which are in complete alignment with God's evaluative point of view, their evaluative points of view are to be regarded as being 'true'. And because Jesus and the narrator are thus made out to be representatives of truth, the extent to which they do or do not approve of other characters, such as the disciples or the Jewish crowds or the Jewish leaders, informs the implied reader of the extent to

---

5.   J.D. Kingsbury, *Matthew: Structure, Christology, Kingdom* (Philadelphia: Fortress Press; London: SPCK, 1975), chs. 1–3.

which he or she is to take the evaluative points of view of these other characters to be credible.

Hill disputes my claim that the implied author of Matthew has established God's evaluative point of view as being normative in his story.[6] He counters this claim with two fundamental assertions, from which he draws conclusions, and with a statement in which he gives his own position. The first assertion is that the same kind of evidence which I muster to prove that God's evaluative point of view is normative in Matthew's story can also be found in the stories of Mark and of Luke, which indicates, he argues, that the matter of God's evaluative point of view does not nearly possess the importance that I ascribe it. The second assertion is that the emphasis throughout Matthew's story is squarely on Jesus, which shows, he maintains, that it is the evaluative point of view of Jesus and not that of God which is determinative of Matthew's story. And the position that Hill then adopts for himself on this issue is that the 'God-orientation' of Matthew's story is to be seen as constituting 'background, not foreground'.

It is neither the assertions Hill makes nor the final position he takes with which I disagree but the conclusions he draws from his assertions. There is no question but that the 'God-orientation' of Matthew's story is background and not foreground, for this story is not, strictly speaking, that of God but that of the life of Jesus. Nor is there any question but that the emphasis in Matthew's story is squarely on Jesus. And it is indeed the case that the same kind of evidence to which I appeal to insist that God's evaluative point of view is normative in Matthew's story can also be found in the stories of Mark and Luke, not to mention John. But to affirm these insights is not to detract in the least from the correctness of the claim that, again, it is God's evaluative point of view which is made normative in Matthew's story.

Basic to this discussion is the matter of 'authority'. Part and parcel of the claim that in Matthew's story God's evaluative point of view is normative is the recognition that precisely the Jesus who occupies the foreground of this story and is the focus of attention is notably characterized as being the supreme agent of God who speaks and acts, not of his own will, but on the authority of God. Miraculously conceived by God's Spirit (1.18, 20), the Matthean Jesus is Emmanuel, or 'God with us' (1.23), whom God empowers with his Spirit for messianic ministry

6.   Cf. Hill, 'Response', pp. 82-86.

(3.16). Jesus himself declares: 'All things have been delivered to me by my Father; and no one knows the Son except the Father, and no one knows the Father except the Son and any one to whom the Son chooses to reveal him' (11.27, RSV); and again: '... he who receives me receives him who has sent me' (10.40). As regards the question of evaluative point of view, what observations and references such as these indicate is that the implied reader of Matthew's story is in no wise invited to construe Jesus as being first of all the spokesman of his own private mind and only secondarily or incidentally as being the mouthpiece of God. Quite the opposite, they indicate that what Jesus does, in setting forth his evaluative point of view, is to reveal the evaluative point of view of God. Then, too, the fact that the implied authors of Mark, Luke, and John are likewise concerned to lay heavy stress on the 'God-orientation' of Jesus is a sign, not that this motif is of little significance, but that, on the contrary, it possesses paramount significance. In sum, the argument stands: in Matthew, the one, overarching, consistent evaluative point of view in the world of the story which serves as the norm of 'truth' and 'falsehood' is none other than that of God. In the idiom of 16.23, 'truth' in Matthew's story is 'thinking the things of God'. In that the implied author continually presents Jesus, and the narrator as well, as in fact 'thinking the things of God', he gives the implied reader to understand that they are the ones in his story who can be counted on as being wholly 'reliable'.

III

Hill rightly recognizes that the claim that it is God's evaluative point of view in Matthew's story which is normative, if conceded to be correct, holds profound implications for understanding the christology of Matthew.[7] On two occasions in Matthew, in the scene following the baptism and at the transfiguration, God enters the world of the story as 'actor', and both times his purpose is to declare Jesus to be 'my beloved Son' (3.17; 17.5). If God's evaluative point of view is normative in Matthew's story, it follows that Jesus is preeminently the Son of God.

To assert that Jesus is preeminently the Son of God, however, is manifestly not to suggest that other titles or terms of respect ascribed to Jesus are unimportant. On the contrary, the meaning and the function of each

---

7. Cf. Hill, 'Response', p. 83.

one of these must be carefully assessed.[8] Still, what it does suggest is
that the principal, even if not exclusive, answer to the question of 'who
Jesus is' is, again, that he is the Son of God.

Why does the implied author of Matthew hold the title of Son of
God in such high esteem? From what can be determined from his story,
his answer is that since 'Son of God' betokens, in a way that is true of
no other title, the unique filial relationship that Jesus has to God, it is
this 'God-orientation' of Jesus, which is not without far-reaching soteriological implications, which is so fundamental to 'who he is'. As the Son
of God, Jesus is miraculously conceived by God's Spirit (1.18, 20), is
empowered by God's Spirit for messianic ministry (3.16), is attested to
by God's voice from heaven (3.17; 17.5), and gives demonstration that
he is stronger than Satan because he is 'perfect', that is, of one heart,
soul, and mind with God (4.1-11). As such, he is the one through whom
God reveals himself to humans (11.25-27), whose death becomes the act
whereby God proffers to all the forgiveness of sins (cf. 26.28 to 27.40,
43, 54), and who is the founder of God's eschatological people, the
church (16.15-19). As the Matthean Jesus announces in the parable of
the wicked husbandmen, it is the Son of God who is God's decisive
agent in the whole of the history of salvation (21.33-46; cf. 21.37-38, 42;
22.1-10).

Hill takes exception to my views on the title of the Son of God and on
the christology of Matthew on the grounds that they lack balance: too
little is made of Jesus as 'servant', and neither the meaning nor the
function of 'the Son of man' is properly defined.[9] On the question of
Jesus as 'servant', it is important to specify where the difference
between us lies. At issue is not whether Isaianic servant-traditions have
been taken up into Matthew, for plainly they have been (cf., e.g., 3.17
and 17.5 ['in whom I take delight']; 8.17; 12.18-21). Instead, the debate
is over whether the presence of these traditions authorizes one to impute
to the implied author of Matthew a distinct and highly profiled servant-
christology in the sense that 'Servant' can legitimately be made into a
title of majesty for Jesus. Whereas Hill finds just such a christology in
Matthew, as his repeated capitalization of 'Servant' and of 'Servanthood'
reveals, I do not.

8.   This is a task to which I have in fact devoted myself in a variety of
publications, but cf. esp. *Matthew*, ch. 3, and my *Matthew as Story* (Philadelphia:
Fortress Press, 1986).

9.   Cf. Hill, 'Response', pp. 89-91, 93-95.

What is the evidence for finding in Matthew a highly profiled Servant christology? At 8.17 and 12.17-21, formula quotations occur which draw on the servant-traditions of Isaiah. These quotations, however, are of the nature of what literary-critics term 'asides'. In them, the implied author, through the voice of the narrator, pauses to speak directly to the implied reader. The purpose of such direct address is to convey information to the implied reader which will enhance his or her understanding of the story. By the same token, characters within the story are not made privy to 'asides'. The upshot is that 'asides' stand apart from a story: they belong to its 'frame', not to its 'plot'. Instead of advancing the action of the story, they comment on it, but again, to the implied reader.

To return with these thoughts in mind to 8.17 and 12.17-21, it becomes evident that the function of these formula quotations is such as to permit the implied author, through the voice of the narrator, to inform the implied reader that Old Testament prophecy associated with the servant of Isaiah is to be seen as coming to fulfillment in the life and ministry of Jesus. By informing the implied reader of this, the implied author is enriching the reader's understanding of the Jesus whose story is being told. But since the implied author imparts this information exclusively to the reader and not to any character within his story, what he is not doing with these formula quotations is compounding types of christology. Or to put it differently, the fact that Jesus is to be seen as fulfilling servant-traditions does not therefore make it appropriate for the implied reader to construct a christological category that makes of Jesus the 'Servant', just as the fact, for example, that Jesus ascends the mountain and teaches the people does not justify establishing 'New Moses' as a christological category.

To argue that the implied author of Matthew has not created a peculiar category of Servant christology is not to argue that there is no concern on his part to present Jesus as one who serves. Just the reverse, the theme that Jesus serves is pervasive in Matthew. Merely to cite but one example, θεραπεύειν, the main verb that is used to describe the healing activity of Jesus, means 'to serve' as well as 'to heal'. Since this verb is closely associated with the formula quotation of 8.17, it is not misguided to claim that all of Jesus' 'healing' in Matthew's story is to be construed by the implied reader as 'serving'. But christologically (and a passage such as 20.28 notwithstanding; cf. below on the force of 'the Son of man'), the title of majesty with which the notion of serving is most frequently and directly linked is that of Son of God. Thus, the Son in whom God takes delight God chooses for a messianic ministry that ultimately leads to the cross, that is, God places the Son in his special service (3.16-17; 17.5; 27.40, 43, 54). Or again, the Isaianic formula quotation of 12.17-21 virtually echoes the words God speaks in the presence of Jesus following the baptism and at the transfiguration (cf. 12.18a to 3.17; 17.5). In this quotation, the term παῖς occurs, which can mean 'son' or 'servant'. Since this is the only time in Matthew's story that παῖς occurs, perhaps both meanings are intended. If that is the case, the relationship between 3.17 and 17.5 on the one hand and 12.18a on the other seems to be the following: the Jesus whom God, entering into the world of Matthew's story, declares to be his beloved 'Son' (3.17; 17.5) is, the implied reader is to know, precisely the 'son' in whom the Isaianic prophecy concerning the 'servant' reaches its fulfillment. To sum up, if the evidence is not such as to permit one to make of 'Servant' a distinct and highly profiled christological category, it does portray Jesus as the Son who is chosen by God for a messianic ministry in which he serves to the uttermost and in the course of which he fulfills the servant-traditions of Isaiah.

To turn to the designation of 'the Son of man', Hill charges that I have misconstrued Matthean usage of it in terms of both its meaning and its function.[10] On the matter of function, Hill challenges my position that 'the Son of man' is not used to inform the implied reader of the identity of Jesus by countering that, on the contrary, it does serve to inform the implied reader of '*who Jesus says he is*' (italics his). On the matter of meaning, Hill rejects my proposal that one can capture the force of 'the Son of man' in English by substituting for it each time it occurs the expression 'this man', or 'this human being', and argues instead that in a passage such as 9.8 it is non-titular and signifies 'a man', whereas in the passage 26.64 it is titular and identifies Jesus with the heavenly being of Daniel 7. As Hill sees it, the implied author of Matthew exhibits no consistent understanding of 'the Son of man' so that it is each scholar who must decide for himself or herself, under 'consideration of what is traditional and what is redactional', what this term means at any given point in Matthew's story.

Does 'the Son of man', or does it not, function in Matthew's story to inform the implied reader of the identity of Jesus? This is perhaps the

10. Cf. Hill, 'Response', pp. 93-95.

first question that must be answered if one is to gain a proper understanding of this term. Because I have already detailed in programmatic
fashion in my article the several reasons why I believe that the implied
author of Matthew's story does not employ 'the Son of man' to inform
the implied reader of the identity of Jesus (i.e. of 'who Jesus is'),[11] I shall
restrict myself here to explaining why Hill's view according to which
'the Son of man' is used in Matthew to permit Jesus to state 'who he
says he is' seems to me to be untenable.

To begin with, Hill avers that the very fact that 'the Son of man' is a
'self-designation' proves already that he is correct in maintaining that it
stipulates 'who Jesus says he is'.[12] In this connection, Hill rightly
observes that I, too, readily acknowledge that 'the Son of man' is a self-
designation, as when I note that, since it occurs exclusively in the mouth
of Jesus, it can be seen to belong to his peculiar phraseological point of
view or argue, further, that it is a technical term, or title. But why is
there this concern on the part of Hill to stress that on this point I agree
with him? The answer is that Hill believes that to acknowledge 'the Son
of man' to be a self-designation is to compel the conclusion that, again,
'the Son of man' stipulates 'who Jesus says he is'. In other words, Hill is
of the opinion that he has, in this instance, turned my own method on
me, for had I been, as he puts it, a 'sufficiently sensitive literary critic', I
should as a matter of course have been so guided by my method as to
arrive at his conclusion.

Hill errs, however, in claiming so easily that the conclusion that 'the
Son of man' functions to stipulate 'who Jesus says he is' necessarily
follows from the acknowledgment that 'the Son of man' is a 'self-designation'. Suppose for the sake of argument that the expression 'this
man' adequately captures in English the force of the Greek original in
Matthew of 'the Son of man'. If the Matthean Jesus is indeed referring
to himself as in effect 'this man' each time he utters the term 'the Son
of man', then he is not, in making use of it, stating 'who he is', and yet
this does not in the least alter the circumstance that 'the Son of man'
shows itself to be (a) a self-designation, that is, a term by which Jesus
distinguishes himself from others, (b) a term that occurs exclusively in
Jesus' mouth and is thus indicative of his phraseological point of view
(i.e. of his peculiar speech), and (c) a technical term, in the sense that
Jesus employs it in such fashion as to associate it with himself (present

11. Cf. Kingsbury, 'Figure of Jesus', pp. 68-73.
12. Cf. Hill, 'Response', p. 93.

work, suffering, and vindication) in a way in which it can be associated
with no other human being. The point that needs to be seen is this: Hill
cannot prove his thesis that the term 'the Son of man' is used in
Matthew to permit Jesus himself to state 'who he is' unless he can
produce a passage in which either Jesus asserts, 'I am the Son of man',
or some other character says, or asks whether, he is the Son of man.
And as is well-known, it is just such a passage that is nowhere to be
found in Matthew.

Along this same line, a second reason why Hill's thesis that the
Matthean Jesus uses 'the Son of man' to state 'who he is' falls short is
that it is unable to come to grips with a Son-of-man passage such as
16.13 and the pericope in which it is embedded (16.13-20). In 16.13-20,
Jesus himself broaches the question of his identity. Now should Hill be
right in insisting that Jesus employs 'the Son of man' in Matthew to
state 'who he is', and should Hill furthermore be right in urging that it is
Jesus' evaluative point of view and not that of God which is determinative of Matthew's story, then how is one to understand that Jesus guides
the disciples, neither in 16.13-20 nor in any other pericope in Matthew's
story, to confess him to be 'the Son of man'? Is it that Jesus does not
elicit from the disciples, at least not here in 16.13-20, the confession that
'he is "the Son of man"' because they are as yet ignorant that he must
suffer and die and so would not know the deeper meaning of such a
confession? But against an objection of this nature, one could argue
equally well that Jesus could indeed guide the disciples here to confess
him to be the Son of man and then command them to silence, after the
manner of the last verse of this pericope (16.20), until such time as they
would be able to comprehend the full meaning of their confession. Still,
all such thoughts aside, the fact of the matter is that the term 'the Son of
man' does occur in this pericope (16.13). Noteworthy in this respect is
the way in which it functions. For example, one can observe that it does
not occur in a confessional statement such as one finds in 16.16, which
has the specific purpose of setting forth the identity of Jesus, of expli-
cating 'who he is'. On the contrary, it occurs instead in the opening
question of 16.13, 'Who do men say that "the Son of man" is?'
Occurring as it does in 16.13, 'the Son of man' functions not only not
to divulge the identity of Jesus, not to explicate 'who he is', but as a
term that is itself in need of explication, as is evident from the rest of the
conversation between Jesus and the disciples beginning with 16.14. The
point, finally, is this: Hill flatly declares that 'the Son of man' functions

in Matthew so that Jesus, in uttering it, informs others of 'who he is', and yet in this pericope, which is devoted to the very topic of Jesus' identity, 'the Son of man' is not at all functioning in any apparent way to explicate 'who Jesus is' but, quite the opposite, gives every indication that it is itself a term in need of explication.

This discussion of the function of 'the Son of man' in Matthew leads to yet a third problem that challenges the viability of Hill's thesis. If 'the Son of man' were in fact being employed by the Matthean Jesus to inform others of 'who he says he is', how is it to be explained that Jesus, in the full hearing of the 'crowd(s)',[13] of the 'Jewish leaders',[14] and of the 'disciples',[15] unabashedly refers to himself as 'the Son of man' and yet, whenever the question of his identity arises, none of these groups of characters ever affirm, or for that matter even entertain the idea, that, indeed, 'Jesus is "the Son of man"'. The crowds at least query, even though they anticipate a negative answer, whether Jesus is 'the Son of David' (12.23). The disciples, having initially asked what sort of man this is that even winds and sea obey him (8.27), subsequently confess Jesus, first on the sea and then in the person of Peter near Caesarea Philippi, to be 'the Son of God' (14.33; 16.16). Once again the disciples, this time as spokesmen for various segments of the Jewish public, tell Jesus that whereas some people think him to be John the Baptist, others think him to be Elijah, and still others think him to be Jeremiah or one of the prophets (16.14). At his trial, the high priest suddenly arises and demands of Jesus that he make known before the Sanhedrin whether he is 'the messiah, the Son of God' (26.63). And as Jesus stands before Pilate, the first thing Pilate does is to put to him the question, 'Are you the King of the Jews?' (27.11). To repeat, if Jesus uses 'the Son of man' in Matthew to state 'who he says he is', then why is this term, though uttered by Jesus openly and publicly, so conspicuously absent whenever characters such as the above actually speak to the issue of Jesus' identity, that is, of 'who he is'?

Hill makes no attempt to deal with this question, which in my judgment constitutes a serious weakness in his reply to my article. Neither does he advance his own proposal for understanding the function, and

13. Cf. 8.20 with 8.18; 9.6 with 9.8; 11.19 with 11.7 and 11.16.

14. Cf. 8.20 with 8.19; 9.6 with 9.3; 12.8 with 12.2; 12.32 with 12.24; 12.40 with 12.38.

15. Cf. 8.20 with 8.18, 23; 10.23 with 10.5; 12.8 with 12.1; 13.41 with 13.36; 16.13.

then also the meaning, of 'the Son of man' in Matthew, something one might claim he was not obligated to do. But from the remarks Hill does make, some of his views on 'the Son of man' do come to light. Thus, it is apparent that he regards 'the Son of man' as being used in Matthew in at least two senses, one that is titular and one that is non-titular.[16] In such passages as align themselves with 9.6, the Matthean Jesus is, in designating himself as 'the Son of man', merely referring to himself as 'a man' ('But that you may know that "a man" has authority on earth to forgive sins'). But in such passages as align themselves with 26.64, the Matthean Jesus goes beyond this and employs the self-designation of 'the Son of man' to apply to himself the prophecy of Daniel 7 concerning the heavenly being ('... hereafter you will see "the heavenly being spoken of in Daniel" seated at the right hand of power, and coming on the clouds of heaven'). Plainly, the critical difference between these two types of Son-of-man passages is whether a reference or allusion to Daniel 7 can be discerned.

The difficulty with the views Hill does express on the use of 'the Son of man' in Matthew is that they seem to be inconsistent with one another. Hill's fundamental assertion is, again, that the Matthean Jesus employs 'the Son of man' to state 'who he says he is'. But if this is the case, how is one to square with this assertion the notion that 'the Son of man', in a passage such as 9.6, denotes no more than 'a man'? If in speaking of himself as 'the Son of man' Jesus is simply saying that he is 'a man', how can it be said that he is thereby employing 'the Son of man' to state 'who he says he is'? Saying that one is 'a man' is obviously not divulging one's identity. And what is to be made of a Son-of-man passage such as 16.13? To take it to read, 'Who do men say that "a man" is?', is almost as unsatisfactory as to take it to read, 'Who do men say that "the heavenly being referred to in Daniel" is?' Yet another option, of course, is to construe 'the Son of man' in 16.13 as the equivalent of the pronoun 'I', in which case the question reads, 'Who do men say that "I" am?' While it is true that this reading makes good sense, and while it is also true that Hill is content with the idea that 'the Son of man' in Matthew possesses no single, consistent meaning, this 'pronominal option' is not one to which he would, or could, agree. The reason for this is not difficult to discern: were Hill to grant that 'the Son of man' in 16.13 is the essential equivalent of 'I', he would at a stroke

16. Cf. Hill, 'Response', pp. 94–95.

negate his own fundamental assertion according to which 'the Son of man' in Matthew stipulates 'who Jesus says he is'. If 'the Son of man' essentially means 'I', Jesus is clearly not, in using it, setting forth his identity. To sum up, although Hill roundly rejects my proposal that one can capture in English the force of 'the Son of man' if one substitutes for it each time it occurs in Matthew the expression 'this man', it is hard to see that the views he himself advances on the use of 'the Son of man' in Matthew have much to commend them. On the contrary, what one is offered are a handful of statements which are either at odds with one another or unable to deal with a 'test case' such as 16.13.

It remains to explain briefly what leads me to render the Greek term underlying 'the Son of man' as 'this man' and to designate 'the Son of man' as a 'technical term', or 'title'. On the question of the meaning of 'the Son of man', my position, which Hill misrepresents,[17] is that the proper translation of the Greek that underlies 'the Son of man' is 'the man', or 'the human being'.[18] But technically accurate as this translation is, one encounters a problem if one attempts simply to substitute, in each Son-of-man passage in Matthew, the expression 'the man' for 'the Son of man'. The problem is that such a simple substitution does not always make it as obvious to the implied reader as it must be that 'the man' refers, without exception, only to Jesus. To illustrate this problem, consider the following translation of the first Son-of-man passage that occurs in Matthew (8.20): 'Foxes have holes, and birds of the air have nests; but "the man" ["the Son of man"] has nowhere to lay his head'. Because this saying is aphoristic in nature, it would make good sense, on the surface of things, to think that 'the Son of man' is being used here in a generic sense, in which event one would take the saying to mean: unlike even birds and beasts, 'man' has no settled home. But this saying of 8.20 is located within the specific context of Matthew's story, and in this 'world' the implied reader discovers that 'the Son of man' is consistently used by Jesus to refer exclusively to himself. Given this fact, one is compelled to ask if there is not a way to render 'the Son of man' in 8.20 so as to make it clear that it is not first of all a reference to 'man' in general and only secondarily a reference to Jesus as a member of the species, but is instead, already at the primary level, a specific reference to Jesus himself which is embedded in an aphoristic saying designed to inform the implied reader about his peculiar style of life? The answer

17. Cf. Hill, 'Response', p. 94.
18. Cf. Kingsbury, 'Figure of Jesus', pp. 73 and 75 n. 63.

to this question is, in my judgment, that one can achieve the desired objective by rendering 'the Son of man', not only here in 8.20 but each time it occurs in Matthew, with the expression 'this man'. 'This man' is what may be termed the 'translational equivalent' of 'the Son of man': it captures the force of 'the Son of man' by regularly indicating that Jesus is 'the man' being referred to. In his remarks on my treatment of the meaning of 'the Son of man', Hill takes no account of the distinction I make between direct 'translation' ('the man') and 'translational equivalent' ('this man'). The result is that he rules that the use of 'this man' to convey the consistent meaning of 'the Son of man' is 'simply not an available option' on the grounds that it is not an exact translation of the underlying Greek.[19] From my perspective, where Hill goes awry in making such a pronouncement is, of course, in not recognizing that the central problem I was concerned to address is not that of how best to translate the Greek term underlying 'the Son of man' but that of how best to capture in English the force it has in Matthew. Incidentally, since writing my article, I have noticed in the American edition (1984) of Geza Vermes's book, *Jesus and the World of Judaism*, that he is of the opinion that the new Spanish Bible, in rendering as 'este Hombre' ('this man') Jesus' references to himself as 'the Son of man', has captured accurately the force not only of the Greek but also of the underlying Aramaic.[20] Here, then, is support from another quarter for the position I arrived at by narrative-critical study.

But if the proper translation of the Greek of 'the Son of man' in Matthew is 'the man' and the translational equivalent 'this man', can 'the Son of man' justifiably be called a 'technical term', or 'title'? Hill thinks not.[21] The reasons why I have not hesitated to call 'the Son of man' a 'technical term', or 'title', are (a) that it applies to Jesus in Matthew in a way in which it can be applied to no other human being (earthly, suffering, vindicated), (b) that it is indicative of Jesus' phraseological point of view (i.e. of his peculiar speech) in the sense that it occurs solely in his mouth, is always definite in form ('"the" Son of man'), and refers exclusively to him, and (c) that it marks Jesus as fulfilling Old Testament prophecy. Because the question of how to

19. Cf. Hill, 'Response', p. 94.
20. Philadelphia: Fortress Press, 1984, pp. 98-99. In checking, I see that Vermes first expressed this opinion in the original edition of his article, 'The Present State of the "Son of Man" Debate', *JJS* 22 (1978), p. 134.
21. Cf. Hill, 'Response', p. 94.

categorize any given designation is obviously one of criteria, the issue is, finally, whether these criteria are sufficient for describing 'the Son of man' as a 'technical term', or 'title'. I believe that they are, despite the fact that I also firmly maintain that 'the Son of man' in Matthew does not set forth the identity of Jesus. Then, too, it should likewise not go unnoticed in this connection that I have taken care in two key sentences to place the word 'title' in apposition to the word 'technical term'.[22] The purpose of this is to indicate that, while I do indeed believe that the criteria cited above are sufficient to call 'the Son of man' a title, it is nonetheless a title 'with a difference'. 'This difference' is precisely that it does not (as do, e.g., 'messiah', 'the Son of David', 'the King of Jews', and 'the Son of God') inform the implied reader of 'who Jesus is'. For his part, Hill, glossing over the circumstance that 'title' has thus been placed in apposition to 'technical term', highlights only the word 'title', asserts that 'the Son of man', translated as 'the man', will 'not act as a title', and contests on these grounds the legitimacy of my understanding of 'the Son of man'.[23] By way of response, I should simply like to say that my view is that, regardless of whether one finally decides to regard the designation of 'the Son of man' as being, more minimally, a 'technical term' or, more maximally, a 'title', this will not affect the validity of the overall understanding of it I have advanced in my article. My task is, as I see it, to define exactly on what basis I characterize it as I have, and that I have done.

IV

The discussion thus far has covered such points of disagreement between Hill and me as have to do with literary-critical method, the importance in Matthew's story of God's evaluative point of view, and matters of christology. The last major topic focuses on aspects of the structure of Matthew.

In my article on the figure of Jesus, the structure of Matthew per se is not an object of investigation. Instead, the goal is to show that a literary- or narrative-critical approach to Matthew does not overturn but, happily, corroborates conclusions about structure which I had otherwise arrived at through the use of as different a method as redaction criticism.[24] In

22. Cf. Kingsbury, 'Figure of Jesus', pp. 48, 73.
23. Cf. Hill, 'Response', p. 94.
24. Cf. Kingsbury, 'Figure of Jesus', pp. 47-48 with *Matthew*, ch. 1.

disputing my statements on the structure of Matthew, Hill makes such random points as the following:[25] (a) the first main part of Matthew's story encompasses, not the section 1.1–4.16 with 3.17 as the climax, but chs. 1–2, which constitute the prologue and reach their culmination in 2.15; (b) standing apart as it does from the prologue, ch. 3 begins the main body of Matthew's Gospel-story; (c) the contention that 16.21 marks the beginning of the third main part of Matthew's story is unfounded because this verse is at the center of a single pericope that begins at 16.13 and includes not only Peter's confession of Jesus (16.16) but also Jesus' rebuke of Peter (16.23); and (d) indicative of the bias that characterizes my outline of the structure of Matthew's story is my failure to call attention to the five times that the expression 'And when Jesus had finished these sayings...' is used as a marker or divider in the story.

To give answer to Hill on these points, let me first call to mind how I construe the structure of Matthew. Matthew's story divides itself, as I see it, into three main parts. The first part (1.1–4.16) presents Jesus to the implied reader. The second part (4.17–16.20) tells of Jesus' public ministry to Israel of teaching, preaching, and healing (4.17–11.1) and of Israel's repudiation of Jesus and of its wonderment and speculation about his identity (11.2–16.20). And the third part (16.21–28.20) describes Jesus' journey to Jerusalem and his suffering, death, and resurrection. The verses on which this understanding of Matthew's structure hinges most are 4.17 and 16.21 (together with 1.1 supplemented by 3.17). In assessing the function I attribute these two verses, Hill charges that I conceive of them as creating 'great structural divides'[26] within the story of Matthew. But in point of fact, the notion of 'outline' with which I operate in dividing Matthew into three main parts is not the static one Hill imputes to me, whereby the purpose of an outline is conceived to be that of marking off something like hermetically-sealed, self-contained blocks of material, but rather a dynamic one according to which the purpose of an outline is to signal the onset of important new phases in a story's developing plot. To ascribe primary significance in an outline of Matthew to 4.17 and 16.21 is to claim that, given the many turns that Matthew's story takes, the greatest turning-points are those marked by these verses.

The tenor of Hill's first two criticisms as listed above is that not the

---

25. Cf. Hill, 'Response', pp. 86-90.
26. Cf. Hill, 'Response', p. 87.

section of 1.1–4.16 but chs. 1–2 form the first main part of Matthew's story.[27] According to Hill, chs. 1–2 comprise the story's prologue (they 'stand outside the flow of the story [as part of the "frame"]'), and ch. 3 begins the main body.

Hill's understanding of the structure of the first chapters of Matthew is conventional but untenable. To begin with, chs. 1–2 cannot be made into the 'prologue' of Matthew even on the basis of Hill's own definition of the term. Literary-critically, 'frame' material does indeed stand apart from the flow, or plot, of a story. Most frequently, it occurs at the beginning or at the end of a story, as the implied reader is led into, and then out of, the story. But it can also occur within the body of a story, as when the narrator makes comments, or 'asides', to the implied reader which no character within the story is privileged to hear. A glance at Matthew shows that while the genealogy (1.2-17) does in fact constitute frame material, the story about Jesus' life begins, as the narrator himself indicates, at 1.18: 'This is the story of the birth [origin] of the Messiah' (NEB). From this point on, the narrator relates the things that characters within the story experience, think, say, and do (cf. 1.18b-21, 24-25).

But if chs. 1–2 cannot be marked off as the first main part of Matthew on the grounds that they are 'prologue', neither can it be maintained that 2.15 is the climax of these chapters. Verse 15 is a stellar example of an 'aside' that the implied author, through the voice of the narrator, makes directly to the implied reader. Such an 'aside' exercises no influence on the plot of a story, since it is not 'heard' by any character within the story. Instead, its function is to enhance the implied reader's understanding of the story. But since an 'aside' serves the purposes of the implied reader and does not affect the plot of a story, it can neither form the climax of a story or of some portion of a story nor detract from the significance of some feature that does prove to be part of a story's plot. Applied to Matthew, this means that the 'aside' of 2.15 does not in the least diminish the critical significance of the 'event' of 3.17 in which God himself enters the world of the story as 'actor'. In short, Hill's analysis of the role both of chs. 1–2 within the structure of Matthew and of 2.15 within chs. 1–2 fails.

The second aspect of Hill's understanding of the structure of Matthew's first chapters, namely, that the main body of the Gospel-story begins with ch. 3, is equally untenable. A fundamental reason for

---

27. Cf. Hill, 'Response', pp. 86-88.

construing the section 1.1–4.16 as being the first part of Matthew's story is that everything prior to 4.17 is preliminary of Jesus' public ministry to Israel and, in one way or another, prepares the implied reader to understand this ministry aright. For example, the purpose of John's ministry (3.1-12) is to show that whereas the people hear the message John proclaims and are in this sense ready for the 'Coming One' to begin his ministry of teaching, preaching, and healing (4.17, 23-25), the Jewish leaders evince no such readiness (3.5-6, 7-10). Having accomplished its purpose, John's ministry ends even as he is imprisoned (4.12). But since the express purpose of John's ministry is to make Israel ready for that time when Jesus will begin his ministry, John's ministry proves itself to be of a piece with all those events that lead up to, but are not themselves a part of, the public ministry of Jesus (cf. 1.1–4.16). Then, too, as one goes about determining the 'structural place' of John's ministry in Matthew's story, it is idle to appeal to a thirty-year jump in events between chs. 2 and 3,[28] for the narrator, far from highlighting this temporal gap, says simply, 'Now in those days came John the Baptist...' (3.1). Nor does the circumstance that John preaches the same words in 3.2 as Jesus does in 4.17 suffice to group John's ministry with that of Jesus.[29] Although the words are the same, the intention of the message in each case is not. When John summons Israel to repentance in view of the approaching Kingdom, he has his eye on the final judgment that, he proclaims, the Coming One, whose appearance is imminent, will immediately carry out (3.11-12). When Jesus summons Israel to repentance in view of the approaching Kingdom, he places the emphasis on the salvation which he is even now proffering to Israel. One place where this contrast becomes strikingly evident is in the later exchange that occurs between the imprisoned John and Jesus (11.2-6). Exactly because Jesus has not fulfilled John's expectation and carried out the final judgment, John, through his disciples, asks of Jesus, 'Are you the Coming One, or shall we look for another?' And exactly because the concern that has guided Jesus since the beginning of his ministry has been that of proffering salvation to Israel, Jesus replies, 'Go and tell John what you see and hear: the blind receive their sight... and the poor have good news preached to them... and blessed is he who takes no offense at me.' To sum up, the treatment of John's ministry in Matthew does not at all invite the implied reader to conjoin it to the ministry of Jesus in such

28. Cf. Hill, 'Response', p. 87.
29. Cf. Hill, 'Response', p. 87.

fashion as to regard the main body of the Gospel-story as beginning with ch. 3; on the contrary, one does best to look upon the 'preparatory section' of 1.1–4.16 as comprising the first main part of Matthew.

The third of the criticisms cited above which Hill raises contests my view that the second main part of Matthew's story comes to an end with 16.20 and that 16.21 begins the third main part.[30] In Hill's perspective, the unit 16.13-20 is not climactic in nature and 16.20 and 16.21 cannot be placed in different parts of Matthew's story but must be seen as standing at the center of a single pericope that begins with 16.13 because Jesus' rebuke of Peter in 16.23 shows that Peter's confession of Jesus in 16.16 is not 'unambiguously correct' but 'inadequate' and that Peter and the disciples 'do *not* really know who Jesus is' (italics his). In my judgment, the fatal weakness of this argument is that it claims for the implied author in 16.13-20 and 16.21-23 a position that the implied author does not claim for himself: whereas the implied author distinguishes between a correct understanding of the identity of Jesus on the one hand and a refusal to accept the truth that death is his destiny on the other, Hill insists that it is the position of the implied author that unless there is an acceptance of the truth that Jesus' destiny is death there can be no correct understanding of his identity. At least one passage (and perhaps two) stands against Hill's argument. In 16.17, Jesus responds to Peter's confession that he is the messiah, the Son of God, with a beatitude: 'Blessed are you, Simon Bar-Jona! For flesh and blood has not revealed this to you, but my Father who is in heaven!' Where, one is compelled to ask, is there any hint in this beatitude either that Peter's confession is 'inadequate' so that the disciples 'do not really know who Jesus is' or that the revelation God has imparted is only partial or in some sense lacking? But although Peter and the disciples do correctly know who Jesus is (cf. also 14.33), they have not as yet been told by Jesus that his destiny is death. This explains why Jesus commands the disciples in 16.20 to silence concerning his identity: perceiving aright his identity, they are nonetheless silenced and not commissioned, until they also perceive aright his destiny, to undertake their mission to the nations (28.16-20). In any event, the beatitude of 16.17 strikes at the heart of Hill's argument.

Hill's final criticism listed above is that I ignore, so as to validate my own threefold division of Matthew, the fivefold use in Matthew of the

---

30. Cf. Hill, 'Response', pp. 90-92.

clause 'and when Jesus had finished these sayings...' (7.28; 11.1; 13.53; 19.1; 26.1).[31] It is well known that the purpose of this clause is to flag the end of the great speeches of Jesus. If one will look at how I deal with these speeches in my article, one can easily see what value I ascribe to these clauses. These clauses are indeed markers in Matthew's story, but they do not alert the implied reader to the most important turning-points of the story. To illustrate this, observe how smoothly the speeches with which this clause is associated can be integrated into the structure of Matthew's story as I understand it. The second part of Matthew's story (4.17–16.20) tells of Jesus' public ministry to Israel of teaching, preaching, and healing (4.17–11.1; 4.23; 9.35; 11.1) and of Israel's repudiation of Jesus (11.2–16.20). In line with this scheme, the Sermon on the Mount is the example par excellence of Jesus' teaching (5.2; 7.28-29), and in ch. 10 Jesus instructs his disciples in a ministry to Israel of preaching and healing (10.5b-8) which is an extension of his own (10.1). As Israel repudiates Jesus, Jesus shows through his parable speech that, on the one hand, Israel is a people that is blind, deaf, and without under-standing (13.10-13) but that, on the other hand, the disciples are given to know the mysteries of the Kingdom (13.11, 51). In its third part, Matthew's story tells of Jesus' journey to Jerusalem and of his suffering, death, and resurrection (16.21–28.20). On his way to Jerusalem, Jesus instructs his disciples, and in ch. 18 he speaks to them of their life together. In Jerusalem, Jesus describes for the disciples by way of pre-diction, immediately before his passion, the things they will encounter after his death and resurrection as they move towards his Parousia (chs. 24–25). In sum, Hill errs when he charges that I avoid dealing with the fivefold clause because it will make the task of establishing the three-fold division easier. Quite the opposite, the five speeches have their nec-essary place in the narrative-structure of Matthew precisely as I delineate that structure.

V

In concluding his response to my article, Hill makes it clear one final time that he looks upon my literary-critical probe of the figure of Jesus in Matthew's story as in effect a failure. For my part, as I reflect on his response and this rejoinder to his response, what strikes me most is that it appears we have reached an impasse as far as the way in which we

31. Cf. Hill, 'Response', p. 90.

approach and interpret Matthew is concerned. Since neither of us has persuaded the other, it will be for third parties to read the initial article and the subsequent exchange and decide for themselves which understanding of Matthew seems to make the most sense of the data. That should bring others into the fray, and from this all students of Matthew will benefit.

MARK

JSNT 6 (1980), pp. 17-41

MARK 9.1: SEEING THE KINGDOM IN POWER

Kent Brower

The enigmatic logion in Mk 9.1 has always been a *crux interpretum*, a fact reflected in the wide variety of interpretations given to it from the second century onwards.[1] The problem, of course, is the apparent discrepancy between the words 'there are some standing here who will not taste death before they see that the kingdom of God has come with power', and the facts of history: the parousia did not occur within the lifetime of the original audience.[2] It may even be argued that the problem

1. Some of the Fathers explained the passage in terms of the Transfiguration. But Origen, while noting its popularity, rejected it in favour of his characteristic spiritualization (in his Commentary of Matthew). Cf. those cited by H.B. Swete, *The Gospel according to St Mark* (London: Macmillan, 1902), p. 186 and V. Taylor, *The Gospel according to St Mark* (London: Macmillan, 1952), p. 385. For a full survey of the treatments, cf. F.J. Schierse, 'Historische und theologische Exegese der synoptischen Evangelien: Erläutert an Mk 9.1 par', *Scholastik* 29 (1954), pp. 520-36.

2. It can scarcely be doubted that the expectation of an imminent, probably even immediate, parousia was characteristic of certain segments of the early church. Paul must seek to explain the apparent delay to some of his converts as reflected in 1 Thess. 4.13-18. That the delay of the parousia presented an increasing problem which is reflected in the Synoptic Gospels has become an axiom of many New Testament scholars. Of significance is the treatment of the problem by E. Grässer, *Das Problem der Parousieverzögerung in den synoptischen Evangelien und in der Apostelgeschichte* (BZNW, 22; Berlin: Töpelmann, 2nd edn, 1960) who holds that Jesus himself envisaged no delay between his death and the coming of the kingdom, and thus the delay was strictly a community problem, with all texts which suggest any delay, including Mk 9.1, community formulations. Several scholars have responded to this perspective, including S.S. Smalley, 'The Delay of the Parousia', *JBL* 83 (1964), pp. 41-46, who denies the presence of a problem created by the non-return of Jesus, and the full-scale treatment by A.L. Moore, *The Parousia in the New Testament* (NovTSup, 13; Leiden: Brill, 1966), who denies the presence of any 'delimitation' of the parousia in the New Testament.

was perceived by Luke, if he was using Mark at this point.[3] Nor has the discussion abated in recent scholarly circles.[4] A consensus has yet to emerge, but with the recent mushrooming of Markan studies, further light may be shed upon this crux.

I

The majority of the recent attempts to penetrate this difficult passage have been conducted within the context of the discussion regarding the authenticity of the logion. It is possible, thus, to classify most of these proposed solutions into two sections: those which proceed from, or lead to, the view that the logion is authentic, and those which do not. Since the rise of form criticism, most scholars, regardless of their view of authenticity, have regarded the logion either as a completely isolated saying,[5] or as the conclusion to the preceding section.[6] Nevertheless, its present position has been regarded by some to capture the actual conceptual context of the original, authentic logion in spite of its apparent independent character.[7]

3.   Cf. for example H. Conzelmann, *The Theology of St Luke* (trans. G. Buswell; London: Faber and Faber, 1960), p. 104, who believes that Luke was cognizant of the problem presented by the terms ἐληλυθυῖαν and ἐν δυνάμει, rightly perceiving them as a 'realistic description of the Parousia', and therefore they are excluded. In this way the saying becomes independent of time.

4.   Two recent treatments are A. Ambrozic, *The Hidden Kingdom: A Redaction-Critical Study of the References to the Kingdom of God in Mark's Gospel* (CBQMS, 2; Washington: Catholic Biblical Association, 1972), esp. pp. 203-42, and B.D. Chilton, *God in Strength: Jesus' Announcement of the Kingdom* (SNTU, 1; Freistadt: Plöchl, 1979; repr. The Biblical Seminar, 8: Sheffield: JSOT Press, 1987); *idem*, 'An Evangelical and Critical Approach to the Sayings of Jesus', *Themelios* 3 (1977–78), pp. 78-85. Reference to Chilton's discussion is confined to the *Themelios* article.

5.   Cf., for example, R. Bultmann, *The History of the Synoptic Tradition* (trans. J. Marsh; Oxford: Basil Blackwell, 1963), p. 121; Taylor, *Mark*, p. 380; E. Schweizer, *The Good News according to Mark* (trans. D.H. Madvig; London: SPCK; Atlanta: John Knox, 1970), p. 178; H. Anderson, *The Gospel of Mark* (NCB; London: Marshall, Morgan & Scott; Grand Rapids: Eerdmans, 1976), p. 220.

6.   Cf., for example, E. Trocmé, 'Marc 9.1: Prédiction ou réprimande?', in *SE*, II (TU, 87; Berlin: Akademie Verlag, 1964), pp. 259-65; W. Lane, *The Gospel of Mark* (NIC; Grand Rapids: Eerdmans, 1974), p. 312.

7.   This is a thrust of the valuable study by Chilton, 'Sayings of Jesus', pp. 78-85.

For those who regard the saying as authentic, one of the more common interpretations is that it refers to the parousia.[8] Indeed, it seems likely that this is the construction placed upon it by Matthew.[9] This, of course, immediately thrusts one into the heart of the problem.[10] For if Jesus promised that the kingdom would come ἐν δυνάμει during his lifetime or shortly thereafter, the inevitable consequence is that he erred, raising serious questions about his own eschatology and its ultimate validity.[11] Two methods of dealing with this problem are adopted. The first is to admit that Jesus' knowledge of the End was limited. On this view, Jesus fully expected the parousia to occur within his own lifetime in accordance with the apocalyptic climate of his day.[12] Either he expected the End to come through his own life and work or that the End would come shortly after his death, which would be the point at which the Son of Man (SM) would come.[13] But subsequent events proved him wrong: the End did not come in the near future. To handle this problem, the logion was slightly modified by Mark (or the

8.   Cf. Ambrozic, *The Hidden Kingdom*, pp. 209-10.

9.   Mt. 16.28 may indicate that Matthew viewed Mk 9.1 in this manner, making what he considered Mark's meaning clear by substituting τὸν υἱὸν τοῦ ἀνθρώπου ἐρχόμενον ἐν τῇ βασιλείᾳ for Mark's τὴν βασιλείαν τοῦ θεοῦ ἐληλυθυῖαν ἐν δυνάμει. Cf. Swete, *Mark*, p. 186: D.E. Nineham, *The Gospel of St Mark* (PGC; Harmondsworth: Penguin; New York: Seabury, 1963), p. 232; D. Hill, *The Gospel of Matthew* (NCB; London: Marshall, Morgan & Scott; Grand Rapids: Eerdmans, 1972), p. 266, who, following Taylor, *Mark*, p. 385, views Mark as referring to the church. It is a matter of debate, however, whether the Matthean or Markan form of the saying is original. Cf., for example, F.H. Borsch, *The Son of Man in Myth and History* (London: SCM Press, 1967), p. 380, who regards the Matthean form as original, while A.J.B. Higgins, *Jesus and the Son of Man* (London: Gerald Duckworth, 1964), p. 104 prefers the Markan form (following Tödt).

10.   Cf. Nineham, *Mark*, p. 231, and the full-scale investigation by Moore, *The Parousia in the New Testament*.

11.   For valuable discussions about attempts to deal with the problem, cf. Ambrozic, *The Hidden Kingdom*, pp. 215-17.

12.   The position is that advocated by A. Schweitzer, *The Quest of the Historical Jesus* (trans. W. Montgomery; New York: Macmillan, 1910), pp. 51-53, and followed by a number of scholars to the present.

13.   Whether or not Jesus viewed himself as the coming SM has also been the subject of intense debate. Several excellent bibliographical essays may be consulted for the description of the debate; for example, I.H. Marshall, 'The Synoptic Son of Man Sayings in Recent Discussion', *NTS* 12 (1965–66), pp. 327-51 and 'The Son of Man in Contemporary Debate', *EvQ* 42 (1970), pp. 67-87.

community), adding the words εἰσίν τινες ὧδε τῶν ἑστηκότων as an attempt to admit that some who originally heard the words would die.[14] This expedient, of course, could only work until the final member of the audience died, at which time the modification could not help in any case. Thus Luke removes the idea from the realm of parousia expectation entirely and eliminates the problem of *Parousieverzögerung*.

The second method has been to postulate alternative interpretations of the phrase τὴν βασιλείαν τοῦ θεοῦ ἐληλυθυῖαν ἐν δυνάμει. This question hinges upon the decision about the precise character of the Kingdom of God (KG) in power and the force of the perfect participle ἐληλυθυῖαν. One solution which attracted wide debate was part of the 'realized eschatology' of C.H. Dodd. For Dodd, the participle was to be translated with a distinct past sense in line with its dependence upon the aorist subjunctive ἴδωσιν: 'there are some who stand here who will never taste death until they have seen that the kingdom of God has come with power'.[15] Thus, he held that the logion meant that the kingdom had already arrived when Jesus was speaking but that they would come to realize that it had been present only later. The point of realization he placed at Pentecost.[16] Dodd's focus upon ἐληλυθυῖαν, though perhaps leading to an extreme conclusion, was nevertheless important since the perfect participle should not be viewed as precisely equivalent to Matthew's ἐρχόμενον (16.28).[17]

Dodd's exegesis of this passage has been almost universally rejected by subsequent scholarship.[18] Almost all scholars who follow him insisted

14. Ambrozic, *The Hidden Kingdom*, p. 214 concludes that he finds it 'practically impossible to doubt that the phrase "some standing here" reflects the church's experience of the delay of the parousia, and that its present formulation should be attributed either to pre-Marcan tradition or to Mark himself'.

15. C.H. Dodd, *The Parables of the Kingdom* (New York: Charles Scribner's Sons, rev. edn, 1961), p. 28. Dodd has notably revised his earlier editions of *Parables* in the direction of his shift of thinking shown in *The Coming of Christ* (Cambridge: Cambridge University Press, 1951), pp. 13-15. For a full discussion of Dodd's position, cf. N. Perrin, *The Kingdom of God in the Teaching of Jesus* (London: SCM Press, 1963), pp. 58-78.

16. Dodd, 'The Kingdom of God has come', *ExpTim* 48 (1936–37), p. 141.

17. RSV translates as 'has come', showing the importance of Dodd's point. But the translation rightly rejects his rendering of the previous clause, since it is slightly tendentious. The ambiguity is preserved by translating ἴδωσιν in combination with γεύσωνται as 'they see'.

18. This is not to reject the importance of 'realized eschatology' as a feature of a

that the logion must have a future reference.[19] But widely differing opinions were held as to precisely what was intended by 'the kingdom of God in power'. One possible suggestion has been that it referred to the Fall of Jerusalem. This is the suggestion of R.T. France, who makes the point that the 'seeing' must be understood in the same sense as in 13.26 and 14.62, which he takes to imply a visible manifestation of the Lordship of Jesus in history.[20] In spite of Cranfield's summary dismissal of this point without so much as a refutation,[21] the view must be given full weight. To be sure, it has long been one of the solutions proposed,[22] and the full discussion of the Mark 13 data by France adds considerable credibility to its plausibility.[23] Following earlier scholars,[24] France argues that the whole of Mk 13.1-31 refers primarily to the Fall of Jerusalem and only 13.32-37 refers to the parousia. In his view, the introduction of the parousia into Mark 13 before v. 32 is 'quite gratuitous, and destroys the natural sequence of thought'.[25] The key to this interpretation rests upon the character of judgment attached to the coming of the SM, dependent in turn upon Dan. 7.13, the fact that the events are to occur before 'this generation' has passed (13.30), and the new subject introduced by the phrase περὶ δὲ τῆς ἡμέρας ἐκείνης (v. 32), and the dis

full-orbed New Testament eschatology, a discussion of which is beyond the scope of this paper.

19. Cf. Perrin, *Kingdom*, pp. 79-81 for his discussion of this point.

20. R.T. France, *Jesus and the Old Testament* (London: Tyndale, 1971), pp. 140, 142 and 235-37. See also K.E. Brower, 'The Old Testament in the Markan Passion Narrative' (unpublished PhD thesis, University of Manchester, 1978), pp. 367-68, 437-38. A slight variation on this is A. Vögtle, 'Exegetische Erwägungen über das Wissen und Selbstwusstsein Jesu', in J.B. Metz *et al.* (eds.), *Gott im Welt* (Festschrift Karl Rahner; 2 vols.; Freiburg: Herder, 1964), I, pp. 608-67, who sees it as a genuine temple saying like 13.30.

21. C.E.B. Cranfield, *The Gospel according to Saint Mark* (CGTC; Cambridge: Cambridge University Press, 1972), p. 287.

22. Cf. A. Plummer, *The Gospel according to S. Luke* (ICC; Edinburgh: T. & T. Clark, 1900), p. 249 for a comprehensive list of the proposed interpretations of the logion as well as the proposers from the nineteenth century.

23. France, *Jesus and the Old Testament*, pp. 227-39.

24. France, *Jesus and the Old Testament*, p. 231 n. 13 for reference to the fact that this perspective was held by pre-critical scholars as well as some contemporary scholars. But it must be noted that those who support this view are in the minority.

25. France, *Jesus and the Old Testament*, p. 232.

avowal of any knowledge of the timing of the End (vv. 32-37) in marked contrast to v. 30.

The possibility that France may be right adds a dimension which places a different light upon our logion. It increases the probability that it also refers to a visible, historical manifestation of the KG within the present generation, and draws our attention to 'seeing' as one of its keys.[26] If the event is a visible, historical, soon-to-occur manifestation of the KG in power, the Fall of Jerusalem fits the data fairly well.

One of the more popular solutions throughout the whole of the Christian era has been that the logion finds its fulfilment in the Transfiguration. Few scholars, if any, however, consider the connection between the logion of 9.1 and the pericope of 9.2-10 to be the original context.[27] The problem is set out admirably by Nineham,[28] who notes that the Transfiguration could scarcely be called the coming of the KG in power, nor is it likely that anyone could actually say with a solemn expression like ἀμὴν λέγω ὑμῖν that some people who are listening will actually be alive in six days' time: 'if Jesus solemnly affirmed that some at least of his hearers would survive his prediction by one week he was uttering ridiculous bathos'.[29]

In spite of this, several scholars have held that this is precisely how *Mark* viewed the logion.[30] Few modern exegetes understand this as the

26. Even if France is wrong about the meaning of 9.1, 13.26 and 14.62 on the lips of Jesus, the usage by Mark of this word and his intention by it stands or falls independently of the issue of Jesus' meaning.

27. Chilton, 'Sayings of Jesus', p. 84 comes close to claiming that the authentic logion was spoken by Jesus with the Transfiguration in view, but stops short of complete connection. Rather, he states that 'Mark placed this saying before the transfiguration precisely because Jesus is speaking of figures similar to those which appear in that pericope'.

28. Nineham, *Mark*, p. 236.

29. C.K. Barrett, *Jesus and the Gospel Tradition* (London: SPCK, 1967), p. 85. Cf. also Moore, *The Parousia in the New Testament*, p. 94 n. 3.

30. Cf. Cranfield, *Mark*, p. 288 for a useful summary of the argument which he, almost reluctantly, accepts. Other proponents of the view include G.H. Boobyer, 'St Mark and the Transfiguration Story', *JTS* 41 (1940), pp. 117-40; U. Mauser, *Christ in the Wilderness* (SBT, 39; London: SCM Press, 1963), p. 111; R. Pesch, *Naherwartungen: Tradition und Redaktion in Mark 13* (KBZANT; Düsseldorf: Patmos, 1968), pp. 187-88; and *idem, Das Markusevangelium*, I (HTKNT, 2.1; Freiburg: Herder, 1977), pp. 59, 65-66. For earlier attempts, cf. Plummer, *Luke*, p. 249.

total picture, however. R. Pesch, for example, sees it as a reference to the Transfiguration which, in turn, 'für die ausgewählten Jünger eine Prolepse der Gottesreicherfahrung bedeutet'.[31] Closely related are others who see it as a proleptic parousia reference.[32] Cranfield sees it as referring to Transfiguration, which in turn 'points forward to, and is a foretaste of the Resurrection, which in turn points forward to, and is a foretaste of, the Parousia, so that both the Resurrection and the Parousia may be said to be proleptically present in the Transfiguration'.[33]

Many scholars have rejected the suggestion that Mark viewed the Transfiguration as fulfilment of 9.1, and offer other solutions. Taylor looks to the church age,[34] while Schmid points to the end of the world or possibly the church age.[35] Pentecost has also been seen as the fulfilment, with the coming of the Holy Spirit and power in the early church seen as the KG in power.[36] Closely aligned to this view is one which sees the fulfilment in the actions of the early Christians, while Dodd's view that the KG was already present in power in the ministry of Jesus draws attention to the word ἐληλυθυῖαν. Others simply suggest that Mark has misunderstood the original context, which may have referred to the Fall of Jerusalem,[37] and then placed it juxtaposed to the Transfiguration. Crucial to the difference between some of these views is the understanding of ἴδωσιν: those who look for a fulfilment of 9.1 in

31. Pesch, *Das Markusevangelium*, p. 67. Similarly, Mauser, *Christ in the Wilderness*, p. 111 as a theophany which reveals God's power.

32. Cf., for example, Boobyer, 'St Mark', pp. 117-40. He regards 9.1 as a parousia prediction and the Transfiguration as a parousia manifestation. Moore, *The Parousia in the New Testament*, p. 127 notes the change in Jesus (μετεμορφώθη), the clouds and voice as temporary but real manifestations of the parousia, adding that the context reveals that the Transfiguration is viewed, in some sense as fulfilment.

33. Cranfield, *Mark*, p. 288. The question of whether or not 9.2-8 is a misplaced resurrection narrative is not relevant to this study. Cf. the careful study by R.H. Stein, 'Is the Transfiguration (Mk 9.2-18) a Misplaced Resurrection Account?', *JBL* 95 (1976), pp. 79-96.

34. Taylor, *Mark*, p. 386 followed by Nineham, *Mark*, p. 232.

35. J. Schmid, *The Gospel according to Mark* (RNT; trans. K. Condon; New York: Mercier, 1968), pp. 168-69.

36. Swete, *Mark*, p. 186. The problem for this position is that Luke alters the saying to remove the difficulty rather than apparently understanding it as pointing to Pentecost and the Holy Spirit, two of his favourite themes.

37. Cf. Moore, *The Parousia in the New Testament*, p. 104 for criticism of this position.

history take the term to mean 'see' as in 'behold' in a physical sense,[38] while those who understand the focus in a non-specific sense take the word to mean 'see' as in 'experience' or 'perceive'.[39]

All of the above suggestions have been made by those who consider the saying to be authentic, although any of them could also be advanced by those who regard it as inauthentic. By far the most popular view of the saying by the latter group is that it was constructed in the face of the increasing anxiety resulting from the *Parousieverzögerung*. On this view, the community perceived that things were going increasingly bad for Judaism (if the book was written before AD 70) or that Jerusalem had fallen (if written after AD 70), and this was interpreted as fulfilment of the apocalyptic expectations of the End, probably understood in terms of Mark 13.[40] Thus, the statement that the KG would come in power before all of the first generation of Christians would die, was constructed and placed upon the lips of Jesus as a *Trostwort*.[41] This was to encourage Christians in the face of persecution by giving them hope

38. Cf. France, *Jesus and the Old Testament*, p. 140.

39. So, most recently, Chilton, 'Sayings of Jesus', p. 84. A serious methodological question is at stake here, however. He likens the present use of 'see' to that used by Jn 3.3, where a logion of Jesus uses the phrase ἰδεῖν τὴν βασιλείαν τοῦ θεοῦ in a context which cannot mean anything but 'experience'. (Cf. R.E. Brown, *The Gospel according to John I–XII* [AB, 29; Garden City, NY: Doubleday, 1966], p. 130.) Chilton has already established to his satisfaction that the core of the logion is authentic by a judicious use of redaction criticism. Because he sees the construction of the logion in Mark as Semitic (based on a textual judgment which is far from commanding universal support) and authentic, he believes that he can readily move from Mark to a logion in John, which, in his judgment, is also Semitic and authentic, to understand the meaning of 'seeing' in the present context. But this type of methodology is hazardous in the extreme. Chilton does not discuss the use of ὁράω by Mark in places like 13.30, 14.62 or 15.32 which should be considered far better commentary on Mark's usage than Jn 3.3 (it may be argued that these passages support his contention, however, but see below), nor does he consider the wider contexts of either Jn 3.3 or Mk 9.1. In Jn 3.3, one would no more expect ἰδεῖν to be a literal usage than expect γεννάω ἄνωθεν to be a physical birth. In Jn 3.3 ἰδεῖν is paralleled by εἰσελθεῖν in 3.5, defining its meaning in clear terms. But in Mk 9.1, the interpretation of 'seeing' must depend, in large measure, upon its wider context which includes 9.9, a clear reference to a visual perception, whatever its actual form.

40. It is almost universally held that Mk 13.3-23 refers to the Fall of Jerusalem. Some extend this meaning to 13.31 (see above).

41. Bultmann, *The History of the Synoptic Tradition*, p. 121; Grässer, *Das Problem der Parousieverzögerung in den synoptischen Evangelien* and others.

that, while the End was not yet, it was indeed imminent—indeed, the suffering which they were currently experiencing was, in fact, part of the immediate prelude. Perrin, who had earlier held that the saying was authentic and represented the genuine tension between the present and future aspects of the KG in the teaching of Jesus,[42] later abandoned this view in favour of a form of *Trostwort* idea, which was intended to encourage the readers to steadfastness.[43] In Mk 9.1, the readers were to understand 'some standing here' as members of the church undergoing persecution, while in 13.30, the addressees were all who would overhear or read it ('this generation').[44]

II

The variety of interpretations given in analyzing this logion indicates that there still remains a presentation of the evidence which can account for all of the features in the text *as it appears in front of us*. A significant advance in the study of the Gospel of Mark has been precisely this emphasis upon the text and its structures as a key for ascertaining the evangelist's understanding of his material.[45] This approach has called forth a new methodology which builds upon the tools used in the past, but is not dependent upon them.[46] It takes the evangelist seriously as a

---

42. Perrin, *Kingdom*, pp. 137-39.

43. Perrin, *Rediscovering the Teaching of Jesus* (London: SCM Press, 1967) and 'The Composition of Mark 9.1', *NovT* 11 (1969), pp. 67-70.

44. Perrin, *Teaching*, p. 201 and *idem*, 'The Composition of Mark 9.1', p. 62.

45. Cf., for example, P. Achtemeier, 'Mark as Interpreter of the Jesus Tradition', *Int* 32 (1978), p. 340 for a concise statement about Mark's method, accurately summarizing this advance in our view of the Gospel. He notes that the 'idea of collecting the traditions about Jesus into a story whose order and arrangement itself would provide, with a minimum of editorial comment, the context for understanding and interpreting those traditions is apparently the invention of Mark himself'.

46. Form criticism has proved a useful tool in understanding the original context of a saying or pericope and helping to penetrate its meaning in its original context. But the gains for interpreting the text as we have it have been minimal. Redaction criticism has been much more successful in illuminating the narratives of Matthew and Luke, but it encounters significant problems in the study of Mark. (Using the tool of redaction criticism in a highly skilled manner, Lane has produced one of the more significant commentaries on Mark in recent years, providing illumination accessible to the skilled, but non-specialist interpreter. Lane, however, strays from a strictly *redaktionsgeschichtliche* approach, being much more eclectic in his use of the tools.)

purposeful writer who has skilfully selected and arranged the traditions available to him, moulding them into a cohesive, overall picture of Jesus.[47] Achtemeier has the balance maintained in this new approach to the text exactly right when he characterizes Mark's technique as follows:

> Rather than choosing a form in which incident is interlaced with comment on the way the incident was to be understood, Mark chose to let the traditions speak for themselves. It was the interpretative context that was to be the key, not the author's own theological expositions. In that way, the traditions would remain free to make their original points, but the way they were arranged and juxtaposed would provide the clue as to the overall context within which these points were to be understood.[48]

This approach, applied to this text, proceeds from an analysis of the logion itself, to a determination of its place within the surrounding context, to an estimate of its contribution to the Gospel as a whole.[49] Only upon completion of these analyses is it possible to proceed to a strictly redactional study, or to determine its precise form, content and meaning on the lips of Jesus.[50]

A. *The Text*

Several points of importance emerge from a careful consideration of the text, as well as some additional problems.[51] In the first place, the phrase

47. Cf. Brower, 'The Old Testament in the Markan Passion Narrative', *passim*, where I have attempted to show that the selection and use of the Old Testament citations and allusions in the Markan passion narrative is according to Mark's own design, while faithful to the general tradition, and further, that the whole is one piece, neither an appendix to, nor the first part of, his work.

48. Achtemeier, 'Mark as Interpreter', p. 340.

49. It is immediately obvious that this approach is concerned with neither historicity nor authenticity. It seeks only to determine the precise meaning of the logion as used in the Markan context. Perhaps it is not too impertinent to observe that this may be more valuable than either of these other enterprises, since it is the Gospel of Mark which we have in canon, not this or that level of tradition alone.

50. To use the Markan text to determine the form, content and meaning of the saying on the lips of Jesus and then to use this insight as a determinative tool in exegesis of the Markan text is slightly circular. Chilton, 'Sayings of Jesus', pp. 78-85, for example, is much more persuasive in establishing authenticity than successful at exegeting the text in Mark.

51. Cf. Bultmann, *The History of the Synoptic Tradition*, p. 121; Taylor, *Mark*, p. 218; and W. Kelber, *The Kingdom in Mark* (Philadelphia: Fortress Press, 1974), p. 73.

καὶ ἔλεγεν αὐτοῖς has rightly been seen as a connecting link used repeatedly by Mark. But it is also important as an indication of the audience. Within the narrative from 8.27-30, the initial teaching on suffering is presented to the disciples (8.27, 31) but the audience is enlarged by the addition of ὁ ὄχλος (v. 34). It is to them that the following statements are addressed. The probability is strong, therefore, that the logion is addressed to all the hearers, in Mark's view, rather than simply to the disciples, especially if 9.1 is seen as playing a significant role in the section from 8.27-30, and especially 8.34-38. However, it cannot be considered conclusive.[52] In either case, the teaching contained in the logion is addressed to those who have already been taught concerning the necessity for suffering, both for Jesus as SM[53] and for those who would follow him.

While one must agree with Chilton that 'Amen' is no guarantee that a saying is dominical, it cannot be doubted that the use of the formula is seen by Mark to introduce a particularly important point.[54] Most of the usages introduce clearly predictive sayings (the exception is 12.43), where the guarantee of Jesus' own person is understood as standing behind the promise. In this instance, Horstmann concludes 'auf unser logion Mk 9.1 bezogen bedeutet das, dass die Gottesherrschaft in einzigartiger Weise an Jesus gebunden ist, der mit seiner eigenen Person für das Eintreffen der Zusage bürgt'.[55] This close attachment of KG with Jesus is crucial to the correct understanding of the passage. The focus is christological, not in the prediction apart from its relationship to the Person of Christ.

---

52. Cf. Trocmé, 'Marc 9.1', p. 263 where he calls the logion 'une protestation supplémentaire contra la couardise de ceux qui, malgré les appels du Maître, se dérobent devant la risque du martyr sous prétexte d'attendre la pleine manifestation du Règne dont Jésus ne peut encore leur montrer que des signes'.

53. The question of whether or not Jesus saw himself as the SM is a moot point. But it can scarcely be doubted that Mark so viewed him.

54. The passages where ἀμὴν λέγω ὑμῖν is used in Mark are 3.28; 8.12; 9.1, 41; 10.15, 29; 11.23; 12.42; 13.30; 14.9, 18, 25, 30. All of them are viewed by Mark as being dominical and all are used to add solemnity to what follows. Cf. Taylor, *Mark*, p. 242, Cranfield, *Mark*, p. 140, Lane, *Mark*, p. 144 and Anderson, *Mark*, p. 123.

55. M. Horstmann, *Studien zur Markinischen Christologie: Mk 8.27–9.13 als Zugang zum Christusbild des zweiten Evangeliums* (NTAbh, 6; Münster: Aschendorff, 1969), p. 61.

The most novel suggestion in Chilton's excellent discussion is the interpretation of τῶν ἑστηκότων as referring to Moses and Elijah. He develops his argument from the *lectio difficilior* reading, inferring from the apparently awkward Markan construction of the phrase τινες ὧδε τῶν ἑστηκότων that '"those standing" was a set phrase which Mark felt was not to be broken up'.[56] Thus, he suggests, this phrase is dominical, being Semitic in construction, and traditional in usage (cf. Mt. 26.73; Jn 3.39; Acts 22.25). Then, by equating 'those standing' with 'some who will not taste death', he states that this latter phrase is 'the equivalent of calling someone immortal',[57] citing *Gen. R.* 9.6 and *4 Ezra* 6.26 as evidence that the phrase was so used to describe such figures as Enoch, Elijah, Moses, Jeremiah and Ezra. Finally, he concludes that the dominical logion is referring to an immortal group, which prompts Mark to place it immediately before the Transfiguration where just such an immortal group is gathered.

The net result of Chilton's study is that the major problems in 9.1 are solved. No longer do we need to struggle to find a period which will adequately explain the prediction of Jesus that 'some standing here will not taste death before they see the KG come in power'. At a stroke, the whole saying is removed from the area of prediction to an instance of a truism: 'Jesus here assures us... that the kingdom, understood as God's revelation on behalf of his people, is a reality. He was as certain of this as he was that the patriarchs, Moses and Elijah, live in the sight of God.'[58] But does Chilton's analysis stand the test of both textual and contextual exegesis?

Several points must be noted about Chilton's argument. First, he far too ready to accept the witness of one codex (Vaticanus) as the basis for his whole discussion. To be sure, he follows one of the accepted canons of textual criticism (along with most critical editions and Taylor and Cranfield), but this canon alone may not be sufficient to dispel any doubts about the original reading. Furthermore, his suggestion that Mk 11.15 shows that the redactor would have preferred the τῶν-ἐκεῖ-ἑστηκότων order is far from unequivocal, while 15.29 and 35, οἱ παραπορευόμενοι and τῶν παρεστηκότων, both similar phrases, indicate that the writer was unafraid to use this participial construction as

56. Chilton, 'Sayings of Jesus', p. 82.
57. Chilton, 'Sayings of Jesus', p. 84.
58. Chilton, 'Sayings of Jesus', p. 85.

a unit. Another consideration is that the phrase occurs in the common Markan construction of εἶναι plus a participle,[59] which does not support Chilton's case, even if it is not decisive against it.

Secondly, Chilton observes correctly that ὧδε has significance as a connecting link to the Transfiguration. But having established this connection does not support his contention that the 'ones here standing' are Elijah and Moses. Rather, it is clear from the context of 9.5 that the ones to whom the ὧδε refers in that instance are the disciples and not Moses and Elijah, and rather than bearing witness to the veracity of Jesus' statement, Peter is shown as misreading the situation entirely. Thus, while a connection is made with the Transfiguration in ὧδε, it is not from the purpose of equating 'those here standing' with Elijah and Moses.

Thirdly, and more significantly, Chilton appears to misread Mark's intention of connecting 9.1 and 9.2-8, implying that the connection was to be seen in the fact that Elijah and Moses are two witnesses of precisely the character required by τῶν ἑστηκότων: deathless figures. Granted that the importance of Elijah and Moses is problematic, it is unlikely that their true significance is found as witnesses to the truth of the logion in 9.1.[60] Elijah in particular is vital to Mark's whole argument in the section 8.27 to 9.13, and his presence in the Transfiguration, from the Markan perspective, should be painted against this wider canvas. The connection between 9.1 and 9.2-8 is vital for Mark, but its point is not to be found in the construction Chilton places upon τῶν ἑστηκότων. In the absence of a more realistic suggestion, these words in the Markan context must refer to some members of the immediate audience, rather than to the esoteric group suggested by Chilton.

Finally, one further note from the text itself must relate to the phrase ἴδωσιν τὴν βασιλείαν τοῦ θεοῦ. The only other occurrence of this phrase is in Jn 3.3, where the meaning must be taken as 'experience' rather than perceive visually. But recourse to John is not justified in this instance, since ὁράω is an important word in Mark's Gospel.[61] Considering the text in isolation, it is difficult to determine with any degree of certainty whether Mark intends ἴδωσιν to be a visual or

---

59. Taylor, *Mark*, p. 45.

60. To be sure, Chilton does not directly attribute their presence in 9.2-8 as witnesses to the truth of the logion in 9.1, but he does imply that Elijah and Moses are in Mark's mind, functioning as witnesses (or guarantors) in 9.1.

61. The importance of the word is considered below.

perceptual phenomenon. But even in this case, one should not press the distinction between visual and perceptual too hard, since Mark is not writing about 'seeing' a static entity but rather 'seeing' the arrival of God's rule in power. This may well be observed in visually perceivable phenomena as evidence for the presence of the KG, but these phenomena cannot be considered the kingdom itself. The point is well made by Mark's phrase: what they will 'see' is the KG ἐληλυθυῖαν ἐν δυνάμει.[62]

B. *The Context*

Unfortunately, the full significance of Mark's contextualization of 9.1 has only rarely been appreciated.[63] Few, if any, studies of the logion have sought to draw out its significance with direct reference to the context, thus tending to isolate the logion from its moorings in the Markan structure. Significant insights are to be gained, however, from a contextual analysis, including its contacts with the surrounding verses, those with similar verbal structures, and the connections in motif structure which the logion acquires by its position and content.

It is generally agreed that Mk 9.1 is placed in its present context by the evangelist.[64] The introduction of the logion by the phrase καὶ ἔλεγεν αὐτοῖς is the most important clue to this original isolation along with the introduction of 9.2 with καὶ μετὰ ἡμέρας ἕξ. This indicates that the whole connection between 8.38 and 9.1, and 9.1 and 9.2 is a Markan construction. But since E. Haenchen has shown that the whole of Mk 8.27–9.1 is Markan,[65] we should take seriously the structure of this whole unit in any attempt to isolate the underlying motif structure. Furthermore, the Transfiguration narrative may well be introduced precisely at this point, bracketed by 8.27–9.1 and 9.9-13.[66] If this is correct,

---

62. Contra Chilton, 'Sayings of Jesus', p. 85, who confuses evidence for the coming of the KG with the KG itself.

63. Cf. especially Horstmann, *Studien zur Markinischen Christologie*, and Kelber, *The Kingdom in Mark*.

64. Cf. Bultmann, *The History of the Synoptic Tradition*, p. 121; Taylor, *Mark*, p. 218; and Kelber, *The Kingdom in Mark*, p. 73.

65. E. Haenchen, 'Die Komposition vom Mk 8.27–9.1 und par', *NovT* 6 (1963), pp. 81-109. It is not necessary to hold that the pericope is therefore created out of whole cloth. Rather, choice and structure are Markan.

66. The importance of bracketing as a Markan technique is clearly noted by many scholars, including the full-scale study by F. Neirynck, *Duality in Mark: Contributions*

Mark uses 8.27–9.1 and 9.9-13 to interpret 9.2-8.[67] This means that this whole section 'more than any other part of the gospel bears the imprint of a skilfully designed composition'.[68] Thus any analysis which focuses upon the text in isolation must be open to question.[69] As Chilton demonstrates, 'the dual connection of 9.1 in Mark's mind to the Son of man saying which precedes and the transfiguration which follows is therefore established'.[70]

The connection with 8.38 is clear though not unequivocal. Both 9.1 and 8.38 end with a 'coming' reference, viewed by some as an implied contrast between the two, forming a climactic antithesis of warning and promise which brings the pericope to its close.[71] But while the connection is real enough, Trocmé has shown that the whole passage has a severe tone, warning the disciples and other followers against 'la légèreté et la lâcheté' of which he found Peter capable.[72] This view of 9.1 must be seen as a real possibility: the coming of the KG in power may well be related to the coming of the SM in the judgment implied by 8.38. The combination of 'glory' (v. 38) and 'power' (9.1) is very evocative of 13.26, which is by no means an unambiguous promise of hope.[73] If France is right in holding that Mk 13.3-31 is related to the Fall of Jerusalem,[74] then the context is very much one of judgment, a point drawn directly from the Dan. 7.13 roots of 13.26. Thus, the 'coming of the KG in power' has as much to do with judgment as it does with hope, and the logion may well be a threat that 'some of those here standing' shall not escape the imminent coming of the SM in power and judgment.

The connections with the following passage are no less difficult to understand. Literarily, the two are linked in sequence by Mark's time

---

to the Markan Redaction (BETL, 31; Leuven: Leuven University Press, 1972).

67. Horstmann, *Studien zur Markinischen Christologie*, sees the sequence of thought being broken by 9.2-8 and therefore the whole piece is used as evidence of Mark's christology.

68. Kelber, *The Kingdom in Mark*, p. 67.

69. Contra W.G. Kümmel, *Promise and Fulfilment: The Eschatological Message of Jesus* (SBT, 23; London: SCM Press, 2nd edn, 1961), p. 25.

70. Chilton, 'Sayings of Jesus', p. 82.

71. Perrin, 'The Composition of Mark 9.1', p. 68.

72. Trocmé, 'Marc 9.1', p. 260.

73. Cf. the 'Day of the Lord' imagery in Amos 5.18-20, clearly a judgment context.

74. Cf. above, note 20.

reference,[75] but this has more to do with his overall view of the progress from confession to cross than to the actual historical events. This whole central section of the Gospel is framed by comments on the 'way' (8.27 and 10.52 bracket the whole, with other 'way' references occurring at 9.33, 34 and 10.17, 32), a motif which gives Jesus' progress towards Jerusalem and the cross both purpose and choice.[76] But the way is not only seen as Jesus' way—the disciples are also to follow him: discipleship consists in following Jesus.[77] This path is a path of suffering which leads to vindication, and just as Jesus must walk this path, so too must his disciples, a point made repeatedly throughout this section (explicitly in 8.34-38 and 10.35-45).

The idea of progress scarcely exhausts the connection between the two, however. It cannot be denied that Mark viewed the revelation of Christ in the Transfiguration as in some sense an illumination of the logion in 9.1. But it is equally unlikely that it was seen as the fulfilment of 9.1. Two key points make this impossible: the juxtapositioning of the futuristic εἰσίν τινες ὧδε ἑστηκότων οἵτινες οὐ μὴ γεύσωνται θανάτου and μετὰ ἡμέρας ἕξ, a combination as unlikely in the Markan narrative as it is on Jesus' lips, if the one is to be fulfilled in the other, and, secondly, the fact that the likely evidence of 9.1 was the disciples plus ὁ ὄχλος (8.34) while the Transfiguration was for the three disciples κατ' ἰδίαν μόνους (v. 2). It is certainly likely that the scene containing a mountain (an important setting for Mark, cf. 3.13), probably a mountain of revelation, glory, cloud and a voice all point to a theophany of some sort revealing the glory of Jesus.[78] But it is equally clear that the scene is not limited to this revelation of glory. To be sure, Mark's own commentary on it preserved in 9.9-13 shows that the scene must be viewed from a post-resurrection perspective, but this does not detract from the crucial contribution of the context to the scene. As

75. Cf., for example, M.D. Hooker, *The Son of Man in Mark* (London: SPCK, 1967), p. 123.

76. Cf. Kelber, *The Kingdom in Mark, passim*, and Brower, 'The Old Testament in the Markan Passion Narrative', *passim*.

77. Cf. Kelber, *The Kingdom in Mark*, pp. 70-71. For a discussion of this idea in the passion narrative, see Brower, 'The Old Testament in the Markan Passion', pp. 234-39, 254-55.

78. Kelber, *The Kingdom in Mark*, p. 77 rightly questions the theory that Mk 9.2-8 is modelled on Exod. 24, noting the crucial point that on Sinai, it is Yahweh's glory that is revealed, while here the scene reveals the glory of Jesus.

Achtemeier observes 'it cannot be disputed that the clearest story in Mark of the divine glory of Jesus is placed in the narrative in such a way that it is bracketed by a reference to suffering (8.34–9.1; 9.9-13). Therefore, it again makes that same point: the path to glory begins as the way of the cross'.[79]

This point is supported by two facts often overlooked. First, the perception Peter shows is as faulty here as it was in 8.32-33. Peter here urges Jesus to remain on the mountain of glory. He is quite in favour of the glory which is central to this scene (9.5-6), just as he was unreceptive to the teaching on suffering (8.32-33). In effect, he says that he decidedly prefers a 'theology of glory' to a 'theology of the cross' and sees Moses and Elijah as a confirmation of this glorious state. But the point is clear: they come down from the mountain. The glory of the SM lies by way of the cross, a point only understandable by the disciples after the resurrection. Secondly, while Moses is present in the scene, his part is ignored in the Markan commentary. The attention is focused on Elijah, confirmed in the unusual formulation Ἠλείας σὺν Μωϋσεῖ.[80] Elijah = John the Baptist is clearly seen by Mark as a suffering figure, whose completed work in some way prefigures that of the SM = Jesus. Both are righteous sufferers, both are misunderstood, both are viewed as figures whose true significance is not perceived even by those who should have known them, yet their true roles are grasped by the readers. In 9.11-13, the Markan Jesus notes that the role of Elijah, the forerunner who is also a righteous sufferer, had been completed (6.14-29)[81] according to the Scriptures just as the role of the SM must find completion according to the Scriptures. For both, the path to glory is via suffering.

79. P. Achtemeier, *Mark* (Proclamation Commentaries; Philadelphia: Fortress Press, 1975), p. 102.

80. Note how Peter puts them in their usual order (v. 5), further indication of his lack of perception. M.E. Thrall, 'Elijah and Moses in Mark's Account of the Transfiguration', *NTS* 16 (1969–70), p. 305 sees them as the key around whom the whole story turns. In her view, the narrative draws a distinction between Jesus and the two figures, in that the scene points to the resurrection and Jesus' glory is thus resurrection glory, quite different from that of Elijah and Moses. This view is, to some extent, supported by v. 9 but tends to founder on Mark's view of Elijah. Cf. also W. Liefeld, 'The Transfiguration Narratives', in *New Directions in New Testament Study* (ed. R.N. Longenecker and M.C. Tenney; Grand Rapids: Zondervan, 1974), p. 173.

81. And, hence, he can appear in the Transfiguration, having completed his role.

Important links also occur between 9.1 and other parts of the Gospel, seen in the key words ἴδωσιν and βασιλεία τοῦ θεοῦ. The verb ὁράω occurs in a number of key verses related to 9.1. Regularly noted are 13.26 and 14.62[82] to which should be added 15.32 and possibly 15.39. In each of these instances, we have an ostensibly visual perception which also has a deeper meaning on the reader's level. As noted previously, 13.26 may well have a historical referent, and I have shown elsewhere that 14.62 also finds a preliminary fulfilment in the action of God on the cross (15.33-39), one which has a visual component in response to the mocking request of 15.32.[83] In this latter verse, the chief priests and scribes want to have Jesus act as wonder worker ἵνα ἴδωμεν καὶ πιστεύσωμεν. Immediately they 'see' darkness at noon, the judgment of God on the world, and the rent temple veil, the specific judgment of Israel. Clearly, they do not see what they want to see, but they do see the action of ὁ χριστὸς ὁ βασιλεὺς Ισραηλ in a fashion unmistakable to the reader. This is also one of the responses to Jesus' threat made before the Sanhedrin in 14.62: they see the judgment of the SM upon their institutions by God's direct action in Jesus on the cross.

In 9.1, the object of ἴδωσιν is the KG having come in power. That Mark sees the logion as a prediction of the future from the audience perspective is clear from the seemingly redundant use of τινες... οἵτινες: the group who will see the coming is only part of the audience. On the other hand, the careful choice of ἐληλυθυῖαν must imply that, from the standpoint of those who have not died, the KG will have come in power: a past occurrence with continuing effect. But this does not elucidate Mark's precise understanding of the KG in power—it merely sets historical parameters within which we should look.

A way forward is possible in an examination of Mark's use of the Day imagery. The connection between the KG and the Day of Yahweh has deep Old Testament roots, and, although they should not be understood as coterminous, at least in the New Testament, they are inextricably connected. The relationship, in fact, is precisely suited to this logion, for the Day is regularly seen as the point at which the coming of the KG in power occurs. Just as regularly, this has been linked with the parousia of Christ (cf. 1 Thess. 4.13-18, for example). But it is by no means certain

82. Perrin, 'The Composition of Mark 9.1', *passim*.
83. Brower, 'The Old Testament in the Markan Passion Narrative', *passim* for the whole argument, the barest conclusions of which are presented here.

that this exhausts the idea of 'that Day' for Mark, or, indeed, if it is even primary. A brief look at three of the relevant texts is thus in order: 2.20; 14.62; 15.33-47.

The logion in 2.20 is usually regarded as pointing to the crucifixion,[84] a perspective which is undoubtedly correct on the reader's level. Significant for our purpose, however, is the key link of passion and ἐν ἐκείνῃ τῇ ἡμέρᾳ, a point totally missed by Matthew and changed by Luke to ἐν ἐκείναις ταῖς ἡμέραις to conform it to the first half of the verse (Lk. 5.35a). Given the fact that Mark also uses the plural in 2.20a, it is at least possible that he has deliberately chosen to use this phrase, probably to connect the passion implicity with 'that Day'.

Clearly, on its own, this logion is insufficient to sustain the view that, for Mark, 'that Day' is the day of crucifixion. But the whole death scene in Mk 15.33-39 has distinct Day of the Lord features which make the designation apposite.[85] The cosmic phenomena, presented in undoubted allusion to Amos 8.9, suggest strongly that Mark viewed the crucifixion in this fashion. 'Darkness at noon' is a symbol of God's judgment, which is a key feature of the Day of the Lord. Furthermore, the judgment motif is not limited to 15.33, but is present in 15.38 in the rending of the temple veil. Both these actions are presented structurally as supernatural phenomena, forming the bracket surrounding Jesus' death. By citing Amos 8.9 in 15.33 and enclosing the death of Jesus between this citation and the temple veil rending, Mark shows the cosmic dimension to what is occurring on the cross. The judgment of the world, symbolized by the darkness at noon, is occurring in the death of an apparently pathetic and deluded figure. Here, Mark's skilful use of irony is at its best: it is in the shameful death of Jesus that the readers can discern the judgment of mankind in general (v. 33) and Judaism in particular (v. 38). In the depth of weakness, the power of judgment occurs.

This understanding casts light upon 14.62 as well. The Markan Jesus here states that the audience, in this case the Sanhedrin, will see the SM seated at the right hand of power and coming with the clouds of heaven.

---

84. On which grounds it is often regarded as inauthentic or misplaced. But it is sufficiently cryptic to allow the actors in the scene to miss the meaning and sufficiently clear to allow the readers to grasp its deeper meaning. Cf. Taylor, *Mark*, p. 211 and Lane, *Mark*, pp. 112-13.

85. At this point, I draw heavily upon the results of my previous research, 'The Old Testament in the Markan Passion Narrative', *passim*.

This is usually interpreted to be a parousia reference, but it is well worth considering whether it may not find its initial fulfilment in the judgment exercised by God on behalf of and through the SM at the cross. Thus, the superficially redundant word in Mark 15.32, ἴδωμεν, is seen to be answered in the immediately following events: the chief priests and scribes (v. 31) do see the judgment of God being exercised, they do see 'that Day' arriving, and they do see the KG having come with power. To be sure, they do not recognize its presence—it is the crowning irony of Mark's Gospel that the perception of who Jesus really is, in the final analysis, occurs on the lips of a pagan soldier. It was not the Jewish leaders nor the disciples who, ἰδὼν ὅτι οὕτως ἐξέπνευσεν, confessed that 'Truly this man was Son of God', but the Gentile centurion.

The cross as the decisive point adds a possible further dimension to the meaning of tasting death.[86] While it clearly points to a physical death on the narrative level and therefore helps set historical limits to Mark's meaning, it may have a deeper significance on the reader's level. Mark has just included the paradoxical logion in 8.35 about losing one's life to find it. But it is clear that this laying down of one's life is in following Jesus in cross-bearing. In fact, the Markan Jesus later promises that his followers shall experience death (10.38), but before he goes to the cross, they are only able to follow in amazement and fear (10.32). After Jesus dies on the cross, however, they too must bear the cross and drink the cup, fully 'tasting death' and experiencing it in its paradoxical life-giving function. On the reader's level, then, the reference to those who shall not taste death may have a dual function in parallel to the dual threat/promise motif attached to the KG. On the one hand, the ones who will not taste death may be those who will not escape the judgment of the SM of the cross, while, on the other hand, it may also point to those who will follow Jesus in cross-bearing and therefore participate in the KG after it comes in power through his death.

One final point remains: to stress that the coming of the KG in power must be seen in connection with the death scene does not imply that its meaning is thereby exhausted. The future, both historical and ahistorical, is an integral part of Mark 13, for example. Nor was suffering ever the end in itself for Mark: like the Old Testament psalms of lament, suffering inevitably issues in vindication for the righteous sufferer, in Mark's view.

---

86. I owe this idea to my former student, Mr. Gordon Thomas, who suggested the possibility to me in private conversation after the first presentation of this paper.

Thus, the cross is not the end—only the beginning of the end. To be sure, Mark does not focus upon the resurrection as vindication to any great extent, nor does he ignore it. Rather, it is a key assumption. Jesus will be vindicated in resurrection (8.31; 9.31; 10.37-38; 14.28; 16.7). But even here, the idea of vindication is not exhausted. Mark sees the whole sequence of death/resurrection/exaltation/parousia as part of a continuous whole, inextricably bound up with the person of Jesus. In each of these facets of the same whole, there is to be seen the kingdom in power. It too can only be understood christologically.

III

Any solution to this crux must not elevate one aspect of the logion to the exclusion of another, unless it is impossible to explain it otherwise. Furthermore, it is necessary to hold the two levels of Mark's narrative closely together. It is on the reader's level, however, that the overall motif structure is such an integrating force.

On the narrative level, the meaning must be simply that some of the people present will see the kingdom having come in power. But from the reader's perspective, Mark has already begun to pave the way to perception: the use of the perfect in 1.15 (ἤγγικεν) to describe the nearness of the KG, the allusion to the cross in 2.20 with the phrase 'that Day', also related to the KG, the focus upon suffering from 8.27 onwards, which, retrospectively, explains the long section on the Baptist's death (6.14-29) and prepares the way for the righteous sufferer theme in the latter half of the Gospel. The position of the vital Transfiguration narrative, almost precisely in the centre and bracketed by suffering motifs, shows the vindication and triumph of Jesus but only as it is related to his suffering. Glory only comes by way of the cross. The repeated use of SM in designation of Jesus, with its clear judgmental overtones, also points to the cross, where the judgment of this world, in some sense, occurs, though its final consummation comes in the future (Mk. 13.32-37). From 8.27 onwards, virtually everything ultimately points to the cross as the decisive point in the coming of the kingdom.

In sum, the crucial logion in Mk 9.1 can best be understood as a combination threat/promise that the KG would come in power in the lifetime of at least some of the hearers. These shall see the kingdom in power, albeit power in weakness, and it may not be perceived as power. Nevertheless, in the cross of Jesus, God's rule has been decisively established, shown by the darkness at noon and the rending of the veil, and witnessed to by the Roman centurion. Furthermore, Mark clearly saw the essential unity of the kingdom: its nearness, coming, establishment and consummation are all one Event and all are unified in God's action in Christ Jesus.

JSNT 31 (1987), pp. 3-22

IS MARK 15.39 THE KEY TO MARK'S CHRISTOLOGY?

Earl S. Johnson, Jr

In recent study of the Gospel of Mark the confession of the Roman centurion in Mk 15.39 has become a *crux interpretum* for Markan christology and is frequently seen as the key to a correct understanding of Mark's theology as a whole. Typical in scholarship of the past fifty years is Vincent Taylor's view that Mark regarded the centurion's words at the end of the Gospel to be parallel to the inscription in 1.1, that is, that the announcement in 15.39 is a confession of the deity of Jesus in the full Christian sense.[1]

In most recent studies the centurion's confession has been understood further as the climax of Mark's *theologia crucis*. In light of the spiritual blindness and misunderstanding about Jesus' true identity which dominates the Gospel, scholars have argued that it is 'crucial for Mark's theology'[2] that the reader be shown who Jesus really is at the foot of the cross. As J.D. Kingsbury has concluded, the centurion's acclamation is pivotal because it constitutes the first time in Mark's story that anyone other than Jesus (or God) fully understands who Jesus is; and that understanding comes at the culmination of Jesus' earthly ministry, his death on the cross. The centurion sees (ἰδών, v. 39) what no one else perceives, that Jesus truly is the Son of God; he becomes, in effect, the first Christian convert or disciple.[3]

1. V. Taylor, *The Gospel according to Mark* (London: Macmillan, 2nd edn, 1966), p. 597.
2. H. Anderson, *The Gospel of Mark* (NCB; London: Oliphants; Grand Rapids: Eerdmans, 1976), p. 148.
3. J.D. Kingsbury, *The Christology of Mark's Gospel* (Philadelphia: Fortress Press, 1983), pp. 128-34. The majority of recent studies present the centurion's confession of Jesus as the Son of God as a key to the Gospel. See, for example, R.G. Bratcher, 'A Note on υἱὸς θεοῦ (Mark xv. 39)', *ExpTim* 68 (1956), pp. 27-28;

It has been recognized for a number of years that one of the keys to a correct interpretation of Mk 15.39 and Mark's theology as a whole is a proper understanding of the anarthrous υἱὸς θεοῦ and the meaning of the imperfect indicative ἦν in the centurion's statement ὁ ἄνθρωπος υἱὸς θεοῦ ἦν. Although it has been argued that υἱὸς θεοῦ should be translated 'a son of god', indicating that the centurion was only intimating that Jesus was a hero or a demigod,[4] E.C. Colwell's careful grammatical study of the Greek article in 1933[5] convinced scholars that the centurion's confession should be translated 'truly this man was the Son of God', and the major subsequent English translations have supported that conclusion.[6] However, a re-examination of Colwell's 'rule', a study of the use of ἦν in the New Testament, and a consideration of the general reputation which a Roman soldier of a centurion's rank may have had among Mark's readers all demand a reconsideration of this widely accepted interpretation of Mk 15.39.

1. *Colwell's Rule*

Colwell's study examines the interpretative problems created in New Testament passages where even though the definite article is absent before a noun (or a title) it appears that the subject is still intended to be definite. His investigation convinced him that the key to understanding such usage was found in the position of the verb:

A. Blight, 'A Note on Huios Theou in Mark 15.39', *ExpTim* 80 (1968–69), pp. 51, 53; K. Stock, 'Das Bekenntnis des Centurio, Mk 15.39 im Rahmen des Markusevangeliums', *ZNW* 100 (1978), pp. 298-301; J. Gnilka, *Das Evangelium nach Markus*, II (EKKNT, 2.2; Zürich: Benziger Verlag, 1979), pp. 324-25; F.J. Matera, *The Kingship of Jesus: Composition and Theology in Mark 15* (SBLDS, 66; Chico, CA: Scholars Press, 1982); H.L. Chronis, 'The Torn Veil: Cultus and Christology in Mark 15.37-39', *JBL* 101 (1982), pp. 97-114, especially p. 106; K. Brower, 'Elijah in the Markan Passion Narrative', *JSNT* 18 (1983), pp. 85-101; D. Senior, *The Passion of Jesus in the Gospel of Mark* (Wilmington, DE: Michael Glazier, 1984), pp. 128-32.

4.   See the seminal work of E.P. Gould, *A Critical and Exegetical Commentary on the Gospel according to Mark* (ICC; Edinburgh: T. & T. Clark, 1896), p. 295.

5.   E.C. Colwell, 'A Definite Rule for the Use of the Article in the Greek New Testament', *JBL* 52 (1933), pp. 12-21.

6.   The Jerusalem Bible and the translations by Moffatt, Goodspeed and Phillips are notable exceptions.

a definite predicative nominative has the article when it follows the verb: it does not have the article when it precedes the verb.[7]

Although by his own admission Colwell's examination was not exhaustive, it was detailed enough to establish the general validity of his rule. As might be expected in any study of language there were also exceptions to the rule. His statistics were as follows:

I.	Definite Predicate Nouns with the Article	244	
	A. After Verb	229	94%
	B. Before Verb	15	6%
II.	Definite Predicate Nouns without the Article	123	
	A. After Verb	26	21%
	B. Before Verb	97	79%

The evidence can be presented in another way which strengthens the rule.

I.	Definite Predicates after the Verb	255	
	A. With the Article	229	90%
	B. Without the Article	26	10%
II.	Definite Predicates before the Article	112	
	A. With the Article	15	13%
	B. Without the Article	97	87%

Colwell cites a number of cases where although a noun lacks a definite article before the verb the author clearly intended the noun to be definite. These examples, and others, support the widely accepted interpretation of Mk 15.39; Mt. 4.3, 6 (par. Lk. 4.3, 9); 5.35; 14.33; 27.40; Jn 1.1; 9.5; 10.2, 36; 1 Cor. 4.4; 1 Tim. 6.10; Rev. 21.22. In Mark's Gospel there are at least two passages which conform to that rule, 2.28 and 12.35. In some of these cases it may not be Colwell's rule which determines the definiteness of the noun, however, but the fact that there is a definite noun which precedes and determines a second noun. Jn 1.1, 1 Cor. 4.4 and Mk 12.35 are cases in point.

As would be expected, the number of cases where a definite noun appears with the article after the verb is much greater (in Mk 1.24; 2.7; 3.11; 4.3; 6.3; 12.7; 14.61, 71; 15.2). Nevertheless, there are still pericopes in Mark's Gospel where the rule appears to be followed and the proper interpretation is still not clear. In 6.3, a passage where the lack of clarity is relatively inconsequential, Jesus' neighbors are trying to

7. Colwell, 'Use of the Article in Greek', p. 13.

determine his identity and say οὐχ οὗτός ἐστιν ὁ τέκτων, ὁ υἱὸς τῆς Μαρίας καὶ ἀδελφὸς Ἰακώβου...; It is not evident in the text whether Mark intends to indicate that Jesus is *the* son of Mary, as the unique son, or whether he is *a* son, that is, a brother among other brothers of James and the others. Some MSS have υἱός agree with ἀδελφός and adopt the second interpretation. In 4.3, furthermore, it is not certain whether the definite article in ὁ σπείρων is to be stressed. If the sower is *the* sower then in allegorical interpretations he becomes God, Jesus or the Christian preacher. If he is *a* sower then even if he is called the sower the interpretation can be much more generalized, that is, the sower is all Christian preachers, the disciples, or one could even argue that it is the seed or the soil which is significant, not the sower at all.

In other cases where there are exceptions to the rule, as Colwell points out, interpretation becomes especially critical. In 15.18, for example, even though an indefinite noun is used after the verb, Mark intends it to be interpreted definitely: the mockers call Jesus *the* King of the Jews, not *a* King of the Jews. Clearly they do not believe that he is the king, but in order to mock him, and with an ironical twist of the truth, that is what they say.

In other passages it is clear that Mark can use titles or names without articles before verbs and that he intends them to be used indefinitely. In 3.30, where he describes why Jesus' critics are guilty of blasphemy, it is because they say Jesus has *an* unclean spirit: ὅτι ἔλεγον, πνεῦμα ἀκάθαρτον ἔχει. Similarly, in 6.49, when the disciples see Jesus walking on the sea they mistake him for a phantasm, ἔδοξαν ὅτι φάντασμά ἐστιν. In 11.32, furthermore, in a passage which is close in form to 15.39, Jesus' enemies refuse to decide whether John's baptism is from heaven or not, because it is clear to them that he is a prophet or one of the prophets:

ἅπαντες γὰρ εἶχον τὸν Ἰωάννην, ὄντως ὅτι προφήτης ἦν.

Here, even though the form is nearly identical to that in 15.39, prophet is indefinite because the determination is whether John is one of the prophets, not Elijah *redivivus*.

In addition to these exceptions in Mark's Gospel, passages in other New Testament books demonstrate that as well as being able to use an indefinite predicate before a verb and intending it to be indefinite, the authors also felt free (breaking Colwell's rule in the other direction) to use a definite predicate nominative before a verb with an article so that it would be clear that it was definite. These examples show that if Mark wanted to make sure that υἱός was clearly definite he could have done so. Colwell argues that some of these exceptions are not significant, but a number of them appear in critical passages.

Lk. 4.41	ὅτι ᾔδεισαν τὸν Χριστὸν αὐτὸν εἶναι
Jn 1.21	ὁ προφήτης εἶ σύ;
Jn 15.1	καὶ ὁ πατήρ μου ὁ γεωργός ἐστιν
1 Cor. 9.1	οὐχὶ Ἰησοῦν τὸν κύριον ἡμῶν ἑώρακα;
1 Cor. 11.25	τοῦτο τὸ ποτήριον ἡ καινὴ διαθήκη ἐστὶν ἐν τῷ ἐμῷ αἵματι
2 Cor. 3.17	ὁ δὲ κύριος τὸ πνεῦμά ἐστιν

(Other exceptions cited by Colwell include Jn 6.51; Rom. 4.13; 1 Cor. 9.2; 11.3; 2 Cor. 1.12; 3.2; 2 Pet. 1.17; Rev. 19.8; 20.14.)

The other class of exceptions—the omission of the article after the verb—contains more examples, particularly in the writings of Paul (Mt. 20.16; Mk 4.32; 9.35; 12.28; Lk. 20.33; 22.24; Jn 4.18; 18.13, 37; Acts 10.36; Rom. 4.11, 18; 7.13; 8.16, 29; 11.6; 1 Cor. 12.27; 16.15; 2 Cor. 5.21; 6.16; Gal. 4.31; 1 Thess. 4.3; 1 Pet. 5.12; Heb. 11.1).

Thus it can be seen that although a high percentage of cases support Colwell's rule and argue for the traditional interpretation of the centurion's confession, clearly New Testament authors did not always abide by the rule and, indeed, that in several cases the difference was not only significant but intentional. In regard to Mk 15.39, therefore, grammar alone cannot eliminate the possibility that Mark intended the centurion's reference to Jesus' divine sonship to be indefinite. The rule in this case is not an absolute guide to interpretation and translation, and other factors must be taken into consideration in the exegesis.

2. *The Use of* ἦν

A second grammatical problem for the interpretation of Mk 15.39 is the correct understanding of the meaning of the imperfect indicative active of εἰμί, ἦν. If translated 'was', as it is in most English translations, it has one range of meanings, but when translated 'is' it can have quite another. Translation in the present tense is not an impossibility, since the imperfect is frequently taken as a historic present in Mark's Gospel.[8] Such an interpretation would support the recognition that the

8. See Taylor, *Mark*, pp. 46-48.

centurion's confession was one that Mark's readers could identify with and repeat in their own present time,[9] since they knew Jesus to be alive. ἦν, however, is not always to be taken as a present of continuing action in Mark or the rest of the New Testament. As Blass and Debrunner point out, after verbs of perception or belief the imperfect is not in itself temporally relative. Since the present expresses time contemporary with that of the verb of perception the imperfect is often limited to cases where a time previous to the time of perception is to be indicated.[10] Thus the imperfect can be translated 'was' or 'had been' like an aorist or pluperfect, depending on the context. In Mk 15.39 it would be exceptional if Mark transmitted a christological statement in the imperfect, since he consistently places confessional statements in the present tense (1.11, 24; 2.28; 3.11; 8.29; 9.7; 12.35; 14.61-62). In the narrative context of the Gospel, Jesus always *is* the Son of God. The closest parallel to the usage of ἦν in 15.39 is once again found in 11.29-32, where discussion centers around the refusal of Jesus' enemies to tell him who John the Baptist *was*. Since Mark has already recorded John's execution in 6.14-29, Jesus asks his detractors in v. 30,

τὸ βάπτισμα τὸ Ἰωάννου ἐξ οὐρανοῦ ἦν ἐξ ἀνθρώπων; ἀποκρίθητέ μοι.

And they are unable to answer because they know that everyone held John to be a prophet (before he died):

ἅπαντες γὰρ εἶχον τὸν Ἰωάννην ὄντως ὅτι προφήτης ἦν.

In the rest of the New Testament the imperfect indicative is frequently used in reference to past time: in regard to Jesus' typological presence at the exodus (1 Cor. 10.4), ἡ πέτρα δὲ ἦν ὁ Χριστός; God's action in Christ's reconciling life (2 Cor. 5.19), θεὸς ἦν ἐν Χριστῷ; as the God who was from the beginning (1 Jn 1.1), ὃ ἦν ἀπ' ἀρχῆς; as the one

9. Blight, 'A Note on Huios Theou', p. 53. Kingsbury (*The Christology of Mark's Gospel*, p. 134) comments, 'Of course the centurion, having just seen Jesus die, says that Jesus "was" the Son the God. But in the resurrection God overturns this "was" so that it becomes "is": the crucified Jesus, who is said upon his death to have been the Son of God, has been raised and so "is" the Son of God'.

10. F. Blass and A. Debrunner, *A Greek Grammar of the New Testament and Other Early Christian Literature* (trans. R.W. Funk; Chicago: University of Chicago Press, 1961), §330.

who is and was and is to come (Rev. 1.4, 8; 4.8; 11.17; 16.5), ὁ ὢν καὶ ὁ ἦν καὶ ὁ ἐρχόμενος.

Thus in Mk 15.39 it is possible and even likely, from a grammatical point of view, that Mark intends ἦν in the centurion's confession to be taken as an observation of something which from an eyewitness perspective is past and gone:

> Truly, this man *was* (before he died) or *has been*[11] the Son (a son) of God.

The dignified death of Jesus of Nazareth convinces the man of the world that a man of divine origins has passed away.

3. *Centurions and Mark's Readers*

It is necessary to consider the *dramatis personae* in 15.39-41, particularly the role of the centurion in the scene, in order to determine how Mark intends his words in 15.39 to be understood. Although it is unnecessary to speculate who the centurion was historically[12] it is important to understand what experiences Mark's readers might have had with Roman soldiers of a centurion's rank, what their general expectations of a centurion might have been, and the way they might have expected a centurion to act at an execution. Interpretation of the centurion's words must depend, to some extent, on knowledge of a centurion's typical role and reputation. On this basis it will be easier to determine the role Mark intended the centurion to play in the crucifixion scene and in the Gospel as a whole.

The Synoptic Gospels themselves only give us limited clues. In Mark's Gospel the only reference to a centurion is in 15.39-41, and even though he uses a considerable number of latinisms throughout the Gospel[13] the

---

11. See Goodspeed's translation of Mk 15.39 in *The Bible: An American Translation* (Chicago: University of Chicago Press, 1935, 1949): 'And when the captain who stood facing him saw how he expired he said, "This man surely must have been a son of God!"'

12. Attempts were made in later literature to determine the identity of the centurion. See Taylor, *Mark*, pp. 597-98.

13. See Taylor, *Mark*, p. 45; Anderson, *Mark*, p. 26; W. Bauer, W.F. Arndt, and F.W. Gingrich, *A Greek–English Lexicon of the New Testament and Other Early Christian Literature* (Chicago: University of Chicago Press, 1952), pp. xixff. See Anderson's comments (*Mark*, p. 27), who argues that latinisms do not prove that

only direct reference to Rome or the army before Jesus' enigmatic statement about Caesar in 12.13-17, his interrogation by Pilate in 15.1-5 and the scourging by the execution squad in 15.16-20, is in 5.9, where a legion of demons is destroyed. Matthew and Luke make reference to centurions in a very different fashion, however, in keeping with their own distinct theological purposes, and these purposes color their portrayals of the centurion's actions and words at the foot of the cross (Mt. 27.51-54; Lk. 23.44-49). Matthew only uses the word centurion (the Greek ἐκατόνταρχος, Latin loanword κεντυρίων in Mark) outside of the crucifixion scene in ch. 8, where he portrays the Roman as being more Jewish than the most faithful Jew (Mt. 8.10; cf. Lk. 7.9). This is in keeping with his desire to bring or shame, if necessary, his Jewish readers to faith in Christ. Thus in Matthew it is no surprise in 27.51-54 that the centurion and 'those who were with him' respond not to the drama of the crucifixion and a *theologica crucis* but to the coming of the new age in Judaism portended by the tearing of the temple curtain and the opening of the tombs which attend it.[14]

In Luke's Gospel the attitude toward the centurion is even more favorable, but for a different reason. In the passage parallel to Mt. 8.5-13 Luke not only attests to the centurion's superlative faith (7.9) but also reports that the elders of the Jews intercede on his behalf because he is worthy (ἄξιος), loves the Jewish nation and has even built a synagogue in Capernaum (7.4-5)! In the crucifixion scene Luke changes the Markan centurion's confession considerably (possibly on the basis of L) to document the fact that just as one Roman centurion is not in basic conflict with Judaism (ἄξιος) so another centurion makes it clear that Jesus is not in conflict with Rome (ὄντως ὁ ἄνθρωπος οὗτος δίκαιος ἦν, 23.47).[15] Both passages support Luke's consistent desire throughout

Mark is writing to Christians in Rome. Many of them have been embedded in the tradition and merely demonstrate that he is probably writing to a Gentile congregation somewhere in the Empire, but not necessarily in Rome. Taylor (pp. 32-34) reviews various theories about the Gospel's connection with Rome. Other suggested home areas for Mark's readers include Galilee (W. Marxsen, *Der Evangelist Markus* [Göttingen: Vandenhoeck & Ruprecht, 1956, 1959]) and Antioch (H.C. Kee, *Community of the New Age* [Philadelphia: Westminster Press, 1977]).

14. For a somewhat similar interpretation in reference to Mark's portrayal of the centurion, see Chronis, 'The Torn Veil', pp. 97-114.

15. Scholars have usually assumed that Luke intends the centurion to be proclaiming Jesus' innocence. Recently the suggestion has been made that δίκαιος

his Gospel to show his elite Roman readers (1.1; Acts 1.1) that Christianity has a right to exist in the Roman Empire and that it is not seditious or threatening to Roman authority (23.4).[16] This perspective is enhanced in Acts where it is a centurion of the Italian Cohort, a devout man (εὐσεβής) who fears God and gives alms to the poor and prays continually, who enables Peter to see that the Gentile mission is God's will (Acts 10.1-48). Later in Acts centurions play a considerable role in Paul's arrest and transport to Rome (21.32; 22.25-26; 23.17, 23; 27.1, 6, 11, 31, 43) and some of them provide an important part in protecting or 'saving' him (22.26; 23.17; 24.23; 27.43), making sure that he meets his destiny and is enabled to bring the gospel to the ends of the earth, even to Rome itself (1.8; 23.11; 28.14).[17] Although attempts have been made by some scholars, most notably S.G.F. Brandon, to argue that a similar motive is evident in Mark's Gospel, that is, to present an *apologia ad Christianos Romanos* to prevent persecution of Christians after the fall of Jerusalem in 71,[18] subsequent study has not sustained the argument for a late date for the composition of Mark[19] and it is necessary to look beyond Luke's presentation for an understanding of the relationship of Mark's church to the Roman Empire and the meaning of the 'confession' of the centurion.

An examination of the prerequisites and privileges of the rank of centurion in the Roman army provides insights into the way Mark's readers may have understood the confession in 15.39. Historians have documented the fact that the rank of centurion was a respected one

means 'righteous' and that the centurion's proclamation indicates that Jesus shows himself to be God's Son through his righteous behavior. See F.J. Matera, 'The Death of Jesus according to Luke: A Question of Sources', *CBQ* 47 (1985), pp. 469-85; J.A. Fitzmyer, *The Gospel according to Luke X–XXIV* (AB, 28a; Garden City, NY: Doubleday, 1985), p. 1515.

16. See J.A. Fitzmyer, *The Gospel according to Luke I–IX* (AB, 28; Garden City, NY: Doubleday, 1981), pp. 10, 58, 168, 175-76; *Luke X-XXIV*, pp. 1476, 1515. But also see P. Walasky ('*And So We Went to Rome': The Political Perspective of St Luke* [SNTSMS, 49; Cambridge: Cambridge University Press, 1983]), who argues that Luke is presenting an *apologia pro imperio* to his church to demonstrate the positive aspects of Roman interaction with the Christian community.

17. See Fitzmyer, *Luke I–IX*, p. 168.

18. S.G.F. Brandon, *Jesus and the Zealots: A Study of the Political Factor in Christianity* (Manchester: Manchester University Press, 1967).

19. For a summary of other criticisms of Brandon's thesis, see Anderson, *Mark*, pp. 26, 42-44.

which found its origins in the Republic.[20] Under Julius Caesar the centurions gained a great deal of respect because it was to them that he entrusted the efficiency of his army.[21] With few exceptions, a centurion was a soldier who had risen to his position through the common enlisted ranks, usually after 15-18 years of service, although it was possible to get a direct commission from civilian life or be promoted from the praetorian guard.[22] Recommendations for promotions from the ranks were usually made by the legionary legates to the provisional governor, and on occasion they were approved by the Emperor himself.[23] The position of centurion was the one to which the common soldier aspired as the culminating point of his career,[24] and once it had been achieved he could try to work through the different grades of centurion (*hastatus posterior, princeps posterior, hastatus, princeps*) to the highest position of honor, *primipilaris*.[25]

The centurion was paid considerably more than a legionary[26] and those who reached the highest rank could look forward to a good pension and retirement,[27] possibly, in rare cases, even to an appointment as a tribune or to a position in the senate (*Cassius Dio* 52.25.6).

It is difficult to compare the responsibilities and privileges of the centurion to those of officers in modern armies because the systems of

20. See, for example, C.E. Brand, *Roman Military Law* (Austin: University of Texas Press, 1968); M. Grant, *The Army of the Caesars* (New York: Charles Scribner's Sons, 1974); H.P. Judson, *Caesar's Army: A Study of the Military Art of the Romans in the Last Days of the Republic* (New York: Biblo and Tannen, 1888); J.E. Sandys, *A Companion to Latin Studies* (New York: Hafner, 1935, 3rd edn, 1963); G.R. Watson, *The Roman Soldier* (Ithaca: Cornell University Press, 1969).

21. See Grant, *The Army of the Caesars*, pp. 19-20.

22. Watson, *The Roman Soldier*, p. 86.

23. Watson, *The Roman Soldier*, p. 86; Grant, *The Army of the Caesars*, p. 74.

24. Sandys, *Latin Studies*, p. 489.

25. See B. Dobson, 'The Significance of the Centurion and "Primipilaris" in the Roman Army and Administration', *ANRW* II.1 (Berlin: de Gruyter, 1974), pp. 395-433.

26. During Augustus's reign the salary within the ranks of the centurions ranged from 3,750 to 15,000 denarii, and it is estimated that the lowest grade of centurion received 17 times as much as the ordinary legionary. See Grant, *The Army of the Caesars*, p. 73. At other times the difference may have been much less. See Sandys, *Latin Studies*, p. 483; Brand, *Roman Military Law*, p. 53; Livy 45.40.5. (References to Greek and Latin literature are from the LCL unless otherwise indicated.)

27. Grant, *The Army of the Caesars*, p. 73.

administration are considerably different. As the one who was ultimately responsible for the training and discipline of the legionaries the centurion functioned like a master sergeant: in his responsibilities to the tribune he was more like a captain. As C.E. Brand puts it,

> In social status, dignity and prestige of position, the centurion was therefore comparable with the First Sergeant in our military establishment. In military authority and responsibility he was captain of his maniple and, technically, major and colonel as well, with far more actual disciplinary authority over his subordinates than any officer of modern armies.[28]

Like master sergeants in most armies today, the centurion was one who had as much experience and as many or more assignments throughout the Empire than almost any other officer. Inscriptions from around 137 AD indicate that during peacetime a centurion had many different functions:[29] he could have general oversight over building projects, be posted to duty in the mines or quarries, be a collector of taxes, an umpire in boundary disputes or, as in Mk 15.33-41, the officer in charge of a security patrol (cf. Acts 21.32; 22.25-26; 23.23; 24.23; 27.1-6; Josephus, *Ant.* 18.6.7 §203), or an execution squad.[30] A representation from a monument dedicated to a centurion of the XVIIIth Legion[31] shows a stern-faced soldier who wears a *corona civica* of oak leaves, and a tunic and cuirass. Two medallions with lions' heads are on his shoulders and in his right hand he carries the vine staff (*uitis*) which was an officer's dreaded emblem of command.

Centurions had a reputation not only of experience and perspicacity but also one of bravery and loyalty. The centurions were the masters of discipline and they were the ones expected to fill the breach. Since they served in the army from the time they were young men until they were well into their fifties or sixties, they were among those who maintained the perpetuity of Roman military tradition. When Augustus reorganized the Roman army he placed primary responsibility in the hands of the centurions because he expected them to be loyal to him.[32] Like all

28. Brand, *Roman Military Law*, p. 54.
29. See Watson, *The Roman Soldier*, pp. 145-46.
30. See Tacitus, *Ann.* 2.65; 13.9; 15.5; Pliny, *Trajan* 10.77.
31. Sandys, *Latin Studies*, p. 488.
32. Grant, *The Army of the Caesars*, p. 75. As J.B. Campbell comments, 'It is plausible... to suppose that centurions were a strongly conservative force, tending to be loyal to the reigning emperor so as not to risk their emolument and careers by

soldiers, the centurion swore an oath or *sacramentum* to his commanding general and more importantly to the Emperor. To break it was desertion, an action which could lead to the severest penalty.[33]

In addition to the respect with which the centurion was regarded he was also the chief enforcer of a brutal system of Roman army discipline. Tacitus (*Ann.* 1.23.12) reports that a centurion Lucilius was nicknamed 'Fetch-another' (*cedo alteram*) because of his habit of breaking his vine-staff over the backs of his soldiers. Punishments for disobeying orders ranged from flogging, to loss of pay and service, to death by stoning or clubbing (*fustarium*)[34] for the most serious offences, and centurions would have been among those primarily responsible for carrying them out. The flogging (Mk 15.15), use of the mock salute (15.18) and the crucifixion itself would not have been an unusual assignment for a centurion accustomed to the brutalities of Roman camp life. Romans regularly used crucifixion as a means of punishment and it is unlikely that soldiers with experience would be moved by one or more incident in which they simply performed their duty. As Martin Hengel demonstrates, educated Romans considered crucifixion to be a demeaning manner of death, generally considered appropriate only for slaves and aliens.[35]

The centurion, therefore, would be known to Mark's readers as the type of man who had vast experience, one who had traveled extensively, one loyal to the Emperor, one who commanded respect in the Roman army and was accustomed to carrying out its discipline.

In regard to the religious propensities of centurions it is not possible to make judgments about the beliefs of individuals in one rank in contrast

---

undisciplined or seditious conduct' (*The Emperor and the Roman Army, 31 BC–AD 235* [Oxford: Clarendon Press, 1984], p. 104). There seem to have been some exceptions, notably in the mutinies of 14 AD (Tacitus, *Ann.* 1.17) and 68-69 AD. See Campbell, p. 107, for full references.

33. On the *sacramentum*, see Grant, *The Army of the Caesars*, p. 79; Brand, *Roman Military Law*, pp. 91-95; Campbell, *The Emperor and the Roman Army*, pp. 19-32.

34. See Sandys, *Latin Studies*, p. 484; Brand, *Roman Military Law*, pp. 58-62, 99-101; Campbell, *The Emperor and the Roman Army*, pp. 303-14.

35. M. Hengel, *Crucifixion in the Ancient World and the Folly of the Message of the Cross* (Philadelphia: Fortress Press, 1977), p. 25. For illustrations of the brutality which often accompanied crucifixion, see Josephus, *War* 5.9.1 §449-451; Tacitus, *Ann.* 15.44; Hengel, *Crucifixion*, pp. 25-32.

to others but some conclusions can be drawn from the information available about the beliefs of Roman soldiers in general. According to Watson, Roman soldiers were introduced to a wide range of religious practices in the midst of their years of service. The deities generally worshipped in the army can be separated into two groups, the gods of the established state religions, whose worship was regulated by official calendars, and those of the cults, mostly non-Roman, which were adopted by military units but not included in official calendars.[36] The official gods who would have their statues in the regimental chapels included the Capitoline triad of *Iuppiter Optimus Maximus, Iuno Regina* and *Minerva Victoria,* besides the god of war, *Mars,* and the goddess of victory, *Victoria.* In addition to these and other gods and goddesses, soldiers were also notorious for the tolerant adoption of cults acquired during their foreign tours of duty and some units were identified with the divinities they had added to their pantheon.[37] The religion which eventually came to be identified with the military was Mithraism, and although it did not reach its peak in popularity until the third century AD it had arrived in Rome as early as the first century BC, brought by the Cilician pirates suppressed by Pompey.[38] Probably a more important religious influence on soldiers at the time Mark wrote his Gospel, however, was the cult of the standards, the religious system through which oaths were sworn to the state, the Roman eagle or *aquila* being a special image of veneration.

Soldiers, furthermore, along with other Romans, also took religious oaths to the Emperor, praising him as a god or a Son of God.[39] Julius Caesar was formally named *Divus* Julius after his assassination,[40] the title passing on to most of his successors. Suetonius, throughout his *Lives of*

---

36. Watson, *The Roman Soldier*, pp. 131-32. See his chapter 'Religion and Marriage', pp. 127-42.

37. See Watson, *The Roman Soldier*, p. 132.

38. Watson, *The Roman Soldier*, p. 132. See A. Harnack, *Militia Christi: The Christian Religion and the Military in the First Three Centuries* (trans. D.M. Gracie; Philadelphia: Fortress Press, 1981 [1905]), pp. 58-64.

39. See L.R. Taylor, *The Divinity of the Roman Emperor* (New York: Arno, 1975 [1931]) for careful documentation, especially 'Caesar's Attempt to Found a Divine Monarchy' (pp. 58-77), 'Divus Julius Enshrined in State Cult' (pp. 78-99), 'Augustus, Son of the Deified Julius' (pp. 142-80).

40. See Tertullian, *Apol.* 5.2-5, who stresses the necessity of the Senate's concurrence.

the Caesars, mentions its application to Augustus, Claudius, Vespasian and Titus. Caesar, he writes, was numbered among the gods, not only by a formal decree, but also in the conviction of the common people (*Caesar*, 88), and Claudius was enrolled among the gods at his burial (*Claudius*, 45), an honor neglected and finally annulled by Nero, but later restored by Vespasian. Although Augustus was hesitant about being called a god or a son of God during his lifetime he did encourage the propagation of the worship of his deified adopted father.[41] Despite his personal preferences about the divine titles applied to himself, history attests to the widespread veneration of Augustus's name. Bureth's collection of titles from papyri, ostraca and inscriptions show that Augustus was widely referred to as

— ἡ καίσαρος κράτησις θεοῦ υἱοῦ
— καῖσαρ θεοῦ υἱός
— καῖσαρ θεοῦ υἱὸς Αὐτοκράτωρ
— καῖσαρ Αὐτοκράτωρ θεὸς ἐκ θεοῦ
— Αὐτοκράτωρ καῖσαρ θεοῦ υἱὸς Σεβαστός
— θεὸς καῖσαρ
— θεὸς καὶ κύριος Αὐτοκράτωρ καῖσαρ
— *Imperator Caesar Divi Filius Augustus.*[42]

Evidence from the same sources indicates that similar titles were also given to Tiberius, Claudius, Vespasian and Titus.[43] By the time Mark wrote his Gospel a regular cult act was performed in the honor of the *genius* or divinity of the Emperor throughout the Empire by pouring out libations to him at public and private banquets (ordered by senatorial decree, 30 AD) and Emperor worship was the center of the state cult.[44] The imperial cult, as is well known, was particularly popular in the army.[45]

41. Taylor, *The Divinity of the Roman Emperor*, pp. 149-51, also the discussion of the process of Emperor deification during the early Empire by A. Wardman, *Religion and Statecraft among the Romans* (Baltimore: Johns Hopkins University Press, 1982).

42. P. Bureth, *Les titulatures impériales dans les papyrus, les ostraca et les inscriptions d'Égypte (30 a.C.–284 p.C.)* (Bruxelles: Fondation Égyptologique Reine Élisabeth, 1964), pp. 23-25.

43. Bureth, *Les titulatures impériales*, pp. 25-41.

44. See Taylor, *The Divinity of the Roman Emperor*, pp. 181-83.

45. See Harnack (*Militia Christi*, p. 65), who writes, 'the cult of the emperor was at its strongest in the army and was hardly avoidable for each individual soldier'. Also

In light of the widespread adherence of Roman soldiers to the Emperor cult and the information Mark could assume that his readers would have about centurions in general, how would he have expected his readers to interpret the centurion's observation in 15.39? Blight has suggested that in 15.39 Mark directly challenges Roman Emperor worship by implying that the centurion's confession means '*This* man, not Caesar, is the Son of God!',[46] but such an interpretation could not have provided a credible narrative for Mark's readers. A Roman soldier's allegiance to the Emperor was expected to be absolute and it is unlikely that Mark's readers would find it believable that a professional soldier would risk his career in order to worship a crucified man, especially if by such a confession he might be risking his own death for treason.[47] A Roman soldier of a centurion's rank and experience would be too sophisticated and would have been exposed to too many gods to make that kind of quick judgment at an execution, and Mark's readers would have known it.

The likelihood that Mark expects his readers to accept the centurion's statement as a full confession in a Christian sense is further diminished by the well-known negative attitudes which Romans had toward foreigners in general and their disdain toward those sentenced to execution by crucifixion in particular. If the Jews thought that nothing good could come out of Nazareth, the Romans surely believed that nothing much of value would be likely to come out of the provinces they were directed by imperial destiny to rule. Roman anti-semitism has been well documented,[48] as has later persecution of Christians,[49] but less well known is the snobbery of the Romans toward provincials in general.[50] If members

---

see Wardman, *Religion and Statecraft*, pp. 99-100.

46. Blight, 'A Note on Huios Theou', pp. 51-53.

47. Josephus (*Ant.* 18.6.10 §227-33) reports that a centurion in charge of Agrippa's guard knew that he was liable to the death penalty just for rejoicing at the false news that Tiberius was dead.

48. J.V.P.D. Balsdon, *Romans and Aliens* (Chapel Hill: University of North Carolina Press, 1979), p. 67; Josephus, *Ant.* 18.1.1-6 §3-5, §25; Suetonius, *Tiberius* 36; *Claudius* 25; Seneca, *Ad Lucilium* 108.22. M. Whittaker, *Jews and Christians: Graeco-Roman Views* (Cambridge: Cambridge University Press, 1984), pp. 3-130, provides full documentation.

49. P. Schaff, *History of the Christian Church* (New York: Charles Scribner's Sons, 1924), II, pp. 41-49; Whittaker, *Jews and Christians*, pp. 133-91; S. Benko, *Pagan Rome and the Early Christians* (Bloomington: Indiana University Press,

of Mark's church were aware of the cultural pretensions of the Romans it is unlikely they would have readily accepted the notion that a Roman soldier proud of his rise to power in the army hierarchy would suddenly jeopardize his seniority because a low-class Galilean had died a noble death. Hengel has demonstrated, furthermore, the derision with which Romans viewed those who were sentenced to execution on a cross and the burden the nature of Jesus' death put on early Christian preaching when missionaries wanted to convince Romans of the centrality of the cross in the gospel. Hengel[51] argues that the Roman disgust toward crucifixion only demonstrates all the more the power of the gospel, but in the case of Mark's Gospel it could signify just the opposite. If even the spokesperson of the disciples is shocked at the suggestion that Jesus is to be crucified (8.32-34, ἀράτω τὸν σταυρόν) and he, along with others, abandons him at the cross, why would Mark's church be expected to understand that a Roman soldier is the only one to comprehend the meaning of Jesus' death? If later Romans believed that Christians worshipped a 'dead god', that Jesus died on a tree of shame, or if contemporaries of Mark thought that crucifixion was 'the most pitiable of deaths' (Josephus, *War* 7.6.4 §202-203), or as Cicero wrote, crucifixion was 'that cruel and disgusting penalty' (*Against Verres*, 2.5.64 §165) Mark could surely expect his readers to assume this centurion would share the common negative Roman opinion of those sentenced to die on a cross.

4. *Conclusions: Future-Determined Christology*

An examination of the centurion's so-called 'confession' in Mk 15.39 in the light of grammatical evidence and the assumption which Mark's readers were likely to have had about a Roman centurion casts significant doubt on the widely accepted conclusion that the centurion's brief observation about Jesus' death is the christological key to Mark's Gospel. The difficulty in attributing the value of a full Christian confession to Mark's centurion is not anchored in doubt that Mark and his

1984); Pliny, *Trajan* 96; Tacitus, *Ann.* 15.44; Suetonius, *Nero* 16; *Mart. Pol.* 9.

50. See R. MacMullen, *Roman Social Relations, 5 B.C. to A.D. 284* (New Haven: Yale University Press, 1974), especially Appendix B, 'The Lexicon of Snobbery', and Balsdon, 'Snobbery Begins at Rome' (*Romans and Aliens*, pp. 18-29), and also his chapters on the Roman outlook toward people of other nations (pp. 59-76).

51. Hengel, *Crucifixion*, pp. 88-90.

readers believed that Jesus was the Son of God, as they most certainly did, or that the cross demonstrated that sonship to them (Mk 8.31, δεῖ) but in the lack of sufficient evidence both inside and outside of the Gospel to compel the contention that such a confession is a necessary or probable conclusion to the Gospel. Robert L. Wilken has recently re-examined the subject of the perception of the Christians by the Romans.[52] The brief examination here of the attitudes Mark's readers may have had toward the centurion suggests that another fruitful area for further New Testament research includes the investigation of the Romans as the early Christians may have seen them. By attempting to determine the cultural dispositions of New Testament readers toward key characters in the Gospel stories it may be possible to understand the assumptions which stand behind them in new and fresh ways.[53]

The re-examination of the evidence also demonstrates how dangerous it is to assume that a single passage or a single theme is a *necessary* key to an entire Gospel, as the long and largely abortive search for the Messianic Secret has shown. If one or two passages must be interpreted in a certain way to bring a thesis to a conclusion it should be clear that the entire thesis may be liable to be, and should be, called into question.

In the case of Mk 15.39 the search for supporting evidence for the confessional status of the centurion's statement has frequently gone beyond that which the Gospel itself provides. If it has been argued, for example, that the centurion's confession is to be understood in some way as a 'conversion', as if the pagan soldier somehow turns away from viewpoints that would normally be expected of such a person,[54] it has been ignored that although conversion is a prerequisite of faith in the gospel (1.15), Mark gives no examples of such a radical change any-where else in his Gospel, and in fact gives no evidence that anyone, not even any of the disciples, has changed enough to perceive fully who Jesus is.[55] In Mark's Gospel, following Jesus is necessary for true

52. R.L. Wilken, *The Christians as the Romans Saw Them* (New Haven: Yale University Press, 1984).

53. Recent studies which have examined Mark's Gospel from substantially new perspectives include those by V.K. Robbins, *Jesus the Teacher: A Socio-Rhetorical Interpretation of Mark* (Philadelphia: Fortress Press, 1984) and D.O. Via, *The Ethics of Mark's Gospel: In the Middle of Time* (Philadelphia: Fortress Press, 1985).

54. Kingsbury, *The Christology of Mark's Gospel*, p. 131.

55. Blind Bartimaeus comes closest to this change but his story is not that of an actual conversion of a disciple but is a paradigm of what conversion and following on

discipleship, but nothing more is said about the centurion. He disappears from the scene as he renders his report to Pilate. And although Luke prepares his readers for the full acceptance and proclamation of Jesus by the centurion of the Italian Cohort (Acts 9), Mark does nothing to prepare his readers to look ahead for a soldier to provide the key to the mystery of Jesus' identity. In Mark's Gospel there are no soldiers whose daughters are healed or who witness his miracles, and no soldiers who show him mercy. Instead in Mark we only have the cold professionalism and political detachment of Pilate, and the expected cruelty of the centurion's execution squad to prepare us for the 'confession' in 15.39.[56]

The argument has also been put forward that the centurion's perception contrasts sharply with that of other characters in the Gospel story who see but do not believe (15.29-32, 33-36)[57] because he 'sees' (ἰδών) that Jesus is the true Son of God. The fact is that even though it is true that the cross is central to Mark's theology, as it is to any believer's, no one in his Gospel perceives its full meaning:

> not the disciples (8.31–9.1; 9.30-32; 10.32-34; 14.60-72)
> not his detractors (15.29-36)
> not the women at its foot (15.40, ἀπὸ μακρόθεν θεωροῦσαι)
> not the women who visit the tomb, who see (ἀναβλέψασαι θεωροῦσιν, 16.4) the stone rolled away, see the angel (εἶδον νεανίσκον, 16.5)— and even though they are ordered to observe (ἴδε, 16.6) the empty tomb, and are reminded that they will see (ὄψεσθε, 16.7; cf. 14.28) him in Galilee, they still run away in fear

the way involve. See my article, 'Mark 10.46-52: Blind Bartimaeus', *CBQ* 40 (1978), pp. 191-204.

56. Some scholars disconnect, to various degrees, the centurion from his Roman ethnicity and conclude that his confession is valid from a Christian point of view only because he understands or perceives that Jesus is the *Jewish Messiah*. Cf. Stock, 'Des Bekerntnis des Centurio', pp. 300-301, who argues that he sees what the high priests refuse to see; Matera, *The Kingship of Jesus*, pp. 136-40, who contends that the tearing of the temple curtain and Jesus' cry of dereliction based on Ps. 22 convince him that Jesus is Messiah; or Kingsbury, *The Christology of Mark's Gospel*, pp. 128-33, who thinks that the centurion sees that the King of the Jews or Messiah is the true identity of Jesus in the Gospel. I have argued elsewhere that Messiah, King of the Jews and Son of David are not fully valid christological titles for Mark and his community ('Mark 10.46-52: Blind Bartimaeus', esp. p. 197). It hardly seems appropriate, furthermore, to insist that a Roman centurion has to be more Jewish than the Jewish leaders to bring the Gospel to a proper christological conclusion!

57. Cf. Kingsbury, *The Christology of Mark's Gospel*, p. 129, for example.

not the politicians who sentence Jesus (14.53-65; 15.1-5; cf. 6.14-16)
and certainly not the soldiers who put him to death.

While there is no secret as such to Mark's readers who Jesus is (1.1; 9.7)
the characters in the Gospel story never perceive its full truth and it is
left to the readers to be the ones who truly see and have the eyes of
faith.[58]

While it is difficult to determine with precision how Mark does intend
the centurion's statement to be understood since it could have had such
a wide range of meanings to Mark's readers[59] it is likely that in the context of the passion narrative it stands along with other ironic statements
at the foot of the cross about who Jesus is:

15.2, 9	King of the Jews
15.31	Savior
15.32	Christ, the King of Israel
15.36	One connected with Elijah
15.39	a son of God.

Even though all of these titles come close to the truth in the context in
which they are found or on the lips of those who speak them they do
not contain the full truth which the church needs to sustain its faith and
follow Jesus. When the reader asks 'Who is this Jesus really?' the

---

58. I have explored the importance of 'seeing' Jesus and the centrality of Mark's
theme of blindness and sight elsewhere. See 'Mark 10.46-52: Blind Bartimaeus',
pp. 191-204; 'Mark VIII.22-26: The Blind Man from Bethsaida', *NTS* 25 (1979),
pp. 370-83.

59. M. Hengel, *The Son of God: The Origin of Christology and the History of
the Jewish-Hellenistic Religion* (trans. J. Bowden; Philadelphia: Fortress Press,
1976), lists the numerous possibilities in the Hellenistic world. In relation to the title
theios aner, C.R. Holladay has shown that it had at least four distinct meanings
during the time the Gospels were written, indicating that it is not useful to utilize it in
discussions of Mark's christology (*Theios Aner in Hellenistic Judaism: A Critique
of the Use of this Category in New Testament Christology* [Missoula, MT: Scholars
Press, 1977], p. 40). For other decisive critiques of the attempt to find a *theios aner*
christology in Mark's Gospel or a reaction to it by Mark, see Anderson, *Mark*,
pp. 49-51; Kingsbury, *The Christology of Mark's Gospel*, pp. 31-37. It is possible
that the centurion is merely reacting in awe to a portent, the darkened sky or the loud
cry of Jesus. Cf. Acts 12.21-22; Josephus, *Ant.* 19.8.2 §345-47, where Agrippa is
regarded as a god because of the brilliance of his silver robes in the sun; Acts 28.6,
where Paul is regarded as a god because a snake bite is not fatal. Whittaker (*Jews and
Christians*, p. 135) contends that the centurion merely sees something superhuman in
Jesus, the kind of thing familiar to him from many stories of Greek demi-gods.

answers which Mark provides run the gamut of human imagination: he is the Holy One of God (1.24), a blasphemer (2.7), a lunatic (3.21), the Son of the Most High God (5.7), a carpenter (6.3), a prophet (6.15), John the Baptist risen from the dead (6.16), a φάντασμα (6.49), the Messiah foreseen in Isa. 35.5-6 (7.37), the Son of Man (8.31, 38; 9.9, 12, 31; 10.33, 45; 13.26; 14.21, 41, 26), the Son of David (10.47-48; 11.10; 12.35-37), the Christ (14.61-62), the King of the Jews (15.2, 9, 18, 62), even the Son of God (1.1, 11; 9.7). Looked at this way, the Gospel does not require a fixed or complete christology because, ending with no one fully understanding who Jesus is and the women fleeing from the tomb without experiencing the appearance of the risen one who could settle the question once for all, Mark extends the question of Jesus' identity fully into the future. The answer will not be found in Jesus' past, in the belief or lack of belief of the Gospel characters, or even in the perception of those who witnessed the crucifixion, but will only be found in the Christian church in which Jesus is found, understood and followed by those with the eyes of faith. It is in this church that the true confession of Jesus will be made and the true meaning of the cross will be discovered and lived.

JSNT 35 (1989), pp. 3-18

MARK'S CHRISTOLOGICAL PARADOX

Philip G. Davis

As many histories of scholarship show, the christology of the Gospel of Mark has long been a lively topic of investigation and debate. Since William Wrede opened the twentieth century with *Das Messiasgeheimnis in den Evangelien*,[1] two of his insights have proved almost unassailable for subsequent research: first, that Mark is a theological work; and secondly, that christology lies at or near the heart of Mark's theological scheme. The continuing stream of literature attests not only the validity of Wrede's insights, but also the fact that no interpretation of Mark thus far has been able to win widespread, lasting acceptance. Rather, as new methods and assumptions come into play, the characteristics attributed to Mark's message vary accordingly, only to change again with still newer fashions. Thus, for instance, various theories which explained Mark's christology in terms of his use of, or opposition to, an alleged 'divine man' concept current in his time have come and gone.[2] So too, in large measure, has the hope that redaction criticism would unlock the special message of the second Gospel.[3]

Obviously, a truly compelling interpretation of Mark has yet to be offered. While there is no hope of this article filling that void, it seems important to suggest some avenues of approach which are not being

1. W. Wrede, *Das Messiasgeheimnis in den Evangelien* (Göttingen: Vandenhoeck & Ruprecht, 1901); ET *The Messianic Secret* (trans. J. Greig; Greenwood, SC: Attic Press, 1971).

2. See, for instance, the appraisal by J.D. Kingsbury, *The Christology of Mark's Gospel* (Philadelphia: Fortress Press, 1983), pp. 33-37.

3. The turn away from redaction criticism is well exemplified by R.C. Tannehill, 'The Disciples in Mark', *JR* 57 (1977), p. 386; C.L. Mitton, 'Some Further Studies in St Mark's Gospel', *ExpTim* 87 (1975-76), p. 300; Kingsbury, *The Christology of Mark's Gospel*, pp. 37-40.

followed at present, and which may help to show a way out of the flux of radically different reconstructions which comprise the history of Markan scholarship.

Earl S. Johnson has recently argued that a recurring difficulty in interpreting Mark, particularly Mark's christology, arises from over-emphasizing and misinterpreting the centurion's confession in Mk 15.39.[4] He points to features in the original Greek which weaken the verse's impact as a statement of faith: the imperfect tense of the verb and the lack of the definite article in the predicate, 'son of God'. Further, he argues that an unnamed and otherwise insignificant Roman centurion is a highly improbable vehicle for Mark's climactic revelation of the truth about Jesus. He concludes that, while Mk 15.39 thus cannot be the key to Mark's christology, we should not seek to ascribe that honour to some other verse in its stead; no single key is to be found in the text itself. Rather, 'the Gospel does not require a fixed or complete christology because, ending with no one fully understanding who Jesus is...Mark extends the question of Jesus' identity fully into the future. The answer... will only be found in the Christian church...'[5]

It is the purpose of this article to argue two points: first, that Mk 15.39 is, indeed, Mark the evangelist's decisive statement on Jesus; and, secondly, that part of the ongoing difficulty in interpreting Mark arises from the fact that this verse, so frequently recognized as a key to Mark's thought, has nonetheless not been properly applied to the door.

1. *The Climax of the Gospel*

Several passages in the Gospel have, on occasion, been treated as keys to Markan theology. Wrede himself, for instance, rested much of his theory of the Messianic Secret on the implications of Mk 9.9;[6] James Robinson expounded Mark's message largely in terms of what he found in the temptation scene, 1.12-13;[7] T.J. Weeden chose the Caesarea

---

4. E.S. Johnson, 'Is Mark 15.39 the Key to Mark's Christology?', *JSNT* 31 (1987), pp. 3-22, now reprinted above, to which page numbers will refer.

5. Johnson, 'Mark 15.39', p. 162.

6. Wrede, *Messiasgeheimnis* (Göttingen: Vandenhoeck & Ruprecht, 3rd edn, 1963), especially pp. 66-69.

7. J.M. Robinson, *The Problem of History in Mark* (SBT, 21; London: SCM Press, 1957).

pericope of 8.27-33.[8] There are good reasons for all these choices, even if the results of these studies have not been widely accepted. Even better reasons, however, direct us to the consideration of 15.39. On the level of narrative, it is clearly the climax of Mark's story; on the level of theology, it pulls together some of the most potent of Mark's themes. It is upon these two observations that I wish to expand here.

The overstated description of Mark as a passion narrative with an extended introduction has often been repudiated, but there can be little doubt that the crucifixion of Jesus is the goal towards which the whole Gospel moves.[9] As early as 2.6-12, Jesus is in conflict with the religious authorities, and his death is mentioned already in 3.6; from 8.31 on, Mark rarely departs from this or related themes for any extended time. Even the muted *dénouement*, devoid not only of resurrection appearances by Jesus but of any tone of celebration whatsoever, throws the emphasis back upon the passion itself.

Just as the passion is the climactic element of the Gospel as a whole, so too the passion narrative has a climax of its own. This clearly comes in 15.39 with the centurion's confession. Dramatic tension builds through ch. 15 as we pass from the trial before Pilate to the crowd's rejection of Jesus, then through the preliminaries to the crucifixion itself. The taunts of the scribes, the supernatural darkness, and the cry of dereliction successively compound the horror of the scene until Jesus finally expires. Simultaneously with his death, the temple veil is torn and the centurion makes his statement. As D. Juel has shown, 15.38-39 forms a double climax, bringing to culmination the twin themes of temple and christology which run through the passion story (14.58, 61-62; 15.29-32).[10] Of these, the accent is clearly on the latter.

Immediately after these events, attention is abruptly turned away from the cross. Indeed, vv. 40-41 are almost a digression, with their painstaking identification of the women and their respective origins. Thereafter we find only the burial of Jesus and the joyless discovery of the empty tomb. Thus, just as the drama continuously builds towards

8. T.J. Weeden, *Mark—Traditions in Conflict* (Philadelphia: Fortress Press, 1971), pp. 52-59.

9. So also D. Senior, *The Passion of Jesus in the Gospel of Mark* (Wilmington, DE: Michael Glazier, 1984), p. 131.

10. D. Juel, *Messiah and Temple* (SBLDS, 31; Missoula, MT: Scholars Press, 1977), pp. 137-38.

15.39, so also nothing that follows this verse detracts from its singular impact upon the reader.

The importance of 15.39 is, then, virtually self-evident; hence the widespread recognition of its importance documented by Johnson. Despite this recognition, in actual fact there have been few, if any, efforts to use the centurion's confession as the key to Mark's christology; rather, it tends to be treated as the capstone to an edifice erected on the basis of other considerations, and interpreted so as to harmonize with them. What do we find if, recognizing 15.39 as the climax of what Mark had to say, we let it govern our approach to the rest of his Gospel?

2. 'This Man'

While all three Synoptic Gospels report a pronouncement by the soldier(s) at the foot of the cross, no two agree precisely on what was said. Lk. 23.47 is so different as to be irrelevant here. On the other hand, every word found in Mt. 27.54 is found also in Mk 15.39, though the word order varies. Mark differs from Matthew in one crucial respect: the subject of the sentence is not οὗτος, 'this', but οὗτος ὁ ἄνθρωπος, 'this man/human being'. This is, indeed, the only significant agreement between Mark and Luke! Is Mark making a particular point by referring to Jesus' humanity at this juncture?

A quick reading of Mark may suggest that Jesus' humanity, as a theme, is no more than implicit in the Gospel. There is no evidence of docetism. Further, Mark's vivid writing sometimes leads him to speak less reverently of Jesus than do the other evangelists: the Spirit 'drives' Jesus into the wilderness (1.12); he becomes angry (3.5; 10.14); his sanity is doubted (3.21); he is sometimes unable to perform miracles (6.5). Such hints may indicate a deeper appreciation on Mark's part of the humanity of Jesus.[11]

To perceive the full import of this theme, however, we must recognize that Mark's worldview is based on the notion of a divine-human dichotomy. God and humanity represent two contrasting extremities within the whole of reality, each of which exerts a focal point of orientation in opposition to that of the other. Though the briefest of the Synoptic Gospels, Mark contains the greatest number of pointed

---

11. A more extensive list of such features is given in R.P. Martin, *Mark—Evangelist and Theologian* (Exeter: Paternoster Press, 1972), pp. 107-108.

contrasts between God's majesty and human weakness and moral inferiority (7.8; 8.33; 10.9, 27; 11.30; 12.14). What is divine is right; what is human is wrong.

A dualistic worldview has frequently been attributed to Mark, but almost always in terms of an opposition between God and Satan. The fact is, however, that Satan has a minimal role in the Gospel. He is mentioned by name or title only five times in Mark (as opposed to nine in Matthew and ten in Luke). More importantly, the evangelist never clearly postulates a God-Satan dichotomy in the manner of the divine-human dichotomy and never refers to the final destruction of the devil (contrast Mt. 25.41).

Several scholars have highlighted the role of Satan by laying great stress on Mark's account of the temptation as being programmatic for the entire ministry.[12] It seems unlikely, however, that this scene is intended to bear the theological weight which is thus put upon it. The passage is simply too vague and too short; indeed, the motifs of conflict and victory are entirely absent. Surely it is illegitimate to read into these verses a struggle of the sort portrayed by Matthew and Luke.

Mark's most extended discussion of Satan occurs in 3.22-27. Verses 23-26 are a purely theoretical discussion of Satan's role in Jesus' exorcisms; indeed, the theory turns out to be wrong. The important verse is v. 27, wherein Jesus predicates his ability to exorcize on his previous binding of the 'strong man'. The narrow meaning of the verse is indisputable; the question is whether exorcism, as the continued struggle against Satan's kingdom, is a paradigm for the whole ministry of Mark's Jesus. If that were so, it would require that all non-Christians, especially the enemies of Jesus, be explicitly under Satan's control. Mark, however, never suggests this; it is not Jesus' enemies but random members of the usually favourable 'crowd' who suffer from possession. As we see also in 4.15-19, Mark views Satan as one of the several threats to human well-being, not as the primary target of Jesus' struggle.

In the case of Mk 8.33, where Jesus addresses Peter as 'Satan', we must note two further points. First, when Jesus goes on to spell out his dissatisfaction with Peter, he makes no further reference to Satan; he phrases his critique in terms of the divine-human dichotomy. Secondly,

12. So Robinson, *The Problem of History in Mark*, p. 28; W. Kelber, *The Kingdom in Mark* (Philadelphia: Fortress Press, 1974), p. 15; M. Hooker, *The Message of Mark* (London: Epworth Press, 1983), pp. 14-15.

the reference does not cite Satan as a supernatural, active personage; Jesus *addresses Peter* as 'Satan'. Peter is likened to Satan as the theoretical paradigm of evil and/or tempter, not aligned with him as a present and active being.

We see, then, that a struggle between God and Satan is not Mark's paramount concern. The real issue is the divine-human dichotomy, and it is here that Jesus' humanity becomes significant. It is, indeed, a paradox: Mk 15.39 pointedly applies to Jesus a word which, elsewhere in the Gospel, represents opposition to God.

3. *Humanity Transcended*

Having seen that Mark affirms Jesus' humanity against a thematic background which sets humanity against God, we must note that he is also at pains throughout the Gospel to show that Jesus transcends the purely human. He preaches of the approach of God's kingdom, which is originally known to him alone (John knew of his coming but not that of the kingdom [1.7-8]). His teaching is unique, not like that of recognized instructors (1.22). He can heal diseases which have resisted all attempts at cure (5.26) and cast out demons which defeat even his own disciples (9.17-18). He can even work his will on the natural order (4.39).

Those who witness these events recognize the uniqueness of the man who performs them. Repeatedly, in the first half of the Gospel, where most of these occurrences are described, Jesus' actions provoke an outpouring of awe and wonder. It is interesting to note that every major element of Jesus' ministry is capable of eliciting this response: teaching (1.22, 27; 6.2; 11.18), healing (2.12; 7.37), exorcism (1.27), power over nature (4.41). His entire public career is cause for astonishment (6.2; 7.37). This ongoing litany of wonder makes plainly evident, in terms of normal human perception, the presence of a more-than-human element at work; indeed, this is clearly one of the purposes of Mark's presentation. What is it that makes Jesus such an uncommon man in the Second Gospel?

At Jesus' first public appearance, we are told what it is: 'he taught them as one who had authority, and not as the scribes' (1.22). A few verses later, Jesus' first exorcism is attributed to his 'new teaching with authority' (1.27). Jesus' teaching, which actually embraces his entire ministry, is unique by virtue of the authority inherent in it. As is well known ἐξουσία incorporates the motifs of 'power' and 'right'. Jesus' power is evident in the wonders he performs and in the widely noted sovereign freedom in which he goes forward to his death. That death is brought about by those who deny his right to do what he does (2.7; 3.6). Between 1.21 and 3.6, Jesus' authority is linked to every major strand of the Gospel story: teaching, healing, exorcism, the call of disciples, rejection, and death. It is unquestionably central to Mark's christology.

What is the nature of this authority? This is precisely the question which Mark has the leaders put to Jesus in 11.28. Jesus' authority must have come from somewhere, and the only alternatives available are 'heaven' and 'men' (11.30). In the Markan frame of reference, this is tantamount to a question of truth and falsity, of good and evil, of legitimacy and illegitimacy. The authority of Mark's Jesus is unequivocally grounded in the divine dimension of reality.

The reactions of Jesus' enemies substantiate this: they recognize the claim for what it is. In 2.7, their very first expression of resistance to him, they accuse him of blasphemy in a way which makes Mark's conception of blasphemy evident: it is the ascription of divine status to that which is not God (compare 3.28-29). Significantly, it is from the self-same charge of blasphemy that Jesus' condemnation by the Sanhedrin arises (14.64). From beginning to end, the conflict between Jesus and the authorities is centered upon the Markan understanding of what is involved in blasphemy: the claim to transcend the radical distinction between the divine and the human.

4. *The Son of Man*

This is no place to raise the larger questions associated with the phrase 'son of man', but the foregoing observations do permit us to take a fresh look at Mark's use of this designation.[13] It has such prominence in the Gospel that we cannot overlook the term ὁ υἱὸς τοῦ ἀνθρώπου in

---

13. As Kingsbury notes (*The Christology of Mark's Gospel*, pp. ix, 53-55), there have been challenges to the very idea of emphasizing Mark's use of christological titles. I myself have questioned the widespread assumption that such titles possess inalienable meanings which can be uncovered through painstaking motif research covering all extant sources; cf. P.G. Davis, 'The Mythic Enoch: New Light on Early Christology', *SR* 13 (1984), pp. 335-36. In a case like this, however, Mark obviously makes conscious and deliberate use of these phrases; what he meant by them is, therefore, an important object of investigation.

our discussion of Jesus as ἄνθρωπος.[14]

At the outset, we may observe that Mark seems to have understood the phrase in a fairly literal way, as designating someone on the human side of the divine-human dichotomy. He alone of the Synoptists refers to the human race as 'the sons of men' (3.28), so it is likely that the singular form shares with the plural the meaning of 'human being'.

The most striking feature of Mark's employment of the phrase, however, is its intimate association with the motif of Jesus' authority.[15] As we have seen, the essential nature of this authority is revealed when it is challenged or denied: it is such as to elicit a charge of blasphemy (2.7; 14.64). Given Mark's definition of blasphemy, it must be significant that both charges of blasphemy are coupled with sayings of Jesus about the authority of the Son of Man (2.10; 14.62). These are, in fact, the first and the last of Mark's Son of Man sayings; we should probably let them govern our understanding of the others.

The common practice in analyses of the Son of Man sayings has been to divide them into three categories as they pertain to Jesus' career, his passion, or his eschatological return. Mark's handling of the first category is unique in two respects: first, he confines them to the very early part of his Gospel (2.10, 28); secondly, Mark has no sayings which portray the humble circumstances of the Son of Man on earth, emphasizing instead his authority to do God-like things such as forgiving sins and ruling over the Sabbath. Here we see more deeply into Mark's paradox: the Son of Man is the man who does what only God can do.[16]

Having introduced the title in this way, Mark evidently expects the reader to understand its subsequent appearances in the same light. This is straightforward in the case of the eschatological sayings (8.38; 13.26; 14.62). The purpose of his coming is judgment: he will save the elect (13.26-27) at the expense of the adulterous and sinful (8.38) and of his own opponents (14.62 is, after all, a threat). In the biblical tradition, of course, it was normally God who was expected to 'come' and 'judge'

---

14. Compare P. Hoffmann, 'Mk 8,31: Zur Herkunft und markinischen Rezeption einer alten Überlieferung', in P. Hoffmann *et al.* (eds.), *Orientierung an Jesus: Zur Theologie der Synoptiker* (Festschrift J. Schmid; Freiburg: Herder, 1973), p. 199.

15. Compare J. Swetnam, 'On the Identity of Jesus', *Bib* 65 (1984), p. 415; M.E. Boring, 'The Christology of Mark: Hermeneutical Issues for Systematic Theology', *Semeia* 30 (1984), p. 133.

16. On 'the Son of Man' as a riddle, see also Hoffmann, 'Mk 8,31', p. 199.

(e.g. Ps. 96.13; Isa. 30.27-28).[17] The manner of Jesus' coming is also instructive. The fact that he is to be accompanied by subordinate angels is a striking indication of transcendent majesty (8.38; 13.27). Even more so is the claim that he will return in glory (8.38; 13.26; cf. 10.37). As Kittel has shown, the New Testament use of δόξα as 'glory' can be explained only from the Septuagint, where it normally refers to 'the divine mode of being'.[18] Mark's Jesus claims that he himself, though a man, will act as surrogate for God at the climactic moment of history; the Son of Man will come in a God-like state of glory and exercise the God-like function of judgment. Apart from such a claim, the blasphemy charge in 14.64 is virtually unintelligible.

This puts us in a better position to understand the remaining Son of Man sayings, specifically in the way Mark uses them to link the motif of Jesus' authority to the passion. On one level, Jesus' suffering arises from the fact that his claim to authority is repudiated by the religious leadership.[19] On another, Jesus' sovereign acceptance of his fate as being the will of God is an expression of his authority, not the renunciation of it.[20] Most importantly, the passion is to Mark the decisive soteriological event (10.45; cf. 14.24); it is, therefore, the event in which Jesus' transcendent authority is most fully revealed. We see this confirmed in the way that several of the passion sayings echo the divine-human dichotomy with a Son of Man-men dichotomy. This is clearest in 9.31, the prediction that 'the Son of Man will be delivered into the hands of men'. A related case is 14.21, where the Son of Man is set in tension with 'that man' who betrays him and who would have been better unborn. Finally, in 14.41 the Son of Man is betrayed into the hands of 'sinners'. The verbal resemblance to 9.31 is immediately evident. Moreover, the thematic equivalence of 'men' and 'sinners' is inherent in the divine-human dichotomy; it is out of the heart of man (and not, be it noted, from Satan!) that all evil comes (7.20-23). Thus, a major element in Mark's understanding of the passion is expressed in terms of the dichotomy

17. Cf. H. Ringgren, *Israelite Religion* (trans. D. Green; Philadelphia: Fortress Press, 1963), pp. 75-79; D.S. Russell, *The Method and Message of Jewish Apocalyptic* (Philadelphia: Westminster Press, 1964), pp. 92-93.

18. G. Kittel, 'δόξα', *TDNT*, II, pp. 247-48.

19. Hooker, *The Son of Man in Mark* (Montreal: McGill University Press, 1967), p. 108.

20. H.E. Tödt, *The Son of Man in the Synoptic Tradition* (trans. D.M. Barton; London: SCM Press, 1965), p. 221.

between Jesus, the man who is on God's side, and 'men'. Again, Jesus appears as surrogate for God.

There is a still more important point to be made. All the passion sayings point ahead of themselves to the saving event which comprises the death and resurrection of Jesus. When the event finally takes place, the Son of Man title is superseded: 'Truly this man was the Son of God'. In undertaking his unique role as the one who must suffer, die, and rise again in order to bring salvation, Mark's Jesus does more than vindicate his authority in a general sense. He proves that his 'blasphemy' is true.

5. *The Son of God*

We must, then, come to grips with the divine dimension of Mark's Jesus. This is the heart of Mark's christological paradox, which identifies Jesus as the man who does what only God can do. Given Jesus' role as saviour in the context of Mark's divine-human dichotomy, the genuineness of his humanity leads us to expect some sort of genuine divinity as well.[21] Taking our lead again from Mk 15.39, we must address three questions. First, does the grammar of this verse allow us to interpret υἱὸς θεοῦ as a title bespeaking divinity? Secondly, is such an interpretation historically plausible in the context of early Christianity? Thirdly, is such an interpretation consistent with the rest of the Second Gospel?

As Johnson notes, the great majority of scholars have accepted the work of E.J. Colwell as demonstrating the validity of a titular interpretation of this phrase.[22] 'Colwell's rule' holds that determinate predicate nouns which precede the verb do not require the article in order to be treated as definite. Johnson, like P.B. Harner[23] before him, marshalls a number of parallel constructions in which Colwell's rule does not hold in order to question the rule's applicability to 15.39; both maintain that if Mark really intended υἱὸς θεοῦ to be taken as definite and titular, he would not have used such an ambiguous construction. These well-researched arguments overlook a simple point. The intended reader of Mark's Gospel, if puzzled by the form of 15.39, would not search out

---

21. Compare Hoffmann's suggestion ('Mk 8,31', pp. 197-98) that Mark's story is told on two levels, the divine and the human, and that this twofold motif is reflected in Mark's christology.

22. Johnson, 'Mark 15.39', p. 145.

23. P.B. Harner, 'Qualitative Anarthrous Predicate Nouns: Mark 15.39 and John 1.1', *JBL* 92 (1973), pp. 75-87.

other anarthrous predicate nouns which precede the verb in order to clarify the problem; rather, he would read 15.39 consistently with previous references to Jesus' sonship to God. When this sonship is predicated of Jesus (omitting the vocative in 5.7 and the textually uncertain 1.1), we find that these previous references do possess the definite article (1.11; 3.11; 9.7; 14.61).[24] There is, therefore, every likelihood that Colwell's rule does hold for 15.39 and that the phrase is to be taken as titular.

What, then, does it mean? Much of what has been written on this subject has been based, explicitly or implicitly, on certain conclusions about the provenance of the Gospel. Those who see Mark as reflecting a pagan environment have tended to interpret the title in terms of a 'divine man' concept allegedly current in the first century.[25] Others affirm a Palestinian Jewish setting in which 'Son of God' was part of the nomenclature of the royal messiah.[26] Again we must recall a very simple point. Mark's *immediate* background was neither paganism nor Judaism but Christianity.[27] There is ample evidence that pre-Markan Christianity

---

24. M. Zerwick found that, throughout the New Testament, the predicate use of the title 'Son of God' virtually always conforms to Colwell's rule: *Biblical Greek* (trans. J. Smith; Rome: Pontifical Biblical Institute, 1963), §175, p. 56.

25. See Kingsbury's discussion and the sources cited there: *The Christology of Mark's Gospel*, pp. 25-45.

26. Kingsbury himself shares this point of view, though he rarely addresses the issue of background directly: *The Christology of Mark's Gospel*, p. 64.

27. It is certainly not my intention to argue that Markan Christianity was impervious to outside influences. Yet, we must recognize that Mark does not represent the first generation of Christianity; there was already a strong body of Christian tradition by the time he wrote, and it is this that would have the most immediate influence on the writing of his Gospel. Further, any survey of the literature will show that there is no generally accepted answer to the question of this Gospel's provenance. As my teacher, Professor Ben F. Meyer, repeatedly told me, historical investigation is a matter of moving from the known to the unknown. In this case, Mark's broader cultural setting is not a 'known'; only the text itself meets this requirement. It would, therefore, be a mistake to let any particular reconstruction of Jewish or Hellenistic beliefs dictate the interpretation of Mark; rather, by interpreting Mark on its own terms first, we may come closer to solving the question of provenance. Here I agree with Kingsbury's statement that the key to Mark must be found within the Gospel, not outside it (*The Christology of Mark's Gospel*, pp. 40-41); unfortunately, Kingsbury himself is all too quick to resort to Old Testament and Jewish ideas when he turns to the task of interpretation.

could speak of Jesus in a way which was, at the very least, open to the notion of his divinity; in some cases, divinity and humanity are linked in christological formulae much as they are in Mk 15.39 (consider Rom. 1.3-4; Phil. 2.6-11; Gal. 1.1, which sets up a dichotomy of God and Christ versus men; Gal. 4.4; 2 Cor. 4.4; 8.9; Col. 1.15-20; Eph. 1.3-7). There is, therefore, nothing implausible about Mark, as a first-century Christian, ascribing genuine divinity to Jesus.

More importantly, other evidence within the Gospel itself supports this interpretation. As we have seen, Jesus' role as saviour is to overcome the divine-human dichotomy; since his own genuine humanity appears to be an important part of Mark's presentation, it is natural to expect it to be accompanied by something approaching genuine divinity. Let us, then, survey briefly the other ascriptions of divine sonship in Mark.

The fact that Mark begins his Gospel with the baptism scene has often been taken to indicate his espousal of adoptionist christology which excludes any attribution of intrinsic divinity.[28] On the whole, this proves to be untenable. Mark specifically identifies John's baptism as the beginning of the gospel, not of Jesus; there is no denial of Jesus' personal preexistence, a necessary corollary of divinity. On the contrary, even though the ascription of sonship in 1.11 is phrased in terms of Ps. 2.7, the specifically adoptionist element of that verse is omitted. Instead of 'this day I have begotten you', we read, 'with you I am well pleased [εὐδόκησα]'.[29] The aorist εὐδόκησα probably indicates that God's pleasure in Jesus is already established and does not arise as a sudden whim;[30] Mark began his Gospel with one of his rare biblical citations in order to show that the events he narrates are part of God's longstanding plan (1.2-3). This leaves us with two logical alternatives for the origin of God's pleasure: Jesus' preexistence, or his uniquely pleasing earthly life before his baptism.

Clearly, the former is to be preferred. If Jesus' adoption at the baptism was the reward for his previous deportment, how could Mark refrain

28. E.g. P. Vielhauer, 'Erwägungen zur Christologie des Markusevangeliums', in E. Dinkler (ed.), *Zeit und Geschichte* (Festschrift R. Bultmann; Tübingen: Mohr, 1964), p. 162.

29. E. Haenchen, *Der Weg Jesu* (Berlin: Töpelmann, 1966), p. 52.

30. This is probably what Zerwick calls a 'global' aorist: M. Zerwick and M. Grosvenor, *An Analysis of the Greek New Testament* (Rome: Pontifical Biblical Institute, 1981), p. 101; it simply states a bald fact without specifying factors such as duration (Zerwick, *Biblical Greek*, §253, p. 83).

from describing that meritorious early life? More importantly, Mark's divine-human dichotomy is too radical to allow for the implication which arises from adoptionism, which is that the gulf could be bridged from the human side (8.37-38). Finally, given the wide attestation of divine-human christology in Christian sources earlier than and contemporary with Mark, any espousal of adoptionism would need to be quite pointed; but this we do not find.

We do, however, find that Mark's references to Jesus' relationship to God lend themselves to the suggestion of intrinsic divinity. They issue largely from supernatural beings, either God (1.11; 9.7) or demons (1.24; 3.11; 5.7), implying that these are supernatural revelations about a supernatural person.[31] Mark's handling of the transfiguration as a whole raises Jesus above Elijah and Moses, emphasizing that he alone is the Son of God, to whom human beings must listen;[32] he alone overcomes the dichotomy. Further, the parable of the vineyard (12.1-11) contains enough evidence of allegorization that the sending of the (already existing) beloved son in 12.6 is most plausibly understood as implying Jesus' personal preexistence, much like Gal. 4.4.[33]

These observations are not undercut by 13.32 and the Gethsemane scene, both of which illustrate Jesus' subservience to God. Just as angels serve Jesus without forfeiting their superhuman status (1.13; 13.27), so Jesus' obedience to the Father confirms his own place on the divine side of the dichotomy. Mark likely thought in terms of a divine hierarchy; Nicaea and Chalcedon are yet a long way off.

Finally, we must consider Mk 14.61. It has been suggested that Jesus' reply to the high priest, a Son of Man saying, serves to correct the titles used in the question: 'the Christ, the Son of the Blessed'.[34] This overlooks a vitally important fact. Unlike Matthew and Luke, Mark has Jesus answer the high priest with an unequivocal affirmative: ἐγώ εἰμι

31. See also H.-J. Steichele, *Der leidende Sohn Gottes* (Biblische Untersuchungen, 14; Munich: Münchener Universitäts-Schriften, 1980), p. 281.

32. See also J.A. McGuckin, 'Jesus Transfigured: A Question of Christology', *The Clergy Review* 69 (1984), p. 279.

33. J. Schreiber, 'Die Christologie des Markusevangeliums', *ZTK* 58 (1961), p. 167; C.R. Kaczmierski, *Jesus the Son of God: A Study of the Markan Tradition and its Redaction by the Evangelist* (Forschung zur Bibel, 33; Würzburg: Echter Verlag, 1979), p. 127; Kingsbury, *The Christology of Mark's Gospel*, p. 115.

34. N. Perrin, 'The Christology of Mark: A Study in Methodology', *JR* 51 (1971), p. 121.

(interestingly, all three Synoptists have Jesus give an equivocal answer to Pilate's 'King of the Jews' question). Mark's Jesus accepts the attribution of sonship to God, and merely clarifies and reinforces it with his reply. His interrogators know what he means, and convict him of blasphemy.[35]

This interpretation is further confirmed by comparing the way 'Son of Man' and 'Son of God' are used syntactically. 'Son of Man' is virtually always the subject of a clause or sentence, the exceptions to this being superficial (9.12; 14.62). This title points to the saving activities of Jesus: his authoritative ministry, his necessary death, and his return as judge. 'Son of God' and analogous phrases, on the other hand, are almost always predicates. The Son of God, as such, does not do things; he is. The point of this title is not to describe Jesus' accomplishment of salvation but to account for it by identifying him as the divine person Mark believed him to be and proclaimed him to be, above all in 15.39.

The use of the imperfect ἦν in the centurion's statement presents no particular difficulty for this interpretation.[36] The confession must be considered in its context. In terms of the narrative, the centurion speaks at a point when Jesus is dead but not yet risen; the use of any other tense at this junction would sound odd in the extreme. Further, there are cases in classical Greek of the use of imperfect of εἶναι, generally accompanied by ἄρα, 'to denote that a present fact or truth has just been recognized, although true before'.[37] Despite the absence of ἄρα, which might be put down to Mark's generally inelegant Greek style, we may have here a clue to the intended significance of the evangelist's phraseology.

35. Like many, Kingsbury states that the high priest, in an instance of Markan irony, proclaims a truth of which he is ignorant (*The Christology of Mark's Gospel*, pp. 22, 120-21). The trial scene, however, with its climax in which Jesus is condemned for blasphemy, loses most of its power unless we recognize that the priests of Mark's story knew perfectly well that Jesus meant and consciously rejected his claim.

36. As argued by Johnson, 'Mark 15.39', pp. 147-48.

37. H.W. Smyth, *Greek Grammar* (rev. G.N. Messing; Cambridge, MA: Harvard University Press, 1956), §1902, p. 426. I owe this information to Dr. David Buck of the Department of Classics, University of Prince Edward Island.

6. *The Role of Mark 15.39*

It is evident, then, that the centurion's confession is not only the narrative climax of the Second Gospel but the christological climax as well. The whole of the preceding story has presented the paradox of the man who does what only God can do, and this paradox has undergirded much of the plot, accounting for both Jesus' successes and the fatal enmity he aroused. The reader is periodically tipped off as to the truth behind the paradox (indeed, the intended readers probably knew the answer before they started), but that truth breaks into the narrative proper only twice: once to be denied (14.61-63) and once to be affirmed (ἀληθῶς, 15.39). The man who does divine things is himself divine.

What of the centurion himself? He certainly is, on the surface, an unlikely mouthpiece for Mark's decisive statement about Jesus. It may be, as some have suggested, that the response of this Gentile is intended as a contrast to the Jewish leadership.[38] It is also possible that his being a centurion is not particularly important. Mark wanted the truth about Jesus proclaimed at the moment of his death, but all the disciples had fled, the mocking scribes were obviously inappropriate for the task, and the women's ignorance had to be preserved for the sake of the tomb scene. Who else was left to witness and interpret the decisive saving event?

It should be emphasized that the centurion's insight is no more unlikely than the obtuseness of those who had followed Jesus and had been told clearly and repeatedly of his impending fate. Arguably, the apparent inappropriateness of the centurion makes the confession itself that much more dramatic. One might quarrel with Mark's choice of a spokesman for the reasons which Johnson suggests,[39] but this does not gainsay the importance of what the centurion is made to say.

The issue, after all, is not what Mark's readers thought of the centurion and the quality of his faith; it is what they were to think of Jesus. The closest witness to the saving event announces the true identity of Jesus and the formal resolution of Mark's christological paradox. The divine-human dichotomy is overcome by the man who is truly the Son of God. Mk 15.39 really is the key to Mark's christology.

---

38. Senior, *The Passion of Jesus*, p. 131.
39. Johnson, 'Mark 15.39', pp. 149-58.

JSNT 34 (1988), pp. 3-20

THE PROLOGUE AS THE INTERPRETATIVE KEY TO MARK'S GOSPEL

Frank J. Matera

Few things are more essential to appreciating a story than understanding the manner in which the narrator begins. Readers who misunderstand the beginning almost inevitably misunderstand the conclusion. At the beginning of a narrative, the narrator establishes the setting, introduces the characters, and lays the foundation for the plot.

Markan scholars have learned that the Gospel's prologue[1] provides the reader with essential information for interpreting the rest of the Gospel. B. Standaert says that from a dramatic perspective the prologue functions as an 'avant-jeu' which is formally separate from what follows[2] and provides the reader with information unknown to the characters of the story. M.D. Hooker writes, 'here Mark is letting us into secrets which remain hidden, throughout most of the drama, from the great majority of the characters in the story'.[3] And W.L. Lane notes that the prologue 'suggests the general plan of the work by anticipating the crucial points in the history he relates'.[4]

Restricted by the genre of their works, however, most commentators deal with the several textual problems the prologue presents, its extent, and the significance of the opening verse. Only a few scholars have endeavoured to relate the prologue to the rest of the Gospel.[5]

---

1. Scholars do not agree about the extent of the prologue. Below, I argue that it consists of 1.2-13.

2. B. Standaert, *L'évangile selon Marc: Commentaire* (Lire la Bible, 61; Paris: Cerf, 1983), p. 42.

3. M.D. Hooker, *The Message of Mark* (London: Epworth Press, 1983), p. 6.

4. W.L. Lane, *The Gospel according to Mark: The English Text with Introduction, Exposition and Notes* (NICNT; Grand Rapids: Eerdmans, 1974).

5. The most notable examples are L.E. Keck, 'The Introduction to Mark's Gospel', *NTS* 12 (1965–66), pp. 352-70; J.M. Robinson, *The Problem of History in*

With the application of literary criticism to biblical studies,[6] however, it appears that the time is ripe for examining anew the question: how does the Markan prologue prepare the reader for the story which follows? Divided into three parts, this study begins by discussing the extent of the prologue. Next, it reviews the major themes of the prologue. Finally, it demonstrates the essential connection between these themes and the rest of the Gospel. It suggests that the dramatic irony of the narrative derives from the fact that the readers possess inside or privileged information, given in the prologue, which the characters of the story (Jesus excepted) do not know. As in all good narratives, the narrator does not reveal everything to the readers at the beginning. The information given in the prologue tells who Jesus is (the Son of God), but does not disclose the full significance of his person through this title. This information must be supplemented by what is told in the rest of the narrative. Thus, by the end of the narrative the readers discover that they must integrate their knowledge of Jesus learned in the prologue with their knowledge of him learned in the light of the cross and resurrection.

1. *The Extent of the Prologue*

At the beginning of this century, most commentators assumed that the prologue consisted of 1.1-8. Their reasoning was clear: the preaching of John the Baptist was the beginning of Jesus' public ministry. Thus these verses were understood as referring to John's work; the beginning of the Gospel of Jesus Christ was the preaching of the Baptist. Toward the

Mark (SBT, 21; London: SCM Press, 1957). My references are to the reprinted edition, J.M. Robinson, *The Problem of History in Mark and Other Marcan Studies* (Philadelphia: Fortress Press, 1982).

6.   I am referring to the application of contemporary literary criticism to biblical studies. For an introduction to how this method is applied to the Gospel of Mark, see P.J. Achtemeier, *Mark* (Proclamation Commentaries; Philadelphia: Fortress Press, 2nd edn, 1986), pp. 41-52; F.J. Matera, *What Are they Saying about Mark?* (New York: Paulist Press, 1987), pp. 75-92; D. Rhoads and D. Michie, *Mark as Story: An Introduction to the Narrative of a Gospel* (Philadelphia: Fortress Press, 1982). For the application of the method to the other Gospels, see R.A. Culpepper, *Anatomy of the Fourth Gospel: A Study in Literary Design* (FF; Philadelphia: Fortress Press, 1983); J.D. Kingsbury, *Matthew as Story* (Philadelphia: Fortress Press, 1986); F.J. Matera, 'The Plot of Matthew's Gospel', *CBQ* 49 (1987), pp. 233-53; R.C. Tannehill, *The Narrative Unity of Luke–Acts: A Literary Interpretation. I. The Gospel according to Luke* (FF; Philadelphia: Fortress Press, 1986).

middle of this century, however, R.H. Lightfoot argued that despite the manner in which Westcott and Hort paragraphed their text of the New Testament (a major break after Mk 1.8), the prologue should be extended to v. 13.[7] Lightfoot's reasoning was insightful: 'only in verses 9 to 13 do we learn that He is Jesus from Nazareth of Galilee, and that He, Jesus of Nazareth, is the unique or only Son of God'.[8] For several years, Lightfoot's position was accepted by most commentators.[9] In 1966, however, L.E. Keck wrote an article which argued that the prologue should be extended to 1.15.[10] He contended that the use of εὐαγγέλιον ('gospel') in 1.14-15, as well as in 1.1, suggests that these verses belong to the prologue.[11] Furthermore, he maintained that the handing over of John (παραδοθῆναι) related in 1.14 is primarily of theological interest, and only secondarily, if at all, of biographical interest.[12] The imprisonment of John is not a break in the text, rather 'vv. 14f. are a climatic statement that fulfils the word of John about Jesus, while at the same time it rounds out the over-arching interest in τὸ εὐαγγέλιον'.[13]

7.	R.H. Lightfoot, *The Gospel Message of St Mark* (Oxford: Clarendon Press, 1950), pp. 15-20.

8.	Lightfoot, *Gospel Message*, p. 17.

9.	Thus most of the standard commentaries accept this position: C.E.B. Cranfield, *The Gospel according to St Mark: An Introduction and Commentary* (CGTC; Cambridge: Cambridge University Press, 1959); Lane, *The Gospel according to Mark*; J. Schmid, *The Gospel according to Mark* (RNT; New York: Alba House, 1968); E. Schweizer, *The Good News according to Mark* (Richmond, VA: John Knox, 1970); V. Taylor, *The Gospel according to Mark: The Greek Text with Introduction, Notes, and Indexes* (New York: St Martins, 2nd edn, 1966).

10.	Keck, 'The Introduction to Mark's Gospel'. Other authors later argued for this position. See J.M. Gibbs, 'Mark 1.1-15, Matthew 1.1–4.16, Luke 1.1–4.30, John 1.1-51: The Gospel Prologues and Their Function', *SE* VI (ed. E.A. Livingstone; TU, 112; Berlin: Akademie Verlag, 1973), pp. 154-88; R. Pesch, 'Anfang des Evangeliums Jesu Christi: Eine Studie zum Prolog des Markusevangeliums (Mk 1.1-15)', in *Die Zeit Jesu: Festschrift für Heinrich Schlier* (ed. G. Bornkamm and K. Rahner; Freiburg: Herder, 1970), pp. 108-44.

11.	Keck, 'The Introduction to Mark's Gospel', pp. 359-60.

12.	Keck, 'The Introduction to Mark's Gospel', pp. 360-62.

13.	Keck, 'The Introduction to Mark's Gospel', p. 361.

Keck's position seems to have won the day among many commentators.[14] Most now extend the prologue to 1.15, interpreting 1.1 as a superscription which covers the content of the whole work.[15]

It seems to me, however, that R.H. Lightfoot's position remains essentially sound. As he and others correctly noted, 1.1-13 is delimited in terms of locality and by its references to the Spirit. In 1.1-13, the locality is the wilderness: John preaches in the wilderness, and Jesus is baptized and tested in the wilderness. In 1.14 the locality changes. 'Jesus leaves the desert and goes back to Galilee to begin his ministry there.'[16] In addition to locality, the Spirit plays an important role in these verses. John says that Jesus will baptize with the Spirit (1.8); the Spirit descends upon Jesus (1.10); and the Spirit thrusts Jesus into the wilderness (1.12). The fact that the Spirit plays a relatively minor role in the rest of the Gospel also suggests that these verses form a unit.[17] Finally, J.M. Robinson notes that there is a difference between John's preaching (something will happen) and Jesus' proclamation (something has happened: the Kingdom has drawn near).[18]

In addition to these traditional arguments, I would add yet another from the point of view of literary criticism. In 1.1-13 the narrator[19]

---

14. Thus the most recent commentaries view the prologue as consisting of 1.1-15: H. Anderson, *The Gospel of Mark* (NCB; Grand Rapids: Eerdmans, 1976); J. Ernst, *Das Evangelium nach Markus* (RNT; Regensburg: Pustet, 1981); J. Gnilka, *Das Evangelium nach Markus 1: Mk 1–8.26* (EKKNT, 2.1; Zurich: Benziger Verlag, 1978); C.S. Mann, *Mark: A New Translation with Introduction and Commentary* (AB, 27; Garden City, NY: Doubleday, 1986); R. Pesch, *Das Markusevangelium 1: Einleitung und Kommentar zu Kap. 1.1–8.26* (HTKNT, 2.1; Freiburg: Herder, 4th edn, 1984).

15. It should be noted that even those commentators who view 1.1-13 as the prologue tend to understand 1.1 as a superscription to the entire work.

16. U. Mauser, *Christ in the Wilderness: The Wilderness Theme in the Second Gospel and its Basis in the Biblical Tradition* (SBT, 39; London: SCM Press; Naperville, IL: Alec R. Allenson, 1963), p. 79.

17. Lane, *The Gospel according to Mark*, p. 48.

18. *The Problem of History*, p. 72.

19. Throughout this study I employ the term 'narrator' to designate the voice of the one who tells the story. Literary critics make a conceptual distinction between the real author and the voice the author employs to narrate the story. In modern literature this distinction is important because the real author does not always employ a reliable narrator, i.e., one who can be trusted to tell the story accurately. This technique does not occur in the Gospels, nevertheless it is important to maintain this conceptual

communicates privileged information about John and Jesus to the reader. Thus the narrator informs the reader that John the Baptist is to be understood in light of the quotation attributed to Isaiah (1.2-3), that the Spirit has come upon Jesus (1.10), that the Father identifies Jesus as his beloved Son (1.11), and that Jesus has confronted Satan in the wilderness (1.12-13). All of this information, vital for understanding the person of Jesus, is communicated *only* to the reader; none of the human characters within the narrative (Jesus excepted) is privy to it. The crowds that come for John's baptism have not heard the narrator identify John in terms of the scriptural quotation attributed to Isaiah. And no one, not even John, realizes that the Spirit has descended upon Jesus, that the Father calls Jesus the beloved Son, and that Jesus struggles in the wilderness with Satan. From the point of view of the narrator, the events of these verses are different from those communicated in the rest of the narrative (1.14–16.8) inasmuch as they are told solely for the reader's benefit;[20] the characters of the story (Jesus excepted) are not aware of them. In contrast to these verses, the events beginning with 1.14 are public in nature.[21] The narrator's summary of Jesus' preaching (1.14-15) and the report of John's imprisonment, for example, are not meant for the reader alone; John's imprisonment is public knowledge and Jesus' proclamation is the kind of preaching which the characters of

distinction because it reminds us that our concern is the narrative world of the narrator, not the historical world of the real author. Thus I am not employing Mark's Gospel as a window through which to peer into the situation of his church or community, the so-called referential fallacy; I am concerned with the narrative world which the narrator creates for the reader. On the literary use of the narrator, see W.C. Booth, *The Rhetoric of Fiction* (Chicago: University of Chicago Press, 2nd edn, 1983), pp. 149-65; S. Chatman, *Story and Discourse: Narrative Structures in Fiction and Film* (Ithaca: Cornell University Press, 1978), pp. 196-262; S. Rimmon-Kenan, *Narrative Fiction: Contemporary Poetics* (London: Methuen, 1983), pp. 86-116.

20. I am aware that there are many moments in the Gospel when the narrator communicates privately with the reader. The use of *gar* clauses (11.13) and other side comments (7.19) are examples. Furthermore, the whole narrative, inasmuch as it is a narrative, is primarily directed to the reader. My point is that the extraordinary events of this section, unlike the events in the rest of the Gospel, are not known to the characters of the narrative (Jesus excepted).

21. Even events such as the transfiguration are public in nature inasmuch as human characters within the narrative witness them. By contrast, no human character of the story hears the Isaiah quotation, the Father's baptismal declaration, or witnesses the struggle in the wilderness. Jesus, of course, is aware of these events.

the story hear, and will hear again. In a word there is a change in the way the narrator speaks to the reader after the testing of Jesus in the wilderness. To this point, the narrator has communicated inside information to the reader. After this point, the events which are narrated are public in nature in the sense that they are accessible to the characters of the story.

But what of Keck's argument that the appearance of εὐαγγέλιον in 1.1 and 1.14-15 binds these verses together? Keck and others correctly argue that 1.1 is a superscription which includes the content of the entire Gospel. But if 1.1 is a superscription to the entire work, then it is not surprising that the word 'gospel' is found again at the beginning of Jesus' public ministry (1.14-15). Furthermore, even if 1.1 and 1.14-15 form a bracket, this does not mean that 1.14-15 is part of the prologue. Rather one could argue that since 1.1 is a superscription to the entire work, it is not part of the prologue proper (1.2-13), which is delimited by references to the wilderness and the Spirit, as well as by the unique nature of the information it communicates.[22] The most telling clue to the extent of the prologue is not the bracket formed by 1.1 and 1.14-15 but the shift of narrative point of view. Prior to 1.14 the narrator tells the reader of events which the characters of the story (Jesus excepted) do not know. After 1.14 the narrator tells the reader of events which the characters of the story will participate in or observe. As for Mk 1.1, it is indeed a superscription covering the entire work. It might be paraphrased as follows: the origin of the proclamation about Jesus Christ the Son of God which is proclaimed in the church today is the account of Jesus which will be narrated as follows.[23] The prologue proper consists of 1.2-13.

22. J. Drury ('Mark', in *The Literary Guide to the Bible* [ed. R. Alter and F. Kermode; Cambridge: The Belknap Press of Harvard University, 1987], pp. 402-17) writes: 'Verse 1 belongs in the present of Mark's Christian readers. "The gospel of Jesus Christ, the Son of God", is their book about their master. From that near present they are suddenly taken far back in time. Verses 2 and 3, quoting Exodus, Isaiah, and Malachi, fasten Jesus' story to the sacred past as strongly as verse 1 has fastened it to the sacred present' (p. 407).

23. Keck ('The Introduction to Mark's Gospel', pp. 366-67) makes a similar point.

2. *The Prologue and the Reader*

The Markan prologue (1.2-13) presents the reader with information essential for understanding who Jesus is. This section will try to state that information as clearly as possible.

a. *The Relationship between John and Jesus (1.2-8)*

The prologue begins with a scriptural quotation attributed to Isaiah (1.2-3) which introduces the work of John and explains his relationship to Jesus. The quotation does not derive wholly from the prophet. It is a mixed quotation. Verse 2 is based upon Exod. 23.20 and Mal. 3.1; v. 3 comes from Isa. 40.3. In its original context, Exod. 23.20 referred to the angel God sent ahead of Israel to protect it on its way to the promised land. The quotation from Mal. 3.1 refers to the messenger God sent to prepare for the day of his appearance. In Mal. 3.23, LXX 4.5, that messenger is identified as Elijah; and in rabbinic exegesis the texts from Exodus and Malchi were later combined, identifying the messenger of both texts as Elijah.[24] The quotation from Isaiah is the beginning of Deutero-Isaiah's prophecy announcing that God is about to redeem Israel from exile by a new exodus. For our purpose it is not necessary to determine if the evangelist, or his tradition, realized the mixed nature of this citation. As it stands, the entire text is attributed to Isaiah. Its function is to identify who John is. It answers that he is the messenger of the covenant, the eschatological prophet foretold by 'Isaiah'. His task is to prepare the way of the Lord[25] for God's final act of salvation, a new exodus. From the opening of the narrative, therefore, the reader knows the correct relationship between John and Jesus. John is not the Messiah; he is the precursor, the promised Elijah as even his garb suggests (cf. 1.6 with 2 Kgs 1.8). When John makes his appearance (1.4-8), the reader, unlike the crowds, knows exactly what his function is.

To further distinguish John from Jesus, the narrator has John contrast himself with the Coming One. The one who will come after John is more powerful (1.7a). John is not worthy to loosen his sandal straps (1.7b). John baptizes with water, but Jesus will baptize with the Holy Spirit.[26]

---

24. Str-B, I, p. 597.

25. Here, the narrator intends that the reader refer 'Lord' to Jesus the Messiah, whereas in its original context 'Lord' referred to God.

26. A few texts read 'with the Holy Spirit and with fire' but the reading appears to be an assimilation of the texts of Mt. 3.11 and Lk. 3.16. So, B.M. Metzger, *A Textual*

John's baptism is described as a baptism for the forgiveness of sins (1.4), but Jesus' preaching is described as the gospel of God (1.14). At John's preaching, all the inhabitants of Judea and Jerusalem go out to be baptized (1.5). Jesus stands apart from those to be baptized inasmuch as he alone is from Galilee. In sum, the first part of the prologue identifies John and explains his relationship to Jesus. It authenticates his mission by interpreting it in light of a quotation attributed to Isaiah. Those who are privy to this information will have a proper understanding of the relationship between Jesus and John. Those who are not will misinterpret their relationship, their identities, and their missions (2.18-19; 6.14-16; 8.27-28; 9.11-13; 11.27-33; 15.35).

b. *The Identity of Jesus (1.9-11)*

Having identified John and his relationship to Jesus, the narrator now focuses upon Jesus. The description of Jesus as coming from Nazareth of Galilee (1.9) immediately distinguishes him from the crowds of Judeans and Jerusalemites. It establishes a contrast between all the people of Judea and Jerusalem on the one hand, and a single representative from Galilee on the other.[27] The crowds from Judea and Jerusalem do not recognize the lone Galilean, but the reader does.

Immediately following Jesus' baptism, a number of important events occur. Jesus rises from the water (ἀναβαίνων ἐκ τοῦ ὕδατος), he sees the heavens open (εἶδεν σχιζομένους τοὺς οὐρανούς), the Spirit descends upon him (καταβαῖνον εἰς αὐτόν), and a voice from heaven declares: 'Thou art my beloved Son; with thee I am well pleased'. These verses confront the interpreter with several difficulties, for example, the imagery of the dove,[28] the meaning of ἀγαπητός,[29] the descent of the Spirit,[30] the source of the scriptural allusion.[31] But despite these

Commentary on the Greek New Testament (London: United Bible Society, 1971).

27. Lane, *The Gospel according to Mark*, p. 55.

28. Taylor (*The Gospel according to Mark*, p. 161) offers rabbinic evidence that the imagery of the dove 'is connected with the picture of the Spirit of God brooding or hovering creatively over the primaeval waters (Gen. i. 2)'.

29. ἀγαπητός can be translated as 'beloved' or 'only'. It can be taken with υἱός ('my beloved Son', 'my only Son') or it can be taken as a separate designation ('my Son, the Beloved', 'my Son, the Only One').

30. Most commentators interpret εἰς αὐτόν as the descent of the Spirit 'upon' Jesus rather than 'into' him.

31. The text can allude to Gen. 22.2, Ps. 2.7, or Isa. 42.1. The choice made here is

difficulties the basic thrust of the text is clear: Jesus is identified as the
Spirit-empowered Son of God. Precisely why God is pleased with him,
the text does not say, nor does it explain the nature of Jesus' sonship.
Such information is withheld from the reader. What is clear is that no
human character (Jesus excepted) within the story, including John, has
seen the Spirit descend upon Jesus or heard the voice.[32] For John and
the crowds this is just another baptism.

Once more the reader is privy to inside information essential for
understanding Jesus' identity. While the crowds and John see Jesus as
another penitent, not even aware that he comes from Galilee, the reader
knows that he is the Spirit-empowered Son of God.

c. *Jesus and Satan (1.12-13)*

In the final section of the prologue, Jesus confronts Satan. Once more
the reader is given privileged information. The same Spirit which
descended upon Jesus now sends him into the wilderness to confront
Satan. No sooner is Jesus identified as the Son of God than he is driven
(ἐκβάλλει) into the wilderness to meet the adversary. No human character within the narrative apart from Jesus is aware of this struggle,
either now or later. As with Jesus' baptism, the scene has an other-
worldly dimension: the testing of God's Son by Satan and the presence
of angels who serve his needs.

Again the text presents problems of interpretation. Do the wild beasts
symbolize a restoration of the situation which prevailed before Adam's
fall, thereby suggesting that Jesus has conquered Satan? Or, do they
symbolize the hostile environment in which Jesus finds himself during
his time of testing?[33] Do the angels serve Jesus to sustain him against

crucial since it can result in understanding Jesus' sonship in terms of Isaac imagery
(Gen. 22.2), royal imagery (Ps. 2.7), or servant imagery (Isa. 42.1). I do not think it
inconceivable that the narrator intends the reader to see an allusion to all of these
texts. Thus, Jesus is the royal Son of God who comes as the Lord's Servant to
surrender his life.

32. The voice is spoken solely to Jesus whereas in the transfiguration it is spoken
to the disciples (9.7). In Mt. 3.17, by contrast, the Father's declaration is in the third
person.

33. Anderson (*The Gospel of Mark*, p. 82) writes, 'The idea may also be present
that Jesus has restored the situation that obtained before the fall when Adam was king
of paradise and Lord of the wild animals'. But Mauser (*Christ in the Wilderness*,
p. 101) contends: 'They [the wild beasts] represent the horror and the danger which

Satan, or because he has overcome Satan? The text does not explicitly
say. Nonetheless, the basic movement of the narrative is clear. The Son
of God does not fail during his period of testing, for he returns from the
wilderness with the gospel of God (1.14).[34] The reader now knows the
secret of Jesus' authority over unclean spirits; he has been tested by the
prince of unclean spirits in the wilderness, and has not failed. Thus when
Jesus tells the scribes that 'no one can enter a strong man's house and
plunder his goods, unless he first binds the strong man' (3.27), the
reader understands what the scribes do not. Jesus is the one who
plunders Satan's house because he has already confronted Satan.

A summary of our results discloses that the reader has been given the
following information, unknown to the characters of the story besides
Jesus. First, John the Baptist is the promised Elijah, Jesus' precursor.
Second, Jesus is the Spirit-empowered Son of God, the one in whom the
Father is pleased. Third, Jesus has confronted Satan in the wilderness
and has not succumbed to his temptations.

3. *Mark's Narrative in Light of the Gospel Prologue*

Markan scholars have not been able to agree upon the outline and structure of the Second Gospel.[35] Nevertheless, most would concur that
Peter's confession at Caesarea Philippi and the centurion's confession at
the cross are major turning points in the narrative. At both moments
human characters within the narrative come to a deeper understanding
of Jesus' identity: he is the messiah (8.29); he was God's Son (15.39).

---

faces man in the desert. Possibly in New Testament times the animals were associated
with demons.'

34. Keck ('The Introduction to Mark's Gospel', p. 362) writes, 'Mark's Jesus is
the victorious Son of God who returns from the testing-ground with the εὐαγγέλιον'.

35. For a summary of different proposals, see H.C. Kee, *Community of the New
Age: Studies in Mark's Gospel* (Philadelphia: Westminster Press, 1977), pp. 56-64.
In my opinion, the placement of Peter's confession (8.27-30) is crucial for determining the Gospel's structure. Does it conclude the first part of the Gospel, or, as
most commentators believe, does it begin the second part? If it concludes the first part
of the Gospel, it is easier to view Peter's confession more positively as the climax of
part one. But if it begins the second part of the story, there is a tendency to view the
confession negatively since Peter's objection to Jesus' passion prediction immediately follows. I believe that the confession climaxes the first part of the story. I hope
to deal with this pericope and the structure of the Gospel in a later article.

The reader, of course, knows this information from the prologue while the human characters within the narrative, except Jesus, continually struggle with the question of his identity. In this section, I will trace the quest by the human characters of the story to identify Jesus. An overview of Mark's narrative will show that the human characters of the story are puzzled by Jesus' identity because, unlike the readers, they have not been privy to the prologue. If they are to attain an understanding of who Jesus is, they must arrive at it by the way of the cross.

a. *Jesus is the Messiah (1.14–8.30)*

The first half of Mark's Gospel is marked by a series of questions and misunderstandings concerning Jesus' identity and ministry. These misunderstandings and questions involve all of the human characters within the narrative: the religious leaders, Jesus' family and compatriots, Herod, the crowds, and the disciples. Only the demons, beings who belong to another realm, know who Jesus is and what his mission entails. They correctly refer to him as ὁ ἅγιος τοῦ θεοῦ ('the Holy One of God', 1.24), ὁ υἱὸς τοῦ θεοῦ ('the Son of God', 3.11), and Ἰησοῦ υἱὲ τοῦ θεοῦ τοῦ ὑψίστου ('Jesus, Son of the Most High', 5.7). Furthermore, the demons seem to know the purpose of Jesus' mission: he has come to destroy them (1.24). Indeed, his very presence torments them (5.7). Because the demons have this knowledge, Jesus commands them to be silent (1.25, 34; 3.12). For reasons which are not disclosed at this point, a public proclamation of Jesus' identity as God's Son is premature.

The source of the demons' knowledge comes from the events which occur in the prologue. In the wilderness Satan tested the Son of God (1.12-13). Consequently, his subordinates are aware of Jesus' identity. They know who he is and why he has come. Their public proclamation of his identity is an attempt to undermine his mission by revealing who he is apart from the cross.

In contrast to the demons, none of the other human characters of the narrative knows Jesus' identity or mission. They must come to an understanding of it by witnessing and properly interpreting what Jesus says and does. A perverse interpretation comes from the religious leaders who form a monolithic block of opposition against Jesus. They question his authority to forgive sins, interpreting his words as blasphemy (2.6-7). They do not understand why Jesus' disciples do not fast (2.18); they accuse the same of violating the Sabbath (2.24) and the traditions of the elders (7.5); and they go so far as to say that Jesus is possessed by an unclean spirit (3.22, 30). They even ask Jesus for a sign from heaven (8.11) after he has fed 4000 with bread in the wilderness. Finally, their intention to destroy Jesus (3.6) reveals their animosity.

The reaction of Jesus' family and compatriots is also characterized by misunderstanding and opposition. Jesus' family comes to take him home because of reports that he is mad (ἔλεγον γὰρ ὅτι ἐξέστη, 3.21). The manner in which this episode involving Jesus' relatives (3.21, 31-35) encloses the Beelzebul controversy (3.22-30) suggests that the narrator intends the readers to see a parallel between the reactions of the religious leaders and Jesus' family: both misunderstand Jesus. Finally, when Jesus returns to his own country (6.1), his compatriots are scandalized by him Because they know Jesus' natural family, they think that they know who he is. Believing that they know who he is, they question his wisdom and power (6.2-3).

The reaction of the crowd and Herod is also one of misunderstanding. The crowd is amazed at Jesus' authoritative teaching which manifests itself in his power over demons (1.22, 27-28). The crowd speculates that Jesus is John the Baptist, Elijah, or one of the prophets (6.14-15; 8.28). Herod, however, is convinced that Jesus is John come back to life (6.16).

The reaction of the disciples to Jesus is the most complicated of all. On the one hand, the disciples enjoy a special relationship to Jesus. Not only does he call them to follow him and to be with him (1.16-20; 3.13-19), he also makes a distinction between them and the crowd, explaining to them the mysteries of the Kingdom of God (4.10-12, 33-34). At several points, however, even the disciples show that they do not understand Jesus' true identity or the full significance of his mission. When Jesus calms a storm on the lake, they ask, 'Who is this, that even wind and sea obey him?' (4.41). And despite the feeding of the 5000 and the 4000, they misunderstand the meaning of his mission (8.14-21).[36] Nevertheless, by the middle of the Gospel, the disciples arrive at a certain knowledge of who Jesus is. At Caesarea Philippi, after they rehearse what others think of Jesus (8.28; cf. 6.14-15), Peter correctly confesses that Jesus is

36. The two feeding stories (6.31-44; 8.1-10) bracket Jesus' discourse on clean and unclean (7.1-23). The first occurs in Jewish territory and the second on the other side of the lake, in Gentile territory. These stories suggest that Jesus' mission extends to Gentiles as well as Jews, a point reinforced by Jesus' declaration that all foods are clean (7.18-23).

the messiah (8.29).[37] His confession seemingly derives from what he has seen Jesus say and do thus far. The first part of the Gospel concludes with the beginning of an awareness of Jesus' identity: knowledge which the reader already possesses from the prologue.

Except for Peter's confession, the first half of Mark's narrative is filled with questions and misunderstandings concerning Jesus' identity and mission. The answers to these questions and the information necessary to avoid these misunderstandings are found in the prologue. Thus the religious leaders do not comprehend how Jesus can expel demons because they do not know that he is the Spirit-empowered Son of God who has confronted Satan in the wilderness. Jesus' family and compatriots are scandalized because they do not realize that he is more than the son of Mary: he is the Son of God. Herod confuses Jesus with John because he does not understand the proper relationship between John and Jesus: John is Jesus' precursor; Jesus is not John *redivivus*. Even the disciples are puzzled about Jesus' identity and mission because they have not been privy to the Father's baptismal declaration. The one who calms the storm and feeds the multitude is the Son of God. In a word, all of these misunderstandings result from ignorance of information found in the prologue: the relationship between John and Jesus; the declaration of Jesus' sonship; the conflict between Jesus and Satan in the wilderness.

b. *The Son of Man Will Suffer and Rise (8.31–10.52)*
In the second part of the Gospel, Jesus does something which he did not do in the first part. He explains to his disciples that he will suffer and rise again (8.31; 9.12; 9.31; 10.33-34). Confronted by these predictions, the disciples rebel against this fate (8.32), do not understand it (9.10, 32), and act in a way incongruous with Jesus' words (9.33-34; 10.35-41). This misunderstanding is complicated by the fact that at the transfiguration there is a reprise of a major theme found in the prologue. The Father declares that Jesus is his beloved Son (9.7), and this time three disciples hear the declaration.[38] After the transfiguration, Jesus discloses that John was Elijah (9.11-13). Despite this privileged information, the

37. Not all commentators agree that Peter's confession is correct. For a discussion of those who view this confession negatively, and so in need of correction, see Matera, *What Are they Saying about Mark?*, pp. 18-27.

38. The narrator uses the third person here whereas the second person was employed at the baptism (1.11).

disciples continue to misunderstand Jesus. Why?

The answer is suggested by the Father's declaration, 'This is my beloved Son; listen to him' (9.7). Unlike the baptismal declaration which was addressed directly to Jesus, the Father now speaks to three of the human characters within the story. Moreover, the declaration concludes with a command, 'listen to him'. If the disciples are to understand that Jesus is the Son of God then they must listen to and accept what he says about the fate of the Son of Man: he must suffer, die, and on the third day he will rise from the dead. The disciples, however, do not understand or accept the fate of the Son of Man (8.32; 9.10, 32; 10.35-41). Therefore, they do not comprehend the full significance of the declaration made at the transfiguration. In a word, the privileged information granted on the mountain does not aid them because of their refusal to 'listen to him'. Only Bartimaeus, who acclaims Jesus as the Son of David (10.47-48), seems to understand something of Jesus' person inasmuch as he follows him 'on the way' (10.52), an expression which refers to the destiny of suffering facing Jesus.

By way of summary, this section suggests that as important as the inside information of the prologue is, it is not sufficient for a full appreciation of Jesus' identity. Even those who know that Jesus is the Son of God and that John is Elijah can remain blind to Jesus' true identity if they do not 'listen to him'. The readers of the Gospel must beware, therefore, lest they take their privileged information, gained from the prologue, for granted. They must integrate the information learned from the prologue with the mystery of the dying and rising Son of Man.

c. *From the Entry into the Temple to the Prediction*
of its Destruction (11.1–13.37)
Except for a brief incident (10.2-9), the religious leaders do not play an important role in 8.31–10.52. In chs. 11–12, however, they do. After Jesus cleanses the temple, they ask him by what authority he acts, and who gave him the authority for such action (11.28). Then in a series of controversies, they test Jesus further (12.13-34).[39] At the conclusion of

---

39. In 8.11; 10.2; 12.15 the narrator employs the verb πειράζειν to describe the activity of the religious leaders. The only other occurrence of the verb in Mark is 1.13, Satan's testing of Jesus. The narrator draws a parallel between the activity of the religious leaders and that of the Satan *vis-à-vis* Jesus. Both test him in order to dissuade him from his mission.

these controversies, Jesus challenges the traditional scribal understanding of the notion that the messiah is the son of David (12.35-37), and then condemns the scribes (12.38-40). In the midst of these controversies, however, there are important allusions to information found in the prologue. Thus, when the religious leaders challenge Jesus' authority, he questions them about the significance of John's baptism (11.30), and then tells the parable of the vineyard (12.1-11) in which he echoes the Father's baptismal declaration (12.6). The religious leaders, however, refuse to answer the question about John's baptism (11.31-33) and take offense at the parable, realizing that it is directed at them (12.12).

These 'echoes' of the prologue (the origin of John's baptism, the beloved son) explain why the religious leaders misunderstand Jesus. First, although all Judea and Jerusalem went out to be baptized by John (1.5), the religious leaders never understood or accepted the origin of his baptism. Secondly, because they did not comprehend the significance of John's ministry, they do not understand that Jesus is the Father's beloved son (1.11; 9.7), even when Jesus imparts this information by way of parable (12.6). As in the previous section (8.31–10.52), the narrator is making an important point. Knowledge found in the prologue is essential for understanding Jesus and his mission, but even this knowledge can be rendered useless by hardness of heart. There is still an opportunity for the religious leaders to acknowledge the origin of John's baptism, and Jesus even discloses that he is the beloved son, but they refuse to 'listen to him'. Once more the reader is being warned that knowledge gained from the prologue must not be taken for granted. Such knowledge can be rendered useless by hardness of heart.

d. *The Recognition of Jesus as the Son of God (14.1–16.8)*
Throughout the narrative thus far, no one has been able to pierce the secret of Jesus' identity or fully understand his mission. This misunderstanding continues throughout the passion narrative. Judas betrays Jesus (14.10-11), all of the disciples flee (14.50), and Peter denies him (14.66-72). Moreover, the religious leaders (14.65), the Roman soldiers (15.16-20), the passers-by (15.29-30), the chief priests and the scribes (15.31-32), and even criminals (15.32) mock Jesus as a false messiah. After Jesus has died, however, a Roman centurion finally realizes that he was truly the Son of God (15.39).This confession is the climax of the Gospel and the final reprise of the Father's baptismal declaration.

The scene of Jesus' death (15.33-39) is related to the prologue in three ways: the reference to Elijah (15.36), the tearing of the temple curtain (15.38), and the centurion's confession (15.39). First, those standing around the cross misinterpret Jesus' great cry as a last desperate call for Elijah. Their misunderstanding manifests ignorance of information found in the prologue. The reader knows that Jesus is not calling Elijah because Elijah has *already* come in the person of John the Baptist. If the bystanders knew this, they would not confuse or mock Jesus' cry as a call for the prophet. But because the bystanders do not understand the proper relationship between John and Jesus, they do not understand that cry.

Secondly, at the moment of Jesus' death the curtain of the temple is torn (ἐσχίσθη) from top to bottom.[40] The word employed here is the same word used to describe the opening (σχιζομένους) of the heavens at the moment of Jesus' baptism (1.10). At that moment the Spirit descended upon Jesus, and the Father declared that Jesus is his beloved Son. Now the curtain of the temple is torn from top to bottom and the centurion confesses what the reader already knows from the baptism, that Jesus was truly the Son of God.[41]

40. Mk 15.38, the tearing of the temple curtain, presents two exegetical problems. First, it seems to interrupt the narrative flow of vv. 37 and 39. Secondly, it raises the question, which curtain? The inner curtain before the Holy Place or the great outer curtain? H.L. Chronis ('The Torn Veil: Cultus and Christology in Mark 15.37-39', *JBL* 101 [1982], pp. 97-114) and H.M. Jackson ('The Death of Jesus in Mark and the Miracle of the Cross', *NTS* 33 [1987], pp. 16-37) have shed light on these questions by the use of literary criticism. Although their answers differ, both convincingly show that the centurion's cry is related to the tearing of the temple curtain, arguing that what the centurion sees is related to the tearing of the curtain. For Chronis 15.38 is a 'cipher for theophany' (p. 110). When the narrator says that the temple curtain was torn, he means that the centurion is the recipient of a theophany. 'Standing in the presence of the dying Jesus, he feels himself to be standing in the divine "presence". Looking into the face of the crucified Jesus at the instant of his death, he sees (as it were) the very "face" of God' (p. 111). Jackson also argues for the narrative logic of 15.38 and 15.39. For him the event is more than a metaphor for a theophany. The breath/spirit of the dying Jesus (ἐξέπνευσεν) 'rends the outer curtain of the Temple, and this is what the centurion saw' (p. 27). Thus the centurion's confession is based upon a divine prodigy: the tearing of the gigantic outer curtain by the expulsion of Jesus' breath/spirit.

41. S. Motyer ('The Rending of the Veil: A Markan Pentecost?', *NTS* 33 [1987], pp. 155-57) draws out the similarity between the rending of the heavens at Jesus' baptism and the rending of the temple curtain. He writes: 'In both places something is

Thirdly, the centurion's confession is a moment of revelation similar to and related to the theophanies at Jesus' baptism and transfiguration. Then the Father declared that Jesus is his beloved Son, now the centurion confesses what no human character has been able to say: Jesus was truly God's Son. The precise motivation for this confession is not clear, but it has something to do with what the centurion has seen (see note 40). Most importantly, the confession occurs after Jesus has died, for only in the light of his death can the full significance of the title 'Son of God' be understood. After Jesus has died, the secret of his identity can be disclosed because there will be no mistaking the nature of this sonship: Jesus is the Father's beloved Son inasmuch as he is the Son who obediently accepts suffering and death (see 14.36). Once more the reader discovers that the privileged information gained from the prologue requires deeper insight. In the prologue the narrator tells who Jesus is (the Son of God) but not the full significance of this title (the Son of God is the Crucified messiah who must suffer, die and rise from the dead).

4. *Conclusion*

This study has argued that the Markan prologue contains essential information for understanding Jesus and his mission. This information concerns the proper relationship between John and Jesus, Jesus' divine sonship, and his confrontation with Satan in the wilderness. In the first part of the Gospel (1.14–8.30), the characters of the story misunderstand Jesus because they do not have this information. Nonetheless, on the basis of Jesus' words and deeds, the disciples come to an initial awareness of him as the messiah. In the second (8.31–10.52) and third (11.1–13.37) parts, the prologue is recapitulated in terms of John (9.11-13; 11.29-33) and Jesus (9.7; 12.6), but the human characters of the story do not understand. The disciples remain blind because they do not 'listen' to what Jesus says about the Son of Man. The religious leaders do not repent because they do not 'listen' to what Jesus has to say about the beloved son in the parable of the vineyard. In a word, direct information

rent, the verb being σχίζω; in both cases the rending involves a theophany, an opening of the Holy Place; in both something descends, whether the Spirit-dove or the tear in the curtain; in both Elijah-symbolism lies close at hand and informs the meaning' (p. 155).

does not help them. In the final section of the Gospel (14.1–16.8), the prologue is recapitulated once more.[42] This time, after Jesus dies, someone recognizes that he was truly the Son of God. This study suggests that the hermeneutical key to Mark's Gospel is the information found in the prologue, information which must be read by the light of the cross.

42. The third element of the prologue, the testing of Jesus in the wilderness, is not recalled as explicitly in the second, third, and fourth sections of the Gospel as in the first. In part, this is due to the fact that all of the exorcisms, except 9.14-29, occur in the first section. Nevertheless, the testing of Jesus by the religious leaders (10.2; 12.15), as well as the mockery of Jesus (15.29-32), recall Satan's testing of God's Son. Most importantly, by his death, Jesus overcomes Satan's power.

JSNT 40 (1990), pp. 15-32

THE GOSPEL OF MARK:
EVOLUTIONARY OR REVOLUTIONARY DOCUMENT?

L.W. Hurtado

Introduction

The commonly accepted view that the Gospel of Mark was the first attempt to produce a written narrative portrait of Jesus' ministry, and that it was the major narrative source used by the writers of Matthew and Luke obviously makes Mark a historically significant document that had immediate and far-reaching acceptance and influence. Mark's distinction as the apparently pioneering Gospel makes important the question of the relationship of this document to the rest of first-century Christianity.

My purpose in this paper is to evaluate a couple of recent attempts to portray Mark as radically disjunctive in its first-century context. In brief, both works to be discussed offer a view of Mark as a revolutionary text, although they differ considerably from each other in what it is about Mark that was revolutionary. I refer to Werner Kelber's *The Oral and the Written Gospel*,[1] and Burton Mack's *A Myth of Innocence*.[2] Because each of the authors rests his case for Mark on a larger conceptual framework, and not primarily on an exegesis of Mark, it will be necessary to interact with these wider issues. I shall argue that neither of these major attempts to portray Mark as a revolutionary text is successful and that an evolutionary model, which allows for ample continuity and significant developments, best serves us in grasping the relationship of Mark to its early Christian setting.

1. W.H. Kelber, *The Oral and the Written Gospel: The Hermeneutics of Speaking and Writing in the Synoptic Tradition, Mark, Paul, and Q* (Philadelphia: Fortress Press, 1983).
2. B. Mack, *A Myth of Innocence: Mark and Christian Origins* (Philadelphia: Fortress Press, 1988).

Werner Kelber: Mark the Creator of 'Textuality'

Although Kelber's programmatic study, *The Oral and the Written Gospel*, has already received some criticism, his portrayal of Mark as the revolutionary emergence of 'textuality' in the Jesus tradition has received acceptance among others.[3] The problems in Kelber's case, however, are so major that his proposal must be judged to be a failure.

His rather over-strict distinction between 'orality' and 'textuality', the conceptual basis of his case, is perhaps the first major problem that can be addressed from several points.[4] Kelber uses this distinction to argue that Mark constituted a veritable and probably deliberate revolution in the Jesus tradition, which had previously been transmitted in an oral mode with very different features. In defining the distinctive nature of oral tradition, he invokes the research by students of oral poetry such as A.B. Lord, but has failed to take seriously Lord's emphasis that his characterization of oral poetry applied *only* to societies that were *pre-literate*. Lord makes it clear that once literacy appears in a society things change considerably. Thus, Lord's characterization applies to situations of what we may call 'pure orality'.[5] And, in spite of Kelber's attempt to minimize the extent of literacy in the Greco-Roman world, it is evident that in Gentile and Jewish circles the preparation and reading of texts was a pervasive part of the culture.[6] We are still developing the means of

---

3. See the discussion of Kelber's views in *Semeia* 39 (1987), esp. T.E. Boomershine, 'Peter's Denial as Polemic or Confession: The Implications of Media Criticism for Biblical Hermeneutics', pp. 47-68. The somewhat uncritical acceptance of Kelber's position is reflected, e.g., in E. Richard, *Jesus, One and Many: The Christological Concept of New Testament Authors* (Wilmington, DE: Michael Glazier, 1988), p. 100.

4. This distinction underlies the whole of Kelber's book, but is expressed explicitly in, e.g., *Gospel*, pp. 14-34.

5. A.B. Lord, *The Singer of Tales* (Cambridge, MA: Harvard University Press, 1960), e.g., pp. 20, 129-35.

6. See, e.g., C.H. Roberts, 'Books in the Graeco-Roman World and in the New Testament', in *The Cambridge History of the Bible*, I (ed. P.R. Ackroyd and C.F. Evans; Cambridge: Cambridge University Press, 1970), pp. 48-66. Cf. Kelber, *Gospels*, e.g. p. 17, who quotes a statement by D.J. Wiseman out of context here. See also M. Hengel, *Judaism and Hellenism*, I (London: SCM Press, 1974), pp. 78-83 (on Jewish schools in Palestine), and pp. 110-15 (on Jewish literature). For surveys of Jewish literature, see R.A. Kraft and G.W.E. Nickelsburg (eds.), *Early Judaism and its Modern Interpreters* (Atlanta: Scholars Press, 1986); M.E. Stone, *Jewish Writings of the Second Temple Period* (Philadelphia: Fortress Press, 1984).

defining and measuring literacy in contemporary societies such as North America, and any precise claims about literacy rates in ancient societies amount to little more than guess-work. But it is clear that a great deal of 'textuality' characterized the Greco-Roman world, both among the highly educated elite and among many from more humble circles. The thousands of surviving Greek letters from antiquity alone, which come from a broad range of cultural levels, testify to a widely distributed, though variegated, literacy.[7]

It is not necessary for everyone, or even a majority of people, in a group to have sophisticated literacy for the group to be heavily influenced by 'textuality'. Kelber fails to recognize that even if only some of the leaders, the opinion formers, the activists, have some literacy, the group will be exposed to, and be influenced (perhaps dominated) by, texts and 'textuality'. Certainly, all evidence indicates that early Christianity was from the first a fervently writing and reading movement, and comparisons drawn with illiterate circles of oral poets do not seem particularly valid. Kelber's attempt to make earliest Christianity a rural phenomenon and his characterization of rural areas as essentially uninfluenced by 'textuality' are unpersuasive.[8]

Furthermore, as others have already indicated, Kelber has not adequately allowed for the interplay and influence of orality and textuality in the Greco-Roman era.[9] Although he grants this interplay in general statements, in practice he writes as if Greco-Roman appreciation for oral communication means a lack of influence of textuality. Students of Greco-Roman literature regularly point out that many of the techniques and characteristics which originated with oral communication and were meticulously analyzed and categorized in the ancient study of rhetoric, influenced the nature of texts as well.[10] In addition, most texts of Greco-Roman antiquity were prepared to be 'performed' before a group, read aloud, with all the techniques of oral communication

---

7. For an introduction to the literary background of early Christianity, see D.E. Aune, *The New Testament in its Literary Environment* (Philadelphia: Westminster Press, 1987). On the epistolary materials, see S.K. Stowers, *Letter Writing in Greco-Roman Antiquity* (Philadelphia: Westminster Press, 1986).

8. Kelber, *Gospel*, pp. 17-18, relying on Walter Ong's work.

9. Boomershine, 'Peter's Denial'.

10. See, e.g., G.A. Kennedy, *New Testament Interpretation through Rhetorical Criticism* (Chapel Hill, NC: University of North Carolina Press, 1984).

available to the reader.[11] So, in the Greco-Roman world, we have a rich mixture of oral and written communication, with each mode of communication affecting the other, and the sharp distinctions Kelber tries to make between oral and written compositions seem extreme and inappropriate. The Greco-Roman world prized effective oral communication, to be sure, but Greco-Roman orality existed side by side with, influenced and was influenced by, widespread literacy. And the influence of textuality is revealed in various forms (high literature, popular literature, letters, commercial documents, inscriptions, etc.) in all levels of the society.[12] The 'orality' of the Greco-Roman world was not that of a pre-literate or newly literate culture, but was the orality characteristic of cultures with heavy influence of textuality. Therefore, Kelber's characterization of Greco-Roman orality is inappropriately based.

Moreover, Kelber's characterization of texts as fixed and frozen is too simplistic and anachronistic. Kelber has failed to recognize that there was no such thing as a fixed, frozen text prior to Gutenberg.[13] So long as a text had to be copied one character at a time by a human hand, there was always the opportunity to introduce all sorts of changes, accidentally and deliberately—deletions, additions, rearrangements, and rewordings in the interests of style and preferred meaning. Ancient writers were certainly aware of this, as is indicated for example by the stern warning in Rev. 22.18-19. Greater familiarity with the textual tradition of the New Testament might have spared Kelber from assuming that the fixed nature of modern printed texts can be attributed to ancient manuscript textuality.[14] As far as his understanding of ancient textuality is concerned, he seems to commit the kind of anachronism he

11. For a relevant discussion of Greco-Roman reading techniques, see now M.A. Beavis, 'The Trial Before the Sanhedrin (Mark 14.53-65): Reader Response and the Greco-Roman Readers', *CBQ* 49 (1987), pp. 581-96; and *idem*, *Mark's Audience: The Literary and Social Setting of Mark 4.11-12* (JSNTS, 33; Sheffield: JSOT Press, 1989). Note, e.g., the little comment directed to the public reader of Mark in 13.14.

12. See, e.g., W.W. Tarn, *Hellenistic Civilisation* (Cleveland: World, rev. edn, 1952), pp. 268-94.

13. I develop this point in my essay, 'Greco-Roman Textuality and the Gospel of Mark: A Critique of Werner Kelber' (unpublished).

14. For an introductory survey of the changes that affected the New Testament texts, see e.g. J.N. Birdsall, 'The New Testament Text', in *The Cambridge History of the Bible*, I, pp. 332-57.

characterizes in others as marching along 'the Gutenberg galaxy'.[15]

But even without an acquaintance with the New Testament manu-script tradition (*terra incognita* to far too many New Testament scholars today), the major modifications of their Markan source by the writers of Matthew and Luke demonstrate that the contents of ancient texts were by no means automatically sacrosanct and fixed. The adaptive renditions of Markan material in Matthew and Luke are major evidence that Mark did not 'freeze' the Jesus tradition but that it remained fluid and adaptive in its written mode as well as in oral form.

As for Kelber's breach between Mark and the pre-Markan tradition, this seems far too overdrawn.[16] We do not know what exact sort of oral narratives of Jesus' ministry circulated in the pre-Markan decades, but there is good evidence that there were such narratives. For example, R.B. Hays has shown that Paul's argument in Galatians 3 presupposes a familiarity with a story of Jesus, that the Pauline kerygma included 'a basic narrative pattern similar to that which informs the canonical gospels', and that 'Paul's letters mark a point within a historical devel-opment *towards* the formulation of "gospels", i.e., explicit literary articulations of the Jesus-story'.[17]

From another quarter, Kloppenborg has criticized Kelber's assump-tion that Mark can be distinguished from Q, portrayed by Kelber as 'an oral genre' with contemporizing interests rather than Mark's histori-cizing tendency. Kloppenborg insists that Q was, like Mark, a literary work, and that Kelber has mistakenly read his distinctions between Markan 'textuality' and Q 'orality' into the evidence. Indeed, Klop-penborg finds in Q historicizing and *bios*-oriented features, concluding that the movement from Q to the Synoptic Gospels was a development of 'inner dynamisms' within Q and characteristic of the ancient instruc-tional genres to which Kloppenborg likens Q.[18]

Given the focus of the earliest Christian tradition on the figure of Jesus, and given the Greco-Roman interest in *bios* literature, it is not at all surprising that Gospels were written. Mark is notable as the first, but

15. Cf. Kelber's critique of previous study of the pre-canonical tradition, *Gospel*, pp. 1-43.

16. Cf. Kelber, *Gospel*, pp. 90-139.

17. R.B. Hays, *The Faith of Jesus Christ* (SBLDS, 56; Chico, CA: Scholars Press, 1983); see e.g. pp. 256-58.

18. J. Kloppenborg, *The Formation of Q: Trajectories in Ancient Wisdom Collections* (Philadelphia: Fortress Press, 1987).

it is hardly the revolutionary development Kelber asserts. The Gospels are organically connected to the oral tradition about Jesus and reflect wider tastes and trends in Greco-Roman culture.[19]

In short, and without going further into other problems in Kelber's views of Mark and other early Christian writers, Kelber's case for Mark as a revolutionary development in early Christianity rests upon an inaccurate description of the oral and written culture of the Greco-Roman era and upon an inaccurate grasp of the nature of the pre-Markan Jesus tradition. He is right to underscore the importance of Mark and to focus attention on the question of why the text was written, but his own answer to this question must be rejected and his case for a revolutionary Mark must be judged to have failed. As I will indicate briefly in the final section of this paper, the evidence suggests that Mark is much more organically connected with pre-Markan tradition.

Burton Mack: Mark the Inventor of Myth

Even more daring in thesis and more ambitious in scope, Burton Mack's 1988 large volume aims to re-orient the entire investigation of Christian origins. Mack's book bristles with controversial assertions and positions, some of them simply long-outdated, many others inconsistent with the evidence or resting on unsubstantiated assumptions. It would take a

19. On the origins of *bios* literature, see e.g. A. Momigliano, *The Development of Greek Biography* (Cambridge, MA: Harvard University Press, 1971). On the relation of the Gospels to Greco-Roman *bios* literature, see e.g. Aune, *New Testament*, pp. 17-76; C.H. Talbert, 'Biographies of Philosophers and Rulers as Instruments of Religious Propaganda in Mediterranean Antiquity', *ANRW* 2.16.2, pp. 1619-57; H. Cancik, 'Die Gattung Evangelium: Das Evangelium des Markus im Rahmen der antiken Historiographie', in *Markus-Philologie: Historische, literargeschichtliche und stilistische Untersuchungen zum zweiten Evangelium* (ed. H. Cancik; WUNT, 33; Tübingen: J.C.B. Mohr [Paul Siebeck], 1984); A. Dihle, 'Die Evangelien und die griechische Biographie', in P. Stuhlmacher (ed.), *Das Evangelium und die Evangelien* (WUNT, 28; Tübingen: J.C.B. Mohr [Paul Siebeck], 1983), pp. 383-411. On the distinctions between the Jesus tradition and ancient Jewish rabbinic traditions about sages, see J. Neusner, *Why No Gospels in Talmudic Judaism?* (Atlanta: Scholars Press, 1988); P.S. Alexander, 'Rabbinic Biography and the Biography of Jesus: A Survey of the Evidence', in *Synoptic Studies: The Ampleforth Conferences of 1982 and 1983* (ed. C.M. Tuckett; JSNTS, 7; Sheffield: JSOT Press, 1984), pp. 19-50. For a general review of the question, see R. Guelich, 'The Gospel Genre', in Stuhlmacher (ed.), *Das Evangelium*, pp. 183-219.

much longer paper than is possible here to detail all the problems in the book. I shall restrict myself to matters directly relevant to the central question of whether Mack's view of the origin of Mark stands up under critical analysis. I think it does not, and I shall provide some reasons for this judgment by way of examining major components of Mack's case.

For Mack, the revolutionary thing about Mark is not its 'textuality' but its content. In Mack's view, Mark succeeded in single-handedly redrawing the nature of Christian faith and consciousness, influencing all subsequent views of Christian origins with its mythic picture of Jesus as the eschatological redeemer figure. Thus, the crucial event for subsequent Christianity was not Jesus' ministry and execution, or the 'Easter' events and religious activities of the early decades, or the career of Paul and the success of the Gentile mission. Instead, it was the composition of Mark.[20]

In brief, Mack sees Mark as a novel achievement that combined imaginatively 'two distinctively different types of written material representative of two major types of early sectarian formation': one type was 'movements in Palestine and southern Syria that cultivated the memory of Jesus as a founder-teacher', and the other type was 'congregations in northern Syria, Asia Minor and Greece wherein the death and resurrection of the Christ were regarded as the founding events'.[21]

The first major problem is in Mack's portrayal of earliest Christian history, upon which his presentation of Mark rests. Mack sees the historical Jesus as a teacher of aphorisms, likening him to a wandering Cynic sage, and rejects the widely shared view that Jesus' message involved an eschatological orientation.[22] After Jesus, the earliest Christian groups, 'Jesus movements' located in Palestine, were essentially 'synagogue reform movements' in which Jesus was seen as the ideal teacher of a preferred form of Jewish practice.[23] The true nature of Jesus' ministry and the earliest forms of the Jesus movement, however, have been lost, and subsequent Christianity derives from Mark's adaptation of the

---

20. Mack, *Myth*, e.g. pp. 8-9. And it is clear that in Mack's view the alleged revolutionary influence of Mark's picture of Jesus was unfortunate and distasteful (e.g. p. 245). Indeed, Mack attributes to Mark an even wider negative influence, blaming the author for several bad features of Western culture, including modern imperialism (pp. 368-75).

21. Mack, *Myth*, p. 11.

22. Mack, *Myth*, pp. 53-77, esp. pp. 63-74.

23. Mack, *Myth*, pp. 78-97.

kerygma of the 'Hellenistic Christ cult', an 'aberration' which developed in Antioch at a sufficient distance from 'hasidic' influences in Jerusalem.[24] The christology of this Christ cult, into which Paul was converted, developed in two major stages: first a 'martyr myth' ('the earliest "christology"'),[25] then a more developed kerygma of Christ as dying/rising savior-god with attendant features of a cultus ('mythic ritualization of the meal', baptism and its symbolic associations, the notion of 'spiritual presence', and 'liturgical materials, including acclamations, doxologies, confessions of faith, and hymns').[26] Mark's distinctive and revolutionary creation was the use of the kerygma of this 'Christ cult' as a framework to reinterpret the ministry of Jesus and present it in narrative form.

In his picture of Jesus the sage, Mack is able to point to a few others who are attempting to overthrow the notion that Jesus' ministry should be seen in the context of ancient eschatological thought.[27] But the basis for the wholly non-eschatological Jesus offered by Mack does not seem to me sound, leaving far too much unexplained to be plausible. Mack is simply not able to explain satisfactorily how a teacher of simple aphorisms about daily life became the object of a new religious movement so devoted to him as the center of attention. It is even more difficult to see how this Cynic-sage Jesus became the focus of the proliferation of the 'Jesus movements' Mack portrays. That there is no fully analogous development focused on any other wandering teacher of aphorisms in Greco-Roman antiquity is surely further reason to treat Mack's proposal as dubious.[28]

Although Mack describes as new this picture of Jesus as a simple teacher of wisdom, it is questionable that the basic picture is really new. There is a somewhat quaint lustre, reminiscent of nineteenth-century views such as Harnack's.[29] Occasionally, older views have been discarded

---

24. Mack, *Myth*, e.g. pp. 276, 315-24.

25. Mack, *Myth*, p. 109 n. 8. Mack's portrait of the 'Christ cult' is in pp. 98-123.

26. Mack, *Myth*, p. 100 n. 21.

27. For another non-eschatological portrait of Jesus, see M.J. Borg, *Jesus, a New Vision: Spirit, Culture, and the Life of Discipleship* (San Francisco: Harper & Row, 1987).

28. Especially relevant are the studies by Neusner and Alexander, cited above, of biographical traditions in other Jewish groups.

29. A. Harnack, *What is Christianity?* (New York: Harper & Row, 1957 [German, 1900]).

without adequate reason, but there were and there remain good reasons for finding inadequate and tendentious the picture of Jesus as the simple teacher of ethics.[30]

There is even more of the old-in-new-dress in Mack's sketch. Mack reflects the currently fashionable emphasis upon the 'social settings' of early Christian groups;[31] but, with allowance for some cosmetic retouching, the basic two-stage schema of Palestinian Jesus movements and the 'Hellenistic Christ cult' appears to be an adaptation from Bousset's *Kyrios Christos*, published in 1913.[32] However, instead of an apocalyptic *Ur-Gemeinde* focused on 'the Son of Man', Mack offers a 'synagogue reform movement' with a non-eschatological view of Jesus the sage.

But neither Bousset's two-stage schema nor Mack's takes adequate account of other evidence. Early Christianity was by no means uniform, but the roots of the cultic reverence of the exalted Christ go right back into the earliest observable circles of Christianity; and the basic conceptual categories of early christology do not derive from pagan mythology and religiosity but are attested in Jewish sources of Palestinian provenance. The 'mutation' in Jewish monotheistic praxis and thought represented in early Christianity, which I have analyzed elsewhere, cannot be written off so easily as Mack supposes as an 'aberration' distinctive of the Antioch church or other circles of 'Hellenistic Christianity' under the influence of pagan religiosity.[33]

Methodologically, it should give us pause that Mack's schema of earliest Christian groups rests upon the assumptions (never justified but relentlessly employed especially in the first eight chapters) that the various forms of material in the Synoptics (e.g. miracle stories, parables, wisdom sayings) reflect differing circles of the Jesus movement and that these formal categories correspond directly to the beliefs and social

30. For recent studies of Jesus, see e.g. E.P. Sanders, *Jesus and Judaism* (London: SCM Press, 1985); R. Leivestad, *Jesus in his Own Perspective* (Minneapolis: Augsburg, 1987).

31. See e.g. Mack, *Myth*, pp. 15-24.

32. W. Bousset, *Kyrios Christos* (Göttingen: Vandenhoeck & Ruprecht, 1913, 1921). The English translation is cited in this essay (Nashville: Abingdon Press, 1970). See, e.g., pp. 31-56, 119-52. For criticisms of several major aspects of Bousset's work, see my essay, 'New Testament Christology: A Critique of Bousset's Influence', *TS* 40 (1979), pp. 306-17.

33. See my book, *One God, One Lord: Early Christian Devotion and Ancient Jewish Monotheism* (Philadelphia: Fortress Press; London: SCM Press, 1988).

characteristics of these hypothetical groups. This assumption, on which some so-called 'sociological' investigation of the New Testament is based, is, unfortunately, a major example of a 'referential fallacy' and has already been cogently criticized.[34] In a setting of cultural mixture such as the Greco-Roman world, it would have been natural for any one religious group to reflect various rhetorical forms and various emphases. Mark's heterogeneous incorporation of Jesus material confirms that various types of collections of Jesus tradition were common property of many early Christian groups.

In Mack's case for early Jesus movements with a non-kerygmatic aphoristic message, he invokes some recent investigations of Q, but here too there are problems, both of a general methodological nature and in more specific matters. With great respect for the painstaking studies of the Q material of recent years, it is not clear that one can build so elaborate a case as Mack does on this work.[35] The Q source remains a hypothesis, useful primarily for explaining the curious 'double tradition' in Matthew and Luke, not the only hypothesis, but the most widely accepted one, which I too find sufficiently plausible to use for this purpose. But inherently less plausible is the hypothesis that Q is the product of a circle of Christians who held a view of Jesus as merely a teacher, for this simply assumes without corroboration what in fact has to be demonstrated: that a Q document (or earlier sayings collection) without a passion account was the fully representative expression of the beliefs and religious pattern of the group(s) in which this hypothetical document might have been composed and used. Instead, that 'Matthew' and 'Luke' have apparently incorporated much or all of the Q material into texts which are governed by the kerygma of Jesus' death and resurrection makes it evident that Q circulated among groups which espoused that form of Christian message, and makes it plausible that it was among such groups that the sayings collections originated.[36]

---

34. See, e.g., E.S. Malbon, 'Galilee and Jerusalem: History and Literature in Marcan Interpretation', *CBQ* 44 (1982), pp. 242-55; the review of G. Theissen by B.J. Malina in *CBQ* 41 (1979), pp. 176-78; R.L. Rohrbaugh, '"Social Location of Thought" as a Heuristic Construct in New Testament Study', *JSNT* 30 (1987), pp. 103-19.

35. Cf. Mack, *Myth*, pp. 85-87 nn. 6-7.

36. See similar observations in G.N. Stanton, 'On the Christology of Q', in B. Lindars and S.S. Smalley (eds.), *Christ and Spirit in the New Testament* (Cambridge: Cambridge University Press, 1973), pp. 27-42.

To move from general methodological qualms to a more specific matter, although Mack claims that the most recent work on Q justifies his notion of early non-kerygmatic Jesus movements that espoused an essentially aphoristic wisdom message, even this is not so clearly the case.[37] Mack refers to Kloppenborg, who hypothesizes two stages of Q tradition, the earlier stage exhibiting aphoristic emphases and the later stage characterized by a 'deuteronomistic' theology and a more eschatological tone. But Kloppenborg emphasizes that his analysis applies only to the literary history of the Q document in Greek and does *not* allow one to construct a tradition-history of pre-literary material or a religious history of Christian groups, such as Mack offers. Indeed, Kloppenborg suggests that some of the eschatologically oriented sayings in his second stage of Q probably reflect Jesus' teaching and that at least some of the aphoristic sayings of his first stage of Q are perhaps younger and less authentic as representations of the message of Jesus and the earliest Christian circles.[38]

Another major problem with Mack's case for Mark's originality is the way the evidence from Paul is mishandled. Mack's attempt to limit Paul to an acquaintance with the message of the 'Hellenistic Christ cult' is no more persuasive than Bousset's attempt of seventy-five years ago.[39] In the decades since Bousset, surely several things about Paul have become clear.[40] He was authentically and thoroughly at home in

37. See Mack, *Myth*, e.g. pp. 84-87 and nn. 6-7.

38. Kloppenborg, *Formation*, e.g. p. 262 (on the biographical tendencies of Q), p. 324 (on the distinctions between the Q wisdom material and Cynic thought), pp. 244-45 (on the distinction between the literary history of Q and the tradition history of earliest Christianity). As for Kloppenborg's sketch of the history of Q, he assumes too easily that the complexity in Q material requires a developmental process, and that differing forms of material require, and can furnish the basis for, a theory of different provenances for the different forms. Cf. A.D. Jacobson, 'The History of the Composition of the Synoptic Sayings Source, Q', in *SBLSP* (ed. K.H. Richards; Atlanta: Scholars Press, 1987), pp. 285-94. R.A. Piper, *Wisdom in the Q-Tradition: The Aphoristic Teaching of Jesus* (SNTSMS, 61; Cambridge: Cambridge University Press, 1989), analyzes the tradition history of Q, arguing that, though at least some of the sapiential sayings may go back to Jesus, the collections of such material lying behind the Q document were later than Jesus and may have come from a particular circle of early Christians. However, unlike Mack, Piper does not attribute to this group a distinctive, non-kerygmatic christology.

39. Cf. Mack, *Myth*, pp. 98-100; Bousset, *Kyrios Christos*, p. 119.

40. As representative of Pauline studies in recent decades, see e.g. K. Stendahl, *Paul among Jews and Gentiles* (Philadelphia: Fortress Press, 1976); J.C. Beker, *Paul*

his Jewish tradition prior to his calling/conversion to apostleship. His Christian contacts, both before and after his calling/conversion included the Jewish Christians in Palestine, Diaspora Jewish Christians of various leanings, and Gentile Christians of various persuasions. His own emphases and orientation were not as influential or as broadly shared as some have assumed, but his acquaintance with Christian circles ('from Jerusalem and as far round as Illyricum', Rom. 15.19) was hardly narrow. Thus, in principle, we simply cannot marginalize his explicit statements and the implicit evidence he offers about the nature of early Christian faith, as Mack tries to do. Nor can Mack sensibly describe Paul as a 'second generation' Christian, given that the probable date of his conversion/calling is sometime in the first few years of the Christian movement.[41]

The letters of Paul are full of indications that early Christianity had its differences, and Paul certainly espoused a somewhat distinctive program of Gentile mission.[42] But even the most bitterly contested differences between Paul and others, including Palestinian-based Jewish Christians, such as the 'false brethren', and the 'certain men from James' mentioned in Galatians 2, seem to have involved basically three things: the legitimacy of his own apostleship, the importance and legitimacy of his Gentile mission, and what we may call various *implications* of the kerygma of Jesus' death and resurrection/exaltation which Paul considered crucial. Paul knew of Jewish Christans who did not share his views about these implications of the crucifixion and resurrection of Christ for Gentile salvation, but there is no hint that Paul knew of 'Jesus movements' in which a basic kerygma of Jesus' death and resurrection/ exaltation formed no part of their beliefs. Given the importance of this kerygma to Paul, his readiness to criticize Christians whose theology he found seriously deficient, and his wide-ranging acquaintance with early

the Apostle (Philadelphia: Fortress Press, 1980); E.P. Sanders, *Paul and Palestinian Judaism* (Philadelphia: Fortress Press, 1977); W.A. Meeks, *The First Urban Christians* (New Haven: Yale University Press, 1983).

41. Cf. Mack, *Myth*, e.g. p. 121. In references to Paul, Mack repeatedly places him in the fifties, the time of Paul's letters, suppressing the fact that Paul's calling/conversion and acquaintance with Christian faith took place in the first few years of the Christian movement. On the importance of chronology, see M. Hengel, *Between Jesus and Paul* (London: SCM Press; Philadelphia: Fortress Press, 1983), pp. 30-47.

42. For discussion of Paul's relationship with various early Christian circles, see B. Holmberg, *Paul and Power* (Philadelphia: Fortress Press, 1978).

Christian groups, Paul's silence about 'Jesus movements' with no
kerygma of Jesus the crucified messiah is much more damaging to
Mack's case than he grants.

In fact, in 1 Cor. 15.1-11 Paul makes the unambiguous claim that a
kerygma of Jesus the Christ's death and resurrection was the common
tradition of his Gentile mission and the Palestinian Jewish churches.
Mack's desperate attempt to avoid the force of this and other such passages in Paul which reflect the beliefs and cultic practices of Jewish
Christian groups, probably including Palestinian groups (e.g. Rom. 1.3-4;
Phil. 2.5-11; 1 Cor. 16.22), is not persuasive.[43]

I have dealt at length with problems in Mack's basic characterization
of early Christian history and beliefs because he makes his scheme so
important for his thesis of Mark as an imaginative and revolutionary
rewriting of Christian faith. His view of Mark does not seem to have
arisen from an inductive exegesis of the text; instead, it seems to be a
hypothetical 'What if' (to use Mack's own words, p. xii). Thus, to cite
another example, his claim that Mark invented the idea that Jesus
fulfilled an eschatological divine plan is not justified by any Markan evidence and flies in the face of Pauline references indicating that such a
view of Jesus was commonly accepted in Christianity several decades
earlier than Mark (e.g. 1 Cor. 15.3-5; Gal. 4.4; 1 Thess. 1.10).

It appears then that, although Mack attempts a revolutionary
redrawing of Christian origins, his case for Mark as a revolutionary document does not stand up to critical scrutiny.[44]

Evolutionary Mark

Examination of the works of Kelber and Mack, the major full-scale
attempts to portray Mark as a revolutionary document, indicates that
neither attempt succeeds, and suggests that the revolutionary model for
understanding the appearance of Mark is not promising. The alternative,
an evolutionary model for understanding Mark's relationship to first-
century Christianity, therefore remains preferable.

Although this, apparently first, attempt to produce a written portrait
of Jesus' ministry in narrative mode was a significant step in the literary
history of early Christianity and a significant influence upon subsequent

43. Cf. e.g. Mack, *Myth*, p. 113 n. 11.

44. See O.L. Cope's appraisal of Mack's book in *RSR* 15 (1989), p. 160: 'the
creative imagination on display here is Mack's, not Mark's'.

Jesus tradition, it was also dependent upon and reflected the narrative presentations of Jesus' ministry already in use orally in pre-Markan Christian circles. Mark represents a notable development, but hardly a revolution.

Mark itself clearly reflects the presupposition that the preached 'gospel' includes narrative(s) of Jesus' ministry, as indicated in the pericope about the anointing in Bethany (14.9), and in allusions to figures and events the author expects his readers to know already, such as the mention of the father of Alexander and Rufus (15.21), and Pilate, who likewise appears without introduction or identification (15.1). Moreover, the casual way the author opens the book by linking the narrative with 'the gospel of Jesus Christ' (1.1) suggests that he expects his audience to recognize his work as in fundamental continuity with previous Christian tradition. Nothing in Mark itself reflects the tension of an author making a revolutionary step in the Jesus tradition. There are emphases in his presentation distinctive in comparison with the other Synoptics, but there is no justification or overt defense of his work, such as one would expect from an author imposing a radically new construction on his subject.[45]

The great gulf Kelber fixes between the pre-Markan oral tradition and written Mark seems far too exaggerated. As Joanna Dewey has shown recently, Mark's narrative is full of the imprints of oral structuring of narrative, which also suggests something considerably less than the radical break with pre-Markan orality that Kelber asserted.[46]

Likewise, Mack's attempt to make the content of Mark revolutionary seems falsified by the data. I have already indicated that the rigid distinctions between the beliefs of Mack's 'Jesus movements' and the 'Hellenistic Christ cult' do not rest on solid footings. I suggest also that Mack's claims about Mark's provenance and purpose are based on faulty analysis of the text.

Although the material in Mark contains many hints that the tradition derived from Palestinian Jewish Christian circles, there are clear indications that Mark itself was written for churches of the Gentile mission,

---

45. Cf. Josephus's clear indication that he wishes to set the record straight concerning the Jewish people in *Apion* 1.1-5. Even Lk. 1.1-4 is closer to being a hint that the author is trying to present a more correct or suitable picture of Jesus than in other accounts.

46. J. Dewey, 'Oral Methods of Structuring Narrative in Mark', *Int* 43 (1989), pp. 32-44.

not a failed 'synagogue reform movement': for example, the numerous explanations of the Palestinian background and Jewish customs and terms (e.g. 5.41; 6.17-29; 7.1-13, 34; 12.18), and the implicit and explicit affirmations of the Gentile mission (e.g. 13.10). Recently, Hengel has shown that a possible Roman provenance, for example, is still an attractive option.[47]

Mack's claim that Mark was intended to reconstitute the message of a failed 'synagogue reform movement' by embedding their Jesus tradition in the mythic framework of the Hellenistic Christ cult is surely off course by 180 degrees. The dynamics in Mark are the opposite.[48] Writing for Christians of the Gentile mission already familiar with the kerygma of Jesus the Son of God, Mark drew upon the Jesus tradition to emphasize Jesus' ministry and fate as the basis of, and model for, the confession and discipleship of these Christians. This accounts for such things as the emphases that allegiance to Jesus requires one to 'follow' Jesus (e.g. 8.34-38), and that Jesus' crucifixion is the pattern of discipleship as well as the redemptive basis of the elect (in the central section, 8.27–10.45, esp. 10.42-45). As another indication of Mark's purpose, note the distinctive Markan combination of the cultic imagery of 'baptism' and the 'cup' to describe Jesus' mission and fate, in the pericope about the request of James and John for special honors (10.35-40). This indicates an audience already familiar with the cultic meal, and suggests that the author was trying to deepen and make specific the meaning of familiar cultic actions.[49]

Other evidence for this view of the author's provenance and purposes could be given. As a final example, it seems likely that the author's desire to make Jesus both the basis and model of Christian life best accounts for the overall shape of the Markan narrative, which begins

47. M. Hengel, *Studies in the Gospel of Mark* (London: SCM Press, 1985), pp. 1-30. See also D. Senior, ' "With Swords and Clubs"... The Setting of Mark's Community and his Critique of Abusive Power', *BTB* 17 (1987), pp. 10-20.

48. See K.G. Reploh, *Markus—Lehrer der Gemeinde* (SBM, 9; Stuttgart: Katholisches Bibelwerk, 1969).

49. Mark (10.35-40) alone joins the 'cup' and 'baptism', the two chief cultic actions associated with participation in early Christian groups, as symbols for Jesus' coming fate and the discipleship for which the disciples must be prepared. Mt. 20.20-23 mentions only Jesus' 'cup'. The images of 'cup' or 'baptism' are found separated in other sayings; see Mk 14.36 // Mt. 26.39 // Lk. 22.42; Lk. 12.49. Note also Mark's use of eucharistic language in the account of the feeding of the 4000 (Mk 8.6-7).

with Jesus' baptism, portrays Jesus in mission and in conflict with opposition, and culminates in his obedient death and vindication by resurrection. As Mark 13 indicates, the themes of mission, opposition and mortal threat, and the hope of ultimate vindication, all of which correspond to the story of Jesus, characterize the author's hints about the situation of his audience (see esp. vv. 9-27).[50]

There is still much to learn about the Gospel of Mark and about the relationship of this book to first-century Christianity. Nothing in this essay is intended to minimize the importance of this document or its distinctives, and the discussion will no doubt continue about the exact nature of Mark's originality and dependence upon other Christian tradition. But the recent attempts to portray Mark as a revolutionary document do not commend themselves under critical scrutiny. It seems clear, therefore, that a basic evolutionary model best enables us to approach the question of why and how this important document was written. An evolutionary model does not imply any particular development as inevitable or insignificant, nor does it imply a unilinear development. The evolutionary model does, however, allow us better to take into account the complexity of the evidence concerning the Gospel of Mark and its relationship to the rest of early Christianity.[51]

50. The author systematically denies that any of the events listed in Mk 13.5-23 is the sign of the end, even the 'desolating sacrilege' of v. 14. The events are all 'historicized', made events within history, not markers of the end, and the hearers are given various practical instructions about how to cope with these events, emphasizing the dangers of being led astray by false eschatological claims (e.g. vv. 5, 7, 8, 10, 13, 14-23). The primary eschatological condition for the end is the spread of the gospel to 'all nations' (v. 10), and the eschatological appearance of the Son of Man is only 'after that tribulation' (v. 24) and the 'all things' warned of in vv. 5-23. See Hengel's discussion of Mark 13 in the light of Roman history: *Studies in the Gospel of Mark*, pp. 14-28.

51. After this essay was in press, there appeared the stimulating essay by P.J. Achtemeier, *'Omne Verbum Sonat*: The New Testament and the Oral Environment of Late Western Antiquity', *JBL* 109 (1990), pp. 3-27, which confirms further the close connection between 'orality' and 'textuality' in the Greco-Roman world. Also worth noting is the major study by W.V. Harris, *Ancient Literacy* (Cambridge, MA: Harvard University Press, 1989), though I am not sure that all his assumptions about the necessary social conditions for widespread competence are correct.

LUKE

JSNT 15 (1982), pp. 30-41

DID ST LUKE IMITATE THE SEPTUAGINT?

William G. Most

Which expressions in the New Testament are Semitisms? How extensive are they? Are they due to translation or other causes? These and similar questions have occasioned much ingenious research, but, unfortunately, generally accepted results are few.

To give a few examples: A. Deissmann noticed that New Testament Greek is not the same as fifth century Attic:[1] thus the need of looking for Semitic influence was reduced. Still, the search for evidence of translation from Aramaic continued, whether for large stretches of the Gospels and Acts[2] or for just the words of Jesus.[3]

A search for errors in translation from Aramaic produced much work, especially that of C.C. Torrey. This approach rested on the assumption that those responsible for the Greek text of the Gospels, especially Luke, mistranslated, since they were unable to learn Aramaic well, even though they lived with Aramaic speakers.[4] Yet it was thought that modern scholars, with far fewer sources, could learn Aramaic better than those who lived with natives. Further, many of these alleged

---

1. A. Deissmann, *Bible Studies* (trans. A. Grieve; Edinburgh: T. & T. Clark, 1902).

2. E.g., J. Wellhausen, *Einleitung in die drei ersten Evangelien* (Berlin: Georg Reimer, 2nd edn, 1911); E. Nestle, *Philologica Sacra* (Berlin: Reuther & Reichard, 1896); C.F. Burney, *The Aramaic Origin of the Fourth Gospel* (Oxford: Clarendon Press, 1922); C.C. Torrey, *Our Translated Gospels* (New York: Harper & Brothers, 1936); *idem, Documents of the Primitive Church* (New York: Harper & Brothers, 1941); *idem, The Four Gospels* (New York: Harper & Brothers, 2nd edn, 1947).

3. E.g., G. Dalman, *The Words of Jesus* (trans. D.M. Kay; Edinburgh: T. & T. Clark, 1902); M. Black, *An Aramaic Approach to the Gospels and Acts* (Oxford: Clarendon Press, 3rd edn, 1967).

4. Especially Torrey (see n. 2 above).

instances of mistranslation '...are open to grave objection'.[5] Yet that did not stop Black from asserting his own claims that he had found mistranslations.

Others sought, and still seek, explanations not in translation, but in the assumption that there was a Jewish brand of Greek.[6]

Some of the most convincing work on Semitisms has been done by H.F.D. Sparks in his studies on Luke.[7] Sparks was right to focus on Luke, since it is admitted that Luke, though a Gentile, shows far more Semitisms than do the native Semitic writers of the other Gospels. In his 1943 study, 'The Semitisms of St Luke's Gospel', Sparks mentions three possible sources, direct translation from Semitic, use of Semitized Greek translations from Semitic, or conscious imitation of the Septuagint to give what we might call a 'Biblical flavor'.[8]

In 1943, Sparks quickly disposed of the theory of direct translation from Semitic, saying that such a theory 'is ruled out of court'[9] by the Two Source Theory, which he then considered solidly proved. However, later on, in 1951, he spoke differently: 'For myself, I am not wedded to orthodox Synoptic criticism'.[10] Sparks showed foresight and prudent judgment; at present the number of attacks on the Two Source Theory is multiplying.[11]

---

5. Black, *An Aramaic Approach*, p. 5.

6. E.g., N. Turner, 'The Unique Character of Biblical Greek', *VT* 5 (1955), p. 478; H.S. Gehman, 'The Hebraic Character of LXX Greek', *VT* 1 (1951), pp. 81-90; F.L. Horton, 'Reflections on the Semitisms of Luke–Acts', in C.H. Talbert (ed.), *Perspectives on Luke–Acts* (Special Studies Series, 5; Edinburgh: T. & T. Clark, 1982), esp. pp. 13-14, 23.

7. H.F.D. Sparks, 'The Semitisms of St Luke's Gospel', *JTS* 44 (1943), pp. 129-38; 'The Semitisms of the Acts', *JTS* NS 1 (1950), pp. 16-28; 'Some Observations on the Semitic Background of the New Testament', *SNTS Bulletin* 2 (1951), pp. 33-42.

8. Sparks, 'The Semitisms of St Luke's Gospel', pp. 132, 134.

9. Sparks, 'The Semitisms of St Luke's Gospel', p. 129.

10. Gehman, 'The Hebraic Character of LXX Greek', p. 39.

11. Cf. W.R. Farmer, *The Synoptic Problem* (New York: Macmillan, 1976 [1964]); B.J. Orchard, *Matthew, Luke and Mark* (Griesbach Solution to the Synoptic Question, 1; Manchester: Koinonia, 1976); E.P. Sanders, *The Tendencies of the Synoptic Tradition* (SNTSMS, 9; Cambridge: Cambridge University Press, 1969); T.R. Rosche, 'The Words of Jesus and the Future of the "Q" Hypothesis', *JBL* 79 (1960), pp. 210-20; E.P. Sanders, 'The Argument from Order and Relationship between Matthew and Luke', *NTS* 15 (1968–69), pp. 249-61; O.L. Cope, *Matthew: A*

Still another shift appears in his 1951 article. Formerly, Sparks was quite firm in claiming that Luke's Semitisms came from deliberate imitation of the LXX.[12] As part of the support for this theory of LXX imitation, he added that, in Luke, 'only two characteristically Aramaic expressions are at all common', whereas 'several [Semitisms]... can be traced without question to Biblical Hebrew'.[13] This, he thought, pointed to imitation of the LXX, since it seemed unlikely that Luke made such a thorough study of Hebrew as to assimilate Hebrew expressions directly.

But in 1951 he could write: 'we should...be very chary of accepting only one' solution.[14]

Bruce Chilton, in a recent meticulous linguistically based redaction analysis of Lukan passages, has prudently rejected many proposals by others as insufficiently grounded conjectures, and has supported the sound work of Sparks, especially by showing that Luke followed tradition with great care at several points in the passages studied.[15]

We hope to build on this work of Sparks and Chilton by a study of one strictly Hebrew feature of Luke that occurs more frequently than other Semitisms: the apodotic καί.

Other Semitic features in Luke are not frequent enough to make conclusions firm. For example, Sparks noted that Greek ἐνώπιον could reflect Hebrew לפני.[16] Yet he saw that it need not reflect it in every instance, since such uses of ἐνώπιον are found at times even in secular Greek.[17] Again, ἐν τῷ plus the infinitive does correspond well to the Hebrew בְּ with the infinitive.[18] But we cannot be sure of a Hebrew substrate, for that structure is known even in classical Greek. Admittedly

Scribe Trained for the Kingdom of Heaven (CBQMS, 5; Washington: Catholic Biblical Association, 1976), esp. p. 12; J.M. Rist, *On the Independence of Matthew and Mark* (SNTSMS, 9; Cambridge: Cambridge University Press, 1978); H.-H. Stoldt, *History and Criticism of the Marcan Hypothesis* (trans. D.L. Niewyk; Macon, GA: Mercer University Press, 1980).

12. See n. 8 above.

13. Sparks, 'The Semitisms of St Luke's Gospel', pp. 131-32.

14. Gehman, 'The Hebraic Character of LXX Greek', p. 38.

15. B.D. Chilton, *God in Strength: Jesus' Announcement of the Kingdom* (SNTU, 1; Freistadt: Plöchl, 1979), esp. pp. 123-77.

16. Sparks, 'The Semitisms of St Luke's Gospel', p. 133.

17. W. Bauer, W. Arndt, F.W. Gingrich, and F.W. Danker, *A Greek–English Lexicon of the New Testament* (Chicago: University of Chicago Press, 2nd edn, 1979), p. 270.

18. Often with a subject and other words too.

classical Greek does not use it in a purely temporal sense, but it does use prepositions with the articular infinitive so often and in such a wide variety that it would not take much to induce a native Greek speaker like Luke to make the slight extension into the purely temporal use of ἐν τῷ.[19] It is only the frequency of the construction in Luke that does suggest Hebrew influence: Matthew and Mark use it only once; John never employs it; but Luke has it 25 times.[20]

We turn now to the apodotic καί, a true hard-core Hebraism and a relatively frequent one.[21] This is the use of καί to connect the main clause to a preceding subordinate clause. Such a structure is almost unknown in classical Greek, though it does happen to occur once in Homer, *Iliad* 1.478.[22] It does seem to occur before questions but then has a different sense.[23] It is also found in slovenly Greek prose.[24]

However, the Hebrew equivalent, apodotic ו,[25] was very common in Canaanite,[26] and had a wide range of uses in classical Hebrew: after conditional, temporal, relative conditional clauses, and after participles standing for clauses, etc. It became rare in new Hebrew, and was rare in Aramaic. In both it is largely confined to use after conditional or temporal clauses.[27]

Before proceeding with our study of apodotic καί we should notice that sentences that have it very often start with still another Hebraism: καὶ ἐγένετο. This reflects Hebrew ויהי, which is quite normal in classical Hebrew. However, in later Hebrew it retreats under Aramaic influence,[28] and disappears completely in the new Hebrew of the Mishna. The structure is not native to Aramaic, though an equivalent does appear at

---

19. H.W. Smyth, *A Greek Grammar for Colleges* (New York and Cincinnati: American Book Company, 1920), §§2033, 2034-37.

20. Dalman, *The Words of Jesus*, p. 13.

21. Cf. M. Wilcox, *The Semitisms of Acts* (Oxford: Clarendon Press, 1965), p. 180.

22. J.D. Denniston, *The Greek Particles* (Oxford: Clarendon Press, 1959), pp. 308-309.

23. F. Blass and A. Debrunner, *A Greek Grammar of the New Testament* (Chicago: University of Chicago Press, 1961), p. 221, §442.7.

24. K. Beyer, *Semitische Syntax im Neuen Testament*, I (Göttingen: Vandenhoeck & Ruprecht, 1962), p. 68.

25. Beyer (*Semitische Syntax*, p. 30) believes that it is not native to Aramaic.

26. Beyer, *Semitische Syntax*, p. 66.

27. Beyer, *Semitische Syntax*, p. 67.

28. Beyer, *Semitische Syntax*, p. 30.

times in the Targums when they are translating the Hebrew expression.[29] Horton adds that ויהי, when followed by apodotic ו, seems to be absent from the colloquial Hebrew of the time of Christ.[30] He adds that the Greek parallel, καὶ ἐγένετο with a following apodotic καί, is not found in the Greek papyri from Egypt, though it could be found in religious works.[31] He assumes its appearance in these works comes from imitation of the LXX.

We turn now to Luke's use of apodotic καί. It is commonly ascribed to conscious imitation of the LXX,[32] or to translation from a document that imitated the LXX, or to the influence of synagogue Greek which would be affected by the LXX.[33] Yet there seems to have been but little careful investigation. Torrey, in *Our Translated Gospels*, devotes a brief chapter to it, but makes no careful comparison to the LXX usage, nor does he give statistics.[34] He is more interested in a comparison of a few examples from the Old Syriac or Sinaitic version of the Gospels. When he is working from the Greek of Luke, he gives only eight examples, and no statistics. M. Zerwick is more thorough, and distinguishes three patterns after ἐγένετο: (1) without a καί, (2) with an infinitive, and (3) with a καί plus a finite verb (the apodotic καί).[35] Oddly, he says the third one, the apodotic καί, is a 'construction of the LXX—which often omits that καί which is so necessary in Hebrew'. As we shall soon see from Johannessohn, the opposite is true of the LXX.

It is obvious that more careful work is needed to determine whether or not it is really plausible to say that Luke was consciously imitating the LXX, or translating a document which did so. The purpose of such an imitation would be, of course, to give a biblical flavor, such as we would give by injecting *thee* and *thou* and similar forms.

Fortunately, we have a basis of comparison from the solid study of Martin Johannessohn on the biblical καὶ ἐγένετο and its history.[36]

---

29. Beyer, *Semitische Syntax*, p. 30.

30. Horton, 'Reflections on the Semitisms of Luke–Acts', p. 4.

31. Horton, 'Reflections on the Semitisms of Luke–Acts', p. 6.

32. M. Zerwick, *Graecitas Biblica* (Rome: Pontifical Biblical Institute Press, 4th edn, 1960), §389; Sparks, 'The Semitisms of St Luke's Gospel', p. 132.

33. Horton, 'Reflections on the Semitisms of Luke–Acts', pp. 4, 6, 13-14, 23.

34. Torrey, *Our Translated Gospels*, pp. 64-73.

35. Zerwick, *Graecitas Biblica*, §389 and n. 1.

36. M. Johannessohn, 'Das biblische καὶ ἐγένετο und seine Geschichte', *Zeitschrift für Vergleichenden Sprachforschung* 53 (1926), pp. 161-212.

Johannessohn counted only examples of apodotic καί that come after
καὶ ἐγένετο. However, from seeing the attitude of the LXX translators
in that context, we can very reasonably suppose they had a similar
attitude in examples that lacked καὶ ἐγένετο.

Johannessohn tells us that the LXX usually keeps the apodotic καί.[37]
In fact, it always occurs in the books of Numbers, Deuteronomy, Ruth
and 4 Kings where the Hebrew has apodotic ו. Outside these books, says
Johannessohn, there are only occasional omissions. It appears least in
Genesis, but there it is still present 45.83% of the time. Exodus uses it 9
out of 13 times (69.23%). Joshua has it 7 out of 11 times (63.63%).
1 Kings omits it 5 times, but keeps it more than 25 times.

In all, this is a very heavy percentage of cases in which the LXX pro-
duces the Hebrew apodotic ו by καί. In fact, Johannessohn has found 9
places in which the LXX adds the καί where the Hebrew lacks the usual
ו.[38] Of course, it is quite possible that at those points the LXX was
translating from a Hebrew text different from our text.

Obviously, now, if Luke really were imitating the LXX, or using a
source which did so, he too should have had the apodotic καί a very
high percent of the time. Otherwise it would be as odd as if a person
today were to insert *thee, thou*, etc., only a small fraction of the time. It
would sound silly.

Finding no study which gave the count for Luke, it was obviously
worthwhile to make that count myself. But two counts were necessary:
first, one of instances where Luke does use apodotic καί, and secondly,
a count of places where normal Hebrew (and so also the LXX) would use
it, but Luke did not.

The rules in classical Hebrew for this ו were in general very well
observed, though, of course, there were exceptions.[39] It is especially
common in conditional sentences, especially in casuistic statements
(though it would not be used before an imperative in the apodosis). It
was also frequent in causal sentences, very frequent in temporal sentences, and present even after very brief temporal expressions, such as in
Exod. 16.6: 'Evening, and you will know'. It was also quite frequent in
relative sentences.

37. Johannessohn, 'Das biblische καὶ ἐγένετο', p. 184.
38. Johannessohn, 'Das biblische καὶ ἐγένετο', p. 190. 3 Kgs 8.54; 14.28;
15.29; 16.11; 17.17; Judg. 2.19; 2 Chr. 2.4; Ezek. 1.1.
39. P. Joüon, *Grammaire de l'Hebreu Biblique* (Rome: Institut Biblique
Pontifical, 10th edn, 1947), §176.

As to the exceptions: Apodotic καί would not be used before an imperative. But it would be found before the jussive (third person), or the cohortative (first person). It was rarely used before a noun, and not ordinarily found before particles, that is, negatives, adverbs, prepositions, and conjunctions. Finally, when there were two *if* clauses each with its own apodosis, the ꞇ was especially necessary before the second apodosis, but was not used before the first.

When we make our count of the *use* of the apodotic καί, we find Luke has the apodotic καί 17 times,[40] plus two other times in which there is some ambiguity, inasmuch as the καί could have the sense of *also* (11.34 and 12.8). Twelve of these examples open with (καὶ) ἐγένετο.

When we count examples of the *omission* of apodotic καί, we need to distinguish between instances in which classical rules would call for omission, and those in which they would not. Luke omits apodotic καί in 48 instances in which classical rules would not call for the omission, in instances in which no noun or substantive or imperative follows.[41]

He also omits it in 14 instances before nouns, pronouns, and adjectives where classical rules would omit it;[42] and in another 16 instances before adverbs, prepositions, negatives, and interrogatives where classical rules would also omit it.[43]

There are two examples also of omission in double conditions, in which καί is left out in both members: in the first member according to classical rule; in the second, in one example, because a noun follows, in the other, when a negative follows.[44] He also omits it in two instances of genitive absolutes.[45] Such an omission would have been required in classical Greek, but not in Koine Greek. The LXX sometimes uses καί

40. In Lk. 2.21; 2.27; 5.1; 5.12; 5.17; 7.12; 8.1; 8.22; 9.28; 9.51; 13.25; 14.1; 17.11; 19.1; 19.15; 24.4; 24.15.

41. In Lk. 1.8; 1.23; 1.41; 1.44; 1.59; 2.1; 2.6; 2.22; 2.39; 2.42; 2.46; 4.8; 5.4; 5.13; 6.13; 7.1; 7.11; 8.40; 9.18; 9.24; 9.33; 9.36; 9.37; 10.6; 11.1; 11.24; 11.27; 11.36; 12.9; 12.10; 12.45; 15.25; 15.30; 16.9; 16.30; 17.6; 17.15; 17.33; 17.34; 19.5; 19.29; 19.41; 20.1; 21.31; 22.14; 22.66; 24.30; 24.51.

42. In Lk. 2.15; 8.42; 9.29; 9.48; 10.38; 11.19; 11.22; 12.38; 13.3; 13.5; 16.11; 16.12; 18.35; 19.40.

43. In Lk. 6.32; 6.33; 6.34; 10.13; 11.8; 11.13; 11.18; 11.20; 11.21; 12.39; 12.54; 16.31; 18.4; 19.31; 21.20; 23.31.

44. In Lk. 20.5-6; 22.68-69.

45. In Lk. 4.42; 22.10.

after a genitive absolute, for example, 4 Kgs 13.21.

Finally, the καί is omitted in two instances of elliptical protases;[46] classical Hebrew more commonly omitted the ו with these, but not always.

We can sum up our totals thus:

Apodotic καί *used:* 17 clear instances, plus 2 ambiguous ones

Apodotic καί *omitted:*

    a)   When no substantive or particle follows: 48

    b)   Before nouns, pronouns, adjectives: 14

    c)   Before adverbs, prepositions, negatives, interrogatives: 16

    d)   In double conditionals: 2

    e)   After genitive absolutes: 2

    f)   After elliptical protases: 2

Since classical Hebrew rules would often call for ו after *casus pendens*, which resembles a genitive absolute, we may add two instances from Luke to the basic 48 of (a) above to reach a total of 50. Also, since the ו is found at times after elliptical protases, we may reasonably take one of the two examples, to give a total of 51 omissions.

As a result, leaving aside the two ambiguous instances where καί does appear, we have a ratio of 17 uses to 51 omissions. That is, we have 17 uses out of a total of 68 possible uses by classical rules. That means that Luke used apodotic καί just 25% of the time. But, as Johannessohn shows, the LXX reproduces apodotic ו most of the time.

Now suppose someone today wanted to use forms like *thee* and *thou* to give a biblical flavor, but used them only one-fourth of the time: he would not only fail to give the flavor, he would get a bizarre result. We conclude: Luke's use of apodotic καί was not due to imitation of the LXX.

Why then did Luke use apodotic καί? Let us say, tentatively, that Luke got his καί's by translation of Hebrew sources (for that καί was not native to Aramaic).

But now another problem emerges. The use of καὶ ἐγένετο is also a marker of a Hebrew source (it appears in Aramaic only in the Targums when they are translating Hebrew closely). But Luke uses (καὶ) ἐγένετο in 20 instances in which he omits apodotic καί.[47] So, one indication

46. In Lk. 5.36 and 37.

47. In Lk. 1.8; 1.23; 1.41; 1.59; 2.1; 2.6; 2.46; 7.11; 9.18; 9.33; 9.36; 11.1; 11.27; 17.15; 19.29; 24.30; 24.51; 2.15; 9.29; 18.35.

would seem to point to the use of a Hebrew source, while the other would deny it.

However, there is a very plausible solution to the puzzle. We now know that Hebrew was in use in two forms in the first century: in a neoclassical form, and also in a more conservative form in what Fitzmyer calls 'pockets of Palestinian Jews'.[48]

In these 'pockets' people held on to the old language when most of the nation had changed to Aramaic. This shows a conservative bent. Other instances are known in which a language in cut-off areas is very conservative; thus, in some parts of the eastern USA there are areas in which a much older form of English is spoken.[49]

In contrast, it is also well established that the apodotic καί had almost vanished in the revival of the new Hebrew.[50]

So then, if Luke really did, as he says in his preface, use documents, it easily could have happened that he would have used two kinds of Hebrew documents: one with the apodotic ו, one without it. Yet in both the ויהי could occur.

Are we straining evidence like Procrustes? Not at all. First, there is no doubt that the two kinds of Hebrew existed. Further, we know definitely that the apodotic ו was almost gone in the new Hebrew;[51] but we also know that the ויהי was not entirely gone in the new Hebrew.[52] And really, this sort of difference is what one would expect: the very odd apodotic ו would more readily disappear than the not-so-strange ויהי. So we can have two kinds of Hebrew, both with ויהי, but one lacking the apodotic ו, one still able to have it, out of conservatism.

48. J.A. Fitzmyer, 'The Languages of Palestine in the First Century AD', *CBQ* 32 (1970), pp. 501-31, at p. 531.

49. Cf. H.L. Mencken, *The American Language* (New York: A.A. Knopf, 3rd edn, 1923), pp. 71-72: 'In remote parts of the United States there are still direct and almost pure-blooded descendants of those seventeenth century colonists. Go among them, and you will hear more words from the Elizabethan vocabulary, still alive and in common service, than anywhere else in the world, and more of the loose and brilliant syntax of that time and more of its gipsy phrases.' Cf. also T. Pyles, *The Origin and Development of the English Language* (New York: Harcourt Brace Jovanovich, 2nd edn, 1971), p. 273.

50. Beyer, *Semitische Syntax*, p. 67.

51. Beyer, *Semitische Syntax*, p. 67; Horton, 'Reflections on the Semitisms of Luke–Acts', p. 4.

52. Beyer (*Semitische Syntax*, p. 30) says that it retreats, 'geht...zurück', but that it does not completely disappear until the Mishna.

But we should make our percentages more precise. To do that, we begin by noticing that the nice distinction about omitting the apodotic ו before nouns and particles could fall into disuse in the course of time even in the conservative form of Hebrew. Even in classical times, these fine rules were not always observed, though they were for the most part. Now Luke, though he regularly does seem to keep the old rule of omitting καί before particles, ignores it often before αὐτός: we find that in 9 out of 17 of our clear examples of the use of apodotic καί, he has καὶ αὐτός.[53] In contrast, the Hebrew Old Testament has the equivalent apodotic ויהי infrequently.[54] So we have reason to suspect that, at least in regard to substantives, the old rules had fallen partly into disuse. If this is the situation, we can reasonably add 14 omissions (in which a substantive opens the main clause) to our previous 51 omissions— thinking the 14 omissions are not really due to classical rules. Then we would have a ratio of 65 omissions to 17 uses, which would mean Luke used the apodotic καί only 20.73% of the time.

But since we cannot be certain about the small rules, it is best for us to use a bracket, and say that Luke uses apodotic καί from 20% to 25% of the time (for, as we saw, without the extra 14 omissions, we would have 25%).

To omit the καί from 75% to 80% of the time surely means he was not using the καί to imitate the LXX.

Further reinforcement of this conclusion comes from some added facts. The typical sentence with καὶ ἐγένετο consists of three members: (1) καὶ ἐγένετο, (2) a time expression, (3) the apodotic καί with the following clause.

We turn to the second of these elements. Johannessohn tells us that the LXX prefers to translate such time expressions (which in Hebrew are commonly ב with an infinitive) by a dependent clause with a finite verb, introduced by ὡς, καθώς, ἡνίκα or ὅτε.[55] But Luke shows the reverse preference. He uses a preposition with the infinitive (commonly ἐν τῷ, corresponding to Hebrew ב with infinitive—but with no equivalent in

---

53. In Lk. 2.27; 5.1; 5.17; 8.1; 8.22; 9.51; 14.1; 17.11; 19.1; 24.4; 24.15.
54. Johannessohn, 'Das biblische καὶ ἐγένετο', p. 190. It occurs mostly only in 1 Kgs and 3 Kgs.
55. Johannessohn, 'Das biblische καὶ ἐγένετο', pp. 199, 201.
56. Johannessohn, 'Das biblische καὶ ἐγένετο', p. 199.

normal Aramaic[56]) 21 times,[57] while he has the dependent clause only 4 times, with ὡς.[58]

Now the fact that this sort of time structure is not striking means it would be a poor means of giving a biblical flavor. For certain, Luke's pattern in it is not the way to imitate the LXX, which has the reverse preference.

What is our conclusion? I suggest that we take seriously what Luke says in his prologue, namely, that he did use written sources. The sparse distribution of apodotic καί shows that he was not just imitating the LXX but was translating, and translating slavishly.[59] He must have been translating Hebrew sources at certain points, not Aramaic—for καὶ ἐγένετο, ἐν τῷ with the infinitive, and apodotic καί are not Aramaic but Hebrew. Further, because he often uses καὶ ἐγένετο without apodotic καί, he must have had two types of Hebrew sources: some in new Hebrew, some in conservative old type speech, from the 'pockets' of Hebrew.

Such slavish translation is, of course, known elsewhere, for example, in the Old Latin versions of Scripture. And the reason for its appearance is obvious and well known: the translator had such great respect for his text, and used such extreme care for accuracy that he went to the extreme of introducing foreign structures into his translation. Therefore we may assume that Luke must have been a meticulous author.

The careful analysis of Bruce Chilton, mentioned above, by showing Luke's great care to follow tradition, gives us at least some corroboration for our conclusion that Luke was meticulous. For if Luke so carefully followed tradition (as Chilton finds), then that tradition is apt to be more substantive than just imitating the LXX—it would be following traditional Semitic sources, written or oral.

What of the fact that Luke's style is so very different in different passages, that is, that he does at times write a good quality of normal

57. Johannessohn found only 19 instances. I found 21 as follows: in Lk. 5.1; 5.12; 9.51; 14.1; 17.11; 19.15; 24.4; 24.15; 1.8; 2.6; 8.40; 8.42; 9.18; 9.29; 10.38; 11.1; 11.27; 17.15; 18.35; 24.30; 24.51. The first 8 examples have apodotic καί, the latter 13 do not.

58. In Lk. 1.23; 1.41; 19.29; 2.15. No apodotic καί in these examples.

59. For an interesting discussion of the influences of bilingualism, see M. Silva, 'Bilingualism and the Character of Palestinian Greek', *Bib* 61 (1980), pp. 198-219. Of course, bilingualism could not account for using a structure only 20-25% of the time.

Greek? Could it be that Luke just *chose* to use different styles at different times? We must say no. For if it were just a *free choice* by Luke, we would have to ask: Why the choice? Writers do not normally shift style that way. Luke could hardly have chosen to imitate the LXX closely at times to provide a biblical favor, and then without reason have dropped that imitation. We could not imagine what such a reason would be. But we can, on the contrary, see a very plausible reason for the variation if we take Luke at his word and affirm that he did use documents.

JSNT 21 (1984), pp. 53-65

THE PURPOSE OF LUKE

J.L. Houlden

The title requires comment. In saying *The Purpose of Luke*, the intention is not to exclude Acts but to direct attention behind the writings to the author and his setting. And in speaking of 'purpose', two things are in mind. First, this article is a reaction to Robert Maddox's study, *The Purpose of Luke–Acts*,[1] which was, in my terms, largely devoted to the purpose of Luke. Secondly, while plainly it is unsatisfactory to isolate it from other matters, the present concern is with only one aspect of Luke's purpose, namely his attitude towards Judaism. The contention is that on this subject Maddox has told only part of the tale and omitted its more remarkable and problematic aspects. If we take note of those aspects, then we find in Luke evidence of a quite distinctive element among the range of early Christian attitudes and opinions on this matter. We find also that we are confronted with some teasing hermeneutical and theological questions.

What would Maddox have us believe? He himself is reacting to those, notably Jervell and Kilpatrick,[2] who have presented a strongly Jewish view of Luke; that is, that far from being the Gentile enthusiast, intent on demonstrating God's grand design whose climax and goal is the Gentile mission, Luke is out to show how God fulfils his purpose for his

---

1. (Edinburgh: T. & T. Clark, 1982). Robert Maddox died in the same year.
2. Ch. 2 of Maddox's book is chiefly in view. The works in question are J. Jervell, *Luke and the People of God* (Minneapolis: Augsburg, 1972), and G.D. Kilpatrick, 'On γραμματεύς and νομικός', *JTS* 1 (1950), pp. 56-60; *idem*, 'The Gentile Mission in Mark and Mark xiii.9-11', in D.E. Nineham (ed.), *Studies in the Gospels* (Festschrift R.H. Lightfoot; Oxford: Basil Blackwell, 1955), pp. 145-58; *idem*, 'Mark xiii. 9-10', *JTS* 9 (1958), pp. 81-86; *idem*, 'λαοί at Luke ii. 31 and Acts iv. 25-27', *JTS* 16 (1965), p. 127; *idem*, 'The Gentiles and the Strata of Luke', in O. Böcher and K. Haacker (eds.), *Verborum Veritas* (Festschrift G. Stählin; Wuppertal: Brockhaus, 1970), pp. 83-88.

people Israel, a process which involves associating Gentiles with Israel. No, says Maddox, that goes much too far. Luke's apparently pro-Jewish elements are not to be explained thus. Judaism is fulfilled but also superseded in the new Christian community. Though no one can deny the thoroughness of Luke's presentation of the Church's Jewish antecedents, this is accounted for by nothing more positive than the wish to describe clearly the foundations of the glorious new structure which has arisen. His dominant attitude to the Judaism of his day is hostile and is marked above all by the theme of judgment. The teaching of Jesus and the missionary work of the early Church are full of the conviction that Judaism is under judgment for its rejection of Jesus and of the message that stems from him. The theme is plain, from the sequel to Jesus' Nazareth sermon in Luke 4, when his end is dramatically foreshadowed, to the final episode in Acts, when Paul, addressing a large gathering of Jews, quotes Isaiah's testimony to their blindness to the purposes of God. It is indeed already adumbrated in Simeon's words to Mary (2.34). And it is reiterated not only frequently but with great severity, especially when God's judgment is seen (so it appears) through the events of AD 70 (19.43-44).

As far as social and religious setting is concerned, Maddox suggests that the emphasis on this doctrine is explained by the need to fortify Christians against Jewish propaganda. In the face of a newly regrouped Judaism, towards the end of the first century, some Christians may have felt uncertain about their status as God's people. As Maddox represents their inner questioning: 'How could non-Jews hope to find any value in something which has its roots in Judaism, yet seems to be repudiated by the leaders of the Jews?' (p. 184). In this case, as Maddox points out, the problem is not unlike that faced by Paul in Romans, only 'the breach with Judaism is now wider and deeper; for Luke there is apparently no longer any reason to hope that the Jews as a whole will accept the gospel'.

Now all this evidence is of course undeniable. The only question is whether Maddox has placed it in the correct focus. Two factors raise the suspicion that he has not. The first of a more general character, and in its case the suspicion may be capable of being allayed. The other specific, and, on the principle that it is narrow gates which lead to good effects, this is the one on which to concentrate.

The general factor may be stated in the form of a question: Has Maddox's picture done justice to the positive aspects of Luke's portrayal of Judaism? These fall into a number of categories which admit of different explanations in terms of Luke's theological or ecclesiastical position.

There is first his striking picture of the scale of the Christian mission's success in the Jerusalem area. The three thousand converts of Pentecost (Acts 2.41) are shortly followed by five thousand more (4.4) and the 'large crowd' of priests referred to in 6.7. By 21.20, it is a matter of μυριάδες, a term plainly intended to convey the impression that the Jerusalem church became a major community in that city. The impression is fortified by elements in the Gospel, where, notably in the Passion Narrative, Luke introduces signs of support and pity for Jesus among the populace. The weeping of the women of Jerusalem (23.27-28) forms a counterpart to Jesus' own earlier weeping over Jerusalem (19.41), and the crowds go home after the crucifixion 'beating their breasts' (23.48).

This material sits uneasily with the blanket condemnations of Israel elsewhere; and if Luke's dominant attitude towards Judaism is to emphasize God's well-merited judgment upon it, then it is hard to understand his deliberate introduction of episodes which point the mind in another direction. The success-story of Acts is certainly easier to explain than the Gospel material which, perhaps wrongly, I have linked with it. Even reprobate Judaism yielded converts, Luke may be saying— brands snatched in advance from imminent burning. Though he pays little attention to Jewish converts in the Gentile world (there are Aquila and Priscilla, 18.2; Crispus, 18.8; and the anomalous Apollos, 18.24— otherwise, apart from this curious concentration in ch. 18, only generalized references), Luke could not deny the existence of such converts in Jerusalem. Yet he seems to go out of his way to draw attention to their strength, as indeed to their continued zealous adherence to the Law (21.20). One way or another, both in the time of Jesus and in the time of the Church, Luke does not see the judgment on Judaism as incompatible with substantial Jewish support for Jesus and the Christian cause.

There is, secondly, Luke's depiction, unparalleled in the New Testament, of the solid Jewish background to Jesus and the Church. The birth stories provide the major evidence, supported by the genealogy, which, however, transcends mere Jewishness, in tracing Jesus' ancestry back to Adam and so to God himself, Adam's creator-father. According to Luke, Jesus springs from the most unimpeachable and devout Jewish setting. Of David's line, he is related to a working priest of the Temple, and his birth in such a context is endorsed by angels from on high. The Temple continues to figure in his infancy and childhood, as the holy man Simeon and the prophetess Anna, stepping out of the past in order to illuminate the present, endorse his role; and the child Jesus learns Torah from the horse's mouth, as the patient tenant of his father's house.

Now all the material of this kind might be aimed to say no more than that Jesus and his message fulfil Judaism. But that was a truism by the time of Luke, and in his first two chapters Luke may be said both to labour the point and, in a sense, to make it less clear than he might have done. If, as Maddox suggests, his aim was to reassure Christians that they were God's true people and Jewish attacks were to be rejected, it might be felt that Luke's approach in those chapters is too gentle and eirenical, too little directed to show how Jesus fulfilled the Scripture, in a word too unlike Matthew. If resistance to a Jewish cause is to the fore, then these stories seem somewhat casual as a way of stating it.

A third aspect of Luke's positive portrayal of Judaism deserves note. Not only Jesus but also his followers lean, in certain respects, in a Jewish direction. The notable case is the obscure episode of Paul's nazirite vow, so hard to credit as an action of the historical Paul (Acts 18.18); and there is also both Paul's and the apostles' earlier temple-attendance (Lk. 24.53; Acts 2.46; 3.3; 5.21, 42; 21.26), which, in view of the parallel material concerning Jesus in Luke 1–2, it is hard to see as free from deliberate point, whatever its historical basis. It is true that in the case of Paul's purificatory visit in Acts 21.26, as in his adoption of the Pharisaic banner in 23.6, his behaviour may be seen as purely opportunistic and no deep doctrine may be implied. But the other statements, especially the concluding verse of the Gospel, surely indicate a positive attitude to the Temple, which is at first sight oddly at variance with both Jesus' condemnatory prophecies of its destruction (Lk. 21.6) and Stephen's speech in Acts 7.

As in relation to the other matters, Luke's demonstrable selectivity means that his inclusion of this material cannot be put down to mere faithfulness to the facts. It is deliberate and is, to say the least, confusing to readers who are, if Maddox is right, meant to be strengthened in their anti-Jewishness.

It seems then that if Luke's dominant view of Judaism is that it lies under God's judgment, even if he also believes it to be the progenitor of Christianity, he has laid a number of false trails and gone to unnecessary lengths to create a quite different and more positive impression.

So much for the general factor which raises a certain suspicion that Maddox's account is unsatisfactory. The specific factor pointing in the same direction concerns four statements, which then lead to a consideration of others, less immediately striking. They are: (1) 'Father, forgive them, for they know not what they do' (Lk. 23.34); (2) 'Lord, do not hold this sin against them' (Acts 7.60); (3) 'I know that you acted in ignorance, as did also your rulers. But what God foretold by the mouth of all the prophets, that his Christ should suffer, he thus fulfilled' (Acts 3.17); (4) 'For those who live in Jerusalem and their rulers, because they did not recognize him nor understand the utterances of the prophets which are read every sabbath, fulfilled these by condemning him' (13.27). The first is of course dubious textually, and perhaps one of the strongest arguments for its authenticity is simply its part, alongside Acts 7.60, in a pattern of parallels between the passion of Jesus and that of Stephen.

The four passages state a remarkable doctrine. Though Luke can maintain that Jesus was 'crucified and killed by the hand of lawless men' (Acts 2.23; cf. 3.14), nevertheless two factors set their wicked act in a special light. In the first place, it happened 'according to the definite plan and foreknowledge of God' (2.23), a point made also, in one way or another, in the two most striking of the four passages before us, Acts 3.17 and 13.27. In the second place, the act is excusable on the ground of ignorance; and perhaps the same idea is implicit in Stephen's petition (7.60). The persecutors were not culpable, even acted in good faith, and may be forgiven by the powerful prayers of righteous men, as Scripture taught (Prov. 15.29; Ps. 34.15; cf. Jas 5.16). And it will not do to say (as is sometimes said) that Luke differentiates between the Jewish rulers, who are wicked, and the people at large, who are either fickle or virtuous; for in the two Acts speeches (chs. 3 and 13) the rulers are specifically included in the exoneration, as they are by implication in the petitions of Jesus and Stephen. Luke's teaching is that though the Jews as a body, or perhaps Judaism as an institution, are under heavenly judgment, as the events of AD 70 have made abundantly plain, nevertheless even those who killed Jesus cannot be held responsible, and both they and Stephen's persecutors are able to be forgiven by God. As one begins to praise Luke more for his charity than his coherence, other evidence makes the picture even stranger.

From the point we have reached, we may see Luke developing his view in two directions. As to responsibility for Jesus' death, it is not merely the Jews, rulers and people alike, who are discharged; it is also those of Jesus' own entourage, who in the earlier Gospels are heavily and deliberately involved in guilt. Judas the betrayer acts not of his own volition, but because Satan 'entered into him' (Lk. 22.3)—though, as with the Jews, that did not prevent his subsequent ghastly fate. Yet even so that fate is not presented as an act of divine retribution, as it surely is in Matthew (27.3-10; cf. 16.27), but as a kind of accident, humanly speaking, which occurs in fulfilment of Scripture (Acts 1.16-20). As for Peter the denier, he too is 'got at' by Satan (22.31) and lapses only temporarily by reason of cowardice, as do the sleeping disciples on the Mount of Olives who are overtaken by grief or, perhaps better, the stress (λύπη) of the situation (22.39-45).[3] Taking the evidence as a whole, Luke's position seems to be that it is none other than God, by his scripturally promulgated purpose, who is fully responsible for the death of Jesus, assisted by what can only appear as a Book-of-Job-like, cooperative Satan. The point is most clearly made in Lk. 24.26: 'Was it not necessary that the Christ should suffer these things, and enter into his glory?' (cf. 24.44; Acts 2.23). At some stage, the question must be faced, whether Luke has reached this position with full deliberateness or by a series of vagaries, so that it is the unfortunate result of his having been moved by a number of other motives, such as the wish not to present the future leaders of the Church in a bad light. It is a position whose various aspects do not on the face of it readily cohere, and one is inclined to settle for the view that Luke is simply better at stories than at concepts.

The exoneration of Jesus' crucifiers connects not only with that of other participants, but also with some of the positive elements which we observed in Luke's attitude to Judaism. Though there is clearly a distinction between, for example, the supportive women of Jerusalem and the elders, chief priests and scribes who condemn Jesus, yet they all receive a welcoming and tender response from Jesus. Even the worst in Judaism, it seems, let alone the best, is within the scope of salvific treatment, even though judgment must also be endured.

Now it may be that the forgiving attitude displayed by Jesus and Stephen (supporting Lk. 23.34 to be authentic) is to be viewed in a christological or ethical perspective, and not at all in relation to the

---

3.   See B.E. Beck, *'Imitatio Christi* and the Lucan Passion Narrative', in W. Horbury and B. McNeil (eds.), *Suffering and Martyrdom in the New Testament* (Festschrift G.M. Styler; Cambridge: Cambridge University Press, 1981), pp. 39-40.

question of attitudes to Judaism. That is, Jesus is shown practising, even in his extremity, what he had preached (cf. Lk. 6.27-28, 37). Or else, he demonstrates, for consumption by Luke's readers, the way a Christian should endure suffering and death. As perhaps, in his extensive reporting of Paul's trials, he is providing guidelines for potential martyrs. Undoubtedly, these elements play a part; but they do not necessarily exclude the Jewish perspective which, on any showing, is present in Luke's mind as he considers where (if anywhere) guilt is to be assigned. It is not as if forgiveness of persecutors was part of the stock-in-trade of martyrdom. Jesus shows no hint of it in the other Passion Narratives, despite Matthew's stress in his Gospel on the duty of forgiveness and love for enemies (but Matthew 23 shows that he was not imaginative in applying that injunction). Nor do the Maccabean martyrs: they are much more inclined to die breathing threats of retribution. Nor exactly do the righteous in the Wisdom of Solomon, a work which may have contributed much to Luke's picture of Jesus, even to his substitution of δίκαιος for υἱὸς θεοῦ in the centurion's saying at the cross, terms which in Wisdom are synonymous to describe God's faithful ones.[4] So if the dying petition for forgiveness is a distinctive feature in Luke, it needs explaining. It is certainly of a piece with his other ethical emphases (on generosity, humility and patience), but it may also both contribute to and be dictated by his beliefs about those within his story most obviously and controversially in need of forgiveness, namely the Jews who rejected Jesus to the point of death and killed Stephen his follower. It seems that the prayers for forgiveness uttered by Jesus and Stephen cannot be categorized merely as shining examples, much less as illustrations of piety in extremity. Their role is more serious and more significant doctrinally: their place is where we have put them—with the two Acts statements exonerating the Jews on the grounds of ignorance.

Let us now pause to survey the perhaps incongruous elements which can be discerned in Luke's attitude to Judaism:

1. Judaism is, profoundly and pervasively, the historical and religious rock from which Jesus was hewn.

2. Judaism, in noble exemplars alive at the time, welcomed his birth.

3. Judaism was the source of many of the Church's early adherents, above all in Jerusalem.

---

4. Lk. 23.47. See Beck, '*Imitatio Christi* and the Lucan Passion Narrative', pp. 28-47.

4. Even in his lifetime, Jesus was met, even to the end, with sympathy as well as hostility and misunderstanding from Jews.

5. The Scriptures of Judaism have been fulfilled by Jesus.

6. Christians share important tenets with Pharisees, notably belief in resurrection.

7. While Christians are severely critical of the Jewish Law where they encounter it, especially with regard to circumcision, sabbath and table fellowship with Gentiles (i.e., where it specially impinges on the Gentile mission), they do not reject it root and branch and (in a perspective not easy to elucidate) do endorse parts of it, even including some of its dietary provisions.

8. Judaism, in the purposes of God, is (and has been shown to be by the time Luke writes) under judgment, and Jesus foresaw this. Indeed, as Stephen's speech shows, grave inadequacies have long been present. Nevertheless, Jesus saw this coming fate as not only inexorable but deeply regrettable: it was no cause for vindictiveness or grim sense of retribution, much less satisfaction. In Luke, he wept over Jerusalem (19.41). It is, it seems, to be accepted as part of God's inscrutable purpose as flowing from Jesus' death, which is itself necessary as part of his journey to glory, which is his goal.

9. So Jesus (and the Church) is not so much hostile to Judaism as able to look back upon it (or across to it) as playing a necessary part in God's plan; and the Church stands on its shoulders. Thus, both Jesus and the apostles visit the Temple as of right—it is the Father's house; and teach there, as of right. By Acts 15, the Church, now a Jew-Gentile amalgam, has come of age: the child has eclipsed the parent in the parental home. This may be the point of the Apostolic Decree, which, like so much in Luke, is to be seen in a historical perspective and not, as it appears, in relation to observance of Torah. Its source is not in misty Noahic commands but in Deuteronomy 12, where, on the eve of entry into the land (and surely the Church fulfils that type), Israel is urged to abstain from idolatry and, while eating what they will (clean and unclean persons alike), to abstain from blood (Deut. 12.16). The Council is the Church's coming of age as the fulfiller and heir of Israel.[5]

10. Jesus (and the Church) is not even hostile to those in Judaism who are most clearly due for condemnation. On the contrary, their fault

---

5.   This view is well argued in the unpublished Oxford D.Phil. thesis by J.L. Keedy, *St Luke's Account of the Travels of St Paul* (1970).

was excusable, their forgiveness is sought. God's ways are indeed inscrutable.

It remains to ask in what perspective these varied elements may be held together; and then, in what Lukan situation this perspective may best be envisaged. If the choice is merely between Luke's being pro-Jewish and anti-Jewish, then incongruity is inescapable. If Luke is pro-Jewish, why the severity of his prophecies of judgment and the anti-Temple speech of Stephen? True, by various devices, these elements can be explained, most commonly by appealing, especially in the case of Acts 7, to sources which Luke has only imperfectly tailored to his doctrines. On the evidence of his Gospel, it seems improbable that Luke would do any such thing. In relation to our own question, there is evidence in the Gospel of his care in adapting his material to his doctrinal ends, especially with regard to audience, as Maddox himself has shown (p. 48). If Luke is anti-Jewish, then his demonstration of Christianity's Jewish antecedents and connections is too thorough and extensive, while still being in some ways inadequate (especially in relation to the detailed fulfilment of Scripture). This simple choice is too straightforward and too constricting.

Two suggestions may enable us to vindicate Luke's intelligence and coherence.

1. Luke's Christians were not directly involved in Jewish relations. While of course the issue of the relationship of the Church to Judaism was not dead and there may well have been occasional flurries and debates, such direct relations were not a major feature of life—unlike the situation among their near-contemporaries, the Johannine Christians, as the Fourth Gospel was being formed. There is an element of detachment, a certain lack of passion in the Lukan attitude. Jews are not hated, because there are others more worth worrying about. 'The Jews' are viewed in a predominantly historical perspective—for what they have been more than what they are. It is true that they rejected Jesus; but in so doing they fulfilled their mysterious God-given destiny and made possible that movement to the Gentiles, which is reiterated in Acts (13.46; 18.6; 28.28) as the key turning-point that made possible the Church as Luke knows it. For this, it is impossible to feel hatred for them; and calm tolerance may, for certain reasons, spill over into exhortation to welcome and forgiveness.

2. The 'certain reasons' concern the chief source of threat as far as Luke was concerned. It came from within, as he shows Paul foreseeing

in his one speech to a Christian audience. Addressing responsible leaders, Paul puts his finger on the coming danger from Christians 'speaking perverse things' (Acts 20.30). And for Luke, I suspect, it was all too true, part of that general crisis in the Church of the late first and early second centuries about the location of authority, when there were diverse views on what Christianity really was.

Inevitably, an essential aspect of that uncertainty, an ingredient in the diversity, was the matter of how Christianity related to Judaism, both in the past (i.e. in relation to Scripture and to Jesus) and in the present (i.e. as two increasingly distinguishable institutions). As we know, or else, where ignorant, surmise, almost every possible position on the subject was taken by some Christian group or other. It would be astonishing if it was left to Marcion to feel that one option was to cut wholly free from Jewish roots and to make of Christianity what was, in effect, the cult of Jesus the saviour who had come out of the blue. It would be almost equally astonishing if such Christians did not look to Paul, viewed through spectacles of their own manufacture, as their inspiration—a Paul who had abandoned the Law and fought Jewish Christians.

Luke's complex posture in relation to Judaism makes considerable sense if viewed as an answer to this teaching. It is an answer from the point of view of one who believed above all in the continuity of the God of the Scriptures with the God of Jesus and the Church. Quite how and why he believed in the vital nature of this continuity and what other beliefs were involved, it is not easy to say. C.H. Talbert, for example, has suggested that an over-realized eschatology was part of the picture and that Luke wished to show that a due historical process must be traversed before the End arrived.[6] Perhaps Luke's determination on this matter arose from his own Jewish background: he is at home in the language and content of the Septuagint and perhaps of other Jewish literature.[7] But his sympathies are wide and his precise provenance is not to be identified. Even his exact relation to the Pauline circle is unclear, though Maddox is convinced that the 'we' element in Acts identifies him as a member of that circle (p. 7). In relation to our suggestion concerning his main interest, he certainly wishes to show Paul as thoroughly

6.   C.H. Talbert, 'The Redaction Critical Quest for Luke the Theologian', in D.G. Miller (ed.), *Jesus and Man's Hope*, I (Pittsburgh: Pittsburgh Theological Seminary, 1970), pp. 171-222.

7.   See the presentation in J. Drury, *Tradition and Design in Luke's Gospel* (London: Darton, Longman & Todd; New York: Charles Scribner's Sons, 1976).

agreeable to his views, and it is not fanciful to see him as looking at Paul in no less inaccurate a perspective than the pre-Marcion Marcionites whom we are postulating. Each side may be seen as taking away one part of Paul's legacy, and, in each case, misrepresenting him.

If this is at all correct, it explains the tightrope Luke walks in relation to our question—just as Matthew, adapting Mark, walked a parallel tightrope in relation to another aspect of the same issue, more directed in his case to the status and observance of the Jewish Law. For Luke, having the concerns which have been suggested, it will not do to be plainly anti-Jewish: the opponents needed no encouragement in that direction. Nor will it do to be plainly pro-Jewish: the facts of Christian origins, above all the fate of Jesus, and of heroes like Stephen, forbade it. What was required was an account of Christian beginnings, especially a historically oriented account, which demonstrated not so much the mechanical fulfilment of prophecies, for they depended for their force on an essentially Jewish approach to Scripture, as the rootedness of Jesus in a warm and attractive Jewish piety. This is precisely the appeal of the Lukan birth stories. And the Lukan genealogy, tracing Jesus back to Adam who transcends the Jew-Gentile divide, but by way of David and Abraham, so that the Jewish point is safely made, reinforces the case, but subordinately, so that it is placed later, in ch. 3.

The puzzling motif of the exoneration of the Jews who crucified Christ may mean that Luke presses one step further. Perhaps he was not only dissuading Christians from an easy dismissal and condemnation of Judaism as a whole, such as Matthew, from a different angle, perpetrated (27.25), but also offering an olive-branch, keeping a path open, which Jews might tread towards the Church, on the basis of a common acceptance of God's inscrutable purposes fulfilled in Christ. If relations with Judaism were the sole interest of Luke–Acts, it would be possible indeed to suggest such an objective as an alternative explanation of the evidence bearing on this subject. But it is not, and, taking the work as a whole, it seems unlikely that it is addressed (primarily, at least) to any other than a Christian audience.

Our problem from the start has been: How does Luke wish his Christians to regard Jews and Judaism? And the answer seems to be that he urges them, on the basis of an essentially historical orientation which alone can serve his purpose, not to abandon their Jewish origins and background. It is much harder to say precisely why he thought this so vital: it has the appearance of an axiom and no theory is provided beyond that of divine purpose revealed in Scripture to await its fulfilment. It is even harder to say whether in some deeper sense he was right theologically, or even whether he gave a workable account of the relationship between Judaism and Christianity. At least it has the merit of a considerable measure of charity.

Finally, it is necessary to say something about the theological aspect which has just been mentioned. It is perhaps the most problematic of all. If this presentation of Luke's setting and intentions were correct, what would it tell us about him as a theologian in the strict sense? It may indicate that his view of God was simply not coherent at all: he allowed it to be thrown into confusion by inferior considerations of policy. But if we strive to give him the credit of having a coherent theology, then it seems to be one which shrugs off all hope of a rational theodicy and, not far removed from the conclusion of Job, sees great events as the responsibility of an inscrutable God whose ways are not our ways and whose thoughts are not our thoughts. He alone brought about the death of Jesus (all others being but unwitting tools), with some Satanic abetting, for the sake of his age-long, deep-laid purposes of salvation. It is a conclusion that makes the sunny, Hellenistic optimism, which many find so congenial in Luke, appear to be a thin veneer. Perhaps it was Luke's religious and dramatic concentration on the heavenly exaltation of Jesus which made it possible for him to be content to leave the mind of God in obscurity: all that really mattered was the clear outcome of the intentions of that mind.

Yet that explanation seems not wholly satisfactory. Perhaps we should refuse to let the doctrinal interest pursue an independent path. That way lies anachronism and an artificial abstraction from life. The doctrine in Luke is surely related to his practical concerns, and it may be that his belief about God's working is, when interrogated, less coherent than we could wish, not simply the result of following one venerable strand in Jewish teaching. It may be also the result of his chief interest lying elsewhere than in the relations of Christians and Jews. The focus of his anxiety is rather, as we have seen, on the differences among Christians, and it is in that perspective that other matters are viewed. In that interest, one may even seek to allay the fears and resentments of Jewish Christians who, with lingering loyalty to their race, felt threatened by the taunts and accusations of the increasing body of Gentiles in the Church, above all perhaps for the crucifixion of Jesus. In other words, in Acts we witness one testimony to the shift of interest in the Church from the conflict with Jews to its own internal disputes, a shift so clearly visible as the Johannine community moves from the time of the Gospel to the time of the Epistles. Internal conflict was, of course, not new—it went back to the time of Paul. What was new was that now it was in the context of a Church much clearer about its separateness from Judaism. In that new distinctiveness, there was less worry about Jews and more energy available for the fresh and never-ending problem of preserving Christian unity and identifying orthodoxy.

APPENDED NOTE

The Wisdom of Solomon, already briefly referred to, may have a bearing on the attitudes which are so problematic in Luke. In Wis. 2.22, we read of the ungodly who persecute the righteous: καὶ οὐκ ἔγνωσαν μυστήρια θεοῦ. Read in conjunction with 3.10, this makes plain that the ungodly both act in ignorance and are punished for their deed. It is virtually the position of Luke, and it may incline us to ascribe his attribution of ignorance to the Jews less to his almost proverbial *mansuetudo* than to a kind of convention or at any rate to a less smiling attitude.

Then, while the NEB takes τοῦ δικαίου (3.10) as neuter (justice, what is right), perhaps Luke (assuming he knew the text) read it as masculine. For Luke, Jesus is ὁ δίκαιος—perhaps for the centurion (23.47) and certainly in Acts (3.14; 7.52; 22.14); and the first use of it may, as we saw, indicate that for him it is the equivalent of υἱὸς θεοῦ. In any case, as a christological term in Luke, it seems to obey the same law as other such expressions in early Christianity: that is, a general term acquires a specific, titular role by its application to Jesus.[8]

Finally, it is interesting to wonder whether the Lukan version of the words that follow the Parable of the Sower owes anything to Wis. 2.22; for Mark's μυστήριον (4.11) he substituted γνῶναι τὰ μυστήρια (8.10). But it may be more convenient to find here ammunition for the view that Luke knew Matthew, who made the identical amendment (13.11).

8. For discerning discussion on this general point, see M.D. Hooker, *The Message of Mark* (London: Epworth Press, 1983), pp. 64-65.

JSNT 22 (1984), pp. 53-80

THE LAW IN LUKE–ACTS

Craig L. Blomberg

Introduction

Luke has the most conservative view of the Mosaic Law of any New Testament writer. Such is the thesis of Jacob Jervell in a series of articles recently collected into his book, *Luke and the People of God*.[1] Jervell defends this thesis most directly in his chapter on 'The Law in Luke–Acts'.[2] Until very recently his work has been the only modern study exclusively devoted to this precise topic;[3] Jervell nevertheless has built on a foundation broad enough to allow David Catchpole to speak of a 'quite remarkable consensus' of scholars which sees Lukan theology in several places as 'fundamentally Mosaic', most notably in Luke's account of the apostolic decree which demands of Gentile Christians that they fulfill that part of the Mosaic Law relevant to them. Catchpole cites as representatives of this consensus, *inter alios*, T.W. Manson, W.G. Kümmel, F. Hahn, L. Goppelt, G. Bornkamm, and H. Conzelmann.[4] Other important studies coming to similar conclusions include Philipp Vielhauer's programmatic essay, 'On the "Paulinism" of Acts', in which he concludes that Acts portrays Paul 'as a Jewish Christian who is

1.   Minneapolis: Augsburg, 1972.

2.   Pp. 133-51. This essay appeared earlier in *HTR* 64 (1971), pp. 21-36.

3.   No similar titles appear in the comprehensive bibliography of Lukan theology in G. Schneider, *Die Apostelgeschichte*, I (HTKNT, 5.1; Freiburg: Herder, 1980), pp. 29-48. Mention must now be made, however, of M.M.B. Turner, 'The Sabbath, Sunday, and the Law in Luke/Acts', in D.A. Carson (ed.), *From Sabbath to Lord's Day* (Grand Rapids: Zondervan, 1982), pp. 99-157. Turner's study is in various respects both narrower and broader than this present one, but his main conclusions coincide remarkably with the independently attained ones offered here.

4.   D.R. Catchpole, 'Paul, James and the Apostolic Decree', *NTS* 23 (1977), pp. 428-29.

utterly loyal to the law',[5] and the recent book by Gerard S. Sloyan, *Is Christ the End of the Law?*, which summarizes the picture of Jesus in Luke's Gospel as one of complete faithfulness to the Law without even a trace of reinterpretation beyond that which was already well known in certain contemporary Jewish circles.[6]

However, students of Lukan theology are now heavily indebted to Stephen G. Wilson's latest monograph, *Luke and the Law*, which subjects Jervell's thesis to a penetrating critique.[7] Wilson concludes that Luke's view of the Law is not nearly so one-sided, noting his many negative as well as positive attitudes toward the Jewish laws and customs. Yet he believes the emphasis remains on the latter, 'that is, the criticism of the law is generally implicit and has to be read between the lines, whereas the affirmation of the law is generally explicit'.[8]

Unquestionably the Mosaic Law plays a distinctive role in Luke's two-volume work. From the infancy narratives to the closing speeches of Paul, Luke portrays believers in the Christ as faithfully adhering to the Law in a wide variety of ways not described identically elsewhere. To begin with, many ordinary Jewish folk receive warm commendation for their faithful observance of all the Lord's commandments and ordinances. Luke calls Elizabeth and Zechariah both 'righteous' and 'blameless' (Lk. 1.6). Six times in Luke 2, Mary and Joseph perform rites which Luke describes as according to the Law or the custom of the Law (vv. 22, 23, 24, 27, 39, 42). Luke also describes Simeon and Anna as righteous and devout and faithful in all the activities of temple worship (2.25, 37). At the end of his Gospel, Luke describes Joseph of Arimathea as 'good and righteous' (23.50) and adds that the women who followed Jesus to the cross rested on the sabbath 'according to the commandment' (23.56). Finally, Luke singles out Gentiles for special mention as God-fearers and lovers of the Jewish nation, especially praising the two centurions of Luke 7 and Acts 10.

Secondly, Luke omits or shortens several narratives which in Mark or Matthew highlight Jesus' criticism of the Law. Thus in the controversy

5. In L.E. Keck and J.L. Martyn (eds.), *Studies in Luke–Acts* (London: SPCK, 1968), p. 38.

6. Philadelphia: Westminster Press, 1978, p. 59.

7. S.G. Wilson, *Luke and the Law* (SNTSMS, 50; Cambridge: Cambridge University Press, 1983).

8. Wilson, *Law*, p. 58.

story with the Pharisees on plucking grain on the sabbath (Lk. 6.1-5), Luke omits Jesus' crucial claim that 'the sabbath was made for man, not man for the sabbath' (Mk 2.27). Mark's account of Jesus' teaching on ritual defilement and purity (7.1-23) disappears altogether from Luke's Gospel, unless Lk. 11.37-41 preserves certain reminiscences of it. Luke also reduces his material on Jesus' criticism of the Old Testament divorce laws from Mark's eleven verses (10.2-12) to only one verse, which is probably non-Markan (Lk. 16.18).[9]

Thirdly, Luke goes to great lengths to emphasize how the Jewish-Christians in the early church did not transgress the Mosaic Law, but faithfully kept its various injunctions. When Stephen's accusers maintain that he has blasphemed 'against Moses and God' and taught that Jesus had promised to 'change the customs which Moses delivered to us', Luke hastens to add that these accusers were false witnesses (Acts 6.11-14). Paul too is regularly charged with teaching men 'to worship contrary to the law' (18.13) and 'to forsake Moses' and his customs (21.21). Yet Luke repeatedly portrays Paul as unequivocally denying these charges, declaring before Felix, 'I worship the God of our fathers, believing everything laid down by the law or written in the prophets' (24.14); before Festus, 'Neither against the law of the Jews, nor against the temple, nor against Caesar have I offended at all' (25.8); before Agrippa, 'I stand here...saying nothing but what the prophets and Moses said would come to pass' (26.22); and before the Jewish leaders in Rome, 'I had done nothing against the people or the customs of our fathers' (28.17). At the same time Luke provides ample positive evidence to sustain Paul's claims as he depicts Paul worshipping in the synagogue (13.14), circumcising Timothy (16.3), assuming a private vow (18.18), and purifying himself with and paying the expenses for four men who themselves had a vow for the express purpose of proving to the Jewish Christians in Jerusalem that he lived 'in observance of the Law' (21.23-24). Nor was Paul the first to behave in this way in Acts. Right from the start, Luke summarizes the activity of the Jerusalem church as including daily temple attendance (2.46; 3.1) and observances of the laws of ritual purity (note Peter's presuppositions in 10.9-16, 28, and the church's reaction in 11.2-3).

---

9.   On the tradition history of this verse, see esp. H. Schürmann, ' "Wer daher eines dieser geringsten Gebote auflöst..." ', in *Traditions-geschichtliche Untersuchungen zu den synoptischen Evangelien* (Düsseldorf: Patmos, 1968), pp. 126-36.

Finally, Luke formulates key summaries of the earliest proclamation (both pre- and post-Easter) in terms of continuity with the Old Testament Law. In addition to the above excerpts from Paul's defense speeches, one finds reference to Jesus approving a lawyer's summary of the way to inherit eternal life in terms of keeping the commandments (Lk. 10.25-28) and to Jesus responding in kind to the identical question from a later inquirer (18.18-20). Elsewhere Jesus declares that 'it is easier for heaven and earth to pass away, than for one dot of the law to become void' (16.17), and he immediately illustrates the point by telling a parable which concludes that Moses and the prophets are sufficient witnesses to the resurrection of the dead (16.29—cf. his teaching in 20.37). More important than these references, which have various parallels in other Gospels, are the unparalleled summaries of Jesus' post-resurrection teaching in Lk. 24.27 and 44. 'And beginning with Moses and all the prophets, he interpreted to them in all the Scriptures the things concerning himself.' And again, 'everything written about me in the law of Moses and the prophets and the psalms must be fulfilled'. Finally in Acts both Peter and Stephen see in Jesus just such a fulfillment of the Mosaic Law when they cite the promise of a prophet like Moses (Deut. 18.15-20) as a reason for heeding the words of Jesus (Acts 3.22; 7.37).

To what do all of these details add up? Are Jervell, Vielhauer, Sloyan, and the consensus claimed by Catchpole correct? Does Luke disclose a theology in which Jewish and Gentile Christians must each keep those parts of the Mosaic Law relevant to them, adding simply the belief in the resurrected Jesus as the promised messiah? Or, following Wilson's more nuanced approach, even if the Law is not required, does Luke still emphasize that it is 'appropriate to the expression of Jewish and Jewish-Christian piety'?[10] Not all would agree. In fact, until recent years most commentators did not think the question of the Law a very important one for Luke at all.[11] J.M. Creed, for example, could write fifty years ago that 'the Pauline controversies about the Law...are not determining factors in St Luke's presentation of the Gospel story'.[12] In

10. Wilson, *Law*, p. 104.

11. R. Banks, *Jesus and the Law in the Synoptic Tradition* (SNTSMS, 28; Cambridge: Cambridge University Press, 1975), p. 6.

12. J.M. Creed, *The Gospel according to St Luke* (London: Macmillan, 1930), p. lxxi.

his important recent monograph, *Jesus and the Law in the Synoptic Tradition*, Robert Banks comes to much the same conclusion, as he not only challenges the 'consensus' that Luke's theology of the Law is very conservative, but also believes that the issue of the Law is very much in the background of Luke's Gospel, emerging only when 'it serves to point up the saving, preaching and healing ministry of Christ, and the corresponding stress upon love and compassion in his teaching'.[13] Others have explained Luke's view of the Law in terms of some type of typological or midrashic correspondence between Jesus and Moses,[14] between the travel narrative and Deuteronomy,[15] between Luke and the entire Pentateuch and between Acts and scattered sequences and motifs from the Old Testament,[16] or between all of Luke–Acts and the Exodus.[17] Clearly the role of the Law in Luke–Acts requires some further careful attention. Moreover, a weakness of almost all of the studies mentioned so far is their lack of close analysis of the function of the various verses and passages on the Law in the structure and progression of Luke's thought. Wilson explicitly admits that his systematic, rather than consecutive, discussion 'can result in distortion';[18] at the very least it would seem beneficial to have both types of studies in order to compare results. Perhaps, therefore, more helpful insights will emerge if the data are examined sequentially as they appear in Luke–Acts, which is surely the better method to determine the impression Luke's work would have made on his original audience.

13.   Banks, *Jesus*, p. 172. G.W.H. Lampe, *St Luke and the Church of Jerusalem* (London: Athlone, 1969), argues that the Law is a very minor issue for Luke, and that what he does say about it stems from his major interest in Jerusalem.

14.   E. Franklin, *Christ the Lord* (London: SPCK, 1975), pp. 72-73; E.L. Allen, 'Jesus and Moses in the New Testament', *ExpTim* 67 (1955–56), pp. 104-106.

15   C.F. Evans, 'The Central Section of St Luke's Gospel', in D.E. Nineham (ed.), *Studies in the Gospels* (Oxford: Basil Blackwell, 1955), pp. 37-53; J. Drury, *Tradition and Design in Luke's Gospel* (London: Darton, Longman & Todd, 1976), pp. 138-63.

16.   M.D. Goulder, *The Evangelists' Calendar* (London: SPCK, 1978), pp. 73-104; *idem*, *Type and History in Acts* (London: SPCK, 1964).

17.   J. Mánek, 'The New Exodus in the Books of Luke', *NovT* 2 (1957), pp. 5-23. The scope of this essay does not permit a detailed consideration of each of these views. Suffice it to say that none has commanded widespread acclaim, and all depend on the presence of parallels between Luke and the Old Testament which are occasionally quite obvious, but more often than not barely perceptible.

18.   Wilson, *Law*, p. 12.

Analysis

Keeping the Law, as noted above, certainly plays an important role in Luke's infancy narratives. In praising the piety of people like Zechariah and Elizabeth, Luke can employ strong words (δίκαιος, ἄμεμπτος) without any hint of the Pauline criticism of Jewish righteousness so well known to readers of passages like Romans 2 and 3.[19] Yet despite these repeated references to the faithfulness to the Law of these humble Jewish people, the emphasis of Luke 1 and 2 falls much more on the coming dawn of a new day, the fulfillment of the promises of redemption long awaited, and the inauguration of a new relationship between God and his people. The various hymns or canticles repeatedly echo these themes as they speak of the remembrance of God's mercy (1.54, 72), salvation for Israel and Gentiles alike (1.68, 79; 2.30-32), and the forgiveness of sins (1.77). This last verse, which also refers to the knowledge of God, brings to mind Jeremiah's new covenant,[20] which was further to involve some kind of change in the relationship between God's people and God's Law. Thus while Luke 1 and 2 offers no positive proof for any coming changes in the Law and even portray pious folk obeying the Law as the appropriate way of serving God at that time, these chapters nevertheless point forward to the advent of a new age. Should changes in the Law be forthcoming, therefore, the reader should not be unprepared for them.

Pau Figueras has recently pointed out some parallels (of quite uneven value) between Simeon and Anna and Moses and Elijah, respectively. Figueras argues that for Luke, Simeon and Anna represent the Law and the prophets which testify to Christ.[21] One of the most interesting parallels comes between the final visions granted to both Moses and Simeon. Like Moses surveying the promised land from afar just before he dies, so Simeon cradles the babe who is to grow up into the long-awaited

---

19. Cf. J. Ernst, *Das Evangelium nach Lukas* (RNT; Regensburg: Pustet, 1977), p. 58, on Lk. 1.6: 'Von der paulinischen Kritik an der jüdischen Gesetzlichkeit ist hier noch nichts zu spüren'.

20. So also I.H. Marshall, *The Gospel of Luke* (Exeter: Paternoster Press, 1978), p. 93.

21. P. Figueras, 'Syméon et Anne, ou le témoignage de la loi et des prophètes', *NovT* 20 (1978), pp. 85-86.

Messiah just before he departs 'in peace'.[22] Figueras's conclusion that
the Law can now be jettisoned, since its role as the precursor of grace is
fulfilled,[23] cannot be justified on the basis of these narratives alone. But
again, if Luke were to teach such a doctrine elsewhere, his careful
readers ought not to be surprised.

In Luke 3 and 4 the new age arrives, climaxed by Jesus' stunning
declaration of the fulfillment of Isa. 61.1-2a in the very hour of his
preaching in the Nazareth synagogue. Lk. 4.31–5.16 then presents a
sample of Jesus' ministry of exorcism, healing, and miraculous power
and authority which his audiences acknowledge as unparalleled (4.36;
5.8-11, 12). No mention of the Law appears in these passages, except
for Jesus' charge to the newly cleansed leper to show himself to the
priest and to make the offering 'as Moses commanded, for a proof to
the people' (5.14). But this last phrase does not suggest that Jesus is
concerned to fulfill the detailed stipulations of the Law.[24] He has already
unnecessarily risked defilement by touching the leper (v. 13—cf. the
unclean woman touching Jesus in 8.44 and Jesus taking the hand of
Jairus's apparently dead daughter in 8.54).[25] Rather the leper's cure
could not be proven to the people until the priest had officially declared
him clean, thereby formally allowing him to return to society.[26]

The next set of passages do deal very directly with Jesus' attitude
toward the Law. Lk. 5.17–6.11 provides a series of controversy stories
with Pharisees and scribes (also known as 'teachers of the law' [5.17]),
in which Jesus repeatedly displays his authority over and above both
the oral and the written law. In forgiving the paralytic's sins, while
Jesus transgresses no commandment, he certainly claims an authority
which can only be justified if in fact he is in some way divinely

22.   Figueras, 'Syméon', p. 90.
23.   Figueras, 'Syméon', p. 98.
24.   *Contra*, e.g., Ernst, *Lukas*, p. 191.
25.   In each of these instances it could be argued that since Jesus' touch produced
instant healing, then he never actually became ritually unclean. But if he was trying to
encourage the people to obey the Law, then he chose a very counterproductive method
of communicating his intentions.
26.   G.B. Caird, *The Gospel of St Luke* (London: A. & C. Black, 1968), p. 98. It is
also possible that the phrase refers to 'evidence to the people of the messianic act
of God in Jesus' (so Marshall, *Luke*, p. 210, following H. Schürmann, *Das
Lukasevangelium*, I [HTKNT, 4.1; Freiburg: Herder, 1969, p. 277], but the text does
not demand this approach).

commissioned.[27] In the calling of Levi, Jesus stirs up Pharisaic discontent by incurring uncleanness when he eats and drinks with 'tax collectors and sinners'. This expression presumably refers to those Jews who, like the Gentiles, had been living ritually unclean lives.[28] In reply to the disciples of John, Jesus stresses the newness of the present age and the impossibility of combining old and new. Luke heightens this sense of newness by adding a verse peculiar to his Gospel in which Jesus comments ironically on the Jews who refused to taste the new wine of his message (5.39).[29]

It is possible to argue that in each of these three pericopes Luke imagines Jesus as transgressing only the oral and not the written law, but there is no hint in the texts that he distinguishes between the two.[30] In the next controversy story, however, Jesus clearly appears to violate the Old Testament sabbath law. Many commentators agree that plucking grain constituted harvesting,[31] and harvesting was definitely forbidden in the Torah (Exod. 16.25-26; 34.21—both before and after Sinai!). Moreover, Jesus' first reply to justify his behavior appeals to a scriptural precedent from the life of David which Jesus specifically says involved that which was not lawful.[32] And the law which David broke could only have been the Torah (Lev. 24.5-9).[33] Finally, Luke's omission of Jesus'

27. Jesus' own words suggest that he understood this prerogative to stem from his being the Son of man (5.24). Cf. Marshall, *Luke*, pp. 210-11.

28. W.R. Farmer, 'Who Are the "Tax Collectors and Sinners" in the Synoptic Tradition?', in D.Y. Hadidian (ed.), *From Faith to Faith* (Pittsburgh: Pickwick Press, 1979), pp. 167-74. *Contra* K.H. Rengstorf, 'ἁμαρτωλός', *TDNT*, I, p. 328, who sees disregard only for Pharisaic principles here.

29. Cf. Marshall, *Luke*, pp. 227-28.

30. Cf. S. Westerholm, *Jesus and Scribal Authority* (Lund: Gleerup, 1978), p. 91.

31. An important exception is Carson, 'Jesus and the Sabbath in the Four Gospels', in Carson (ed.), *From Sabbath to Lord's Day*, p. 61. Cf. also A.T. Lincoln, 'From Sabbath to Lord's Day: A Biblical and Theological Perspective', in Carson (ed.), *From Sabbath to Lord's Day*, p. 361. Carson and Lincoln argue that Jesus never broke the letter of the law during his life because the new covenant was not inaugurated until after his death.

32. Cf. Turner, 'Sabbath', p. 104: 'The point at issue is that the two leaders of Israel, David and the Son of Man (though probably in very different degrees), have an authority that at least occasionally (and in Jesus' case perhaps permanently) transcends the law and the institutions revealed therein'.

33. Cf. Westerholm, *Jesus*, p. 98, where David's example is cited as a case 'where the letter of the Torah is broken'.

statement about the sabbath being made for man does not tone down the radical nature of Jesus' words. If anything, as Banks points out, it causes his declaration, 'the Son of man is Lord of the sabbath', to follow from the illustration about David as conclusion from premise. Thus Luke brings out all the more clearly that Jesus takes a position above the Law, 'so that it is incorporated into an entirely new framework and viewed from a quite different perspective', namely, 'Christ's estimate of the situation'.[34] Attention once again must turn to the question of Jesus' remarkable authority, which surpasses that of anything or anyone in all of Jewish history.

In the final pericope of this section Luke relates the first of three sabbath healings performed by Jesus (6.6-11; cf. 13.10-17; 14.1-6). In these passages one can only demonstrate Jesus to have broken the oral law, but it is not at all obvious how Jervell can claim that the main principle Jesus enunciated was that his behavior was what the written Law demanded.[35] Jesus' own explanation seems rather to depend on the claim to be able himself to perceive what the right thing to do is, regardless of any existing laws, oral or written. In 13.16, for example, Jesus appears to be leading up to an *a fortiori* argument, but rather concludes with a simple common-sense appeal, 'And ought not this woman...be loosed...?'

The theme of Jesus' remarkable authority continues to dominate the subsequent chapters of Luke's Gospel. The sermon on the plain, the healings in Capernaum and Nain, the reprise of the Nazareth synagogue speech for the benefit of John's disciples, and Jesus' scandalous behavior at table with Simon the Pharisee all give rise to the question voiced at the end of this section, 'Who is this...?' (7.49). Through his first seven chapters Luke has set the pace for his entire work which, far from disclosing a nomistic theology, reveals Jesus breaking down legal barriers and shattering Jewish stereotypes rather indiscriminately. But at the same time he is the fulfillment of the hopes of the 'people of the land' who yearn for the redemption promised in the Old Testament. And Jesus is no antinomian. In Lk. 10.25-28 he strongly affirms the double love-commandment and in his subsequent parable of the good Samaritan endorses the broadest possible definition of the neighbor to whom one is required to apply that commandment.

34.   Banks, *Jesus*, pp. 122-23.
35.   Jervell, *Luke*, p. 140.

Again in 11.42, in reprimanding the Pharisees for neglecting justice and the love of God, Jesus at the same time reminds them to continue practicing what Matthew's version considers the less weighty matters of the Law (Mt. 23.23). Yet in Luke's context, the 'other things' not to be neglected (v. 42b) do not obviously refer to anything besides the various tithes mentioned in v. 42a. Moreover, in v. 41 Luke has a phrase not found in the other Gospels: 'and behold, everything is clean for you'. Some scholars argue that v. 41a, 'But give for alms those things which are within', is a mistranslation of an Aramaic original which read, 'purify those things which are within'.[36] There is, however, no manuscript evidence for this suggestion, and it seems more likely that Luke's version is designed to state more plainly what Matthew only implied (23.25-26), that Jesus is turning an illustration about ritual purity into a more widely applicable statement about moral purity.[37] In this view, v. 41b potentially contains some very radical implications concerning the need for the cleanliness laws, paralleled only by Mark's obviously *ex post facto* reflection in Mk 7.19b: 'Thus he declared all foods clean'. Luke makes nothing of this development at this point but proceeds immediately to unleash a scathing attack on Pharisaic and scribal behavior in vv. 42-52. Again one should not be taken aback if later in his writing Luke should support a neglect of ritual cleanliness altogether. Luke's omission of Mk 7.1-23 forms part of his 'great omission', and is no doubt to be explained by one of the reasons advanced for his omitting that entire section, rather than by assuming that he wanted to tone down Jesus' radical teaching concerning the law.[38]

In Lk. 16.16, Jesus utters yet another strikingly radical statement. 'The law and the prophets were until John; since then the good news of the kingdom of God is preached, and everyone enters it violently.' Regardless of whether John is to be seen as belonging with the law and the prophets or with the kingdom of God,[39] and regardless of how one

36. Creed, *Luke*, p. 166; Caird, *Luke*, p. 158.

37. Westerholm, *Jesus*, p. 87; J. Neusner, '"First Cleanse the Inside"', *NTS* 22 (1976), pp. 486-95.

38. See, e.g., the various explanations of Drury, *Tradition*, pp. 96-103; A.Q. Morton and G.H.C. Macgregor, *The Structure of Luke and Acts* (London: Hodder & Stoughton, 1964), pp. 23-33, as well as those of the classic four-document hypothesis.

39. For the former alternative, see H. Conzelmann, *The Theology of St Luke* (London: Faber & Faber, 1961), pp. 22-23; E.E. Ellis, *The Gospel of Luke* (NCB;

interprets βιάζεται in v. 16b,[40] this much seems clear: at least two ages are in view, Jesus belongs to the second age, and that second age has in some way superseded the first age, the age of the law and prophets.[41] Now Jervell denies that v. 16 views the law and prophets as an 'epoch'; he believes that v. 17 proves that Luke believed the Law to be eternally valid.[42] Yet v. 17 only says that the Law will not 'fail' (πεσεῖν). The Matthean form of the saying (Mt. 5.18) and the parallelism between v. 17a and v. 17b suggest that πεσεῖν means substantially the same thing as παρελθεῖν,[43] which Siegfried Schulz rightly interprets in an apocalyptically motivated and pregnant sense. In other words the Law is valid in the age of this world. But with the end of this 'Weltzeit' and the arrival of the kingdom of God and the Son of man, the Mosaic Law loses its validity and becomes superfluous.[44] Thus, *contra* Jervell, v. 18 is not an example of how for Luke Jesus preserves the Mosaic Law unchanged. Granted, the saying differs from Mk 10.11-12, but it nevertheless prohibits what Deuteronomy 24 permits, even as does the Markan passage. Banks rightly sees v. 16 as the main point Luke wants

London: Oliphants; Grand Rapids: Eerdmans, 1974), p. 204. For the latter alternative, see Marshall, *Luke*, p. 628. W. Grundmann, *Das Evangelium nach Lukas* (THKNT, 3; Berlin: Evangelische Verlagsanstalt, 1961), p. 323, takes a mediating position, calling John the 'eschatologische Grenzscheide zwischen den Zeiten'.

40.   *In malam partem*, Ellis, *Luke*, pp. 204-205 (as criticism of the Pharisees); F.W. Danker, 'Luke 16.16—An Opposition Logion', *JBL* 77 (1958), pp. 236-37 (as criticism from the Pharisees). *In bonam partem*, G. Schrenk, 'βιάζομαι, βιαστής', *TDNT*, I, p. 612 (middle voice); G.E. Ladd, *The Presence of the Future* (London: SPCK, 1974), p. 166 (passive voice).

41.   Cf. D. Guthrie, *New Testament Theology* (Leicester: IVP, 1981), p. 679: 'This presumably means that Old Testament revelation has given place to the revelation of Jesus Christ. The one prepared the way for the other. Some indication of this may be seen in the wineskins illustration that Jesus used... '

42.   Jervell, *Luke*, p. 140, and nn. 35, 150.

43.   S. Schulz, *Q: Die Spruchquelle der Evangelisten* (Zürich: Theologischer Verlag, 1972), p. 114, who also suggests that the words may be translation variants.

44.   Schulz, *Q*, p. 116; Ernst, *Lukas*, p. 470; Grundmann, *Lukas*, p. 324; and on the original form of the saying, B.D. Chilton, *God in Strength* (SNTU, 1; Freistadt; Plöchl, 1979; repr. The Biblical Seminar, 8; Sheffield: JSOT Press, 1987), p. 230. Cf. Creed, *Luke*, p. 206, who comments that the new order does not abrogate the Law; the Law stands since it has been fulfilled. The topic of divorce is introduced 'as a striking instance of conflict between the teaching of Jesus and the Jewish law. Therefore it is set side by side with the assertion of the permanence of the law in order to affirm the paradoxical claim that the law is at once ended and in force.'

to stress, but even his judgment—that vv. 17-18 probably results from Luke's faithfulness to tradition even when not yielding to his particular concerns—seems too cautious.[45] Verses 17-18 do illustrate the principle of the new age announced in v. 16, but vv. 17–18 also remind the reader that the Law has not passed away without failing to accomplish everything for which it was intended (cf. Mt. 5.18).

Lk. 18.18-30 narrates a second instance of Jesus answering the question of how to inherit eternal life. As in Lk. 10.25-28, Jesus' reply appeals to the Law, this time to the fifth to the ninth commandments of the decalogue. Yet, as Banks observes, this reference to the Law 'is primarily intended as an endorsement of its value as a testimony to or its forming a springboard for, the more ethically demanding and uniquely personal claim which follows'.[46] The ruler has claimed to have kept all the commandments, and nothing in the text challenges his claim. But Jesus' verdict still renders him outside the kingdom of God (vv. 24-25). The Lukan form of the Last Supper narrative further suggests that Luke, even perhaps more than Mark, is emphasizing that which is new about Jesus' ministry. In the longer text of the words of institution, the originality of which has been ably defended by several recent writers,[47] Jesus proclaims, 'This cup which is poured out for you is the new covenant in my blood'. Here the reference to Jer. 31.31-34, implicit in Lk. 1.77, becomes explicit.[48]

Finally, Luke closes his gospel by summarizing Jesus' post-resurrection ministry in terms of his teaching his disciples to interpret the Old Testament christologically.[49] Indeed this is a prophetic-christological interpretation, for all of Scripture is seen as prophecy, pointing forward

45. Banks, *Jesus*, p. 220.

46. Banks, *Jesus*, p. 164.

47. J. Jeremias, *The Eucharistic Words of Jesus* (London: SCM Press, 1966), pp. 142-52; H. Schürmann, 'Lk. 22.19b-20 als ursprüngliche Textüberlieferung', in *Untersuchungen*, pp. 159-92. Cf. more briefly, I.H. Marshall, *Last Supper and Lord's Supper* (Exeter: Paternoster Press, 1980), pp. 36-38; Ernst, *Lukas*, p. 584; Ellis, *Luke*, p. 255.

48. Cf. Marshall, *Luke*, p. 801.

49. See D.L. Baker, *Two Testaments, One Bible* (Leicester: IVP, 1976), for a survey and evaluation of the various christological (as well as other) understandings of the relationship between the testaments. The term is used here merely as a shorthand description of the contents of Lk. 24.25-27 and 44-47.

to the forgiveness of sins to be accomplished by the Christ.[50] Luke says nothing directly about the relevance of the commandments in the Mosaic Law, but presumably they too are fulfilled in Christ, leaving open the possibility, and perhaps even the probability, that the requirements of the new age might in some way be different. Now Wilson believes that the predictive and prescriptive functions of the Law are left uncorrelated,[51] and this is an accurate description of Luke's explicit discussion. Implicitly, however, a correlation does seem present. Certain laws are fulfilled in Christ's ministry and sacrifice and therefore are not required of Christian believers, as the church of the book of Acts will eventually discover. Others are fulfilled in Christ's ethical demands, summarized by the love commandments cited by Jesus in Luke 10 and 18. Indeed Luke, by introducing his lengthy travel narrative which contains almost exclusively teaching material, seems to suggest that Jesus' own words and not the Law are the commandments of the new covenant.[52] This supposition is strengthened if Lampe is right in identifying the prophecies of Lk. 24.47 as including Mic. 4.1-2 and Isa. 2.2-4 where the proclamation to all nations beginning from Jerusalem is precisely the proclamation of the Law.[53]

The last verse of Luke leaves the disciples in the temple praising God (24.53), which is no doubt what they continued to do as the book of Acts opens with them waiting in Jerusalem, as Jesus commanded, for the coming of the 'promise of the father' (Acts 1.4). Little wonder then that Luke includes in his first summary of the activity of the church that they attended the temple together daily (Acts 2.46). Yet Luke lays no stress on this fact, nor even on the fact that Peter and John went to the temple

50. R.J. Dillon, *From Eye-Witnesses to Ministers of the Word* (Rome: Biblical Institute Press, 1978), pp. 136-37.

51. Wilson, *Law*, p. 102.

52. Cf. Mt. 5.19 and the discussion in D.A. Carson, *The Sermon on the Mount* (Grand Rapids: Baker, 1978), p. 38, on 'these commandments'. Evans's approach (viewing the travel narrative as a Christian Deuteronomy) draws many more parallels than can be justified, but his general idea that Luke was highlighting the correspondence and contrast between gospel and law ('Section', p. 42) is quite reasonable. Cf. also the discussion of exodus motifs in Lk. 9 in W.L. Liefeld, 'Theological Motifs in the Transfiguration Narrative', in R.N. Longenecker and M.C. Tenney (eds.), *New Dimensions in New Testament Study* (Grand Rapids: Zondervan, 1974), pp. 162-79.

53. Lampe, *Luke*, p. 17.

at the hour of the evening sacrifice (3.1).[54] 'Theological questions about the replacement of the temple sacrifices by the spiritual sacrifices by Jesus had probably not yet occurred' to these young Christians.[55] But is Luke trying to emphasize right from the start that Jewish Christians did not forsake the religion of their fathers?[56] This seems unlikely, since the only purpose of Acts 3.1 is to introduce the miracle story and speech by Peter which follow in vv. 2-26. If anything, Luke sees the significance of the hour as the hour not of sacrifice but of prayer (v. 1), since repeatedly in Acts God works in dramatic ways when his people pray.[57]

In Peter's subsequent speech Luke recounts the first of two appeals to Deut. 18.15-20 (cf. Stephen's remarks in 7.37) to identify Jesus with the eschatological prophet that Moses promised. Some have seen these references as support for a 'new Moses typology',[58] or for a proof of Jesus' prophetic office on the basis of his resurrection (from the potential double meaning of ἀνίστημι in the quotation).[59] But surely Peter's main point (and probably Stephen's also) is that if Jesus is the prophet of whom Moses spoke, then one must carefully heed everything he says, specifically the call to repentance which summarizes Luke's understanding of the early Christian kerygma.[60] Continuity with the authority of the Old Testament Law is not the issue. The issue is the urgent appeal to the scripturally prophesied authority of Jesus' own proclamation.

In Acts 6, Luke begins to prepare his readers for the divinely commissioned expansion of the church beyond the city limits of Jerusalem (1.8), for which he sees Stephen's martyrdom as primarily responsible (8.1). Stephen's accusers maintain that he has spoken against Moses, the Law, and the customs (vv. 11, 13 and 14), terms which Luke is presumably using synonymously to include both written and oral law.[61] Luke

54. For the details of this and related ceremonies, see E. Schürer, *The History of the Jewish People in the Age of Jesus Christ* (ed. G. Vermes, F. Millar and M. Black; Edinburgh: T. & T. Clark, 1979), II, pp. 299-302.

55. I.H. Marshall, *The Acts of the Apostles* (Leicester: IVP, 1980), p. 85.

56. E. Haenchen, *The Acts of the Apostles* (Oxford: Basil Blackwell, 1971), p. 192.

57. Cf. P.T. O'Brien, 'Prayer in Luke–Acts', *TynBul* 24 (1973), pp. 111-27.

58. E.g. Allen, 'Jesus', p. 104.

59. J. Dupont, *Etudes sur les Actes des Apôtres* (Paris: Cerf, 1967), p. 249; A. Wikenhauser, *Die Apostelgeschichte* (RNT; Regensburg: Pustet, 1961), p. 61.

60. Haenchen, *Acts*, p. 209; Banks, *Jesus*, p. 77.

61. Cf. Schneider, *Apostelgeschichte*, I, p. 439; G. Stählin, *Die Apostelgeschichte* (Göttingen: Vandenhoeck & Ruprecht, 1970), p. 102.

describes these accusers as 'false witnesses' (v. 13), thereby leading some to argue that, whatever Stephen's true position, Luke wanted to portray him as quite law-abiding.[62] Against this view, however, are two important considerations. First, only part of the accusation need have been false for Luke to call the witnesses false.[63] Interestingly Luke only refers to the more specific testimony of vv. 13-14 as false and not that of v. 11.[64] Secondly, Stephen makes no unambiguous attempt to refute the charges against him in his speech, which was specifically supposed to answer the question of the high priest, 'Are these things so?' (7.1). Now some have suggested that Stephen nevertheless indirectly denies the charges,[65] and I.H. Marshall notices that the two themes of Stephen's speech correspond to the two accusations of 6.14—that it is the Jews who had not been keeping the Law and that God had never been tied down to one place of worship even in the Old Testament.[66] Yet even this does not amount to a denial of the charges against Stephen; Luke knows how to present such a denial much more clearly (cf. Acts 25.8)! Even the positive references to the Law in 7.38 and 53 imply no permanent, unalterable obedience to the Law.[67] Rather, as William Neil concludes after a useful summary of various alternative interpretations, Stephen's speech appears to be

62. So, e.g., M. Simon, *St Stephen and the Hellenists in the Primitive Church* (London: Longmans, Green, 1958), pp. 24-25, 46-48. Simon notes also that Luke omits the parallel charges against Jesus in his trial narrative to minimize any opposition to the Jewish religion in his Gospel. But J.C. O'Neill, *The Theology of Acts in its Historical Setting* (London: SPCK, 1961), pp. 73-74, rightly recognizes that had this been Luke's intention, he could have just as easily omitted all reference to the charges against Stephen here as well.

63. F.F. Bruce, *The Book of the Acts* (Grand Rapids: Eerdmans, 1954), p. 135; Stählin, *Apostelgeschichte*, p. 102; R.N. Longenecker, 'The Acts of the Apostles', in F.E. Gaebelein (ed.), *The Expositor's Bible Commentary*, IX (Grand Rapids: Zondervan, 1981), pp. 335-36.

64. Cf. Schneider, *Apostelgeschichte*, I, p. 436. W. Neil, *The Acts of Apostles* (London: Oliphants, 1973), p. 106, comments, 'if Stephen's advocacy of the Gospel is correctly reflected in his address to the Sanhedrin in chapter seven, the Jews would be entitled to treat this as blasphemy'.

65. E.g. S.G. Wilson, *The Gentiles and the Gentile Mission in Luke–Acts* (SNTSMS, 23; Cambridge: Cambridge University Press, 1973), p. 132.

66. Marshall, *Acts*, p. 132.

67. *Contra* A. George, *Etudes sur l'oeuvre de Luc* (Paris: Gabalda, 1978), p. 111 n. 3.

a subtle and skilful proclamation of the Gospel, which in its criticism of Jewish institutions marks the beginning of the break between Judaism and Christianity, and points forward to the more trenchant exposition of the differences between the old faith and the new as expressed by Paul and the author of the letter to the Hebrews.[68]

As for the reference to Deut. 18.18 in 7.37, 'For Stephen Jesus was the prophet of the final age to call to repentance, to deliver and lead God's people out of bondage, to announce the end time and to introduce the new order'.[69] In the end, though, it is not Stephen's attitude to the Law and temple which Luke describes as triggering his premature execution, but rather the confession of his vision of the 'Son of man standing at the right hand of God' (7.56).[70] One must therefore not exaggerate the importance of the question of the Law too much in either a conservative or a liberal direction.[71]

In fact, the same could easily be said about the role of the Law in all of Luke–Acts up to this point. Luke has left quite a few hints that point toward a reappraisal of the function of the Law in Jesus' teaching and in the life of the early church, but they are hardly prominent enough to suggest that Jesus' disciples ought to have abandoned any of their ancestral legal practices outright. In Acts 10, this state of affairs changes abruptly. God speaks to Peter in a spectacular vision and specifically commands him to kill and eat animals which by Old Testament standards are ritually unclean. Moreover, Peter interprets the vision to apply not only to the cancellation of dietary laws but also the abolition of the barriers banning table fellowship between Jews and Gentiles (10.28; cf. the concern of some of the Jerusalem church in 11.3).[72] Ernst Haenchen properly points out that Luke stresses the conservative piety of

68. Neil, *Acts*, p. 107. So too G.E. Ladd, *A Theology of the New Testament* (Grand Rapids: Eerdmans, 1974), p. 354; Bruce, *Acts*, 136; Wikenhauser, *Apostelgeschichte*, p. 83; Schneider, *Apostelgeschichte*, I, p. 416; M. Hengel, 'Zwischen Jesus und Paulus', *ZTK* 72 (1975), pp. 190-91, 204.

69. J.J. Scott, Jr, 'Stephen's Defense and the World Mission of the People of God', *JETS* 21 (1978), pp. 131-41.

70. Cf. Wilson, *Gentiles*, p. 136; *contra* E. Lohse, *Grundriss der neutestamentlichen Theologie* (Stuttgart: Kohlhammer, 1974), p. 63.

71. J. Bihler, *Die Stephanusgeschichte* (Munich: Hueber, 1963), p. 52; *contra* M.H. Scharlemann, *Stephen: A Singular Saint* (Rome: Biblical Institute Press, 1968).

72. Cf. Bruce, *Acts*, pp. 218-19.

Cornelius prior to his conversion (10.2, 4, 22, 30).[73] But Luke stresses even more the radical implications of Peter's vision and the descent of the Holy Spirit on Cornelius and his companions with his threefold repetition of the narrative in Acts 10, 11.4-18 and 15.7-11.[74] This last account, at the beginning of the apostolic council, not only supports Luke's emphasis that 'the Gentiles should be received into the Church without obligation to the Law',[75] but also challenges Jervell's claim that Luke did not view Jewish Christians as having also received such freedom. For Peter states plainly that the Holy Spirit 'made no distinction between us and them' (15.9; cf. v. 10).[76] Similarly Acts 19.8-10 demonstrates that, apart from possibly in Jerusalem, Luke did not imagine separate Jewish Christian and Gentile Christian communities. Yet without this division it is very difficult to conceive of the Jewish Christians still observing the entire Law of Moses which their Gentile brethren were ignoring.

The more difficult question, returning to the Acts 10 narrative, concerns the moment when God cancelled the dietary laws. Is this a brand-new decree, overturning all the previous evidence of Luke–Acts?[77] If it were, one might suspect Peter's conservatism to cause him to reject the vision as a false one or as perhaps a test of his loyalty to the Law. But in fact Peter had good precedent for obeying the heavenly voice in the teaching of Jesus in Mk 7.1-23. Moreover, it is not unreasonable to

73. Haenchen, *Acts*, p. 357.

74. P.-G. Müller, 'Die "Bekehrung" des Petrus', *Herder Korrespondenz* 28 (1974), p. 373. Müller, p. 375, further observes how this three-fold narrative parallels Luke's three-fold narration of Paul's conversion and concludes that any attempt to view Luke's portraits of either Peter or Paul as 'early catholic' must be abandoned.

75. M. Dibelius, *Studies in the Acts of the Apostles* (London: SCM Press, 1956). Cf. Dupont, *Etudes*, pp. 111-12.

76. Jervell, *Luke*, p. 146, admits that 15.10 goes against the general tendency which he perceives in Luke–Acts. But it is hardly fair for him to dismiss this verse (and 13.38 as well) by speaking of 'reminiscences and echoes from tradition... never developed into a theological concept'.

77. As Wikenhauser, *Apostelgeschichte*, p. 119, and Stählin, *Apostelgeschichte*, pp. 152-53, seem to suggest by declaring that the purity restrictions were dropped in the very moment of God's command to kill and eat. Cf. H. Conzelmann, *An Outline of the Theology of the New Testament* (London: SCM Press, 1969), pp. 147, 212, who sees this narrative and that of Acts 15 as the decisive turning points in Luke's history to show how a church which began with unquestioned adherence to the Law ended up entirely law-free.

speculate that Mark's parenthetical comment in v. 19b came straight from Petrine tradition, which had reflected back upon the significance of Jesus' teaching in light of the later vision in Acts.[78] Nor would Luke be unaware of these developments, as his own 'parallel' in Lk. 11.41 demonstrates. The Acts 10 narrative might even be Luke's 'substitute' for the Markan passage earlier omitted.

In Acts 13.16-39 Luke presents his first major sermon from Paul. This sermon concludes with the clearest parallel to Pauline thought in all of Luke's writing, considering the infrequent appearance of δικαιόω in Luke–Acts and the discussion of the role of the Law in forgiveness.[79] Vielhauer, of course, maintains that v. 39 should be interpreted to mean freedom from those things in the Mosaic Law which were unpardonable (i.e. sins with a 'high hand').[80] Vielhauer, however, stands virtually alone among recent commentators in supporting such a view.[81] The whole thrust of Lukan theology of the forgiveness of sins (cf. Lk. 1.77; 3.3; 4.18; 24.27; Acts 2.38; 5.31; 10.43; 26.18) goes against it,[82] as do Acts' doctrines of *solus Christus* (4.12), *sola gratia* (15.11), and *sola fide* (26.18).[83] Even the following quote from Hab. 1.5 (Acts 13.41) harks back to a context in which the prophet had just lamented how 'the law is slacked and justice never goes forth' (Hab. 1.4), and in which he concludes his first cycle of dialogues by declaring, 'the righteous shall live by his faith' (2.4). Both of these themes, of course, reappear regularly in the epistles of Paul (see esp. Rom. 1.16–3.20).

78. Cf. K. Lake and H.J. Cadbury, 'The Acts of the Apostles', in F.J. Foakes Jackson and K. Lake (eds.), *The Beginnings of Christianity* (London: Macmillan, 1933), I, pp. iv, 115.

79. Cf. Lake and Cadbury, 'Acts', I, p. 157; Wikenhauser, *Apostelgeschichte*, p. 157; Neil, *Acts*, pp. 159-60; and in detail, P.H. Menoud, 'Justification by Faith according to the Book of Acts', in *Jesus Christ and the Faith* (Pittsburgh: Pickwick, 1978), pp. 210-17.

80. Vielhauer, '"Paulinism"', p. 42.

81. One notable expression is Franklin, *Christ*, p. 112: 'Jesus completes what is partially realized in the Law... he remains complementary to it...'

82. Haenchen, *Acts*, p. 412, rightly comments that Luke is intending here to reproduce Pauline theology, and notes that anyone viewing these verses as support for a doctrine of incomplete justification through the Law 'imputes to him a venture into problems which were foreign to him'. H. Conzelmann, *Die Apostelgeschichte* (HNT, 7; Tübingen: Mohr, 1972), p. 85, thinks Luke's use of ἄφεσις ἁμαρτιῶν is un-Pauline but agrees that v. 39 cannot be read as Vielhauer does.

83. Stählin, *Apostelgeschichte*, p. 185.

Similar echoes of Pauline theology come from the mouth of Peter as the apostolic council gets underway in Acts 15.10.[84] John Nolland has recently shown that neither the 'yoke' nor the burden (implied by βαστάσαι) necessarily carries any negative connotations here, but only emphasizes the 'irrelevance' of the Law to salvation for either Jew or Gentile.[85] Yet Luke nevertheless has prepared his reader for the decree in vv. 19-20, which is not intended to be burdensome (μὴ παρενοχλεῖν) in any way. At this point scholars disagree sharply over the purpose and origin of the decree. Catchpole, as noted above, speaks of a consensus which sees these prohibitions as the minimal requirements for Gentiles sojourning among the Jews according to Leviticus 17 and 18.[86] These requirements, though, are hardly the only ones (if in fact that is what they are) which the Law demands of the גר (cf. Exod. 23.12; Lev. 16.19; 20.2; 22.10, 18; Num. 15.30; Deut. 16.11, 14; 26.11). Deut. 31.12 even suggests that in some way the sojourner was expected to obey all the Law. Of course, possibly the later rabbinic tradition of Noahic commands (*b. Sanh.* 56b), including these four, was already being applied to Gentile God-fearers.[87] But the entire tone of the letter which the apostles then draft (Acts 15.23-29) does not sound like even minimal 'legislation'. Verse 29 concludes merely with the mild exhortation, 'if you keep yourselves from these, you will do well'. Surely it is better to see these restrictions, as many commentators still do, as an appeal for the Gentile Christians to abstain from those practices especially offensive to the Jews for the sake of unity in table fellowship.[88] It would certainly not be easy for Jews who had become Christians to

---

84.   Lake and Cadbury, 'Acts', p. 173, call it 'in some ways the most "Pauline" in Acts'. Like Jervell, Haenchen, *Acts*, p. 446, has to explain the existence of this verse as an oversight on Luke's part; he has here 'lost sight of the continuing validity of the law for Jewish Christians'.

85.   J.L. Nolland, 'A Fresh Look at Acts 15.10', *NTS* 27 (1980), pp. 105-15.

86.   See the opening paragraph of this article. So also Franklin, *Christ*, p. 125; Haenchen, *Acts*, p. 450; M. Simon, 'The Apostolic Decree and its Setting in the Ancient Church', *BJRL* 52 (1970), pp. 459-60. See now also Wilson's extended discussion in *Law*, pp. 73-102.

87.   Stählin, *Apostelgeschichte*, p. 205.

88.   Marshall, *Acts*, p. 253; Dibelius, *Studies*, p. 97; Wikenhauser, *Apostelgeschichte*, p. 173; M. Dömer, *Das Heil Gottes* (Cologne: Peter Hanstein, 1978), pp. 173-74; E.F. Harrison, *Acts: The Expanding Church* (Chicago: Moody, 1975), p. 235; J. Munck, *The Acts of the Apostles* (AB, 31; Garden City, NY: Doubleday, 1967), p. 140; Bruce, *Acts*, p. 311; Guthrie, *Theology*, p. 686; Turner, 'Sabbath', pp. 117-18.

overcome instantly all the inhibitions which they had been trained their whole lives to view as God-ordained. And their feelings would have been all the more important to respect if, as Neil suggests, the mission to the Jews was at this stage still as promising as that to the Gentiles.[89]

Verse 21 may then be paraphrased, 'For there have been Jews in all these cities for a long time, and their respect for the Mosaic Law runs very deep indeed'.[90] This follows from vv. 19-20 more naturally then if the decree were interpreted to mean Gentile observance of the part of the Law applicable to them. For in that case, v. 21 would have to be paraphrased, 'For all the Gentiles have had plenty of opportunity to learn about what the Law commands them to do'.[91] But this paraphrase makes v. 21 speak primarily about the Gentiles and their background, while in the actual text all attention, as in the former paraphrase, is focused on the Jews and their background.[92]

The church in Antioch receives the decree with rejoicing (15.31), and Paul and his companions spread the word throughout the churches of Syria and Cilicia (15.41; 16.4). In the course of his traveling, Paul circumcises Timothy (16.3). Luke can hardly have viewed this as contradicting the decision of the Jerusalem council; his juxtaposition of v. 4 and careful explanation of Timothy's background in v. 2 make that clear. Regardless of Paul's preferences, an uncircumcised 'right hand man', who was regarded as a Jew by Jews, would have made Paul's work in the Jewish synagogues impossible.[93] Verses 2 and 4 make Vielhauer's opinion that v. 3 'fits Luke's view that the law retains its full validity for Jewish Christians' indefensible.[94]

In Acts 18.18, Luke notes in passing that Paul cut his hair at Cenchreae, for he had a vow. The reference, however, is entirely incidental and Luke makes nothing of it at all. There would certainly have been nothing un-Pauline in practicing a well known Jewish custom (cf. Josephus, *War* 2.15.1 §309-332) for thanking God for deliverance from

---

89. Neil, *Acts*, p. 171.

90. Similarly Neil, *Acts*, pp. 174-75.

91. Similarly O'Neill, *Acts*, p. 78.

92. For even less likely interpretations of v. 21, see Bruce, *Acts*, p. 312; Dibelius, *Studies*, p. 98; Conzelmann, *Apostelgeschichte*, p. 94.

93. Cf. Wikenhauser, *Apostelgeschichte*, p. 184; Stählin, *Apostelgeschichte*, p. 213; Neil, *Acts*, p. 178.

94. Vielhauer, '"Paulinism"', p. 41. So too G. Bornkamm, 'The Missionary Stance of Paul in 1 Corinthians 9 and in Acts', in *Studies in Luke–Acts*, pp. 203-204.

sickness or preservation from misfortune.[95] More questions might be raised if Paul had completed his vow with sacrifices in the Jerusalem temple, since according to Num. 6.12 those sacrifices included guilt offerings. But Luke says nothing of this, and Paul presumably ends his vow in Cenchreae,[96] not in Jerusalem, and may well have already abandoned the idea of offering sacrifices altogether. Haenchen's analysis that Luke didn't realize that such a vow was 'diametrically opposed to the Pauline doctrine of grace'[97] goes far beyond anything implied by the text. Why then does Luke mention the vow at all? Lake and Cadbury perhaps came closest to the answer. Luke included it 'not, probably, to indicate Paul's obedience to Jewish customs, but to explain his... movements', since it appears in the middle of a section of detailed travel itinerary material.[98]

Acts 21.17-26 again finds Paul involved with a vow, but the details of this story are hard to decipher. Verse 20 introduces the problem. Many of the Jewish Christians in Jerusalem are still 'zealous for the law', and have been hearing rumours which James, and apparently Luke as well, disbelieve. If the reference to Jews in v. 21 is taken literally, the accusation is patently false. Paul nowhere teaches Jews to abandon circumcision or other Mosaic laws. If the reference is to Jewish Christians, however, the matter is less certain. Yet teaching people that circumcision avails nothing (Gal. 5.6) is not quite the same as teaching them *not* to circumcise their children (Acts 21.21). Furthermore, Paul's harsh words elsewhere in Galatians must be seen in light of his opponents' attempts to link law-keeping with justification (cf. Gal. 2.16; 5.4).[99] F.F. Bruce adds that 'we have no indication in Paul's letters of his advice in these respects [the "traditional practices of Judaism as voluntary actions which might be undertaken or omitted as expediency directed"] to Jewish Christians, except that Jewish and Gentile Christians alike should respect

95.   Wikenhauser, *Apostelgeschichte*, p. 216.

96.   Neil, *Acts*, p. 199. Harrison, *Acts*, p. 282, thinks this marks the beginning of the vow, but there is no evidence that Jews ever shaved their heads at the start of such a period of time (Marshall, *Acts*, p. 300), and the imperfect tense suggests that the vow had already been underway for some time.

97.   Haenchen, *Acts*, p. 546.

98.   Lake and Cadbury, 'Acts', p. 230.

99.   *Contra* J.D. Pentecost, 'The Purpose of the Law', *BSac* 128 (1971), p. 227, who sees the issue as one of sanctification.

each other's scruples—or lack of scruples'.[100] If Luke really wanted to present Paul keeping the sacrificial law, he could have done it much more plainly. As it is, all one can derive with certainty from the text is that Paul agreed to identify himself with the four men who were under a vow, and in order to do so, agreed to pay the expenses for their sacrifices, and to purify himself so that he could enter the temple with them.[101] Verse 25 follows with needless repetition on any interpretation of the text; perhaps its presence in a 'we-source' is the best solution.[102] Luke may have retained it to create a three-fold repetition of the decree, just as he emphasized Cornelius's conversion and also Paul's conversion by three-fold repetition.[103] What Luke thought of Paul's behavior will probably never be known. Again the structural function of the passage is not to underline Paul's obedience to the Law, but rather to set the stage for his arrest and imprisonment. In fact Luke's narrative never allows Paul to carry out his plan; the scheme backfires disastrously as the crowd seizes Paul and drags him out of the temple (21.27-30).

From here Luke's story progresses rapidly and inexorably from prison in Jerusalem to Caesarea to Rome. The dominant theme in these final chapters is Paul's defense. In speech after speech Paul proclaims his innocence on the grounds of both Roman and Jewish law. Here, if anywhere, is support for Jervell's claim that Luke's Paul was and is a Pharisee faithful to everything in the Mosaic Law.[104] Yet to see the issue of the Law as the central concern of Paul's defense speeches is to overlook the repeated references to the resurrection as the focal point of controversy. In 23.6, when Paul defends himself before the Sanhedrin, it is the only issue which Luke introduces. In 24.14-25, the law and prophets testify to the resurrection of just and unjust, which again Paul claims is the key issue (v. 21). In 25.8, Paul reasserts his innocence, but the phrase, 'Neither against the law of the Jews, nor against the temple', no doubt refers back specifically to the false charges of 21.28b, and as far as Festus is concerned, it is Paul's final phrase, 'nor against Caesar', which would carry climactic import.[105] In 26.2-8 and 22-23, Paul once

100. F.F. Bruce, 'Is the Paul of Acts the Real Paul?', *BJRL* 58 (1975–76), p. 297.

101. On the various possible reasons for Paul's own purification, see Marshall, *Acts*, p. 345. Cf. Longenecker, 'Acts', p. 520.

102. Marshall, *Acts*, p. 346.

103. See above, p. 255, and n. 69.

104. Jervell, *Luke*, p. 163.

105. A.A. Trites, 'The Importance of Legal Scenes and Language in the Book of

more refers to the resurrection as the fundamental question and appeals
to the testimony of Moses and the prophets to support his belief. Here
Paul recounts his pre-Christian behavior not to justify a claim to be still
obeying the Law, but to highlight that it was not his own will, but
God's, which pulled him forcibly against his original will to break away
from the beliefs and practices of his forefathers (26.9-20).

Finally, before the Jewish elders in Rome, Paul again protests his
innocence under Jewish law, but also again redirects attention to 'the
hope of Israel' (28.20—cf. 26.6 where this phrase refers to the resurrection) as the reason why he is 'bound with this chain'.[106] Thus Paul re-
enacts in the concluding chapter of Acts the identical role played by
Jesus in Luke 24, and even by Simeon in Luke 2. All of Scripture,
including the Law, has abiding, permanent value. This value, though, is
not that of providing a list of commandments forever inviolable, but that
of prophecy—testifying to the resurrection of the dead, and therefore
specifically to the resurrection of the Christ, that 'by being the first to
rise from the dead, he would proclaim light both to the people and to
the Gentiles' (26.23).[107]

Conclusions

In some respects it is not fair to look only to Luke–Acts when trying to
understand Luke's view of the Law. One ought also to examine the
antecedent theology of the Old Testament and intertestamental literature
which influenced Luke, as well as his relationship to the thought of the
other New Testament writers, especially Paul and the author of the letter
to the Hebrews.[108] But granted the limitations of this study, certain

Acts', *NovT* 16 (1974), pp. 278-84, calls attention to the great number of terms and
motifs in these chapters which have, or can have, technical legal meanings. Trites,
p. 283, concludes that the dominance of this imagery helps Luke to show that
Christianity is not a *religio illicita*, by either Jewish or Roman law.

106. For further discussion of the centrality of the resurrection in Paul's defense
speeches, see R.J. Kepple, 'The Hope of Israel, the Resurrection of the Dead, and
Jesus: A Study of Their Relationship in Acts with Particular Regard to the
Understanding of Paul's Trial Defense', *JETS* 20 (1977), pp. 231-41.

107. Cf. P. Schubert, 'The Final Cycle of Speeches in the Book of Acts', *JBL* 87
(1968), p. 16.

108. P. Stuhlmacher, 'Das Gesetz als Thema biblischer Theologie', *ZTK* 75
(1978), pp. 251-80, has supplied such a diachronic treatment, though perhaps

conclusions nevertheless remain fairly clear. To begin with, some interpretations of the role of the Law in the New Testament find little, if any,
support from Luke's writing. In this category fall both the view that
Christianity did away with the oral law but left the written law wholly
intact and the view that Christianity rejected the ritual law (or the ritual
and civil law) but preserved the moral law unchanged.[109] In Jesus' controversies with the Pharisees, Luke makes it very difficult for his readers
to determine whether the laws Jesus broke were written or oral; Luke
apparently cares little for such distinctions. And in at least one place
(Acts 6.11-14), as Wilson emphasizes, Luke uses the terms 'Moses',
'law', and 'customs' interchangeably [110] As for distinctions between
moral and ritual law, Luke portrays Jesus challenging both, with his
teaching on divorce (Lk. 16.18) as well as on ritual cleanliness (11.37-
41), while in Acts the apostolic council rejects entirely the claim that the
Gentile believers had to keep any of the law of Moses. And the stipulations they do lay down (for whatever reason) deal primarily with ritual
matters![111]

overemphasizing the diversity of the various views. Cf. also Sloyan, *Christ*, in more
detail, but with even less satisfactory results.

109. W.G. Kümmel, *The Theology of the New Testament* (Nashville: Abingdon
Press, 1973; London: SCM Press, 1974), pp. 51-53; on the latter see Westerholm,
Jesus, p. 91, and cf. C,C. Ryrie, 'The End of the Law', *BSac* 124 (1967), pp. 239-47.
Contra L. Goppelt, *Theologie des Neuen Testaments*, II (Göttingen: Vandenhoeck &
Ruprecht, 1976), p. 623. Indeed, as Turner, 'Sabbath', p. 111, concludes, 'to bring
such categories into the discussion at this point would be "anachronistic"'.

110. Wilson, *Law*, pp. 1-11.

111. W.C. Kaiser, Jr, 'The Weightier and Lighter Matters of the Law: Moses,
Jesus and Paul', in G.F. Hawthorne (ed.), *Current Issues in Biblical and Patristic
Interpretation* (Grand Rapids: Eerdmans, 1975), pp. 176-92, has cogently argued that
the Synoptists did distinguish between the weightier and lighter matters of the Law
(cf. Mt. 23.23), as did other schools of Jewish thought in and before Jesus' day. But
he has not established anything like a one-to-one correspondence between these two
categories and the moral and ritual law. G. Wenham, *The Book of Leviticus* (NICOT;
Grand Rapids: Eerdmans, 1979), pp. 32-37, is more helpful when he suggests that
'the principles underlying the Old Testament are valid and authoritative for the
Christian, but the particular applications found in the Old Testament may not be'.
Thus, e.g., Luke can still portray Jesus and Paul quoting certain fundamental
principles from the Torah as binding in their situations—see Lk. 4.4, 8, and 12, and
Acts 23.5. Cf. W.C. Kaiser, Jr, *Toward Old Testament Ethics* (Grand Rapids:
Zondervan, 1983), esp. pp. 310-14, with C.J.H. Wright, *Living as the People of God*
(Leicester: IVP, 1983), esp. pp. 148-73.

Nor is the question of justification by law a burning one for Luke. Luke rarely even broaches the topic, and in the one place where he does so in detail (Acts 15), he makes it abundantly clear that Jew and Gentile alike will be saved 'through the grace of the Lord Jesus' (v. 11). But does Luke think that Christians (or perhaps just Jewish Christians) must nevertheless keep the Mosaic Law as 'fruits befitting repentance'? The evidence above surveyed consistently points in the opposite direction. Throughout his Gospel Luke takes pains to point out what is new about Jesus and to highlight the amazing authority which he claimed, even if the implications of this authority with respect to the Old Testament are never explicitly spelled out. Throughout Acts, while many of the first Christians continue to keep various aspects of the Law, Luke makes little of this behavior, and several of the references are remarkably incidental (3.1; 16.3; 18.18). What Luke does stress, through length and repetition of narrative, are the events which lead the early church (both Jew and Gentile) to break away from Judaism and from the Jewish Law—the ministry and martyrdom of Stephen, the vision of Peter and Cornelius's conversion, Paul's conversion, the apostolic council, and repeated rejection of Christianity by the Jews, and the ineffectiveness of Paul's defense speeches. The dominant roles which these themes play call into serious question the view that for Luke the issue of the Law is a minor, background issue. But they do demonstrate the validity of Banks's main thesis which challenges the 'consensus' that claims Luke's theology of the Law to be ultra-conservative.[112]

Even Wilson's view, which recognizes more diversity in Luke–Acts, still reverses the true emphasis of Luke's thought. Those who keep the Law throughout Luke's Gospel do so rightly, from a salvation-historical perspective; the new covenant is not inaugurated until the complex of events stretching from the crucifixion to Pentecost. Those who continue these customs in the book of Acts do so because the implications of the new covenant dawned on them only over time. Wilson almost entirely ignores these important distinctions; the tension he perceives between upholding and abrogating the Law in Luke–Acts is substantially dissipated by this observation. By the time of Luke's writing, after the events of Acts 10 and 15, it is hard to imagine his audience reading these volumes from start to finish in sequence without finding 'freedom

---

112. Cf. George, *Etudes*, p. 120, who concludes that for Luke, 'la loi juive appartient pour lui au temps d'Israël; elle prend fin avec le temps de l'Eglise'.

from the Law' the more dominant theme, and that with respect to both Jewish and Gentile Christians.

Luke's most important understanding of the Law, however, lies in a different direction altogether. This is the understanding which he presents in the infancy narratives, in the post-resurrection narratives, and especially in Paul's defense speeches. For Luke the Law is preeminently prophecy, and specifically prophecy about the coming Christ. Unfortunately Luke recounts none of the details about how Jesus interpreted the books of the Law to refer to himself, and the appeals to Scripture in the sermons in Acts generally cite passages from the prophets and psalms rather than from the Law. But it is not inconceivable that Luke's understanding might have indeed resembled that of Paul or the author of Hebrews, who delve into the promise-fulfillment scheme in more detail.[113] Luke simply does not elaborate; all descriptions of his approach will therefore leave many questions unanswered. It seems fair, nevertheless, to term Luke's view of the Law a christological one and to conclude with Basilios Stoyiannos that he 'interpreted the Law as a prophecy, a prediction of God's revelation in the person of Jesus Christ'. Thus, 'the Law remains an eternal authority, a revelation of God because it speaks about Christ. It is not its moral content that one has to preserve, but rather its prophetic character'.[114] Or as Johannes Munck puts it, the major impression which Luke conveys is that 'Jewish Christianity [and therefore, *a fortiori*, Gentile Christianity as well] had been liberated by Jesus from the Law', and this precisely 'because it read the entire Old Testament as a story about Jesus Christ'.[115]

To a certain extent, Wilson is therefore right in describing the prophetic and prescriptive aspects of Luke's view of the Law as unconnected. But at a deeper level, at a christological level, there is unity. Old Testament prophecy often juxtaposed 'foretelling' with 'forthtelling', and it is frequently unclear in a given passage which of the two functions is primarily

113. On Paul, see esp. D.R. de Lacey, 'The Sabbath/Sunday Question and the Law in the Pauline "Corpus"', in Carson (ed.), *From Sabbath to Lord's Day*, pp. 159-95; on Hebrews, A.T. Lincoln, 'Sabbath, Rest, and Eschatology in the New Testament', in Carson (ed.), *From Sabbath to Lord's Day*, pp. 197-220.

114. B. Stoyiannos, 'The Law in the New Testament from an Orthodox Point of View', *Greek Orthodox Theological Review* 24 (1979), p. 319, applying this statement to New Testament theology in general, as well as to Luke.

115. Munck, *Acts*, p. lxix. Similarly H. Hübner, *Das Gesetz in der synoptischen Tradition* (Witten: Luther Verlag, 1973), p. 208.

in view. For the pious Israelite, however, the prophecy remained God's word in either case, to be believed and/or obeyed. So also Luke sees *all* of the Hebrew Scriptures (Moses, prophets, and Psalms) as fulfilled in Christ—in his commandments and ethical instructions as well as in his actions in life and death. Just as New Testament historical narrative fulfills Old Testament prophecy, New Testament ethical instruction fulfills Old Testament Law. Similarly, Wilson's verdict that 'Luke did not intend to offer a consistent view of the law'[116] is only partially adequate. Luke is no more or less consistent than any other New Testament writer; Matthew, Paul, and the author of Hebrews, for example, are equally notorious for upholding the authority of the Law while radically transforming its application (cf. esp. Mt. 5.17–20 with 21-48; Rom. 3.10-20, 31 with 21-30; Heb. 8.8-12 with 7, 13). The 'inconsistency', perhaps better termed a 'tension', is thoroughly biblical, because the very notion of the new covenant as 'fulfillment' of the old involves both a termination of temporary provisions as well as the preservation of the purposes behind those provisions, albeit sometimes in drastically altered forms.

This study has intended to deal rather exclusively with Luke's own views, without addressing the question of how accurately Luke has characterized the actual course of events during the life of Jesus and the early church. But if the results which have emerged are valid, that is, if Luke's main concern on the topic of the Law has been to describe the origins and underline the significance of a law-free Christianity, then his repeated references to conservative teaching and behavior with respect to the Law acquire a strong likelihood of historicity. This applies especially to the very incidental references, in light of the importance which historians regularly attach to 'unintentional' testimony.[117] And it is these references, not those more critical of the Law, which are often labeled inauthentic or unhistorical.[118]

116. Wilson, *Law*, p. 51.

117. See M. Bloch, *The Historian's Craft* (Manchester: Manchester University Press, 1954), pp. 60-61; C.F.D. Moule, *The Phenomenon of the New Testament* (London: SCM Press, 1967), pp. 56-76.

118. Thus, e.g., R.H. Fuller, *A Critical Introduction to the New Testament* (London: Gerald Duckworth, 1966), p. 44, includes such 'rejudaization' among his criteria for inauthenticity. Such elements ought rather to be seen as very primitive; could the criterion be re-labeled 'pre-Christianization' and applied as a criterion of authenticity, at least as far as Luke's works are concerned? Cf. further Munck, *Acts*, pp. lxvii-lxx.

Be that as it may, Luke's emphasis remains one of portraying Christianity as free from the Law as a regulatory code of behavior. The early church had not arrived at that stage without conflicts, setbacks, or compulsion from without. But in Luke's view, perhaps above all as a result of Jesus' own teaching, the first Christians developed a predominantly christological view of the Law which, as Frances Young observes, 'was a natural extension of the primitive kerygma that the Scriptures had been fulfilled'.[119] The Law was not abolished but it was no longer directly relevant for the church *apart from* its fulfillment in and interpretation by the Lord Jesus.

119. F.M. Young, 'Temple Cult and Law in Early Christianity', *NTS* 19 (1972–73), p. 331.

JSNT 34 (1988), pp. 21-46

THE 'LEAVEN OF THE PHARISEES' AND 'THIS GENERATION':
ISRAEL'S REJECTION OF JESUS ACCORDING TO LUKE

David P. Moessner

'Now when all the λαός and the tax collectors heard this, they declared
God to be right' (Lk. 7.29a—Galilee). 'And immediately he received his
sight... And all the λαός... gave praise to God' (18.43—Journey). 'So
all the λαός would rise early in the morning...to hear Jesus in the
Temple... But the chief priests and the scribes were searching for a
possible way to kill him, since they were afraid of the λαός' (21.38–
22.2—Jerusalem). Thus Luke builds his carefully connected narrative of
Jesus (1.1, 3) to the decisive showdown: the expectant, enthusiastic
people of Israel—who from the first days in Galilee have been 'hanging
on' every word of Jesus (e.g. 4.37—reports everywhere in the surrounding region; 5.26—amazement seized all; 6.17-18; 7.11; cf. 3.21;
19.48)—pitched against a recoiling leadership that also from that
Galilean 'springtime' had been scheming to end Jesus' public influence
(5.17—Galilee, Judea, Jerusalem!; 5.21; 6.7). But surely Luke proceeds
quickly to destroy any credible plot that has thickened when he has
Pilate in 23.13 summon 'the λαός' along with their 'chief priests and
rulers' to have the whole gathering (παμπληθεί) not once, not twice,
but three times all together cry out for Jesus' death (23.18, 21, 23).
'Their presence here is strange', comments Marshall on 'the λαός' in
v. 13.[1] 'Auffällig ist das Zusammenrufen der Behörden und des Volkes',
observes Schweizer.[2] A variety of explanations, both theological[3] and

1. I.H. Marshall, *The Gospel of Luke* (NIGTC; Exeter: Paternoster Press, 1978),
p. 858.
2. E. Schweizer, *Das Evangelium nach Lukas* (NTD, 3; Göttingen:
Vandenhoeck & Ruprecht, 1982), p. 234.
3. E.g. R.J. Karris, *Luke: Artist and Theologian* (New York: Paulist, 1985),
p. 91: 'It seems that the power of darkness has vanquished all humanity'; cf.

source traditional,[4] have been offered for the presence of the λαός before Pilate. But there is growing sentiment that, for whatever reason, Luke has given his story an unfortunate 'twist'.[5] For within the interaction of characters and events of the plot development Luke simply has not provided his readers with an adequate or at least consistent explanation of the λαός's demand for Jesus' death. Perhaps Luke himself was at a loss to comprehend what he possibly could not deny from his source(s).

The situation does not seem to be much better with Luke's handling of the 'Pharisees'. In the Galilean phase, 4.14–9.50, the word occurs some eleven times in six different settings. In four of these scenes the Pharisees are linked with 'the scribes' (οἱ γραμματεῖς, 5.21, 30; 6 7; νομοδιδάσκαλοι, 5.17; or νόμικοι, 7.30), while in the first, the Levi meal, the Pharisees are said to have 'their scribes' present with them (5.30).[6] Once the Journey section begins (9.51–19.44), Luke retains this tandem in three settings (11.37-54; 14.1-24; 15.2 with 16.14 in 15.1– 17.10), whereas the 'Pharisees' are mentioned in four audience arenas without explicit reference to any scribes (12.1 in 12.1–13.9; 13.31-35; 17.20 and 18.10, 11 in 17.20–18.14; 19.39 in 19.28-40). As in the Galilean portion (9.22), the scribe(s) (i.e. a νόμικος, 10.25) are depicted once without the accompanying religious label. These facts are misleading, however, unless it is also pointed out that in both sections Pharisees never seem to be very removed from the scribes in the way Luke has plotted his story. For instance in the controversy over the disciples eating grain on the sabbath (6.1-5) the mention of only 'Pharisees' who protest this sabbath infraction (v. 2) follows on the heels of the

K.H. Rengstorf, *Das Evangelium nach Lukas* (NTD, 3; Göttingen: Vandenhoeck & Ruprecht, 1955), pp. 262-63; F. Danker, *Jesus and the New Age* (St Louis: Clayton, 1972), pp. 233-34; W. Grundmann, *Das Evangelium nach Lukas* (THNT, 3; Berlin: Evangelische Verlagsanstalt, 8th edn, 1978), pp. 425-26.

4.   E.g. J.A. Fitzmyer, *The Gospel according to Luke X–XXIV* (AB, 28A; Garden City, NY: Doubleday, 1985), pp. 1483-84; Marshall, *Luke*, p. 858.

5.   E.g. J. Kodell, 'Luke's Use of *Laos*, "People", Especially in the Jerusalem Narrative (Lk. 19, 28–24, 53)', *CBQ* 31 (1969), pp. 327-43, e.g. p. 332: 'The use of *laos* here seems a serious discrepancy in Lucan style'; Grundmann, *Lukas*, p. 425: 'auffällige Bemerkung'; G. Rau ('Das Volk in der lukanischen Passionsgeschichte, eine Konjektur zu Lc 23.13', *ZNW* 56 [1956], pp. 41-51) proposed an emendation of τὸν λαόν to τοῦ λαοῦ, although there is no textual support for it; see also nn. 1 and 2.

6.   That Luke understands the three terms as semantically functional equivalents is clear by 5.17 → v. 21; 11.45-46 → v. 53.

Pharisees *and their scribes* 'murmuring' against Jesus' disciples' lack of culinary scruples (5.27-32) or of fasting (5.33-39). And Luke follows the sabbath controversy with yet another dispute over sabbath conduct in which it is clear that both 'the scribes and the Pharisees' 'were now in the process of watching (παρετηροῦντο) him' 'in order to find reason to take him to court' (6.7, 6-11). Or again the meal of the 'sinner' with Simon the Pharisee (7.36-50) appears to be a one-act dramatization of the foil between the 'tax collectors and sinners' of the λαός, on the one side, and the Pharisees *and* scribes, on the other, that the narrator has boldly introduced in 7.29-30 and continues to develop in 7.31-35, 36-50. Similarly in the Journey narrative, at least two of the four 'singular appearances' either immediately follow the the activity of both Pharisees and scribes together as in 12.1, where Jesus warns the disciples against 'hypocrisy' (cf. 11.37-54), or directly anticipate the appearance of both groups as in 13.31-35 → 14.1-24, where they are 'watching' (παρα-τηρέομαι, 14.1) to 'trip Jesus up'.

Consequently it is all the more striking, not to say singularly strange, that once Jesus enters the Temple precincts and proceeds to encounter 'scribes' (five instances of γραμματεῖς: 19.47; 20.1, 19, 39, 46) and then is hauled before the Sanhedrin and then Pilate where 'scribes' are accusing him (γραμματεῖς: 22.66; 23.10; cf. 22.2), nowhere do we come across the term 'Pharisee'. The final occurrence of φαρισαῖος (-οι) is back in 19.39 before Jesus enters the Temple from the descent of the Mt of Olives. Often 'theological' explanations are given.[7] Now, however, there seems to be little if any uneasiness among the exegetes concerning Luke's literary skills or the consistency of the portrait that he has painted. Rather, for one reason or another, Luke intentionally absolves the Pharisees from direct involvement in the arrest and execution of Jesus, and/or he knows from his sources that Pharisees befriend and even defend the Christian movement (e.g. Acts 5.34-40; 23.9)— despite the fact that in at least one of his probable sources Pharisees are directly involved in the efforts to arrest Jesus (Mk 12.13-17), while

---

7.　E.g. H. Conzelmann, *Theology of Saint Luke* (London: Faber & Faber, 1961), p. 78; J.T. Sanders, 'The Pharisees in Luke–Acts', in *The Living Text: Essays in Honor of Ernest W. Saunders* (ed. E.E. Groh and R. Jewett; New York: University Press of America, 1985), pp. 142-49, 167-88; J.B. Tyson, *The Death of Jesus in Luke–Acts* (Columbia: University of South Carolina, 1986), pp. 148-53; J.A. Ziesler ('Luke and the Pharisees', *NTS* 25 [1978–79], pp. 146-57) appeals to both theological and source-traditional explanations (pp. 146-47, 149, 151, 153-56).

Matthew places a major part of the responsibility upon the Pharisees for the death of Jesus (e.g. 21.45; 22.15-22, 34-46; 27.62; cf. ch. 23!).[8] Or to rephrase the current consensus, Luke ascribes the 'lions' share' of the 'blame' to the 'chief priests', those responsible for the regulation of the Temple and the assembling of the Sanhedrin, and to the 'scribes', now considered to be either Sadducees or simply 'Jerusalem authorities' represented in the Council (Lk. 19.47; 20.1; 22.52; cf. 9.22; Acts 4.5, 8, 23; 6.12; 23.14; 24.1; 25.15).[9] But then this concentration on the Sanhedrin seems to harmonize perfectly with Luke's emphasis throughout that it is Israel's leaders and not the people who have been the opponents all along and thus must be singled out as the preponderate perpetrators of Jesus' death.[10] Nonetheless, what seems to be left unaddressed or passes unnoticed through the sieve of critical consistency is the role that Luke assigns almost exclusively to 'the Pharisees' and 'their scribes' through the first two-thirds of his Gospel as the *leaders* of the opposition to Jesus. We shall be arguing in the remainder of this study that it is only in perceiving the distinctive way that Luke interweaves the responses of these Pharisees/scribes with the responses of the people in the pre-Jerusalem ministry that his depiction in the Jerusalem and passion narrative—with its mysterious disappearance of the Pharisees and its equally disturbing 'appearance' of the λαός before Pilate—can be elucidated.

8. E.g. Ziesler, 'Luke', p. 154: 'Both in Acts and in his pre-Passion narrative the Pharisees are so depicted that it would be inconsistent to have them as agents in the trial and death of Jesus. The other Gospels however are not trying to exonerate the Pharisees'; cf. C.H. Talbert, *Reading Luke: A Literary and Theological Commentary on the Third Gospel* (New York: Crossroad, 1984), p. 217.

9. E.g. Conzelmann, *Luke*, p. 78; Fitzmyer, *Luke X–XXIV*, p. 1270; Tyson, *Death*, p. 165: 'only the chief priests and their allies'; Kodell, *'Laos'*, p. 329: 'chief priests... archetypal foes... taking the place of the Pharisees'; Marshall, *Luke*, p. 858; D. Juel, *Luke–Acts: The Promise of History* (Atlanta: John Knox, 1983), pp. 47-53; R.J. Cassidy, 'Luke's Audience, the Chief Priests, and the Motive of Jesus' Death', in *Political Issues in Luke–Acts* (ed. R.J. Cassidy and P.J. Scharper; Maryknoll: Orbis, 1983), pp. 146-67.

10. Typical is Kodell (*'Laos'*, pp. 328-33) who argues for Luke's consistent use of λαός in the Jerusalem section, with the exception of 23.13 (see above, n. 5): 'It is precisely Luke who emphasizes the division and lessens the guilt of the Jewish people more consistently than the other evangelists' (p. 335 n. 36); cf. Juel, *Luke–Acts*, pp. 47-53.

I

The problem of Luke's consistency in laying the responsibility for the death of Jesus at the feet of both the leaders and the people is posed actually at the beginning of Jesus' Galilean activity. Already before Jesus enters his home town to encounter the volcanic reaction against him his popularity among the masses has spread throughout the region—'being praised by all' (4.14, 15b). As his activity progresses, one enthusiastic response after another by both larger crowds and smaller gatherings would appear to make the Nazareth pericope an erratic block—however programmatic in its prolepsis—contrasting sharply with the Galilean springtime of Jesus' meteoric rise to fame among the peoples of Israel (Judea and Jerusalem, 4.44; 6.17) and even from the district of Tyre and Sidon (4.36-37, 40, 42; 5.15, 26; 6.17-19; 7.11, 16-17; 8.4, 19, 40, 42b; 9.[7-9], 11 [18-19], 37, 43). It is the Pharisees and the teachers of the law/scribes who set in motion a growing resistance to the integrity and thus authority of this preacher/healer: 'Who can remit sins but God alone?' (5.21); 'Why do you disciples eat and drink with tax collectors and sinners?' (5.30); 'Why are you disciples doing what is not lawful on the sabbath?' (6.2; cf. v. 7); 'And so the scribes and the Pharisees were watching him...in order that they might find ground to bring charges against him in legal proceedings' (6.7b); 'And they were filled with fury and were discussing among themselves what they might possibly do with Jesus' (v. 11). Particularly in the first scene of this evolving opposition Luke has lent programmatic force when Pharisees and scribes 'have come from every village of Galilee and Judea and Jerusalem', sc. the whole of Judea, or precisely the area where Jesus' fame has already penetrated (4.14, 37, 44), and have stationed themselves as a kind of 'official' inspection team to pass verdict on Jesus' teaching. The result is the most serious suspicion of 'blasphemy' (5.21, 17-26).

Thus by the time Luke recounts Jesus' selection of twelve 'apostles' and his manifesto to the masses who have assembled from much of Palestine (6.12-49) the lines of resistance to Jesus are already blurred. Was the attempt to kill Jesus by the Nazareth congregation a freak event, to be pushed out of view for the moment, perhaps as a kind of ingenious literary mnemonic device that for the reader will spark a sense of déjà vu when the people of Israel as a whole cry out for Jesus' death—again at a place of worship—or when a Stephen or even a Paul similarly are met with violent resistance at sanctuaries of the Jewish people?[11] Moreover, what are we to make of the hostility of the Pharisees and, as in 5.30, their scribes, that has already taken on the character of a plot? Is all of this again simply symbolic rehearsal to be taken over by an entirely different cast of characters once Jesus enters Jerusalem? Or, in other words, can the various pieces of opposition be fitted together into any coherent and focused picture, or are we left with various bits that can at best form an impressionistic collage that leaves the lines of organic development fuzzy and disjointed?

Luke himself provides us the answer when crowds and Pharisees and scribes come together in an important Galilean audience arena (7.18-50). After a healing in which Jesus extols the *faith* (πίστις) of a Gentile over against the apparent lack thereof in Israel (7.9b, 1-10) and a raising from the dead which elicits cries among the crowds (ὄχλος, 7.11, 12) of God's visitation in a *great prophet* (7.16, 11-17), John the Baptist, though presumably in prison (3.20), hears about these events and questions Jesus' identity through them all (7.18, 19-20). That Luke understands John's question through his ambassadors to be a doubting in the sense of inadequate *faith* is clear, not only by Jesus' direct rebuff to John and his disciples in v. 23—'Blessed is that one who does not take offense at me!'—but also by Jesus' comments directly to the assembled crowds (οἱ ὄχλοι, v. 24). However great John has been in the fulfillment of Scripture (e.g. Mal. 3.1; Exod. 23.20), even—note— greater than any or all of the *prophets* in this fulfillment (7.26 → v. 16), yet 'the little/or lesser one/or least within the domain/or perspective of the kingdom of God is greater than he' (v. 28). Why?

Luke comments immediately (v. 29) about 'the λαός and the tax

---

11. See e.g. N. Petersen's (*Literary Criticism for New Testament Critics* [Philadelphia: Fortress Press, 1978], pp. 81-92) pattern of plot motivation; J.B. Tyson ('The Jewish Public in Luke–Acts', *NTS* 30 [1984], pp. 574-83) delineates a 'literary device' akin to Aristotle's (*Poetics*) *metabasis* in Greek tragedy in which a crisis in the plot leads to a 'sudden reversal' of the fortune of the hero. Lk. 4.16-30 foreshadows this change which takes place in the arrest of Jesus (Lk. 22.47-53) when the Jewish public 'suddenly reverses its role of popular support to outright rejection'. Although this pattern, which is repeated in the Acts, leads to a 'logical inconsistency' (p. 581) in the overall plot, Luke thereby expresses that initial Jewish acceptance in the Gospel and in Acts has 'either been neglected or suppressed' and that the 'mission to the Jews is terminated in favour of the mission to the Gentiles' (p. 582). For his more detailed argument, see *Death*, pp. 9-16, 19-47, 165.

collectors' in the crowds declaring God to be *right* in Jesus' estimate of John, and they do so because these are the folk who had submitted to John's baptism. In 3.7-22 Luke has already described a group termed 'the λαός' who, coming from the larger group of crowds (ὄχλοι, 3.7, 10), had heeded John's demand of repentance to prepare for the 'mightier one' who was coming and thus receive John's baptism (3.15, 18, 21). In this context of repentance Luke has also, interestingly enough, mentioned 'tax collectors' (3.12). It is clear in 7.29-30 that by λαός Luke is again distinguishing a smaller group from the crowds. For Jesus continues to address these *same* crowds by charging that when John came upon the scene 'neither eating nor drinking', 'You say (λέγετε) he has a demon' (v. 33b). These are hardly the folk who have submitted to John's baptism! Hence it also appears that Luke is depicting the masses or crowds over against this λαός as those who have not or are not repenting in response to either John or Jesus. For again these same crowds are also castigated, because when Jesus 'the Son of Man has come eating and drinking, *you* say, "look, a glutton and drunkard, a friend of tax collectors and sinners"' (v. 34).

But in light of the enthusiastic responses of the crowds to Jesus that Luke has so vividly unfolded, by what right does Jesus make such a scandalous accusation? And who is or are 'the least' (ὁ μικρότερος, v. 28), those who are supposed to be 'greater' than John? Our clues begin to fall into place when we take into account the other half of the narrator's foil in v. 30, viz. 'the Pharisees and the scribes (lawyers)' who 'had rejected the will of God for themselves because they had not been baptized by him (John)'. (1) Thus far it has been only the Pharisees and *their* scribes who have murmured against Jesus' disciples for eating and drinking with tax collectors and sinners, as with Levi and his friends (5.30), and to whom Jesus had retorted that he 'had come (ἐλήλυθα) to call sinners, and not the righteous (δίκαιοι) to repentance' (5.32). (2) They likewise are precisely the group(s) that are mentioned the only time John's asceticism of fasting, that is, of 'neither eating nor drinking', is discussed, again when tax collectors are exhibiting a posture of repentance with Jesus at table (5.27-39). (3) Immediately after Jesus chides the crowds, a Pharisee is again criticizing Jesus, this time directly, for Jesus' own behaviour at table, again with a 'sinner'. If this man were a real prophet—as the crowds suppose, 7.16—he would not be defiled by a 'sinner' at table. And the woman? She is at Jesus' side, submitting to his authority, sc. in a posture of repentance that binds her with the λαός and the tax collectors who have received John's baptism of repentance leading to the removal/forgiveness of sins (3.3). For her *faith*, Jesus declares, has demonstrated that her 'sins are forgiven' (7.50, 47-48). Accordingly, Simon's Pharisee friends question, again as in 5.21b, 'Who is this who can forgive sins?' (v. 49).

The foil of 7.29-30 then could not be more boldly paraded in front of our eyes. The 'sinner' woman, along with the tax collectors and λαός of 7.29 and 7.34, is one of 'Wisdom's children' who in their repentance declare God or Wisdom to be right in sending John and Jesus (ἐλήλυθεν) to Israel. We have, consequently, the following picture of the dynamics of response in 7.18-35, 36-50: (1) The questioning or doubt on the part of a smaller group, viz. John and his disciples, regarding Jesus' identity as expressed in his healings and exorcisms (7.10, 11-17, 21-22) is transmuted by Jesus into a charge of offense against the whole crowd. It is the 'folk of this generation' who, like children in the market place, do not know how to respond to either John's or Jesus' movement (7.31-32).[12] (2) The blanket charge against the whole generation is conceived and formulated as that offense displayed in the resistance of the Pharisees-scribes ('eating and drinking with tax collectors and sinners', 7.34 → 5.30). That is to say doubting or disenchantment with Jesus' activities is perceived by Jesus as a *direct* affront to his authority. Desire for further demonstration of Jesus' credentials is tantamount to rejection. It is rather the submission of repentance or faith in the 'little ones' or 'least' that vindicates God's purpose (βουλή) in Jesus.

We shall have to test whether 7.18-35, 36-50 is not itself an aberrant block in an otherwise consistent landscape. But already we may have opened up the problem of the seeming discrepancy between the response of the crowds and that of the Nazareth congregation. It is precisely when the sabbath congregation is marvelling and wondering if this 'is not Joseph's son', that Jesus reinterprets their questioning as a direct affront. More specifically in both passages: (1) Jesus declares that the Isaianic prophecies of fulfilled salvation are now taking place in his healing and preaching (4.18-19, 21—7.22-23; cf. v. 21). (2) These actions are the object of wonder and raise the issue of Jesus' status or authority (4.22—7.18-21). (3) This question is perceived by Jesus himself

---

12. For various nuances of interpretation of the parable, see esp. Fitzmyer, *Luke I–IX*, pp. 677-82.

as a demand for greater proof of his authority ('Doubtless you will say, "Physician heal yourself". All the things we have heard you have done in Capernaum do here also in your home town', 4.23b—7.22a, 'Go, tell John what you have seen and heard' sc. v. 21, the same events that have already raised questions in John, v. 18a, 7.23—'But blessed is the one who does not find offense in me'). (4) This questioning is in turn regarded as the mis-reception and thus rejection of a *prophet's* sending to Israel (4.24—7.26-27, 29-30, 39). The response of a smaller group (synagogue, 4.16b—7.18-20, John and his disciples) is representative of the rejection of the whole nation (4.25-27—7.31-35 'this generation... you say'). (5) The salvation refused by Israel as a whole is sent by God's messenger-prophet to individual Gentiles or to defiled sinners (4.26-27—7.36-50). Curiously in both passages this salvation is represented at one point as the sharing of food or meal hospitality (4.25-26—7.34; cf. 7.36-50, esp. vv. 44-46).[13] It may be, then, that 4.16-30 is *not just* an anticipatory rejection that initiates some larger (extrinsic)[14] literary pattern of acceptance and rejection but rather, more fundamentally, is also Jesus' own prophetic perception of the intrinsic nature of the crowds' 'enthusiastic' approval.

II

Does the larger and distinctively Lukan Journey section in any way reflect and perhaps develop this particular dynamics of crowds' and leaders' response in 7.18-50? After describing Jesus' commissioning of seventy (-two) more disciples (10.1-20) and further instruction to disciples as the journey begins (10.21-24, 38-42; 11.1-13), Luke once again portrays the crowds (ὄχλοι) thronging about this one who heals and teaches (11.14, 29). 11.14-36 forms *one* large audience arena in which *four* different types of responses *from the crowds* are leveled by Jesus to *one* mass 'of an evil generation' (v. 29). 'Marvelling' (θαυμάζω) amazement by 'the crowds' at the exorcism of a deafmute (v. 14), a charge 'by some from the crowds' of alignment with Beelzebub (v. 15), 'testy' (πειράζω) skepticism by 'others' who 'were seeking a sign

13. On the function of meals in Luke's story of Israel's fulfillment of salvation, see D.P. Moessner, *Lord of the Banquet: The Literary and Theological Significance of the Lukan Travel Narrative* (Philadelphia: Fortress Press, 1988), esp. Parts III and IV.

14. See note 11.

(σημεῖον) out of heaven from him' (v. 16; cf. 10.25—ἐκπειράζω), and admiration and praise for the day Jesus was born from a 'woman from the crowd' (v. 27)—all are transposed by Jesus into the charge of 'seeking a sign' (11.29). If it should seem reasonable that those who do *not* put Jesus in league with 'the ruler of the demons' would receive fairer treatment than those who do, Jesus shatters any such expectation when he claims that the folk of Nineveh will condemn 'this generation' at the final judgment. Jonah was a *sign* (σημεῖον) to the Ninevites who responded accordingly with repentance, that is, they hearkened to his preaching (v. 32b—κήρυγμα → v. 28—ἀκούω); but Jesus, again self-styled as the 'Son of Man' (v. 30   7.34), is also 'a sign to this generation' and in fact, 'look, something greater than Jonah (the prophet) is here' (ὧδε, v. 32b), and yet this generation does not repent. Thus all are in a predicament no better than those equating the 'finger of God' with the 'finger of Satan'—even the *pagan* Ninevites and the Queen of Sheba will stand to condemn them.[15]

It is then 'as he finished speaking' (v. 37a) that a Pharisee emerges to invite Jesus to dine with him where both *Pharisees* (vv. 39, 42, 43; cf. v. 53) and *scribes* (vv. 45, 46, 52; cf. v. 53) are present. The Pharisee 'marvels' (θαυμάζω) that Jesus does not wash his hands before dinner, sc. he *eats and drinks* defiled. In a barrage of six woes (three each against the Pharisees and the scribes) Jesus now ties the Pharisees/scribes directly to 'this generation', and, in so doing, Luke brings together the evolving crowds' and leaders' responses into an illuminating and definitive whole. The Pharisees in their zeal to maintain strict adherence to ritual purity and tithing have actually 'passed by' crucial matters of social justice and love for God[16] and have thus *misled the people* into thinking that they themselves are the people's authentic leaders. By their presence in the 'seats of honor' at worship and their 'greetings' from the people 'in the market places' they are actually defiling an 'unwitting' folk (οὐκ οἴδασιν, 11.44). Thus Jesus turns the Pharisees' obloquy in v. 38 and the accusations of 5.30 and 7.34 ('eating and drinking') on their head. The scribes in turn are loading these same folk with such unbearable burdens of observances (v. 46) that they are actually 'hindering/preventing' (κωλύω) the people from entering into

15. Notice how the 'parables' of the 'lampstand' (11.33) and of 'partial reception' (11.34-36) together illustrate and reinforce this stark 'all or none' judgment.

16. Cf. Grundmann, *Lukas*, p. 248; Marshall, *Luke*, pp. 497-98.

'the knowledge of God' (v. 52). This is the consequence, Jesus charges, of the scribes promoting a long tradition that has become a touchstone in Israel's history: the murdering of Wisdom's prophets and messengers. Ever since the murder of the prophet Abel all the way through to the slaying of Zechariah ben Jehoida in the Temple, Israel has killed the agents of salvation sent to them, and now the *Pharisees*' scribes have the singular honor of setting and decorating the 'cap stones' of this long process of entombment. But, warns Jesus, the blood guilt of this entire history is now shrieking out for retribution; in fact upon the folk of 'this generation' the judgment of God will fall for the murder of all of Israel's prophets (vv. 47-51).[17]

We can draw the following conclusions concerning the responses of the crowds and the Pharisees-scribes to Jesus in both audience arenas, 7.18-50 and 11.14-54: (1) Jesus' healing and exorcisms are met with doubting and disenchantment on the part of some from the assembled crowds (John and disciples, 7.18-20—11.15-16, 'some', 'others'). (2) This dubiety is treated by Jesus as a direct encroachment against his authority, tantamount to a perverse demand for a 'sign' ('go tell John...', 7.22a; σκανδαλίζομαι, 7.23—11.17-22,[18] 23, σκορπίζω; vv. 24-26, χείρονα τῶν πρώτων).[19] (3) This 'demand' for further proof of his identity *on the part of some* Jesus takes and throws back as an evil challenge against his authority *on the part of the whole generation* ('you [pl.] say... ', 7.33a, 34a—11.29, 'this generation is evil... seeks a sign'). Thus by the time the story reaches 11.29 we have the interesting development that the crowds of the whole generation have been stained with the opposition which in the Galilean section emanated from smaller groups of the crowds (Nazareth congregation, John and disciples) and from the crowds' leaders, the Pharisees-scribes.[20] (4) Out from the masks of the

17. For the function of this 'woe oracle' in the overall plot of Luke–Acts, see D.P. Moessner, 'Paul in Acts: Preacher of Eschatological Repentance to Israel', *NTS* 33 (1987), pp. 96-104.

18. In v. 17 the addressees (αὐτοῖς) include the 'others' (ἕτεροι) of v. 16.

19. Partial belief is tantamount to total rejection; see n. 15.

20. In 7.33 Jesus' charge against the crowds of aligning John the Baptist with the demonic realm is echoed in 11.15 as an accusation by 'some' in the crowd that Jesus exorcises demons by 'the prince of the demons'. Again in the opposition experienced John and Jesus are linked in the βουλή of God; cf. 3.20 → 4.29. In both 7.34 and 11.14 Jesus is the 'son of Man' who 'has come' (7.34) or is 'here' (11.30-32) whose authority is greater than even the one who is 'greater than all the prophets' (7.26;

faceless crowds emerge the Pharisees and *their* scribes as the prime
movers or orchestrators (cf. 7.32) of a generation that knows neither
how to dance nor to mourn (7.36-50—11.37-52). For in engaging Jesus
at their meals and addressing him as teacher (7.40b—11.45)—and yet
refusing to repent—they set the beat in the market places and synagogues to which the whole generation marches. Their own offense at
Jesus' eating and drinking (5.30; 7.39—11.38) becomes—precisely at
their own tables—emblematic of their defiling of the whole generation.

But now in 11.37ff. Jesus 'turns the tables' by exposing their infec-
tious influence to be the quintessence of Israel's unrelenting history of
the persecution and murder of the prophets With 11.53-54 and its
notice of the scribes' and the Pharisees' intensifying hostility (6.11 →
11.53)[21] to put an end to Jesus' influence, it becomes manifest that Jesus
has not only aligned himself with the lugubrious legacy of the prophets,
but also that he himself will form the climax to their infamous fate. It is
'this evil generation' spurred on by its leaders that will perform this
crowning deed. Crowds and leaders coalesce into an unbreakable whole
of a nation that refuses to repent. It is as though Luke has drawn a line
from a sample of the evidence (skepticism on the part of some) to an
arraignment of the accused (the whole evil generation) to the prime
source or origin of the crime (the baneful influence of the Pharisees and
their scribes). Thus in the classic strokes of the Deuteronomistic presentation of Israel's history of disobedience[22] Luke forges a growing monolith that will put Jesus the anointed prophet on the cross. And, characteristic of this perspective, the solid front of resistance is brought to light
right against the backdrop of a small minority—a remnant[23] of
'Wisdom's children' (7.35)—who do repent at the 'sign' of Wisdom's

---

11.32b) or than that of the 'wise' king Solomon (11.31b) (cf. 10.24).

21. The adverb, δεινῶς, linked to ἐνέχω, can *only* have an intensifying sense, 'act
very hostilely', and *cannot* mean merely, 'hold a grudge'; cf. BAGD, ἐνέχω, 1, and
LSJ, ἐνέχω, III ('to be urgent against') and δεινῶς, I ('dire', 'fearfully', 'terrible').

22. O.H. Steck, *Israel und das gewaltsame Geschick der Propheten* (WMANT,
23; Neukirchen-Vluyn: Neukirchener Verlag, 1967), esp. pp. 60-80; for this view of
Israel's past as constitutive of Luke's travel narrative (9.51–19.44), see Moessner,
Lord, Part III; *idem*, 'Luke 9.1-50: Luke's Preview of the Journey of the Prophet
Like Moses of Deuteronomy', *JBL* 102 (1983), pp. 600-605; of the larger story of
Luke–Acts, *idem*, ' "The Christ Must Suffer": New Light on the Jesus-Peter,
Stephen, Paul Parallels in Luke–Acts', *NovT* 28 (1986), pp. 220-56.

23. See Steck, *Israel*, pp. 76 n. 3, 111 n. 4, 167 n. 9.

agents sent to Israel (11.49). Yet the whole nation bears the guilt, and consequently, for the first time, but similar to his woes against the Galilean cities that did *not* repent (10.13-15), Jesus sounds the knell of judgment against 'this whole generation'. Gentiles who before the messengers of God *did* repent will be their accusers (11.31-32 → 4.26-27; cf. 10.13). By 11.37-54 it is also clear that the scribes associated with the Pharisees have been earmarked as those in particular who are keeping alive Israel's tradition of killing the prophets, especially in their intensifying scheming to 'catch Jesus at something he might say' (11.53-54). When Luke in the transition between the Galilean and Journey sections (9.1-50) has Jesus prophesy of the Son of Man's death at the hands of 'elders, chief priests, and scribes' (οἱ γραμματεῖς, 9.22), there can be no doubt which scribes are meant!

7.18-50 is therefore no anomalous piece but is part and parcel of a contour that is detectable already in the first part of the journey. Immediately following the Pharisees'/scribes' meal of 11.37-54 Luke mentions that the crowd (ὄχλος) continues to swell to the thousands ('myriads', 12.1). Jesus turns alternatingly to his disciples and to the crowds in another large audience scene (12.1–13.9) in which the masses are never out of range of Jesus' words, even those to his disciples. Jesus warns the disciples first against the 'leaven, that is to say, the hypocrisy of the Pharisees' (12.1b). This metaphor from meal preparation connotes an invisible but highly effective influence which is permeating the crowds of Israel with a darkening malaise. But, says Jesus, this covering will be lifted, and whatever has been concealed from the people will be proclaimed openly and clearly in the public light (vv. 2-3).

That this 'leaven' refers to the Pharisees'/scribes' 'hindering/preventing' the people from repenting in the presence of Jesus becomes clearer as the scene progresses: (a) By warning the disciples further not to fear those who can kill only the body, Jesus incorporates their fate into his own as the one who brings the killing of the prophets to the omega point (vv. 4-7). Yet the disciples themselves face the danger that they will succumb to the leaven and deny the 'Son of Man' before other folk (vv. 8-12). (2) The 'lust for wealth' (πλεονέξια) which is so dramatically presented from one 'out of the crowd' (vv. 13-15) harks back to the 'greed' (ἁρπαγή) of the Pharisees of 11.39 and points forward to 16.14—the Pharisees' 'love of money'. (3) The disciples again are under the same snare as the crowds (12.41); there is the gravest danger that they will 'plunder' the riches of the Kingdom of God as irresponsible and ill-prepared stewards and will not be 'ready' (ἑτοιμός) when the Son of Man comes (cf. esp. v. 44, ὑπάρχουσιν → v. 15). (4) In the concluding address to the crowds, 12.54–13.9, the entire scene is pulled into focus. The crowds are 'on their way' now to a judgment in which the only expedient course is 'coming to terms', 'reconciliation' with the accuser who is *in their midst*: (a) They know how to discern the 'signs' of nature but are completely dense to the signs of the present time (vv. 54-56). (b) This blindness is due to a counter-presence which hinders the crowds from judging 'for and from themselves' (ἀφ' ἑαυτῶν, v. 56) the sign in their midst. That is to say, like the unwitting folk of 11.44 the crowds are unable to judge because of lack of knowledge ('they do not know'—οὐκ οἴδατε, v. 56). Rather, they are letting those who 'have taken away the key of knowledge' control their own discernment (11.52!). (d) Therefore they themselves have become like the Pharisees-scribes: they are 'hypocrites' (v. 56 → v. 1). Their enthusiastic cries of 'teacher' (v. 13) and 'prophet' (7.16; cf. 11.27-28; 13.33) reveal in essence a folk that refuses to repent. (5) In fact, 'at that present time'[24] a calamity experienced by some (Pilate's blood-bath; collapse of Tower of Siloam, 13.1, 4) is a ready illustration of the calamity facing all—unless they all (πάντες) repent. *All* the crowds are as sinful as their acknowledged 'sinners' (cf. 7.29). The time for the fruit of repentance, cultivated by the gardener in their midst, is almost over (vv. 6-9). Once again the point of view of a smaller group from within the crowds (τινες, 13.1) is an occasion for Jesus to *equalize all* the crowds into *one* mass of an unrepentant folk. We have again the Deuteronomistic warning of the nation through the prophet and an unrepentant nation *as a whole* bearing the consequences of its guilt ('fig tree', cf. Hos. 9.10; Joel 1.7 etc.).

To sum up: The nation as a whole, the people and their leaders, are guilty of rejecting God's messenger of repentance sent to them. Even the disciples are placed in a precarious light. By the fluidity of the audience changes, Luke gives dynamic expression to the growing solidarity between the burgeoning crowds and the disciples precisely in the midst of their distinction; to their increasing identification with 'this generation' despite their separate functions vis-à-vis the one who is in their midst. Moreover, it is the influence of the Pharisees and of *the scribes associated with them* that is pinpointed as the primary source of the

---

24. Probably paronomasia on καιρός in 12.56.

hindering of the repentance required of this generation.

As the journey advances through towns where the people's eating and drinking with Jesus begins to resemble his meals with the Pharisees/scribes (13.26-27), the Pharisees in 13.31 try to make good on their attempt to 'trip Jesus up' (11.54) to which Jesus responds with his second judgment oracle against the whole nation together with its leaders (Herod and the Jerusalem-Temple authorities) that 'stone all the prophets' sent to it.[25] Then for the third and final time Pharisees invite Jesus to a meal where again as in 6.7 Pharisees and the scribes are together 'watching' (παρατηρέομαι) Jesus on the sabbath. Now Jesus condemns their eating and drinking as unfit for the Kingdom of God. They and the 'many' (πολλοί, 14.16) they control will be excluded from the banquet of the Kingdom (v. 24), whereas the 'little ones' of Israel—the poor, disabled, blind and lame—along with Gentiles will fill the banquet hall.

Meanwhile 'the crowds' continue to swell (14.25). But Luke concentrates now in the second part of the journey on the oscillation between disciples and Pharisees in Jesus' addresses, though to be sure the crowds comprise again an almost ever present backdrop. All Israel is being gathered (cf. 11.23, 29; 12.1; 13.34b; 14.25; 15.3-10). The Pharisees and the scribes, however, continue to pound the beat that has become a dirge throughout the Gospel: not their 'eating and drinking' but rather Jesus' meals with tax collectors and sinners make him unfit to speak for the God of Israel (15.1-2; 14.1-24). Jesus retaliates with three parables of 'the lost' of Israel who repent while the 'righteous' (e.g. 15.7, 29) refuse to enter the house of the Kingdom of God (15.3-32). It is the scribes' and Pharisees' love for prestige and influence 'with respect to the folk of their own generation' (16.8), Jesus warns the disciples in the shrewd legerdemain of the 'dishonest (ἄδικος) steward' (16.1-9), that disqualifies their management of the riches of the household of God. Their 'love for money' is, in fact, 'an abomination to God' (16.14-15). For in their attempts to present their actions as 'right' and 'just' (δίκαιος) before the people, while excluding 'the unclean' (16.19-31), they actually lead the people down the path of rejecting God's messengers, even if one of these envoys should first 'rise up from the dead' (16.27-31). Even the disciples are in the gravest danger of causing the 'little ones'

25. For the Deuteronomistic patterns in this judgment oracle, see Moessner, 'Paul', pp. 97-98.

(οἱ μικροί, 17.2) in their midst to fall away from hearkening to the voice of the reign of God in their midst. Their own leaders, 'the apostles' (17.5), are exhibiting a demeanor not unlike that of the Pharisees-scribes (17.7-10).

Luke introduces the last large audience theater (17.20–18.14) with the now conspicuous front of hardness of nine Jewish lepers over against the one 'foreigner', a Samaritan, who submits to the authority of Jesus. Pharisees emerge once again from the crowds to question Jesus (17.20-21). The lines of development from the previous large scenes of crowds, Pharisees, and disciples are striking: (1) These Pharisees are wanting Jesus to provide a 'concrete indication' (παρατήρησις) of the Kingdom's coming. They thus speak for the entire generation (11.29), so palpably presented by the Nazareth synagogue (4.22-24). (2) Jesus declares that no 'observable sign' will mark the Kingdom's presence, except of course the 'sign' or 'presence' already in their midst (17.21). Like the 'sign of Jonah' folk will *not* be saying 'look, here it is' (ἰδοὺ ὧδε) or 'there it is', even though 'look, something greater than Jonah is here' (ἰδοὺ ... ὧδε, 17.21 → 11.32b; cf. v. 31b). (3) The disciples now run the risk of falling prey to this same mentality, of wanting concrete signs of the coming 'day of the Son of Man' (17.22-23). Jesus warns them, 'Do not follow or go after such people' (v. 23b). (4) Indeed, the whole present generation during the 'days (pl.) of the Son of Man' is becoming like the 'generations of Noah's' and 'of Lot's days' in which their 'eating and drinking', 'buying and selling' (i.e. trading in mammon), etc., made them deaf and dumb to the pleading of God's messengers (vv. 26-29). Thus, as they were caught 'unprepared', so also will the judgment of the (final) 'day (sg.) of the Son of Man' fall upon this generation that will first put the Son of Man to death (vv. 30-35, 25). (5) Thus the disciples must be especially alert to persist in prayer in order to withstand the crisis that is speeding to a showdown. 'When the Son of Man comes, will he find any faith at all upon the earth/land?' (18.8, 1-8). (6) For already there are disciples who are acting presumptuously as though they were 'right' or 'just' (δίκαιος) while 'snubbing their noses at the rest' (ἐξουθενέω, 18.9). And now, as what should come as no surprise, Luke has Jesus parade the foil of the Pharisee and the tax collector before his readers that Luke has been developing since the beginning of the Galilean days (esp. 7.29-30). Here is the 'righteous' Pharisee (18.11-12) that we have met throughout the story—fasting (5.33); praying (5.33; 11.43) and tithing (11.42), condemning association with the 'unclean sinners' (5.30-32; 7.36-50; 11.42, 46; 14.12-14; 15.1-2) and exalting himself over the 'others' (5.32; 11.43, 46; 14.7-14; 16.14-15);[26] and here is also the repentant tax collector (5.27-29; 7.29, 34; 15.1) who is the one declared by God to be 'right' (18.14; cf. 7.29; 3.12; 19.9).

To summarize: The 'leaven of the Pharisees' has been virulently effective even among the disciples in the midst of the crowds that are consolidating to become 'this generation'. It is not by accident that Luke follows this audience interchange with the disciples trying to 'hinder/ prevent' (κωλύω) 'little ones' from entering the Kingdom of God (18.15-17).

The final events of Jesus' entrance into Jerusalem move quickly but not without a climax commensurate with all that has preceded. When riches *prevent* a 'ruler' from entering the Kingdom (18.18-30), all in the entourage, including disciples (v. 28) who hear, side immediately with the 'godly' prestige of wealth of this leader of the people. Peter's attempt to extricate himself and other disciples from Jesus' rebuke in v. 27 is met with another 'leveling' remark. *All* are called to deny riches and self for the sacrifice required in the present crisis. The vacuity of Peter's claim in v. 28 is brought then into even greater relief in the next episode ('third' passion prediction, 18.31) when the 'way of the cross' demanded ultimately of Jesus' disciples remains completely elusive to the 'twelve' (18.33 → 14.26b-27). But now in contrast—as if on cue—a blind 'beggar' manifesting 'faith' 'hears' and 'sees'[27] but not without having to persist against the *hindering* rebuke of 'those who were leading the way' (v. 39) of the crowds (disciples? Pharisees?). The people, now curiously termed the λαός, respond in kind and 'give praise to God' (αἶνος τῷ θεῷ), aglow with the mighty act of healing they had 'seen' (ὁράω, v. 43). Zacchaeus, a 'chief tax collector' (19.1), a 'sinner' (v. 7), 'rich' (v. 2b), and yet a 'little one' (μικρός, v. 3b) of Israel who 'repents' (v. 8) is—ironically—*hindered* by the crowd from 'seeing' Jesus. When Jesus goes in to lodge with him the response is patent of a generation that has been completely leavened by the hypocrisy of the Pharisees. 'All (πάντες) murmur' (διαγογγύζω, v. 7)

---

26. Notice how the Pharisee's characterizations of the 'sinful rest' (18.11) echo accusations against and caricatures of Pharisees earlier in the narrative (ἁρπαγῆς— 11.39; 16.14, 19-31; ἄδικοι—11.42, 46; 16.1-8; μοιχοί—16.18).

27. And 'follows'; cf. the Gentile centurion who also has 'faith' simply upon 'hearing' (7.1-10).

the same litany of disgust—crowds, leaders, disciples—that has become characteristic of the Pharisees-scribes in the Journey and Galilean sections (19.7 → 15.2 → 7.39 → 5.30). The solidarity of the 'house of scorn' is now in place (cf. 18.9; 17.25).

As Jesus' caravan nears Jerusalem he provides a commentary on his entire journey with the story of the nobleman who, on a journey to receive a kingdom, is told by a select group that the mass of citizens do not want him to 'reign over' them (19.12, 14). For although the crowds have just heard that the Son of Man 'has already come' (ἦλθεν) with 'salvation' to 'children of Abraham' like Zacchaeus (19.9-11a), it is now clear that their expectation that the Kingdom of God was yet to 'appear' in obvious manifest form (19.11b) is tantamount to rejecting the 'sign' of the son of Man that has been in their midst all along. Indeed the multitude of *disciples* within the crowds take up the banner for the whole generation when they ring out in 'praise to God' (αἰνεῖν τὸν θεόν) 'for all the mighty works (δυναμεῖς) they had seen' (ὁράω) (19.37b). For Jesus' disciples these healings are just the signs to convince them that Jesus is a special prophet, an 'anointed king' whose coming to Jerusalem will brook the onslaught of the Kingdom in its final show of power that they had long been hoping for (e.g. 9.20, 52-56; 18.15-17). But coming as it does, as we have seen, at the end of a long series of warnings by Jesus to beware how they 'see' (7.22; 8.10, 18; 10.23-24; 11.33; 12.15, 54; 13.35; 17.22; cf. 5.26; 8.20; 9.9, 27, 32, 36; 10.33; 17.15; 18.15; 19.3; 21.8, 20, 27, 29, 31; 24.39) or 'hear' (6.27, 47, 49; 7.22; 8.8, 10, 12, 13, 14, 15, 18, 21; 9.35; 10.16, 24; 11.28, 31; 14.35; 15.1; 16.29, 31; 18.6; cf. 4.23, 28; 7.3, 29; 9.7; 10.39; 12.3; 19.48; 20.45; 21.38; 22.71; 23.8) or 'be ready' and 'stay awake' (12.35-40, 42-48; 13.24) or how to 'eat and drink' (13.26; 15.5-32; 16.19-31) or how to 'rejoice' (10.20; 15.3-32)—their cries ring 'hollow'. For they are at base a generation that seeks a sign. Appropriately at that moment the now familiar characters who have set the tune all along for this generation, the Pharisees, try again to hinder Jesus' movement (19.39). Jesus, however, this time does not rebuke them but takes the disciples' cry and transposes it into the shrill shriek of the judgment coming upon the whole nation: 'When these become silent, the very stones will cry out' (19.40).[28]

---

28. In Koine ἐάν with a future *indicative* in the protasis can mean simply 'when' 'whenever', referring to a fulfillment of a future (temporal or logical) condition; see BAGD, 2a and BDF, §373(2).

For Jesus knows too well that the hands of this generation—crowds, leaders, disciples—will clasp together to form the specter of the cross. Hence the irony that as he is proclaimed king and bestowed regal honor, Jesus weeps and laments over the destruction awaiting a people that cannot 'see' the sign of the royal 'visitor' in their midst.

III

Jesus enters the Temple immediately from his descent of Olives to find 'this generation' 'buying and selling' and asserts his authority over 'my house' (19.45-46). In the following cross-section of events (20.1–21.36) on 'one of the days' of a longer, indefinite period of teaching—compassed in introductory and concluding summaries (19.47-48; 21.37-38)—it becomes obvious that the Kingdom of God has not come with great signs of power (cf. 19.11); yet like the Galilean and Journey sections the crowds are as enthusiastic as ever, hanging on to every word of Jesus.

But there are signs of important changes: (1) the people who throng to the Temple every day are never termed the 'crowds' (ὄχλοι) but are consistently the λαός (19.48; 20.1, 6, 9, 19, 26, 45; 21.38; cf. 21.23!). (2) The disciples are mentioned only once, 20.45; 'apostle' not at all. (3) And as is well known, the term 'Pharisees' does not occur. (4) Jesus is preeminently the 'teacher' of the people(s) of Israel gathered from Galilee, Judea, and Jerusalem at the central place of worship (διδάσκαλος, 20.21, 28, 39; 21.7; διδάσκω, 19.47; 20.1, 21[2×]; 21.37).

In the first encounter (20.1-19) representatives of the three groups of the Sanhedrin mentioned already in 9.22 directly challenge Jesus' authority to teach in the Temple. In his introduction to this whole period Luke had mentioned, for the first time, a plotting to *put Jesus to death* (19.47). Hence the events that will eventually lead to Jesus' crucifixion are regarded by Luke as an official act of the chief court of the nation. That Luke does not mention religious parties in this first Temple confrontation should be no cause for amazement. Jesus' counter-question over the authority of John the Baptist draws the reader back immediately to 7.18-35 where John's and Jesus' movements are juxtaposed, λαός and tax collectors are placed over against 'the Pharisees and the scribes', and submission to John's baptism is the key link between John's and Jesus' authority in the will of God. Now here as there the scribes are set directly against both John and Jesus since they had not submitted to John's baptism. Chief priests and elders are now conjoined to that stance. But now the λαός are described *not* as having submitted to John's *baptism*, but rather as holding John to have been a 'prophet' (20.6). But that was the posture of the crowds in general (7.26; 9.19; cf. 9.7-8; 1.17, 76) and not of the smaller group of λαός per se in 7.29 who actually were baptized by him (7.29; 3.15, 18, 21). Moreover, Jesus is said, like John in 3.18, to be 'preaching good news' to the λαός who have come out to hear him (19.48). Thus it appears that Luke is presenting another watershed of response that raises the question yet again whether the λαός will actually 'hearken' (ἀκούω, 19.47; 21.38) to Jesus' words and repent or consent rather to the schemings of their leaders who, like 'the scribes and the Pharisees' of 6.11, were wondering what to do (ποιήσωσιν) with Jesus as he taught the people in a place of worship (19.48; cf. 6.11, ποιήσαιεν).

In the continuing parable of the Wicked Tenants (20.9-18) which Jesus addresses to the λαός who, like the crowds in the Journey, form an ever present background, Luke tips his hand.[29] The tenants of the vineyard who persecute and even kill the messengers sent to them match exactly Jesus' description of the scribes associated with the Pharisees at table in 11.45-52. There Jesus had placed the greater responsibility for Israel's unmitigated history of obduracy squarely upon the shoulders of the 'scribes' *of the Pharisees*. And as Luke had made clear in the last Pharisee/scribe meal (14.1-24), God was in the process of removing this leadership from them. When Luke adds at the end of the parable (v. 19), that '*the scribes* and the chief priests...' knew that he had directed this parable at them, there is no doubt about the pivotal significance of this encounter: the crescendoing plot of 'this generation' to put an end to Jesus' sending to Israel of the Galilean and Journey sections is now bracing for fulfillment.

That by οἱ γραμματεῖς in the Temple precincts Luke understands the determinations of the scribes *of the Pharisees* from the pre-Jerusalem ministry to be carried on, is confirmed by the exchanges that follow:

29. As is typical of Lukan plot development, a parable often interprets an event or saying(s) of Jesus that immediately precedes it: e.g. 10.25-29—30, 35; 11.29-32—33, 34-36; 12.13-15—16.21; 12.22-34—35-38, 39; 13.1-5—6-9; 14.1-6—7.14; 14.15—16.24; 15.1-2—3-7, 8-10, 11-32—16.1-8; 16.14-18—19-31; 17.1-6—7.10; 18.35–19.11—12.27.

20.20-26. (1) Like the scribes of 6.17 (Galilee) and 14.1 (Journey) these scribes are 'watching' (παρατηρέω, v. 20) Jesus, and like those of 6.7 explicitly so in order to hand him over *for legal proceedings*.[30] (2) The spies sent are 'pretending' or 'feigning' (ὑποκρίνομαι) a posture vis-à-vis Jesus that again matches the *Pharisees* and their scribes and their influence over the people (12.1, 56; 13.15; cf. 6.42). (3) Their demeanour of δίκαιος is precisely that characteristic which has become a cipher for and even caricature of the Pharisees and their scribes (5.32 → 10.29 → (12.57) → 15.7 → 16.15 → 18.9(14); cf. 7.29, 35; 18.14 by contrast). (4) The only characters described thus far in the story who try to 'catch/seize' (20.20, ἐπιλαμβάνομαι) Jesus' words in order to terminate his influence have been the Pharisees and *their* scribes (11.54, θηρεύω; cf. 14.1; 10.25-29; 17.20). (5) With παραδοῦναι (20.20) Luke is indicating that all of the forces that had already been set in motion and had even given Jesus a prolepsis of his death are now culminating within the Temple jurisdiction. Thus far the only identified antagonists to Jesus have been the Pharisees and their scribes (παραδοῦναι, 9.44 [Galilee] → 18.32 [Journey]).[31] (6) Verse 21. Of the seven occurrences of διδάσκαλε in the vocative (7.40; 9.38; 10.25; 11.45; 12.13; 18.18; 19.39; cf. 20.21, 28, 39; 21.7) thus far, five have come from Pharisees, or from scribes or rulers who on other grounds bear striking resemblances to Pharisees. 'Teacher' has thus become the distinctive address for Jesus on the part of the Pharisees.[32] (7) Verse 26. The only characters to this point who have been 'unable' (ἰσχύω) to 'trap' Jesus and then become 'silent' in the face of Jesus' confutation are the Pharisees-scribes (14.4, 6, ἰσχύω). As before the sharpest minds from the Pharisees' scribes are unable to 'out-wit' Jesus (cf. 5.33; 6.6-11; 10.25-29; 14.1-6).[33]

20.27-44. (8) Luke finds it necessary to identify the next group of examiners who question Jesus about *halakhic* matters as those from the

30. 6.7 most probably refers to the jurisdiction of the Sanhedrin instead of the Roman judicial process as in 20.20.

31. For Herod in 13.31-33, see 'conclusion' (below) on 23.6-12 and n. 36. Though Herod probably did not intend to 'kill Jesus', contra the Pharisees' contention, 13.31-33 may reflect the tradition in Mk 3.6 and 12.13 par. Mt. 22.16 that Pharisees and Herodians were 'in cahoots' in attempting to keep Jesus' influence in check and make him prove his credentials.

32. In both the other two instances, 9.38 and 12.13, individuals are identified as 'from the crowd' (ὄχλος)!

33. As already anticipated in the *Temple* exchange in 2.46-47.

'Sadducees' (vv. 27-38). It is clear, then, that those skilled in the matters of Law or scribes in vv. 20-26 are non-Sadducees and therefore scribes not from the same religious 'party' (αἵρεσις) as the chief priests (Acts 5.17; 23.6-8). The only other αἵρεσις that Luke mentions with those trained in legal questions is 'the Pharisees' (Acts 15.5: 26.5; cf. 5.17; 5.34 [Gamaliel]; 23.9). (9) The scribes who 'answer' in v. 39 have obviously overheard the Sadducees' question, and Luke must be referring back to *non-Sadducean* scribes who were either part of the delegation of 'spies' or are other scribes whom Luke is coordinating with those in v. 19 and the 'watchers' of v. 20: (a) Because they no longer 'dared' to put themselves in another embarrassing predicament, the scribes' 'compliment' in v. 39 cannot mean that these scribes, unlike those of vv. 19-20, were (now) favourably disposed to Jesus. (b) Sadducean scribes according to the information Luke has just provided in v. 27 would very improbably, facetiously or not, ever state that an argument demonstrating 'resurrection of the dead' was 'well done/put'. (c) The strong verb, τολμάω, in an imperfect durative and conative sense fits much better with those who tried *more* than once to trap Jesus, even by sending 'feigners' or 'spies', than with the Sadducees of vv. 27-38. (d) The quandary, 'David's son—David's lord', would have more force for those maintaining some possibility of resurrection after death than for those who did not (v. 27; see Acts 23.8).

20.45-47; 21.1-4. With the change of primary audience from scribes to disciples, with the λαός 'hearing on' in v. 45, Luke brings the three main *dramatis personae* of the Galilean and Journey sections together to expose unabashedly 'the scribes' of the Jerusalem period (now mentioned alone) to be none other than the familiar scribes of *the Pharisees*. The scribes Jesus has just confounded in 20.41-44 are like their earlier counterparts: (10) They like to be 'greeted in the market place' (ἀγορά, 20.46—11.43);[34] (11) 'love the first seats in the synagogues' (20.46—11.43); (12) and 'the seats of honor at meals' (20.46—14.7-11); (13) for the effect on others make their prayers (20.47b—18.11-12); (14) and use their wealth to control others (20.47a—14.12-14; 16.14-15, [19-31]). When Luke then presents a widow whose use of mammon is diametrically the opposite of the scribes'—that is, without thought of personal gain or status—the foil of 7.29-30 is more blatant than ever. It is no wonder, (15) that like the Pharisees' scribes in 11.46-52 these scribes

---

34. 11.45 implicates the scribes under all of the 'woes' of vv. 40-44.

shall 'receive the greater condemnation' (20.47c)!

But as in 7.18-30, 11.14-27 (38-48), 12.13-59, 17.20-21, when the resistance on the part of some to Jesus the Son of Man in their midst becomes emblematic of the opposition of the whole generation, once again in the last phase of Jesus' public ministry the people, disciples, and their leaders consolidate to form the monolith of the λαός of Israel that refuses to repent. Now again, appropriately, as a smaller group representative of the whole λαός addresses Jesus as 'teacher' (21.7) and seeks a 'sign' (σημεῖον, v. 7), Jesus announces judgment against the whole nation (21.6—'not one stone upon another', cf. 19.44). But then each group of characters has continued to play its role with consistency. The people have remained enthusiastic over Jesus' presence throughout, yet without the hearkening to his unique authority that he has demanded. The disciples remain 'caught up' with the people over the power and authority of Jesus in which they participate in a special way and yet are 'caught between' the demands of a new stewardship, on one side, and the patterns of leadership of the Pharisees and their scribes, on the other. And the scribes of the Pharisees together with chief priests and elders of the Sanhedrin continue to scheme for ways to expose and try Jesus as a false teacher and prophet, and yet find it impossible to 'trap' him in anything he says. All the more striking, then, that Jesus does at last give 'this generation' a sign (21.8-36). But now these are signs[35] of the inevitable fulfillment of 'all that is written' of the destruction of 'wrath to this λαός' (21.23b), a folk that continued to eat and drink with 'dissipation and drunkenness' and to 'be weighed down with the affairs of daily life' (v. 34) such that they were not ready to receive the Son of Man when he came (v. 34b; cf. vv. 27, 36 → 17.24, 25-35).

Conclusion

The denouement comes quickly. Right when it appears again that the chief priests and the scribes will be foiled by the people in their attempts to 'lay their hands on' Jesus, 'the hands of this generation' that 'deliver Jesus over' (παραδοῦναι) clasp together with Jesus at table (22.21). As the Son of Man 'goes' as it has been ordained (22.22), the twelve argue which of them is 'the greatest', thus sealing their own incorporation into that generation whose leaders, the Pharisees and their scribes, are

---

35. Verses 8-11, 12-19, 20-21, 24, 25-28, 29-31.

epitomized by their striving for 'rank at table' (22.24-27 → 14.7 → 11.43; cf. 20.46). When the arresting party, now termed (a) 'crowd' (ὄχλος), led by Judas, comes upon Jesus on the Mt of Olives, this member of the twelve 'hands Jesus over' to them (παραδοῦναι, 22.48 → 22.21-22 → 22.4, 6 → 20.20 → 18.32 → 9.44), while the rest of the disciples, rather than being 'awake' and 'ready', are asleep when the 'Son of Man comes' (22.48 → 22.45-46 → 22.33 → 12.37, 40 → 9.32). Only Peter follows at a distance to deny three times any association with the 'Galilean'.

The stage has thus been fully prepared for the grand finale. The whole nation is gathered. The people (λαός), their leaders, their king, their Gentile govenor of the kings of the nations (22.25) all join together to condemn Jesus to death. With the λαός joining the cries of 'crucify him' (23.13ff.), the charges by the chief priests and the scribes of Jesus 'perverting' or of 'stirring up the λαός all over Galilee and Judea' (23.2a, 5) prove most fitting. The leaven of the Pharisees-scribes has carried the day. Jesus has proven to be a false prophet, a messianic pretender, impotent before the king of the Gentiles and silent before tetrarch Herod when any 'sign' would have proved most expedient (23.8 → 9.9).[36] Barabbas had at least made a gallant attempt and now in comparison deserved to be free (23.18, 25; cf. 24.21). 'This generation'—to the end an 'evil generation that seeks a sign'—had spoken.

Luke has thus presented a theological interpretation of the inescapable enigma that Israel as a whole had rejected its messianic fulfiller of salvation. As we have seen, Luke draws on living Deuteronomistic traditions of the unrelenting obduracy of Israel throughout its history to receive God's pleaders of repentance. These traditions were ready to hand as is

---

36. It is clear that Herod retained a fascination with Jesus' activities following on from 9.7-9 and perhaps even entertained the possibility that Jesus was a genuine prophet (esp. 9.7-8). According to Luke his beheading of John the Baptist was *not* due to the Baptist's 'revolutionary' activities as a prophet or messianic contender or of 'stirring up the people' to expect a messiah, but rather simply that John dared to rebuke Herod's 'relation' to his brother's wife and all of his other 'evil things' (3.19-20). That Herod seems totally uninterested in 'killing Jesus' (13.31) in 23.8-12 (and esp. 23.15) indicates again that the Pharisees are out to 'trip Jesus up' and *not* to befriend him in 13.31-33. In fact, with Herod's enthusiasm in 23.8 it becomes manifestly clear that he becomes the quintessential representative, the 'king', of a folk whose 'delight' in signs can transform quickly into the ugly 'sign' of death (4.16-30)!

amply attested in Jewish literature of the second Temple or intertestamental period.[37] When we ask again why it is that Luke fails to use the
word, 'Pharisee', despite his consistent portrayal of their influence in the
Jerusalem and Passion narratives, we may wonder if there are not a
number of clues in his second volume. At two critical points in the persecution of apostles or of Paul by fellow Jews, Luke presents 'scribes of
the Pharisees' who step in to protect them from further abuse (Acts
5.33-40; 23.6-10). Paul himself is depicted as the truest of Israelites precisely as a Pharisee believer in Jesus the messiah who has fulfilled the
Pharisees' hope of resurrection (e.g. 26.4-8). Nevertheless, it is also
certain that it is *Pharisaic* believers from the Jerusalem and Judean
churches that have stirred up the mass of *believing* Jews so hostilely
against Paul and his mission, that James must step in to reduce tensions
(15.1-2, 5; 21.18-25). Now it may not be purely happenstance that Luke
introduces *Pharisaic believers* (15.5) for the first time and in an indirect,
almost delicate way as those who criticize Peter's *eating and drinking
with Gentile sinners* (11.2-3 → 15.1-2 → v. 5). Just as it was true of
Jesus' disciples in the Gospel, so now again it is true of Peter and especially of Paul and his mission that it is their relation to Moses in dietary
and ritual observances that spearheads the larger controversy against
them and their followers. That is to say, in the Pharisees' 'murmuring'
at table in the Gospel we have the prefiguration or anticipatory
rehearsal of this focal controversy in the Acts. And just as the leaven of
the Pharisees manifested especially *at table* in the Gospel becomes the
decisive influence over the whole people's refusal to repent and of their
rejection of Jesus, so also in the developing story of Acts it is the
influence of the Pharisee or 'circumcision party' that is predominant in
forming a growing network of resistance to Paul and his message of
repentance that eventually leads to his near lynching and arrest at the
Temple on the part of the whole Jewish people. The 'double destination'
of leaders and people in both volumes to constitute and continue as the
folk whose 'eyes do not "see" nor ears "hear" nor heart "perceive"
lest they should turn and be healed' (Acts 28.26-27)[38] is played out most

---

37. See Moessner, 'Christ must suffer', p. 230 n. 31.

38. Cf. e.g. the differing views of D. Tiede ('The Exaltation of Jesus and the
Restoration of Israel in Acts 1', in *Christians among Jews and Gentiles: Essays in
Honor of Krister Stendahl on his Sixty-fifth Birthday*, HTS 79/1-3 [1986], pp. 278-
86); R.C. Tannehill ('Israel in Luke–Acts: A Tragic Story', *JBL* 104 [1985], esp.

decisively in the fate of the Pharisees. It may well be that Luke–Acts is an appeal for the unity of the church precisely at a time when Pharisees and their scribal leaders were crucial links between believing and non-believing Israel, when the fate of Israel vis-à-vis its messianic salvation hung in the balance and to a large extent rested on them. At such a time it would be more than understandable why Luke would omit explicit reference to the Pharisees' role in the death of messiah as well as in the near parallel fate of messiah's messenger Paul.

pp. 75-85); D.P. Moessner ('The Ironic Fulfillment of Israel's Glory', in J.B. Tyson [ed.], *Jews and Judaism in Luke–Acts: Eight Perspectives* [Minneapolis: Augsburg, 1988], pp. 35-50).

INDEXES

INDEX OF REFERENCES

OLD TESTAMENT

NEW TESTAMENT

The Synoptic Gospels

INDEX OF AUTHORS